FRAGILE HOPE

SOUTH ASIA IN MOTION

EDITOR
 Thomas Blom Hansen

EDITORIAL BOARD
 Sanjib Baruah
 Anne Blackburn
 Satish Deshpande
 Faisal Devji
 Christophe Jaffrelot
 Naveeda Khan
 Stacey Leigh Pigg
 Mrinalini Sinha
 Ravi Vasudevan

FRAGILE HOPE

Seeking Justice for Hate Crimes in India

SANDHYA FUCHS

STANFORD UNIVERSITY PRESS
STANFORD, CALIFORNIA

Stanford University Press
Stanford, California

© 2024 by Sandhya Fuchs. All rights reserved.

No part of this book may be reproduced or transmitted in any form or by any means, electronic or mechanical, including photocopying and recording, or in any information storage or retrieval system, without the prior written permission of Stanford University Press.

Printed in the United States of America on acid-free, archival-quality paper

Library of Congress Cataloging-in-Publication Data
Names: Fuchs, Sandhya, author.
Title: Fragile hope : seeking justice for hate crimes in India / Sandhya Fuchs.
Other titles: South Asia in motion.
Description: Stanford, California : Stanford University Press, 2024. | Series: South Asia in motion | Includes bibliographical references and index.
Identifiers: LCCN 2023058094 (print) | LCCN 2023058095 (ebook) |
  ISBN 9781503638341 (cloth) | ISBN 9781503639362 (paperback) |
  ISBN 9781503639379 (epub)
Subjects: LCSH: India. Scheduled Castes and the Scheduled Tribes (Prevention of Atrocities) Act, 1989. | Hate crimes—Law and legislation—India—Rajasthan. | Dalits—Crimes against—India—Rajasthan. | Dalits—Legal status, laws, etc.—India—Rajasthan. | Dalits—Political activity—India—Rajasthan.
Classification: LCC KNU6403.95.M56 F83 2024 (print) | LCC KNU6403.95.M56 (ebook)
LC record available at https://lccn.loc.gov/2023058094
LC ebook record available at https://lccn.loc.gov/2023058095

Cover design: Susan Zucker
Cover art: Shutterstock / Whitney Ott

To everyone who told their stories

CONTENTS

Preface: Positioning Accountability ix

Acknowledgments xvii

Main Interlocutors xxi

Introduction 1

PART I
A Kaleidoscope of Imaginaries

1   The Prevention of Atrocities Act 49
    A Social Genealogy

2   Who Owns the Law? 69
    Politics and Intimacies of Atrocity Cases

PART II
When Atrocities Become Cases:
Rewriting Law's Allegiance

3   The Case That Could Not Be 105
    Police Translations at the Margins

4   (Re-)writing Law's Allegiance? 132
    Rumors, Deep Truths, and Strategic Disobedience

5   "You Must Not Compromise!" 160
    Contested Collectives and Complex Complicities

PART III
Law at the Limits of Hate and Hope

6   Fields of Massacre   189
A "Hollow" Law?

7   Habits of Hopefulness   214
Legal Labors for a Better Future

Epilogue   New Directions   241

Appendix   259
The 1989 Scheduled Castes/Scheduled Tribes Prevention of Atrocities Act as per the Amendments of 2015

Glossary   285

Notes   287

References   293

Index   323

PREFACE
POSITIONING ACCOUNTABILITY

In their writings anthropologists have always made a point of thanking their interlocutors: for making their work possible and granting them access to lives, moments, and institutions from which they would otherwise have been excluded. While I, too, am deeply thankful for these opportunities, I also acknowledge that in the context of this project my gratitude must run much deeper.

This book is an ethnographic analysis of the social life of the 1989 Scheduled Castes/Scheduled Tribes (Prevention of) Atrocities Act, as it is engaged by Dalit (former untouchable) communities in the North Indian state of Rajasthan. Sometimes referred to as India's only hate crime law, the Atrocities Act aims to prevent and punish violent manifestations of prejudice and discrimination against Dalits and Adivasis (Indian indigenous groups). As a result, the forms of aggression that are prosecuted under the act are, per definition, deeply traumatic. They are symptoms of systemic social oppression; they rip through families, villages, and the lives of individuals in brutal ways, leaving survivors searching for new hope and sociality.

Hence, any study that explores the social life of the Prevention of Atrocities Act and the landscape of caste-based violence from the ground up, requires insight into intimate narratives that can leave their experiential owners profoundly exposed. For me this insight was made possible by an extensive network of families belonging to Rajasthan's Meghwal community, one of the most populous Dalit *jātis*[1] (subcastes) in the state. These families adopted me—a European woman who grew up in India—as their daughter and made me part of their homes and social networks. Living with two Meghwal families in Rajasthan's northeastern Jhunjhunu district for eighteen months allowed me to trace how incidents of caste aggression are gradually shaped into legal cases. I learned how attempts to seek justice for caste atrocities through special hate crime statutes can fracture kinship relations, professional commitments, and political allegiances.

Over time the families whom I lived with became my own. They, and the survivors, whose cases I followed, did much more than allow me entry into a world I could not have explored without their help: They granted me access to the most vulnerable, most difficult moments of their lives. I may speak of atrocity cases throughout this book, but the word "case" is merely a terminological cover for what are essentially personal stories of loss, determination, and fragile hope for a more equal future, free from caste violence. During my time in Rajasthan, I gathered information about dozens of atrocity complaints. The ones I discuss here are those that were exposed to me deeply, both in procedural detail and in sentiment. Through access to documents, conversations, and simple offers to tag along, the survivors, activists, and lawyers I worked with volunteered their physical, emotional, and intellectual labor to make it possible for me to write this book: they have allowed me to tell their stories and to draw on my own interpretations when speaking about their lives. I want to acknowledge this explicitly! In turn, I have attempted to give their confessions space, write their feelings with care, and allow their own voices to become clearly audible throughout these chapters.

Before I take readers deep into the contested social life of the Atrocities Act, I must outline the implications of my own ethnographic positionality, and frame the ambitions and limits of this study.

Above all, I must recognize that I do not know firsthand what it means to grow up as part of a group that is faced with habitual, and exceptional, forms of violent exclusion. Hence, this book, and the ethnographic work that underlies it, is not intended as, and cannot ever be, a narration or analysis of caste violence as a category of immediate experience. Nor do I mean to offer a reflection on the phenomenology of untouchability or caste oppression, as scholars from Dalit backgrounds have done (e.g., Guru and Sarukkai 2019). My scholarship is not situated to represent these experiences.

Instead, I hope to offer a different perspective: the perspective of someone whose past has granted her the privilege to trace how caste bias is discussed, resisted, and often reproduced at every institutional level in India's legal system. As a young, white woman, who grew up in a North Indian village from an early age, spoke Hindi fluently and without accent, and attended well-respected educational institutions, I inspired a certain confidence among judges and police officers. Yet, being female, unmarried, and youthful in appearance, I was never perceived as a threat by upper-caste legal professionals (who were primarily men). Consequently, even high-ranking police officials or members of Rajasthan's judiciary usually shared their controversial opinions on the Atrocities Act with me candidly, even though they knew their words would make it into my research publications. I believe that this candor has enriched my understanding of the practical and conceptual dilemmas, as well as the public attitudes around the Atrocities Act and hate crime law more widely. These insights form the central contribution of this book.

At the same time, my childhood days in remote areas of North India allowed me to fit comfortably into the families, villages, and towns that atrocity survivors inhabited. To the Meghwal families I lived with during my fieldwork, I was a daughter, whose worldview they instructed. I shared beds with their children, attended their weddings, and helped them with their daily chores—albeit usually quite badly.

Furthermore, I believe that a personal trauma of sexual violence, which I have long carried with me, helped me to listen to the stories of those who had to live through targeted aggression—and especially to the stories of Dalit women—with empathy and care. While no one can claim that they know what to say or do in the face of people's deepest, intersectional injuries, I like to think that my personal history has, at least, taught me what forms of communication to avoid; when to be silent and how to allow survivors to guide the conversation and direct understanding.

I don't claim that I have navigated this morally sensitive and intellectually complex ethical terrain flawlessly. However, throughout my research I have reflected on the boundaries of my own analysis continuously and tried to remain conscious of my own position. Admittedly, I have also sometimes wondered whether I really should be the person to write this book. I, ultimately, came to the conclusion that despite not being a member of the communities I worked with, my ethnographic perspective is a valuable one. It is valuable not just for its multidimensional or multiscalar institutional insights, but also because it is based in intimate, longstanding friendships with, and a deep responsibility towards, the people whose stories I recount in these pages. They wanted me to write this book and I have tried to write alongside them.

A few additional points deserve mentioning. First, due to my own positionality, background, and experiences, the perspective on the everyday life of hate crime law that this book offers is in some ways a gendered one. I did not exclusively study the legal trajectories of Dalit women. Many chapters in this book discuss caste atrocities perpetrated against men and present insights from conversations with male advocates, activists, and politicians. Still, most of my closest Meghwal confidantes were women. Therefore, the legal concerns and contestations I foreground in this book are deeply shaped by intersectional experiences of caste and patriarchal violence.

Second, I am a legal anthropologist, not a lawyer. While I have completed formal certifications in Indian constitutional law and have worked closely with professional advocates and legal scholars while writing this book, this is not a study that foregrounds the procedural aspects of state law.

In his brilliant ethnographic study of terrorism trials in India (2023), Mayur Suresh, a trained criminal lawyer and anthropologist, focuses on legal technicalities and argues that the mundane aspects of criminal trials can serve as a platform for new agencies and intimacies. While this approach is profoundly enlightening, and studies like Suresh's have served as analytical catalysts in these chapters, I represent an opposite approach in this book. *Fragile Hope* focuses on the way legal cases are constituted before, and outside, court trials. As someone who learned about legal processes, technicalities, and rules as I became involved in them, I developed my view and understanding of the Scheduled Castes/Scheduled Tribes (Prevention of) Atrocities Act alongside my interlocutors. I was able to sympathize with the substantive expectations atrocity survivors in Rajasthan have of hate crime law, a type of law that they consider to be for "their" protection. Experiencing the nontransparencies and bureaucratic pitfalls of legal justice-seeking alongside atrocity survivors, I also grew to understand why and how they demanded change from a criminal legal system, which theoretically championed their protection by legislating against caste atrocities, but whose procedures and institutional rules in practice favored the economically powerful upper castes that had harmed them.

As an anthropological researcher, who operates within a wider space of sociolegal scholarship and practice, I am familiar with debates in legal theory, which outline the problems with the special demands hate crime laws make of legal truth regimes: discrimination is hard to prove, motives of bias are difficult to capture evidentially, and reversing or lowering the burden of proof in the context of hate crime laws comes with profound risks. However, the stories in this book nonetheless highlight that Dalit atrocity survivors in Rajasthan felt that laws like the Prevention of Atrocities Act were futile if they were embedded in a general system of criminal law whose procedures were stacked against them. If, as Mayur Suresh argues, the technicalities of law breed new agencies and socialities, my interlocutors argued that some of these technicalities had to be adjusted if the legal system truly wanted to make space for the agencies of the historically marginalized.

Third, I must emphasize that as the first book-length ethnographic study of the Prevention of Atrocities Act, the analyses in this book are, necessarily, incomplete. Truthfully, each chapter in this book touches on questions and issues that deserve to be much more extensively analyzed on their own terms: the gendered experience of hate crime law, questions of police interpretation and translation, the competing truth regimes and different modes of hope and resistance that hate crime laws engender.

When writing this book, I made an executive decision that I wanted to open up all these discussions ethnographically, rather than systematically exploring one issue from all possible angles. Hence, I know that many of the theoretical and practical questions raised here must be studied further by myself, as well as other scholars. These future studies will doubtless provide additional insights and even contradict some of my own arguments. My only hope is that this book can serve as a starting point for further analysis.

For reasons of analytical precision, I have not included complaints filed by Adivasis in this book. Even though Dalits and Adivasis are both protected under the Atrocities Act, the political dynamics around indigenous categorization and issues of land or forest protection that shape experiences of discrimination among India's Adivasis are distinctive and deserve to be explored on their own terms.

Additionally, I must accept that due to a rapidly changing Indian legal landscape and the rather slow nature of academic writing and publishing, the cases in this book, and even the features of the Atrocities Act itself, will have inevitably evolved or changed by the time these pages are published. I conducted the fieldwork for this book between 2016 and 2018. Consequently, my analysis engages with the debates around, and the legal amendments made to, the Atrocities Act in 2015 and 2018. Later modifications to the act are discussed sparingly.

This then leads me to a crucial political caveat. In the five years that have passed since my fieldwork, the current Indian climate of Hindu nationalism has had a profound effect on the landscape of caste resistance in Rajasthan. As a result of the amendment to the Foreign Contribution Regulation Act (FCRA) in 2020, many of the NGOs and legal aid centers that feature prominently in the cases and stories I tell, had to significantly reduce their operations. Thus, anyone who sets out today to conduct fieldwork of the kind I pursued in Rajasthan in 2016 would encounter a very different world of legal activism.

Nonetheless, this book is not itself a study of Hindu nationalism. While Hindu majoritarian attitudes and policies have doubtless exacerbated violence against Dalits in India, the prejudices and forms of exclusion that constitute caste violence are not themselves the result of the recent Hindu nationalist agenda. They are deeply historically ingrained, economically rooted, and culturally multivalent.

Finally, I must honestly highlight where my allegiance as the author of this book lies: Many aspects of cases were discussed with me as a confidante or friend. To protect the identities of my interlocutors and keep them safe, I have chosen to anonymize affected families and individuals, even though atrocity complaints, case reports, and statements have entered the public record. I have not included the numbers of official police reports (FIR numbers) in the text. Additionally, I have changed the names of villages and allowed for ambiguousness in the description of people's public roles. However, I have sometimes chosen to retain the real names of NGOs, who take pride in the public outreach of their work, while ensuring that the personal opinions of individuals within these organizations remain anonymous. Throughout I use the term Dalit to refer to Scheduled Caste complainants under the Prevention of Atrocities Act because most of my interlocutors chose this designation, though sometimes they also referred to themselves by the name of their community, like Meghwal or Bairwa.

Ultimately, my ethical responsibility and my loyalty in this book is to the Meghwal families I lived with, and to the survivors who shared their injuries and stories. It is their notion of justice, their desire for legal transformation, and their vision of the future I foreground in this book. Their truth is the one *Fragile Hope* positions in the spotlight, and their imaginary of justice is the one to which I am accountable.

ACKNOWLEDGMENTS

Fragile Hope does not belong to me alone. It is the result of a series of conversations, professional relationships, and ethnographic engagements that have spanned over a decade. Above all, I thank the people who shared their stories for this book. As I have already stated in the preface, their trust in my ability to tell these stories has been invaluable. I have tried my best to do it, and them, justice!

In Rajasthan, my most profound gratitude goes to the families who helped with my fieldwork and allowed me to make Rajasthan my home through their friendship and care. I thank Akhil, Savita, and Nipu for welcoming me to Rajasthan with open arms. I am deeply indebted to their families, who treated me like a daughter and sister of their own. From the bottom of my heart, I also thank my mentor, friend, and confidante Suman, whose deep knowledge of Rajasthan and profound sensitivity towards people's stories continue to be a source of inspiration. By allowing me entry into her natal home in Jhunjhunu, Suman gave me the chance to truly understand life in Rajasthan. Finally, I cannot forget the children who kept me company. Neha, Toni, Anu, Chaksu, Naytik, Ansh, and Vansh shared big bottles of Pepsi with me on hot Rajasthani evenings and taught me how to fly kites. They made sure that I experienced moments of humor when the stories I encountered were hard to hear.

I am deeply indebted to the Centre for Dalit Rights for its support. I thank Adv. P. L. Mimroth, Adv. Satish Kumar, Adv. Girjesh Dinker, Adv. H. Mimroth, Ms. Indira, Adv. Jajoria, and Ms. Pooja Singh, whose collaboration was of immeasurable value. I also express my gratitude to Navin Narayan at the ActionAid office in Jaipur and to Rakesh Sharma, who has been a great friend and collaborator! I am indebted to Bhanwar Meghwanshi, an incredible writer and activist, who allowed me to follow him around even though he had more important things to do! I also thank Adv. Vinay Pandey, Adv. Mathur, and Mr. Srivastava for their help.

I am grateful to the Indian Institute of Dalit Studies (IIDS), the National Campaign on Dalit Human Rights (NCDHR), the National Dalit Movement for Justice (NDMJ), and the All India Dalit Mahila Manch (AIDMAM) for their support throughout my research. My gratitude especially goes to Prof. Sukhadeo Thorat for giving me my first job out of university. Without this opportunity I would never have written these pages. I also thank Mithika, Vinod, Dilip, Swati, and Sandeep for being wonderful colleagues and dear friends. I express my deepest gratitude to the late P. S. Krishnan, who was instrumental in drafting the Prevention of Atrocities Act, for taking the time to share with me his views on the social genealogy of the act.

In my young career I have been fortunate to have been guided by incredible mentors. At the London School of Economics (LSE), I am profoundly indebted to my supervisors Alpa Shah and Laura Bear, who taught me everything I know about fieldwork and provided intellectual guidance as well as continuous emotional support. They were my biggest champions! I am grateful to Nichola Lacey and the LSE International Inequalities Institute for helping me situate my ethnographic insights within a wider landscape of sociolegal scholarship. Furthermore, I thank Mukulika Banerjee, Michael Scott, Matthew Engelke, Insa Koch, Katy Gardener, and Jonathan Parry for their feedback. I profoundly enjoyed developing my work alongside Anishka Lohiya, Nora Ratzmann, Clayton Goodgame, Miguel Alcalde, Itay Noy, Thomas Herzmark, Megnaa Mehtta, Nikita Simpson, Mascha Schulz, and Jennifer Cearns, who provided insightful comments.

At the University of Edinburgh, I am extremely grateful to Tobias Kelly for guiding me throughout the anxieties of the publishing process as well as through the first years of my academic career. I would not be where I am today without him! My deepest gratitude also goes to David Mosse at School of Oriental and African Studies (SOAS) for providing insightful and constructive criticism on my research findings. I wholeheartedly thank my mentor and friend Julia Eckert at the University of Bern for giving me my first academic position, collaborating with me to explore conceptual questions on hate crime law in India and helping me pave my professional path.

My gratitude also goes to my colleagues Sharib Ali and Surya Ghildiyal for helping me to understand caste atrocities within the wider context of hate crimes in India. I am thankful to Vidhu Verma at Jawaharlal Nehru University for being a wonderful guide throughout my fieldwork. Finally, I also wish to acknowledge my earliest anthropological advisers, Mary-Beth Mills, Britt Halverson, and Catherine Besteman at Colby College, who helped me uncover what unique insights and transformations anthropology can engender.

Parts of this book were published as articles in the *Political and Legal Anthropology Review* (*PoLAR*), *Contemporary South Asia*, *South Asia Multidisciplinary Journal* (*SAMAJ*), and the *Journal of the Royal Anthropological Institute* (*JRAI*). I thank the editors and anonymous reviewers for their constructive feedback.

I wholeheartedly thank the Wenner-Gren Foundation, the Leverhulme Trust, and the Laura Bassi Scholarship for their financial support in making my research possible!

At Stanford University Press I am grateful to my editor, Dylan Kyung-Lim White, for being my trusted shepherd throughout the publishing process. I thank editorial assistants Sarah Rodriguez and Cindy Lim for patiently answering my endless questions, and Susan Olin for her help with copyediting. I also thank Thomas B. Hansen for supporting this book project. Moreover, I am deeply grateful to the peer reviewers for their extensive and constructive feedback. A big thanks goes to my friend and graphic designer Lydia Denno for lending her expertise with map design.

Finally, I want to thank the three most important people in my life! To my parents I wish to say: I could not have finished this book without your continuous support! But mostly, I would have never even begun to ask the questions that have guided this research had it not been for the life you created for us. Not many people find in their parents, friends, intellectual inspiration, and unconditional love. And finally, to George, my husband and the love of my life: Thank you for sticking with someone who endlessly talks about violence and law, and leaves books everywhere. Thank you for keeping me calm when I panic, making me tea when I am overwhelmed, and for telling me that my work matters when I doubt it. Thank you for building a wonderful life with me and our fluffy cat Ella. You are the best (that's all you ever wanted to hear, so here it is in print)!

MAIN INTERLOCUTORS

Note: Everyone on this list has been anonymized.

FIELDWORK FAMILIES

Jhunjhunu Town

Avinesh Meghwal: My friend and a central fieldwork contact in Jhunjhunu.

Rajesh Bhāiia: Avinesh's eldest brother, who accompanied me on interviews.

Randeep Bhāiia: Avinesh's brother-in-law, who also accompanied me on interviews and fact-finding missions.

Badrasar Village

Sonali: A Jhunjhunu-born activist and close friend. Sonali was the convenor of the Rajasthan division of the All India Dalit Women's Forum (All India Dalit Mahila Manch, or AIDMAM) at the time. Her family lived in Badrasar village where I stayed for six months.

Mummy-jī: Sonali's mother and the local kindergarten (*ānganwadi*) worker. She helped me conduct a demographic and agricultural survey of Badrasar.

Aakash Bhāiia: Sonali's brother.

Bitu Aunty: Sonali's aunt and neighbor.

COMPLAINANTS AND THEIR COMMUNITIES
JHUNJHUNU DISTRICT

Bilaria Village (Chapter 2)

Pinky Meghwal: A seventeen-year-old Dalit girl of the Meghwal *jāti* (subcaste) who was gang-raped by four boys of the dominant Jat caste in 2017.

Sundari Devi Meghwal: Pinky's mother.
Rohan Lal Meghwal: Pinky's father.

Puranapura Village (Chapter 4)

Birendra Meghwal: A young man who filed an atrocity complaint after his father's alleged murder.
The late Lakha Ram Meghwal: Birendra's deceased father.
Rani Devi: Birendra's mother.
L. Chaudhary: Phula Ram's higher-caste employer and the accused in Birendra's atrocity case.
Vivek Meghwal: A potential witness to Phula Ram's murder.

Jagta Village (Chapter 4)

Radha Devi: The officially elected village leader (*sarapanca*) of Jagta village.
Krishna Kumar Meghwal: Radha's husband, who takes on most of her public duties. He is a contract lawyer.

Badrasar Village (Chapter 4)

Rahil Meghwal: A distant relative of Sonali's, who filed an atrocity complaint accusing a local member of the powerful Jat caste of hate speech.
Jataram Jat: The accused in Rahil's case.

UDAIPUR DISTRICT

Libasha Village (Chapter 3)

Choti Lal Meghwal: An agricultural laborer, who attempted to file an atrocity complaint against the local council of the powerful Rajput caste.
Suman Devi: Choti Lal's wife.
Kavita: Choti Lal's daughter-in-law.

KARAULI DISTRICT

Kotra Village (Chapter 5)

Roop Singh Jatav: An agricultural laborer, who registered an atrocity complaint after repeated attacks on his body and livelihood.

Preity Devi: Roop Singh's wife.

Raja Ram Chaudhary: The accused, of the influential Jat caste, in Roop Singh's case.

NAGAUR DISTRICT

Dangawas Village (Chapter 6)

The late Ratna Ram Meghwal: A Dalit man who was killed during the Dangawas massacre in 2015 after getting involved in a land dispute with Chinma Ram.

Chinma Ram Jat: The Jat man who laid claim to Ratna Ram Meghwal's plot of land. Chinma Ram died in 2007. His sons, Kana Ram and Oma Ram, are the main accused in the atrocity case filed by Ratna Ram's family after the Dangawas massacre.

Jaipur City (Chapter 7)

Aunty-ji: An upwardly mobile Meghwal woman who lives in Jaipur. She and her husband filed a complaint under the Atrocities Act after their son's suicide.

Ragu: Aunty-ji's youngest son, who committed suicide after being tortured by men of India's highest-ranking Brahmin caste.

Sikar District (Chapter 7)

Anisha: A young girl of the Balai *jāti* (subcaste), whose sisters committed suicide after being raped by two boys of the Rajput caste.

LEGAL AID ACTIVISTS, NGO WORKERS, AND JOURNALISTS

Mr. Nairoth Sr.: Lawyer and founder of a prominent human rights NGO in Jaipur, which provides legal aid to Dalits who want to file atrocity cases.

Mr. H. Nairoth Jr.: Lawyer, activist, and heir to his father's legal aid NGO.

Nivedita Devi: A Dalit woman of the Bairwa *jāti* who worked as the liaison for Mr. Nairoth's NGO in Rajasthan's Dausa district.

Raveen: A journalist of the Meghwal *jāti* from Rajasthan's Udaipur district.

MEGHWAL COMMUNITY LEADERS AND CASTE ORGANIZATIONS

Satyanarayan G.: A prominent and controversial Meghwal leader (*netā*) in Jhunjhunu.

The Jhunjhunu Meghwal Sangarsh Samiti (Jhunjhunu Association for Meghwal Assertion)—JMSS: An association founded by Meghwal men in Jhunjhunu to help atrocity survivors file cases.

POLICE OFFICERS, JUDGES, AND INDEPENDENT ADVOCATES

Mr. X: A high-ranking official in the Police Commissionerate in Jaipur.

Nattu Meghwal: A lawyer from Jhunjhunu.

Adv. Geeta: A female lawyer working for Mr. Nairoth's legal aid NGO.

Adv. Gaurav: An independent lawyer in Ajmer district.

FRAGILE HOPE

INTRODUCTION

SCENE 1

Aunty-jī[1] put down her stitching needles and scrutinized her finished pattern before focusing her eyes on me. "Look at this, Sandhya," she demanded forcefully. I obeyed and inspected her stitching work, which portrayed a delicate, yellow flower. It was beautiful. "I have not made anything so pretty and bright, in a long time," Aunty-jī reflected, tucking a strand of her grey hair under her *dupatta* (headscarf). "I had lost all hope. But I have hope again now. Ragu's case is difficult because the system is corrupt, but we have a way to fight now. I can imagine a world where people like Ragu can live and love happily." I was unsure how to respond. The pain of losing her youngest son Ragu was still raw for Aunty-jī and her hope in legal victory so fragile. One year earlier, in January 2016, Ragu, a promising young doctor, had committed suicide after being kidnapped and brutally tortured by five men of the Brahmin caste.

Aunty-jī and her family were Dalits, India's former untouchables, who occupy the lowest rank in the traditional Hindu caste hierarchy. They belonged to the Meghwal community, one of the most numerically strong and politically influential Dalit subcastes (*jāti*) in the North Indian state of Rajasthan. The family was upwardly mobile, educated, and financially secure. Aunty-jī and her husband lived a comfortable urban life in Rajasthan's capital of Jaipur and had considered untouchability or caste-based violence a matter which would not affect middle-class families like theirs. However, Ragu's tragic fate had taught them that their low caste status still mattered much more than they had previously believed.

At university Ragu had fallen in love with a young girl called Karishma. Karishma was a Brahmin. In India Brahmins are widely considered to occupy the apex of the traditional Hindu caste hierarchy. In the eyes of those who still believed in notions of ritual impurity and bought into the idea of a "proper" caste order, Karishma thus represented the highest possible social status, while Ragu occupied the lowest. The couple had known they would face difficulties, but they had been deeply in love and determined to spend their lives together. And so they had married in secret. But their happiness was short-lived: upon finding out about the union, Karishma's family banished her. Her father announced that he "would have accepted anyone as a son-in-law but not a "damn dirty Dalit (*gandā Chamar, sāla*),"[2] and he disowned his daughter. Karishma had come to live with Aunty-jī and her new husband in Jaipur, grieving the loss of those she once held dearest. However, a year after the wedding, when Karishma was pregnant, things seemed to take a fortuitous turn. Her family contacted the couple and requested they visit them in Delhi. Everyone, including Aunty-jī, had rejoiced, considering the invitation a peace offering. Ragu and Karishma promptly traveled to Delhi to pay their respects. But they walked directly into a trap.

As soon as the couple got out of the car in front of Karishma's parents' home, her four brothers and father overwhelmed Ragu. They beat him violently; they cursed and insulted him and subsequently tied him up and tossed him in a sewage canal in the city of Gurugram (formerly Gurgaon) in the neighboring state of Haryana. Ragu somehow managed to cut the rope tied around his wrists on a rock. He pulled himself out of the canal and found a shop with a telephone landline. There, he called his father, Uncle-jī, who rushed up from Jaipur to help him. However, when Ragu called Karishma, she didn't pick up. The following day, the family received a text message from her. The message broke Ragu's heart. Karishma wanted a divorce. She wrote that marrying Ragu was the biggest regret of her life.

When Uncle-jī arrived in Gurugram, he found a weak and injured Ragu propped up against the wall of a news stall. With the help of his father, Ragu made it safely home to Jaipur and received the necessary medical attention. But he seemed broken. Though he never believed that Karishma had voluntarily forsaken him, he was faced with the reality that he would not get his wife back. Uncle-jī often said that he no longer recognized Ragu after the attack. His charismatic youngest son, the joker and entertainer, had become withdrawn, weeping for his lost love and child. Three days after his return home, Ragu walked out of his family home early in the morning and headed towards the railway tracks south of his neighborhood. There he threw himself in front of an approaching train. At noon, his father received a call from the police, asking him to identify a body. Uncle-jī understood immediately that Ragu was gone. "In my bones, I knew that he left this earth," he told me when we spoke a year later. Ragu left behind a letter for his brother explaining that, abandoned by his wife and humiliated for his status as a Dalit, he no longer wanted to live.

Aunty-jī and her family did not consider Ragu's death suicide: for them it was murder, a death forced on their son by the irreparable trauma of discrimination, hate, and social rejection. And so, Aunty-jī and Uncle-jī decided to call on the only ally they could think of: The 1989 Scheduled Castes/Scheduled Tribes (Prevention of) Atrocities Act. Aunty-jī and her husband knew that the Atrocities Act had been introduced to prosecute violence and discrimination by socially dominant, upper castes against two of India's most historically marginalized groups: Dalits (legally referred to as Scheduled Castes) and Adivasi tribal groups (Scheduled Tribes).[3] And so, they went to their local police station in Jaipur to register a complaint under the Atrocities Act and the Indian Penal Code (IPC), accusing Karishma's family of casteist hate speech, grievous hurt, and of "abetting" Ragu's suicide. Victory in court would be difficult. But Aunty-jī always hoped, her eyes firmly fixed on a horizon of formal, public justice.

As I sat in Aunty-jī's living room that morning in January 2017 and wracked my brain to find an appropriate response to her unforeseen declaration of hope in a legal case that was unlikely to end in conviction for Ragu's tormentors, I was relieved by Sonali. Sonali, an energetic Meghwal woman in her forties, had been resting on a woven bed (*cārapāii*). But now she walked over. "I know it's difficult, Aunty-jī," she said, kneeling down beside the older woman, "but you are doing the right thing. You have hope because you have understood that this law is about the future of our Dalit movement (*āndolana*). We must use this law the right way to change how things work in our society (*samāja*), to change politics and the legal system (*kānūnī* system), so that there are fewer Ragus."

Aunty-jī shook her head: "For *you* it's about the future of Dalits, and law, and the movement," she said, gently pushing Sonali's hand aside, "for me it's still about real justice for *my* son! The right way to use this law is to restore his honor, to lessen the pain of our family." Sonali sighed. This was not the response she had wanted.

I was struck by a sense of déjà vu. This was not the first time I had heard this speech from Sonali. It was also not the first time it had been met with resistance. Sonali was a seasoned legal aid activist and the Rajasthan state convenor of the All India Dalit Women's Forum (All India Dalit Mahila Manch, or AIDMAM), an organization that fought for the rights of Dalit women. A central part of her work was to comfort and advise families like Aunty-jī's, who had lived through horrific experiences of discrimination or had lost loved ones to caste atrocities. Sonali helped them file complaints under the Atrocities Act, which accused upper-caste parties of violence and discrimination against Dalits.

Like many activists I had met during my eighteen months of ethnographic fieldwork in Rajasthan, Sonali saw the Atrocities Act as a weapon to eradicate structural casteism from the ground up and as road map to a more equal Indian society. However, her vision often clashed with the hopes of survivors like Aunty-jī, who were seeking justice for deeply personal traumatic experiences and had to reorient themselves to a social world that had violently marked them as outsiders: often by literally etching caste prejudice onto their bodies and property. Though most survivors were grateful for Sonali's advice, they were often hesitant to register formal complaints under the Atrocities Act. When they did, they rarely pursued their cases according to the parameters Sonali laid out as the "right way." The perceptions of legal success that survivors like Aunty-jī articulated differed drastically from those of activists like Sonali.

SCENE 2

"From the moment the SC/ST (Prevention of) Atrocities Act was ratified as a law someone has always been trying to abolish it! . . . Many people feared this act. They knew it would change privilege and impunity and they did not like it. And look what is happening: dilutions and noncompliance with its rules. This act was seen as a battleground of social power, and we have been battling ever since!"

With those words the retired civil service officer reached for the glass of water on the side table. After a short pause, he continued: "I am proud that we made the issue of caste violence into a matter of law . . . although the law is still not implemented properly by police and courts and people get bullied into out-of-court compromises. This must change if we want more convictions and make this act successful."

I was sitting in the living room of P. S. Krishnan, a former member of the Indian Administrative Service and previously Secretary to the Government of India, and one of the original authors of the Atrocities Act. When I met Mr. Krishnan in January of 2018, I had come to the end of my fieldwork in Rajasthan, during which I had explored ethnographically how the Atrocities Act was mobilized by Dalit communities in the state. As the end of my fieldwork loomed, I had pursued an interview with Mr. Krishnan with an investigative zeal that had left me slightly guilt-ridden considering his age.[4] Admittedly, it was also difficult not to feel pleased, as I looked around his sitting room, clasping my teacup: I had made it to the source.

Yet, I was almost grateful that it had taken me this long to secure the interview. Now, after months of fieldwork, I arrived at Mr. Krishnan's doorstep equipped with a depth of knowledge about the social dynamics around the Atrocities Act that allowed me to situate his bureaucratic, authorial vision against the backdrop of a much wider, political, experiential, and socioeconomic landscape. I knew now that the success or failure of the Atrocities Act could neither be assured through a linear focus on police and courts nor be measured against procedural markers like conviction rates. In Rajasthan the battle for success that atrocity survivors were fighting was more radical: they were fighting to redefine the truth regimes and procedures of a criminal legal system, which was deeply steeped in upper-caste power.

A FAILING VISION OF EQUALITY?

The above scenes offer a first glimpse into the contested political, normative, and affective landscapes that have emerged around the 1989 Scheduled Castes/Scheduled Tribes Prevention of Atrocities Act (henceforth Atrocities Act) since it burst onto India's legal terrain three decades ago. The Atrocities Act, which is currently the only law in the country that bears the contours of hate crime legislation, represents the final instance in a series of legal measures that were introduced in independent India with the goal of weakening the system of caste: a structure of social hierarchy (Srinivas 1962) and status ranking (Weber 1978) whose ritual rules, economic modes of exclusion, and oppressive practices have systematically and violently relegated Dalit (former untouchable) communities to the social margins (Ambedkar 1989b [1936]).

In January 1950, almost three years after India gained independence from the British Empire, the country adopted its new constitution. The chairman of the constitutional drafting committee, legal scholar Dr. B. R. Ambedkar, belonged to the Mahar caste and was himself a member of India's Dalit community. Ambedkar made sure to enshrine the value of nondiscrimination in the foundational legal framework of the postcolonial Indian state and to position the principles of equality, justice, liberty, and fraternity at the center of the constitutional social agenda.[5] Ambitiously, India's constitution banned discrimination based on caste, religion, gender, sex, or birthplace, and it outlawed the practice of untouchability, whereby Dalits were socially ostracized due to notions of ritual impurity.[6] To the authors of the constitution, India was not just meant to be a country that *discouraged* discrimination. It was designed as a democracy, which *encouraged* active resistance to hegemonic power structures amongst its citizens through a mission of transformative constitutionalism (Kannabiran 2012; Bhatia 2019). B. R. Ambedkar was convinced that India's full democratic potential would only unfold if social inequalities were systematically eradicated (Ambedkar 1989a [1917]; see also Linkenbach 2021).

Therefore, India's constitution laid the foundation for a new set of special legal protection mechanisms to compensate members of historically marginalized groups, like Dalits, for the historical injustices they had had to endure (Mosse 2018, 423). The term "Dalit," which translates to "broken" or "downtrodden" in Maharati[7], is a self-designation, adopted by a socially and economically heterogeneous group of low-caste communities across India (Fuller 1996). These communities are unified by a systematic history of exclusion from social and political life: Dalits have been denied access to common water sources and sites of worship, refused ownership of land and other economic resources (Deliege 1999), and forced into demeaning forms of labor like manual scavenging (Omvedt 1995). Above all, they have been subjected to brutal acts of humiliation and violence (Guru 2011). It was this landscape of oppression which the Indian constitution aimed to eradicate by combining two approaches to equality: equality for all on the basis of citizenship, also termed "equality as a right," and special provisions for some on basis of caste or community, often described as "equality as a policy" (Béteille 1998, 224).

In independent India, "equality as a policy" was primarily enacted through state-led affirmative action programs for specially categorized disadvantaged groups (Galanter 1984). When the government introduced proportional reservations for so-called Backward Classes (BCs), 15% and 7% of all government sector jobs and higher education seats were respectively set aside for Scheduled Castes (Dalits) and Scheduled Tribes (Adivasi indigenous groups).[8] Following a report submitted to the government in December 1980, which found that over half of India's population was economically and socially "backward," reservations were also extended to so-called Other Backward Classes (OBCs) in 1990.[9] Affirmative action policies provided an important anchor for the upliftment of Dalit communities and facilitated their access to political institutions (Pande 2003). However, they neither resulted in wide-scale economic advancement nor did they fundamentally undermine caste prejudice (Corbridge 2000; Guru and Chakravarty 2005; Jaffrelot 2006).[10, 11] Hence, Indian lawmakers introduced additional legislation to eliminate practices of untouchability and economic marginalization (chap. 1). Still these laws failed to address the one method of oppression that continuously nourished the framework of caste from within: violence.

Caste-based aggression against Dalits in India has always been a consistent and troublingly varied feature of sociopolitical life. A twice-sharpened blade, violence on the basis of caste has been defined by two simultaneous processes: First, by a mundanity of injury, which weaves various forms of verbal and physical humiliation, discrimination, and symbolic harm into the everyday fabric of Indian social and economic interactions and renders them normal and invisible (Loomba 2016; Muthukkaruppan 2017). Second, by brutal, public outbreaks of mass aggression, whereby upper castes physically etch their perceptions of Dalit inferiority, feelings of disgust, and fear of status loss onto Dalit bodies through physical torture (Sarukkai 2009). Together, these strands of violence have woven a grid of "structural oppression" (Muthukkaruppan 2017, 40), which has been able to rejuvenate the hierarchy of caste whenever it has been under siege.

Eventually, legislators realized that they had to cut off caste aggression at its roots. In 1989 the Atrocities Act arrived on India's social and legal stage, a watershed moment in Indian anticaste legislation. Often referred to as a *special criminal law* in India—a law that creates a specific category of offences for a certain group or subject (Ambasta 2020)—the Atrocities Act is difficult to categorize within a global legislative context. As a statute, which enhances punishments for crimes that are committed against individuals because of their membership in a historically marginalized or oppressed group (Sharma 2015, 206) the Atrocities Act is typically referred to as a hate crime law in the international scholarly literature (Myers and Radhakrishna 2018; Hota 2019). Yet the socially transformative agenda of the act is profoundly reflective of India's unique landscape of caste and civil liberties. Hence, this book highlights the Atrocities Act as a postcolonial example of culturally embedded hate crime legislation.

The Atrocities Act was the first law in India to explicitly criminalize all forms of verbal, physical, and "symbolic violence" (Rao 2009, 174) against Dalits and Adivasi indigenous groups as so-called atrocities. It did so by creating new types of offences not included in the Indian Penal Code (IPC). The current version of the act, which is the result of several amendments in 2015, 2018, and 2020, specifies over twenty discriminatory actions that must be penalized as criminal infractions when they are committed against Dalits and Adivasis by someone not belonging to these groups. Additionally, the law outlines enhanced punishments for certain offences under the Indian Penal Code when they are committed against the aforementioned communities.

Over the past decade the Atrocities Act has gradually emerged as an inspiration for Indian scholars and civil society groups who are advocating for a comprehensive legal framework against identity-based violence for all of India's historically marginalized groups (Bhat 2020b; Perry 2020). Incidents of hate speech and mob violence against Dalits and religious minorities, and Muslims specifically, have risen steeply as India's government has embarked on a policy of majoritarian Hindu nationalism rooted in traditional caste hierarchies (Hansen 2001; Jaiswal, Sreenivasan, and Singh 2018; Chatterji, Hansen, and Jaffrelot 2019). Thus, advocacy groups are increasingly pointing to the Atrocities Act as India's *only* determined effort to systematically punish bias crimes and are demanding an expansion of the judicial ambition it represents (Citizens against Hate 2018).

However, despite, or perhaps because of, its punitive rigor and socially transformative ambition, the Atrocities Act has always been a deeply polarizing law in India, and even a disappointment to many who have fought for caste equality. Today, thirty years after its implementation, scholars have questioned the ability of the act to generate fundamental social change (Baxi 2014; Berg 2020), as most cases registered under the law never make it to court and a negligible number lead to conviction (Carswell and de Neve 2015, 1116; Rameshnathan 2018). Many feel that the Atrocities Act has failed Dalits and Adivasis by allowing their realities of violence to be systematically ignored by police (Khora 2014) and to go unacknowledged in courts (Wire Staff 2018). Cumulatively, these studies suggest that, in the eyes of most, the Atrocities Act is an unsuccessful law.

And yet, most of these critiques have neglected to ask some crucial questions: *What would it really mean for the Atrocities Act to be successful? To whose vision of success are hate crime laws accountable? And how are survivors of caste atrocities, their families, and their communities trying to find success within a legal landscape that is fundamentally stacked against them?*

This book is an attempt to step into this gap. Peeking behind the curtain of official crime statistics and conviction rates, *Fragile Hope* lays bare the social life of India's Prevention of Atrocities Act. It analyzes how the aims, substantive rules, and evidentiary procedures of the act are (re-)interpreted, gendered, and contested by Dalit communities in Rajasthan—a North Indian state which has consistently seen one of the highest rates of caste atrocities in India in the past decade (Press Trust of India 2016; Shakil 2020).

Fragile Hope argues that the Atrocities Act is gradually and invisibly rewriting systems of caste hierarchy and sociopolitical power in Rajasthan, even as the explicit and implicit caste biases of legal actors often undermine individual atrocity complaints. Therefore, the book proposes that previous analyses, which have highlighted the toothless nature or failure of the act, paint an incomplete picture. *Fragile Hope* shows that in Rajasthan, which has never witnessed the large-scale mobilizations that have marked Dalit resistance in other parts of India (Bhatia 2006), the Atrocities Act has emerged as a site for a project of *legal meliorism*: the gradual improvement of oppressive societal conditions (Dewey 1958), which relies on the construction of new strategic legal communities as well as new epistemologies of justice and habits of hope.

As these new practices and modes of sociality have symbiotically grown around the bureaucratic trunk of the Atrocities Act, the law has inspired different stakeholders to question the fundamental assumptions and temporal frameworks underlying criminal truth regimes in India. In microscopic and sometimes controversial ways, survivors, activists, and legal aid NGOs have begun to unlace and rearrange what they consider the structural allegiance of India's criminal legal system to upper-caste worldviews: a system that holds the potential of the Atrocities Act captive.

However, this agenda of institutional transformation is not uniformly conceptualized, experienced, or enacted. The Atrocities Act and the search for justice after violent incidents of discrimination and hate come to bear on individuals and groups in heterogenous and discordant ways. When the Atrocities Act is pulled into the everyday life of families, communities, politics, and activist missions, it becomes gendered, fractured along socioeconomic lines, and can generate new forms of intracommunity hierarchy and even violence. As individuals, and sometimes entire neighborhoods, file complaints, the Atrocities Act embeds itself in intimate ties of kinship, weaves itself into political agendas, and encounters different modes and scales of violence. In the process it gives rise to a mosaic of visions of legal success and to competing sociolegal imaginaries of justice. These visions can be deeply at odds with one another, even within the boundaries of individual family homes.

This book is an ethnographic voyage alongside the Atrocities Act as it springs off the page of bureaucratic imagination and is drawn into the social life of individuals, families, villages, and towns. In the autumn of 2016, inspired by my previous work with human rights organizations in Delhi, I journeyed to Rajasthan with a clear objective: as an anthropologist, rather than as a lawyer, I wanted to explore the everyday discourses around, and approaches to, the Atrocities Act. Over eighteen months I traveled across the state alongside atrocity complainants, activists, and advocates to trace how individual incidents of caste-based violence become legal cases under the act.

In the process I learned that the Atrocities Act is a law that radically challenges juridical and political assumptions about the type of transformation that hate crime laws can and should create. On the one hand, the act exposes familiar, lived dilemmas and evidentiary contradictions that haunt legal attempts to legislate against prejudice and hate at a global level. On the other hand, its social life reveals that in the interstices of daily life (Das 2019), hate crime laws are not the sum of their procedural, juridical obstacles, conviction rates, or individual case outcomes.

Instead, they become open battlefields, on which different stakeholders fight for the right to imprint their vision of equality, justice, and truth onto the epistemologies, temporalities, and procedures of official law. In Rajasthan, the Atrocities Act has become a canvas on which Dalit families and communities paint their own ideas of agency and restitution. In doing so, they actively try to reduce the historical footprint of dominant castes—not just on the Atrocities Act—but on the structure of general criminal law to replace it with their own. Hence, the Atrocities Act raises new, important questions about the way hate crime law generates expectations of institutional transformation and accountability.

REWRITING LAW'S ALLEGIANCE
Challenges of a Postcolonial Hate Crime Law

The theoretical and practical challenges facing hate crime law have been extensively discussed in sociolegal scholarship. "Hate crime," a term deeply steeped in the legacy of the US civil rights movement, has entered common parlance to describe acts of physical and verbal violence directed at (historically) oppressed groups because of certain racial, religious, or gender-based markers. "Hate crime" is a conceptually fuzzy phrase that has no consistent definition across jurisdictions (Hall 2013). Yet scholars fundamentally agree that hate crimes are symbolic acts of harm fueled by the perpetrator's aim to uphold hegemonic power structures (Perry 2001).

While the empirical usefulness of the word "hate" to describe diffuse, cumulative processes of social prejudice is contested (Bowling 1993), the proactively, hostile attitudes the expression evokes are analytically potent in capturing the effects bias generates in everyday social life. Encapsulating a diverse, yet related, set of emotions like paranoia, anxiety, fear, anger, and envy (Ngai 2005) which people in unequal economic and political systems experience, "hate" is not a passive feeling but an active, affective method of social boundary-making (Ahmed 2004). These affective boundaries are often consciously (Chatterjee 2023) or unintentionally (Shoshan 2016) (re)produced by state institutions. In societies defined by increasing diversity and nontransparent economic and political relations, the strategic projection of hate becomes an emotional tool for members of historically powerful groups to differentiate themselves from other communities in a way that allows for a positive perception of their own social group (Ahmed 2004). This projection, which is deeply entwined with fears around status loss (Kimmel 2018), can escalate into targeted acts of violence against minorities, who are perceived as the source of this fear. When groups that have been marginalized demand a type of social change that requires sacrifices from those who have historically had a monopoly on sociopolitical influence, the latter often react violently. This violence is exacerbated when historically powerful communities encounter new financial limitations that give rise to unconscious narratives of perceived loss (Gadd and Dixon 2011).

To govern these practices of violent boundary-making, legislation that targets so-called hate crimes—also variously termed "bias crimes" or "identity-based offences"—has increasingly sprung up in different national contexts (Walters 2022). Proponents of hate crime laws stress their symbolic value. As legal instruments they communicate state opposition to (violent) prejudice and promote social tolerance (Perry and Alvi 2012). Supporters have further suggested that hate crime laws offer a strategic shorthand for historically subjugated communities to translate their unique grievances into a recognized, global language of crime and punishment (Perry 2020).

Meanwhile, critics of hate crime legislation have not only been skeptical of its ability to remedy discrimination (Björgo 1994) but have also expressed concerns that such laws could further entrench identity-based antagonisms (Alongi 2017). Some have doubted the procedural validity of hate crime legislation, as its institutional success hinges on the ability of survivors and legal practitioners to prove perpetrators' hateful *motives*—the reason *why* someone developed an intent (*mens rea*) to commit a crime (Brax and Munthe 2015; Brax 2016)—in court. Others have proposed that hate crime legislation may silence real experiences of discrimination by denying some narratives legal credibility as hateful offences (Walters, Owusu-Bempah, and Wiedlitzka 2018). Finally, some scholars have been skeptical towards the idea that legal officials could function as neutral arbitrators in disputes involving questions of prejudice (Swiffen 2018).

However, India and crimes against Dalits rarely feature in these debates, despite the historical parallels between caste exclusion in India and structural racism in countries like the United States (Thorat and Umakant 2004, xxxix; Myers and Radhakrishna 2018; Wilkerson 2020) and the frequency and brutality of caste atrocities. Additionally, conceptual and empirical analyses of hate crime law have largely been concentrated in the fields of criminology and legal studies and have only sparingly relied on extensive ethnographic research.[12]

This knowledge gap is not simply unfortunate from a methodological or political standpoint. It has hindered scholarly insight into the social and political ramifications of hate crimes, as well as hate crime laws, and slowed down global initiatives for social justice. Legal institutions, policing practices, and evidence regimes in many postcolonial nations remain shaped by colonial hierarchies of power and identity, which have contributed to the political stigmatization of (particular) racial, religious, or ethnic groups

(Baxi 2012; Jauregui 2016; Bhat 2020a). Colonial governments not only introduced new, often antagonistic, categories of social identity (Dirks 2001) but also molded legal and political institutions in line with these categories (Comaroff 2001; Mbembe 2001; Mamdani 2003; Chatterjee 2004; Berti and Bordia 2015). Hate crime laws like the Atrocities Act are embedded in a legal system which is steeped in colonial codes, assumptions, and procedures that aimed to control indigenous populations, who were considered disorderly and inferior (Kolsky 2010).

Therefore, the inner lives of atrocity complaints in India—a postcolonial nation marked by exceptional social diversity and equipped with one of the most comprehensive affirmative action programs in the world—offer promising insights into the unexpected challenges, possibilities, and questions that grow out of legal attempts to prevent and prosecute hate crimes.

In India, the Atrocities Act has been met with similar apprehension as hate crime laws in the global North. Introduced to counteract, punish, and, ultimately, end caste discrimination, the expectations placed on this law have always been high and the disappointments in its shortcomings bitter. Dynamics of caste and casteism are extremely difficult to capture in legal categories of evidence (Waughray 2022). Moreover, legal attempts to punish caste-based violence are themselves enacted within a social and political system which is built on structures of caste hierarchy (Rao 2009; Teltumbde 2018b). Hence, some critics have concluded that the Atrocities Act is paralyzed by the same web of power that it seeks to dismantle (Baxi 2014).

Indeed, evidence suggests that in everyday legal practice the Atrocities Act has often been made to operate in line with upper-caste interests. As India's judiciary remains dominated by the country's highest-ranking castes, and police investigations are subtly influenced by economically and politically dominant caste groups, the sharp arrow of the Atrocities Act is redirected to point at its intended beneficiaries. Through strategic judicial interpretations, or even openly compromised police investigations, the Atrocities Act has frequently seen itself "converted" into a law that unsees caste discrimination in practice and invalidates Dalit experiences in favor of upper-caste narratives (Berg 2020, 153).

Therefore, the Atrocities Act has faced a crisis of purpose: scholars have proposed that it has achieved little more than to permanently mark Dalits and Adivasis as injured identities, whose specific protection under criminal law has produced more hostility and further polarized Indian society (Rao 2009).

Beyond Legal Paralysis
In *Fragile Hope* I do not reject these analyses. Instead I show that they fail to highlight a different dynamic, which India—a country whose constitutional framework encourages active resistance to discrimination—can illustrate better than any other national context: for historically marginalized communities, hate crime laws can become sites for the creation of new social resources and foundational legal epistemologies which aim to eradicate the institutional biases and bureaucratic inequities that make hate crime legislation necessary in the first place.

Many of the stories I encountered during eighteen months of fieldwork in Rajasthan illustrate that the "conversion" of the Atrocities Act (Berg 2020) into an instrument of upper-caste power is indeed a frequent reality. Dalit survivors of caste atrocities regularly struggled to access, and be taken seriously by, the institutions that produce legal evidence, such as hospitals, forensic labs, or police stations. This struggle was compounded as powerful, horizontal upper-caste networks made strategic interventions in investigations that aimed to neutralize the punitive power of the act. These simultaneous processes resulted in a public discourse that painted Dalits as inauthentic or "unreliable" legal narrators (comp. Affolter 2021), and habitually ripped the Atrocities Act from the hands of survivors, leaving them without a sense of justice.

And yet, the window my fieldwork granted me into the social and political life of the Atrocities Act in Rajasthan also shows that analyses, which foreground the reappropriation of the act by higher-caste perpetrators and legal actors, don't tell the whole story. Previous studies of the Atrocities Act, which have focused less systematically and longitudinally on the *lived legal negotiations* in which atrocity complainants engage, have underemphasized that survivors actively and tactically resist the usurpation of "their law" by upper castes. Through a multilayered, multifaceted agenda of legal engagement, survivors, human rights activists, and Dalit political leaders in Rajasthan labored to overcome the networks of power that paralyzed the act. Carefully and gradually, they tried to rewrite the allegiances of legal institutions as well as the epistemological assumptions, temporal frameworks, and procedures of general criminal law in line with the unique subaltern truths of past and present oppression.

Hence, *Fragile Hope* shows that the social life and the transformative potential of the Atrocities Act in Rajasthan do not end at neutralization or "conversion." Instead, they begin there. As Dalit communities try to reduce the upper-caste footprint on formal law, they explore and engage varied legal strategies which aim to incrementally shift ingrained structures of caste power loyalty and institutional bias. Since these strategies can often contradict one another, survivors and their supporters are united neither in hope nor in resignation. However, what they do share is a meliorist outlook: a sense that at least their engagement with the Atrocities Act can make social and legal conditions for Dalits *comparatively* better (Fiala 2019).[13]

The Dalit communities I worked with in Rajasthan—most of whom belonged to the upwardly mobile and numerically robust Meghwal *jāti* (subcaste)—were very aware of the institutional obstacles and dynamics that held the transformative potential of the Atrocities Act hostage. But many were not ready to accept those limits. Through diverse moments of counter-practice, which began long before atrocity complaints went to court, activists, NGO advocates, community leaders, and survivors themselves defiantly moved into legal spaces. Cultivating their own legal personas (chap. 3), out-of-court compromises (chaps. 2, 5), hermeneutic habits (chaps. 4, 7), temporalities and regimes of truth (chap. 4), understandings of restitution (chap. 6), and narrative expressions (chap. 3), different stakeholders in atrocity cases engaged in a concerted effort to turn their own social, economic, and political imaginaries of caste equality into "embodied expressions" of legal resistance (Larsson 2017, 71; also Csordas 1994).

The same way that political elites and upper castes had historically impressed their worldview and hierarchies onto the foundations of the criminal legal system, stakeholders in atrocity cases worked to impress their own concepts of truth and evidence as well as the temporal frameworks that define discriminatory experience onto legal cases (chap. 4). In doing so, they attempted to "deconstruct" the existing relationship between hate crime law and official justice, which they considered to be rooted in mechanisms of power and domination (Derrida 1992), and to reprogram the legal truth-finding procedures.

However, this was a tricky process with complex consequences. To free the Atrocities Act from the state of institutional paralysis it finds itself in, and to make it deliver on its promise of caste equality, survivors, Meghwal politicians, and independent Dalit advocates used the act in creative ways. These engagements were radical attempts to shine the spotlight on the unique truths, historicity, and economic conditions that define caste violence. Survivors proposed that a legal system, which wanted special protection laws like the Atrocities Act to help marginalized groups, must account for the unique features of lived discrimination. However, legal actors from upper-caste backgrounds often (mis-)interpreted these efforts as examples of lawfare—the illegitimate use of legal instruments (Merry 1994; Pinos and Hau 2022).

In Rajasthan, which can only claim a splintered Dalit movement (Rawat 2017), the Atrocities Act has emerged as a new, constitutionally embedded, and bureaucratically sanctioned anchor in the fight for caste equality. As a special criminal law for the empowerment of historically disadvantaged communities (chap. 1), it signals the accountability of the Indian legal system to the narratives, memories, and truths of those who have suffered most at the hands of a caste order, which has long been challenged by the country's foundational legislative structure: the Indian constitution (Director, Centre for Dalit Rights, Jaipur, pers. comm., January 2017).

In *Tools of Justice* Kalpana Kannabiran claims that "the Indian constitution gives voice to counter-hegemonic imaginations of justice" through its insurgent imperative to erode social inequalities in the name of democracy. According to Kannabiran, the Indian constitution positions the right to nondiscrimination so centrally that it creates a space for historically oppressed groups to resist policies and laws which are at odds with this constitutional value (Kannabiran 2012, 10, 1).

Similarly, the Atrocities Act has produced imaginations and strategies among Rajasthan's Meghwals which aim to subvert legal processes that facilitate the conversion of the Atrocities Act into an instrument of upper-caste power. These insurgent activities have also created a polarized discourse around the Atrocities Act on the national political and juridical stage.

A Polarizing Resistance

The independent legal practices and visions Dalit communities in Rajasthan developed in conversation with the Atrocities Act were not only deeply threatening to upper-caste communities but also to many legal professionals (chaps. 4, 7). These professionals saw Dalit efforts to make the Atrocities Act truly "theirs" as a danger to their own vision of law as an institutional and ideological edifice imbued with static, even eternal, authority and general rules. Targeted Dalit engagement with the Atrocities Act publicly highlighted contradictions within the current framework of special criminal laws in India (chap. 1) as well as inconsistencies within legal practice. It shone the spotlight on the structural biases that still permeate legal institutions and, ultimately, called into question the authority and rationality of India's criminal legal edifice itself. Dalit human rights activists in Rajasthan frequently insisted that courts should deliver on the *social objective* of the Atrocities Act—to protect marginalized groups—instead of being a slave to *general evidentiary* categories and criminal *procedures*, which were ill-equipped to capture the temporalities, frameworks of truth, and the institutional obstacles that define experiences of discrimination.

Hence, they demanded conceptual and methodological adjustments within general criminal law to create space for the truth regimes that govern marginalized lifeworlds. By defining criminal law in terms of its intended social effects, Dalit communities turned it into something other than what legal professionals considered it to be (see Cotterrell 1998, 175). Their demand that evidentiary categories and arguments in criminal law should be rethought and potentially transformed brought legal professionals face to face with law's own impermanence as a historically specific assemblage (Vissmann 2008). Hence, Dalit legal engagements in Rajasthan uncomfortably illuminated the ephemerality of criminal law.

These practices often produced immense social backlash against the Atrocities Act among legal professionals even at India's highest judicial level. In a controversial 2018 judgment, the Indian Supreme Court declared the act a vehicle for fraud (chap. 4) and warned that it had become a tool in the hands of "scheming complainants," who use the law as a device for revenge (*Dr. Subhash Kashinath Mahajan v. the State of Maharashtra*). These anxieties resonate with critiques in Indian legal scholarship which dismiss special criminal laws like the Atrocities Act as policies that fly in the face of general principles of justice (Ambasta 2020; see chap. 1).

Such reactions highlight that the implementation of hate crime laws is, ultimately, a battle over social space and power. Hate crime law creates a framework within which historically powerful and marginalized groups compete to bring the foundations of formal law in line with their social imaginaries, epistemologies, and visions of history.

A Fractured Imaginary: Gender, (Masculine) Politics, and the Traps of Professionalism

And yet, the quest to bring the framework of Indian criminal law in line with the truths, needs, and narratives of historically oppressed groups was neither a uniform nor unproblematic endeavor. One of the most striking insights from my fieldwork was that the attempt to remold legal processes in the name of a wider Dalit public was in itself fraught with deep issues of power, and occasionally even intracaste violence. Ideas of what it meant to have a successful case under the Atrocities Act (chap. 2), how such a case should best be pursued (chap. 5), for how long, at what cost, and with what aim (chap. 7) differed drastically among, and within, Dalit communities in Rajasthan.

Perhaps most problematically, the pursuit of a "better" legal structure was often a distinctly masculine quest which relied on and deepened injurious patriarchal structures. As a young, unmarried woman, who was considered a daughter by the Meghwal families I lived with, and who closely worked with a Dalit women's activist, I heard the stories of female atrocities survivors in detail and resonated with them most keenly. Even though I did not focus my fieldwork exclusively on women's issues and also traced atrocity cases involving male survivors, the conversations I had with Meghwal women—especially with those of a younger generation—involved exceptional depth and trust. These interactions taught me that even though caste violence was still disproportionally directed at Dalit women, their ideas of justice, truth, and success usually mattered little in atrocity cases. In one sense, this is hardly surprising considering that Dalit women in India have always faced a compounded type of violence, which is rooted in general caste vulnerability, upper-caste perceptions of Dalit women as usable and disposable bodies, and systems of patriarchy (Ciotti 2012; Baxi 2010; Baxi 2014; Still 2017a,b). However, it also highlights how both the pursuit of a legal framework defined by equality and a fight for the procedural efficacy of hate crime legislation can be profoundly unequitable. It can sideline the most vulnerable sections within marginalized communities and create new forms of gendered violence. To use the Atrocities Act for the greater good of their local village communities or the wider Dalit movement, Meghwal husbands, fathers, and "big" men regularly ignored the injuries which the pursuit of legal cases inflicted on the women in their lives.

However, the fight for the Atrocities Act also threw existing and emerging hierarchies of masculinity into stark focus. Dalit men, who were the heads of their households, often equated a determined pursuit of a legal case in the face of threats, or possible emotional harm to oneself or one's family, with courage and strength. Thus, the willingness to endure a legal fight, which symbolized a struggle for Dalit rights, often became entwined with a particular perception and performance of ethical masculinity.

Specifically, socially mobile Meghwal men fashioned themselves into leaders of purpose and honor: men who were not simply strong and ethical because of "what they had endured" (Cohen 2010, 256) but also because of the assertive way in which they were willing to forge a legal path through this suffering. Just as practices of consumption or sexual prowess can become methods of projecting masculinity in everyday life and differentiating oneself from other, less masculine, Dalit men (Anandhi and Krishnan 2002), the cultivation of legal personhood became a way of establishing new hierarchies of masculinity.

In Rajasthan, the gendered and classist production of the Atrocities Act was often inspired and encouraged by professional Dalit human rights activists, who generally stemmed from upwardly mobile families and lived in urban centers like Jaipur. Despite the genuine empathy that most activists and NGO advocates had for survivors, many also held rigid ideas about the "right way" to fight *through*, and *for*, the Atrocities Act. They thought that the act was a powerful legal document, whose reputation had to be protected for its own sake even if this posed additional challenges for survivors. Taking on the role of legal strategists and with various levels of legal training, professional human rights activists advised poorer, less literate atrocity survivors how to pursue justice "properly." Yet their vision of a "proper" legal fight was often incompatible with the concerns and hopes of survivors, who desired restitution as well as economic and social survival.

Ironically, professional activist efforts to make the Atrocities Act the primary focus of Dalit assertion in Rajasthan were often stopped in their tracks by local Meghwal big men (*netās*), who performed a similar type of assertive privilege but had an entirely different set of political and social concerns and agendas. Meghwal leaders in villages often viewed party politics, not law, as the primary pathway to Dalit assertion. They feared that the stubborn pursuit of legal justice would cost them upper-caste votes in local elections for seats that were reserved for Scheduled Caste (SC) candidates, thereby undermining a sustainable pathway to equality through political representation.

As both activists and *netā*s descended on survivors' families, they often failed to listen to survivors' own desires and understandings of legal success. Echoing the insight that movements of group assertion often have unintended consequences (Cody 2013), the struggle for legal transformation and equality, which the Atrocities Act inspired in Rajasthan, was not in itself an effort marked by equality. Some voices were much louder than others, some types of pain were declared more valid than others, and some ideas of success and justice were systematically prioritized over others.

Still, the voices that were habitually relegated to the sidelines found a way to make themselves heard. Perhaps one of the most encouraging insights of this book is that survivors consistently found subtle ways to make the Atrocities Act serve their own needs and hopes. Despite the new hierarchies and forms of intersectional violence that grew around the act, survivors of all genders frequently managed to integrate the law into their everyday pursuit of justice through micro-agencies which defied the instructions of *netā*s and activists (chap. 5). While the latter frequently lamented such instances as failures of the law, women in particular tended to find a fragile hopefulness and success in precisely those moments.

For some Meghwal women like Aunty-jī, the Atrocities Act in its textual form emerged as a quasi-sacred document, on the back of which they could develop new, hopeful habits and orientations (chap. 7). In the face of profound grief and loss, hate-crime-law-as-text allowed these families to imagine and labor for a future and society that was *better*. While they were astutely aware that the legal system was stacked against them, they looked to the symbolic document of the Atrocities Act as a source of *meliorist thinking*: the idea that this special law was proof that society could be comparatively improved (Dewey 1958).

Amplitudes of Success

At the start I asked: What does it mean for the Atrocities Act to be successful? *Fragile Hope* reveals that this query is neither a purely legal, nor political, nor bureaucratic question. The success of the Atrocities Act has never been either binary or fully scalable.

Behind realities of conversion, legal paralysis, institutional bias, police corruption, and judicial neglect, hate crime laws like the Atrocities Act create a scenery of competing societal visions and imaginaries of justice. These are rooted in contradictory ideas of the "right" pathway to (legal) victory, healing, or social transformation after violent rupture. When we zoom in on the social life of the Atrocities Act, we see that one group's or person's legal failure, success, or restitution rarely maps onto someone else's. When viewed through the lens of conviction rates, the Atrocities Act may have failed; when regarded through the eyes of Mr. Krishnan, its bureaucratic author, its success might hinge on a specific notion of better implementation. However, in reality, the successes of the Atrocities Act are both: already well alive, deeply fragmented, and forever fragile and incomplete.

The best metaphor for the unpredictable patterns of success that the Atrocities Act engenders is perhaps that of *amplitude*: a wave that vibrates at different frequencies over a single time period and within a single space. The voices in this book reveal that the success of hate crime laws is socially situated and individually experiential. It materializes for one survivor and not another in the same family. In Rajasthan, the success of the Atrocities Act emerged at different frequencies across Meghwal communities, as part of a struggle to upend the social allegiances of the legal system.

AN ANTHROPOLOGIST ON THE TRAIL OF HATE CRIME LAW

My scholarly interest in the Atrocities Act has evolved organically. India has been my second home since the age of five. I spent my childhood years moving back and forth between my German hometown and a village in the North Indian state of Uttarakhand where my mother, a trained anthropologist, conducted research on the history of forest protests. Growing up, my life in Uttarakhand shaped me as much as my life in Germany (Fuchs 2020c). We lived with a family, I made friends, and I adopted the local language, mannerisms, habits, and a love for the most dramatic of Bollywood movies without much reflection. I was treated like a daughter by the family of the Rajput caste we stayed with, and I loved them in turn, accepting their authority on local matters in the simple way children do. When *Mata-ji*, the mother of the family, told me that there were certain people—*Harijan*s, as they referred to the local "untouchable community"—that one should not accept food from, I did not question it.[14] But my mother did. It was one of the few times she fiercely instructed me to ignore local practices.

Then, when I was twelve, my father, a sociologist of religion, set out for fieldwork in Mumbai. His work explored how Dalit communities in Dharavi, Mumbai's biggest slum, mobilize religious practices to resist casteist frameworks. The time I spent with my father's interlocutors in Dharavi, and the scholars and activists I was introduced to through his work, caused me to reflect, for the first time, on what caste meant. As I learned about the brutal inequality inflicted by the caste system, I grew uncomfortable with the demands our host family in Uttarakhand had made of me. I struggled to make sense of the fact that the people, who had partially raised me, engaged in practices that were deeply discriminatory, even though they were friendly with particular Dalit individuals.

Reflecting on my own experience, the ease with which prejudice was intergenerationally transmitted, even to supposed outsiders, troubled me deeply. This sense of discomfort stayed with me thereafter. As I maintained my relationship with our host family in Uttarakhand, I increasingly felt like I had to challenge their habits of untouchability more openly. Following the completion of my undergraduate studies in 2012, I therefore joined the Indian Institute of Dalit Studies (IIDS) in Delhi as a researcher.

IIDS had been founded by Sukhadeo Thorat, Professor of Economics at Jawaharlal Nehru University and former Chairman of India's University Grants Commission in 2003. The institute had a small team working on caste-based violence and it was here that I first heard about the Atrocities Act. IIDS often collaborated with the National Campaign on Dalit Human Rights (NCDHR), *Swadhikar* in Hindi. Highlighting the fact that "Dalit rights are human rights," the NCDHR argued that practices of untouchability are in direct violation of the right to human dignity. On World Human Rights Day in 1998, the NCDHR had launched the "Black Paper Campaign," which sought to draw international attention to caste violence and untouchability as a "heinous crime against humanity" (Bob 2007, 180). The NCDHR openly criticized the Indian government's failure to successfully implement India's central safeguard against caste-based atrocities: the Atrocities Act.

I was intrigued by the work of the NCDHR and the way the historically unique phenomenon of caste was being reframed in the language of international human rights law. Therefore, I returned to Delhi in 2014, during my MPhil studies at the University of Oxford, to work as part of NCDHR's international advocacy team. One of the most visible arms of the NCDHR is the National Dalit Movement for Justice (NDMJ), which actively tracks caste atrocities in India and highlights obstacles to the effective implementation of the Atrocities Act. Observing the work of the NDMJ, I began to wonder why constant advocacy around laws like the Atrocities Act was necessary. Why was the act not being implemented "properly"? How did those who experienced caste-based violence experience the potential of the act? And what did "proper implementation" even mean to them, or to organizations like NDMJ?

Moreover, it dawned on me that the Atrocities Act posed broader questions about the intersection between politics, law, and structural violence as well as about the real-life traumatic implications of legal attempts to address and counteract bias and hate. Were the issues facing the Atrocities Act unique to the Indian context, or did they mirror obstacles that faced hate crime laws in other parts of the world?

Another, much more personal reason also drove my interest in the Atrocities Act. During my time at the NCDHR, I became friendly with a group of women who coordinated the All India Dalit Mahila Manch (AIDMAM), a section of the organization which raised awareness around the violence experienced by Dalit women and provided legal aid to victims. I learned that sexual assault and rape were incredibly common forms of caste violence: upper castes tried to inscribe their claim to social power on the bodies of Dalit women, who have been rendered even more economically and socially vulnerable than Dalit men through patriarchal practices (chap. 1). The insights the AIDMAM staff shared made it clear that this vulnerability seeped into the arena of formal law. Dalit women, central targets of caste-based aggression, seemed to have little say in how they wanted to engage with the legal system.

As a woman who had herself experienced a traumatic incident of sexual assault in her early twenties, these stories hit me hard. I wanted to know if the Atrocities Act, as a hate crime law, could bring any sense of justice for women who had survived horrific experiences of identity-based assault. As these questions grew more urgent for me, I decided to place the social life of the Atrocities Act at the center of my doctoral research at the London School of Economics. Even though I did not focus my study exclusively on atrocities against Dalit women, the way hate crime law can produce new forms of gendered violence was a fundamental concern that drove my ethnographic study of the Atrocities Act.

I chose Rajasthan as my field site for several reasons. From a scholarly perspective, serious analytical engagement with the dynamics of caste and law in Rajasthan was pressing. Rajasthan registered the second highest number of caste-based atrocities in India between 2013 and 2015 (Sharma 2016; Scroll Staff 2016), a trend that was reaffirmed in data released by the National Crimes Record Bureau in 2020 (Singh 2020). In 2019 Uttar Pradesh, India's most populous state, which borders on Rajasthan in the southeast, reported the highest number of atrocity crimes against Dalits in absolute terms. However, it was Rajasthan—a state with a Scheduled Caste population of 17%—which had the highest *rate* of atrocity crimes against Dalits (55.6%) in the same year (Shakil 2020). This exceptionally high rate of caste atrocities can partially be explained by Rajasthan's unique feudal history (Zutshi 2009), which has produced fractured movements for Dalit assertion compared to states such as Maharashtra or Tamil Nadu (Bhatia 2006; Rawat 2017). Though regional pockets of Dalits within Rajasthan have become more vocal in their demands, traditional caste hierarchies remain intact in many parts of the state. The high rate of caste atrocities and the absence of large-scale political organization around Dalit issues have turned the Atrocities Act into a crucial instrument of Dalit mobilization in Rajasthan.

I also had personal and ethnographic reasons for focusing on Rajasthan. First, while working with the NCDHR in Delhi in 2014, I had gotten to know members of a human rights NGO in Rajasthan's state capital of Jaipur. This NGO, the Centre for Dalit Rights (CDR), focused on providing legal aid for Dalit survivors of caste atrocities and had networks across the state. Second, I had met an economist in Delhi who belonged to the Meghwal community and had family in Rajasthan's northeastern district of Jhunjhunu. Therefore I already had a solid network of interlocutors in the state. From a linguistic viewpoint Rajasthan was also opportune. Due to my childhood days in Uttarakhand, I spoke Hindi fluently and had an ear for Hindi-based dialects. Hindi is spoken widely across Rajasthan. Most local dialects, like *Marwari*, which is spoken in Jhunjhunu, are related to Hindi in vocabulary and structure. The linguistic landscape and my extensive network across Rajasthan allowed me to conduct a regionally and institutionally multisited ethnography of the Atrocities Act.

TRACING LAW IN RAJASTHAN

The ethnographic subject I engage with, interpret, and conceptualize in this book is the Atrocities Act itself. However, this book does not centrally represent either a discourse analysis of the Atrocities Act as a legal text or an examination of the law as a platform for courtroom arguments (Berti and Bordia 2015). Rather I analyze the Atrocities Act as a social imaginary (Taylor 2004) which is politically, affectively, and economically vernacularized (Levitt & Merry 2009) by its intended Dalit beneficiaries. In this approach I take inspiration from work in legal anthropology, which has positioned chains of political and legal production, or specific legal techniques (Lokaneeta 2020), at its center and highlighted how state policies can become milieus that generate new modes of intimacy and sociality (Nordstrom 2004, 246).

However, for purposes of ethnographic accuracy I ground my analysis in the landscape and history of contemporary Rajasthan. As the largest state in India by size, Rajasthan makes up approximately 10% of the country's total area although it is only India's eighth most populous state. Rajasthan is characterized by extreme differences in climate and agricultural potential, ranging from dry desert regions in the west, to the luscious green hills of Udaipur district in the south, to the semi-arid Shekhawati region in the northeast (fig. 1).

To add to the geographical complexity, the idea of Rajasthan as a uni-

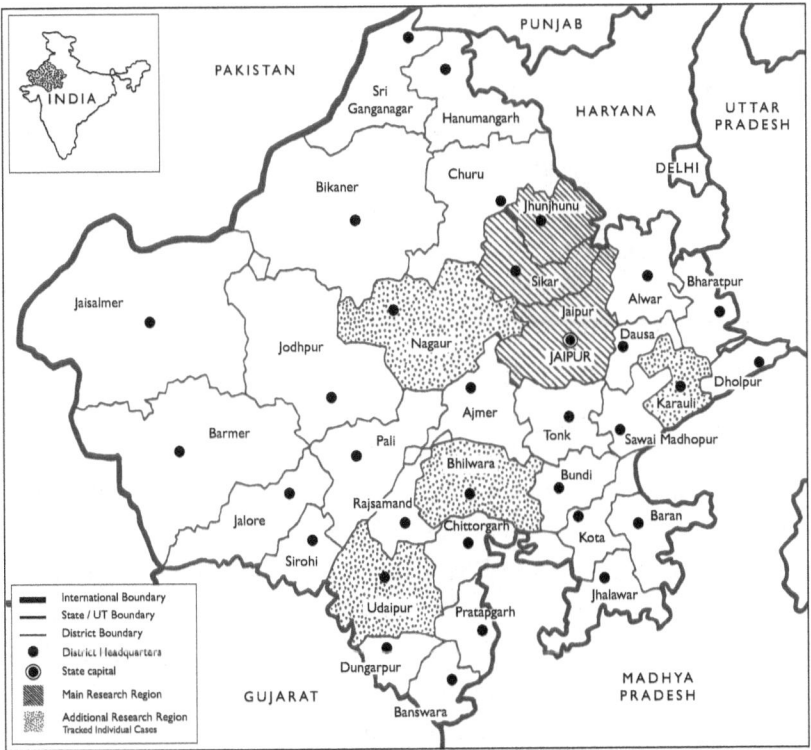

FIGURE 1. District map of Rajasthan pre-2023. On March 17, 2023, the Government of Rajasthan announced the creation of nineteen new districts. In October 2023, three further districts were created. However, this map represents the district boundaries between 2016 and 2018, at the time the fieldwork in this book was conducted. Map created by Lydia Denno.

fied geopolitical entity is recent and obscures a complex (colonial) history that still shapes caste relations today. The modern state of Rajasthan was formed in 1949 out of a conglomeration of former British "princely states" and was known as the Rajputana Agency.[15] Under the British Raj, these princely states were governed through a system of truncated, ambiguous sovereignty, referred to as "indirect rule." Indirect rule signaled a practice whereby a territory was ruled by an indigenous *rāja* (king), who was supervised by an agent of the crown (Rudolph and Rudolph 1966, 138).

The Rajputana Agency consisted of over twenty semi-sovereign states and chieftains with varying levels of political, economic, and social development (Singh 1964; Sisson 1972). However, most princely states shared two common features: They were marked by deep-rooted networks of solidarity between the ruling Rajput clans (Lyall 1884), and they functioned according to rigid feudal structures, which positioned Rajputs at the top of a social pyramid as the landowning elite (Tod 1920). These structures and loyalties naturalized a hierarchical caste organization and gave rise to deeply antagonistic relationships between the Rajputs, the dominant peasant castes (Jats and Gujjars), who were employed as tillers on Rajput lands, and various (largely landless) Dalit communities, who worked as casual laborers (see below).[16]

Rajasthan's history still has significant influence on the way caste boundaries are negotiated and reinforced today (Copland 2005; Kooiman 2003; Zutshi 2009). Since different princely states had different systems of land tenure, caste-based land ownership in contemporary Rajasthan also varies across different districts. While Dalit communities own small parcels of land in some areas of Rajasthan like Shekhawati in the northeast, where I predominantly conducted fieldwork, they often remain landless in southern districts like Udaipur. Hence, Rajasthan is characterized by a plurality of sociolegal orders (Moore 1993), economic relations (Gill 2018), and distinct traditions of caste-based aggression (Shakil 2020).

Rajasthan's past as a group of loosely connected princely states means that the historical source material is far less extensive and less systematically structured than what is available for large parts of British-ruled India. There are no Settlement Reports, and the District Gazetteers I located in the British Library stem from the post-independence era. Furthermore, the classic historical literature on Rajasthan (see, e.g., Tod 1920) almost exclusively focuses on the ruling Rajput elite or the administrative structures of the princely states. Therefore, much of the information on the Dalit communities I worked with, who primarily belonged to the Meghwal *jāti* (subcaste), is based on oral history, NGO reports, and select scholarly publications, which also rely on oral transmissions.

Due to Rajasthan's historical and geographical diversity, I decided to centrally focus my research on the Atrocities Act in the northeastern Shekhawati region, which borders the capital district of Jaipur in the southeast and the state of Haryana in the north. Shekhawati, which fell under the erstwhile control of the Jaipur princely state (Jhunjhunu District Gazetteer 1984), is named after the former Rajput ruling clan: the Shekhawats, who governed the region until the formation of Rajasthan in 1949. It comprises the district of Jhunjhunu, the adjacent district of Sikar, as well as parts of Nagaur, Churu, and Jaipur district (fig. 1). While I also followed complaints in other areas of the state, such as Udaipur in the south (chap. 3), Karauli district in the southeast (chap. 4), and the capital city of Jaipur (chap. 7), most of the legal journeys in this book unfolded in Shekhawati.

I set up two fieldwork bases: The first was in Jaipur, where the Rajasthan High Court, the Jaipur sessions court (the highest criminal court in a district), and the Police Commissionerate are located. Access to these institutions allowed me to observe how atrocity cases were treated at various institutional levels within the criminal legal system. India's judicial system is pyramidal in structure with the Supreme Court at the top and the High Courts and other subordinate courts at the lower levels. The Indian Supreme Court is the country's highest court of appeal (it also has advisory and original jurisdiction in certain matters of law). However, every Indian state also has a designated High Court, which is the highest court of appeal in that state. High Court decisions are binding on all the lower courts of the state over which it has jurisdiction. The High Court appoints judges to the district courts, which deal with judicial matters at the district level in a state. District courts are referred to as sessions courts when disposing of criminal matters. Within districts so-called lower, subdivisional criminal courts are then presided over by magistrates, the lowest-level criminal court judges. In addition, the 2015 amendment to the Atrocities Act had stipulated the creation of exclusive special courts at the district level for the speedy trial of atrocity cases. In areas where there were lower numbers of caste atrocities, the sessions court was designated a special atrocity court. One of Rajasthan's busiest exclusive special courts was located in Jaipur within the boundaries of the district court complex.

I explored the court landscape in Jaipur alongside several human rights NGOs, headquartered in the capital, that provided legal aid for Dalit atrocity survivors. Among them was the CDR. Part of the CDR's work was to run a legal resource center that provides "legal support, assistance and counselling to . . . Dalit and Adivasi victims and witnesses [and] free legal aid . . . in the cases of [an] atrocity" (CDR website 2016). With the dual aim of educating Dalits across Rajasthan about the Atrocities Act and helping victims of violence through the challenging process of filing and fighting criminal complaints, CDR activists liaised with relevant authorities regarding atrocity incidents and coordinated media interventions. Most staff members employed by the CDR came from Dalit communities across Rajasthan, but some belonged to higher castes. Many held a law degree (LLB) and sometimes acted as independent legal counsel for survivors. They intervened when families expressed concern about their assigned public prosecutors (chap. 1) or doubts about their ability to secure evidential documents (caste certificates, medical reports, etc.).

The CDR also had regional offices in several districts across Rajasthan. District headquarters were largely managed by local activists, who worked in close collaboration with the central Jaipur office. Frequently these district coordinators were salaried women who had no legal expertise of their own but were knowledgeable about their areas, enjoyed significant respect in their communities, and had extensive regional networks. I contacted the NGO during my initial visit to Jaipur in the winter of 2015 and they were happy to have me observe their work. The CDR also gave me access to some internal case files. Based in Jaipur, I accompanied CDR staff on fact-finding missions. I also followed independent criminal lawyers to the special SC/ST court that was integrated into the local sessions court, and interviewed High Court judges, magistrates, and police officers in their chambers.

The second leg of my research was based in the district of Jhunjhunu, where I centrally focused on the Meghwal community, the most numerous and socially influential Dalit *jāti* in the region. In Jhunjhunu and the wider Shekhawati region, Meghwals also represented the most upwardly mobile section of the Dalit community. They were very active in local politics, ran most Dalit civil society organizations (chap. 2), and were the most litigious among Shekhawati's Dalit groups. Based on data I obtained from the office of Jhunjhunu's Superintendent of Police (SP), Meghwals had also filed the most complaints under the Atrocities Act in Jhunjhunu in 2016 (see below).

To understand the unique social and cultural perspectives that motivated Dalit engagement with the Atrocities Act in Shekhawati, I lived alternately with two Meghwal families. One was Avinesh's family—the economist I had met in Delhi. Avinesh's family was college educated, upwardly mobile, and resided in Jhunjhunu town. The other Meghwal family I lived with inhabited a village in Jhunjhunu subdistrict, which I will call Badrasar. The eldest daughter, Sonali, coordinated the Rajasthan wing of the AIDMAM in Jaipur and became a dear friend. While Sonali lived in the capital, the rest of her family remained firmly anchored in the village, where her brother worked as a taxi driver while her mother ran the local kindergarten (*anganwadi*) and tilled their small plot of agricultural land.

The demographic make-up of Badrasar mirrored that of other villages in rural Jhunjhunu. Badrasar claims a large, agriculturally wealthy community of the Jat peasant caste (50%) and a substantial Dalit population (15%), consisting mainly of the Chamar, Meghwal, and Nayak *jāti*s. Many Dalits enjoy at least a basic education and own small plots of land. Rajputs, who ruled Shekhawati during the colonial era, constitute about 12% of the village but have lost agricultural wealth to the Jats since independence. Meena Adivasi families make up 6% of the village population. Badrasar also had a sizable Muslim population (10%). Scattered households of Brahmins, Kumbhars (historically potters), or Nais (barbers) make up the rest.

Sonali's and Avinesh's families had relatives and acquaintances across Shekhawati, which embedded me in an invaluable network. As an unmarried young woman who worked on a sensitive subject, setting out alone to contact atrocity survivors, would neither have inspired trust nor been safe. Instead, Avinesh and Sonali set me up with dependable relatives or friends who traveled around the district with me. I was handed down a remarkable web of *bhāiia*s (brothers), uncles, and cousins, who took it upon themselves to get in touch with affected families they knew and helped me understand the local Marwari dialect when terms became too specific for me. Though I was initially unsure about showing up at survivors' homes backed by a group of predominantly male relatives, I soon learned that this method was perhaps my only way to obtain uncensored information on caste atrocities. Many of the villages I visited had never been in direct contact with foreigners, and despite my fluency in Hindi I was immediately perceived as an oddity. However, accompanied by "brothers," I was stamped as a respectable woman, under the explicit protection of a good family. Moreover, the presence of people from their own community reassured survivors of my motives and made them more comfortable sharing their stories.

Throughout this, I always tried to remain mindful of the delicate nature of my work. I didn't want to compound survivors' fear and trauma by forcing them to provide information on my terms. And so I also shared difficult and intimate aspects of my own past with survivors, and especially with the young women I came to know.

In this process, Sonali was a great source of friendship and support. In her capacity as Rajasthan State Coordinator of the AIDMAM, Sonali had extensive experience working with female victims of (caste-based) sexual violence and provided a nuanced gendered perspective on caste aggression. The tact Sonali displayed when talking to Dalit women who had suffered sexual trauma, taught me how to approach topics of a sensitive nature. Her long-term engagement with female survivors also meant that women had time to get to know me gradually and engage if and when they felt ready to do so.

Taken together, the institutional and familial networks that guided my fieldwork allowed me to understand the bureaucratic dimensions of the Atrocities Act in dialogue with the lived aspects of caste violence, which grow out of Rajasthan's unique past.

JHUNJHUNU: HISTORIES OF CASTE AGGRESSION

The district of Jhunjhunu, where Sonali's and Avinesh's families resided, is divided into six subdistricts (*tahasīla*s)—Jhunjhunu, Nawalgarh, Chirawa, Buhana, Khetri, and Udaipurwati (fig. 2)—and shares a border with the state of Haryana (see fig. 1). Jhunjhunu district and the wider Shekhawati region are the ancestral home of some of India's most influential Marwari

FIGURE 2. Subdistrict (Tehsil Map) of Jhunjhunu pre-2023. Map created by Lydia Denno.

business families of the historical *bania* merchant castes, who have invested heavily in the educational uplift of the area.

Jhunjhunu has a Dalit (Scheduled Castes) population of 16.88% (Census of India 2011). Indigenous Adivasi communities only make up 1.9% of the district populace, which is a low percentage compared to other parts of Rajasthan. According to my interlocutors, the majority of Jhunjhunu's Dalit population belongs to the Meghwal *jāti*. Other Dalit groups in the district are Khatiks, Raigers, Jatavs, Balais, and Nayaks.[17] 62% of Dalits in Jhunjhunu still work in agriculture and approximately 33% are agricultural laborers (Alha 2018).[18]

Jhunjhunu's Meghwals have exceptional visibility in legal proceedings under the Atrocities Act. The district police data I secured upon my arrival showed that Meghwals filed 69 out of 116 (59%) complaints registered under the Atrocities Act in Jhunjhunu between January and October 2016.[19] Other Dalit *jāti*s in the region feature much less prominently on the case registry.[20] Similarly, most of the atrocity cases that became the subject of media attention in Jhunjhunu between 2016 and early 2018 involved Meghwals. Three Meghwal caste organizations led efforts to offer legal support to atrocity complainants in Jhunjhunu and exerted active influence over political negotiations in individual cases: The Jhunjhunu Ambedkar Society, the Jhunjhunu Meghwal Samāj (Jhunjhunu Megwhal Society), and Jhunjhunu Meghwal Sangharsh Samiti (Jhunjhunu Association for Meghwal Assertion).

During my fieldwork I closely investigated thirty atrocity cases against Dalits in Jhunjhunu. Out of these thirty cases, eighteen caste atrocities were directed at Meghwals. All but one of the cases involving Meghwals cited members of the Jat caste as the accused parties.[21] Jats belong to the category of Other Backward Classes (OBC) and are the largest landowning caste in Jhunjhunu today.

The high number of Jat-Meghwal atrocities hints at an ambivalent dynamic between the two caste groups in Shekhwati. Understanding this relationship requires a closer look at the formation of the Meghwal community against the backdrop of Shekhawati's history of agricultural relations.

Becoming Meghwal

Meghwals in Rajasthan have a unique history of identity formation that has allowed the group to rapidly grow in size and strength over the past century. The Indian Census of 2011 lists Meghwals as the single largest Dalit community in Rajasthan, with approximately 3.1 million members.[22] This stands in stark opposition to earlier census data, which counted only 22,978 members of the Meghwal *jāti* in 1931 (Cole 1992). This means that in the Rajputana Agency, Meghwals were only the eighth largest Dalit community, while Chamars (766,649), Balais (218,857), and Bambhis (169,803) were listed as the most numerous Dalit *jāti*s in the 1931 census. However, from 1931 onwards, Indian census data reveal a steady growth of Rajasthan's Meghwal population.[23] This rise is socially significant. Over the course of the past century many Dalits in Rajasthan, who historically belonged to the other *jāti*s, have started calling themselves Meghwals (CDR Fact Finding Report 2008, viii).[24] In eastern Rajasthan this process began as early as the 1940s (Shyamlal 2010).

Oral history suggests that the Meghwal community was likely consolidated in Mumbai in the 1930s (Mullard 2010), when members of different low-caste groups from India's northwestern regions flocked to the city in search of work. The 1930s was an important decade for Dalit communities in India. A politically "active, visible Dalit public" (Rao 2009, 88) had begun to emerge in the wake of Ambedkar-led Dalit movements of the 1920s.[25] In Mumbai, members of various untouchable groups (mainly Balai, Chamar), who had traditionally been engaged in "polluting" work with dead animals (e.g., leatherwork), organized themselves by forming a caste council. The community embarked on targeted efforts at social purification and status enhancement, and started calling themselves Meghwal (see Mullard 2010, 71).[26, 27] In Sanskrit *Megh* means cloud or rain, and some sources claim that the designation "Meghwal" derives from Saint Rishi Megh, who had the ability to draw water from the clouds. Meghwal literally translates to "the people who pray for rain" (Helia 2019).

In 1953 the growing Meghwal community drafted a constitution, the *Meghwal Gnati Bandharan*, which was subsequently updated in 1977, 1986, and 1993. The constitution dictated that Meghwals should refuse any involvement in traditionally untouchable occupations, such as the skinning of dead animals. It also stipulated fines for members of the community who broke this rule. The constitution was designed to remove the basis of discrimination against Meghwals within the Hindu caste system.

These efforts of reinvention were underscored by the conscious scripting of a "caste history," which counteracted the idea of Meghwals as untouchables and constructed a respectable caste identity.[28] In Rajasthan, the best-known example of the new Meghwal mythology is the *Meghwansh Itihas* (History of the Meghwals), which was authored by Swami Gokuldas (1998). The *Meghwansh Itihas* links the history of the Meghwal community to the non-Brahmanical deity Ramdev Pir, who is also worshiped among some followers of Shia Islam (Khan 1997). Ramdev was a Rajput warrior who became sanctified. He was rumored to have been born a member of the untouchable castes.[29] In Jhunjhunu many Meghwals worshiped Ram Dev. Avinesh's family had visited his supposed final resting place in Bikaner district multiple times.

Meghwals in Shekhawati: A Tale of Caste Ascendancy

Over the course of the last century, Meghwals in Rajasthan have, thus, been involved in a concerted effort at Sanskritization—the emulation of upper-caste customs (see Srinivas 1952)—to establish themselves as a ritually pure, respectable caste community. However, the growing economic and political strength of Meghwals in Jhunjhunu and the wider Shekhawati region is tied to a different local story of caste mobility: that of the above-mentioned Marwari community of *bania* merchants.

Jhunjhunu is the ancestral home of a group of midranking *bania* (trader) castes often referred to as Marwaris. Some Marwari families, like the Birlas, Dalmias, and Piralams, began their business expansion through the textile industry in the early 1900s. Their meteoric rise on the national and international business scene profoundly shaped Jhunjhunu district. On the one hand, the steady accumulation of financial capital by Marwari families since Indian independence has meant that the district's business networks are now largely monopolized by the *bania* caste (Alha 2018). On the other hand, the charitable arms of business conglomerates like the Birla Group have also invested heavily in the educational uplift of Jhunjhunu, turning certain parts of the district into hubs of (elite) learning. From the 1950s onwards, the growing discourse around progress through education, modeled by wealthy Marwari families, precipitated the growth of the educational sector in the region, and Jhunjhunu gradually emerged as a leading district in primary school enrollment in Rajasthan (Rajasthan Development Report 2006, 297). Along with the neighboring district of Sikar, Jhunjhunu has one of the highest literacy rates in Rajasthan today. According to the 2011 census, Jhunjhunu's literacy rate stands at 74.13% (male 86.9%, female 60.95%), which is 8% above the Rajasthan state average of 66.11%.[30]

Due to these developments, Dalit communities in Shekhawati, many of whom now identify as Meghwal, enjoyed comparatively easy access to education. In the 1970s this opened the door to reserved government jobs under India's affirmative action program for a small group of Meghwal men. Employment in the public sector has produced a section of well-educated and upwardly mobile Meghwal families, who have reinvested some of their earnings into Jhunjhunu's agricultural and property sectors. The educational and economic strength of Meghwals in Jhunjhunu has also allowed the community to grow its political presence. The upwardly mobile Meghwal families in the district now use their educational acumen to run local caste associations like the Meghwal Samāj, the Jhunjhunu Meghwal Sangarsh Samiti, and the Ambedkar Society, which all actively promote local Dalit engagement with the Atrocities Act (chap. 2).

However, the growing economic might of the Meghwal community and the political prominence of its caste associations has become a concern for another caste group in the district, which increasingly fears for its predominant status in Jhunjhunu's agricultural and political landscape: the Jats.

A Battle for Status: Jat-Meghwal relations

In Shekhawati, the Jat community, which is categorized as one of India's Other Backward Classes (OBCs), shares a complex history with the former untouchable groups in the region. Jat and Dalit relations in Jhunjhunu are defined by mutual economic and political dependencies, which trace back to the agrarian property regimes of the colonial Rajputana Agency.

During the Rajputana Agency, agricultural land in Shekawati was mainly administered through the exploitative *jāgīrdari* land tenure system.[31]

Vast stretches of land were controlled by a small, influential group of upper castes (mainly Rajputs), while tenants (mainly Jat and Gujar castes) were the tillers of the land, who managed smaller plots and paid tributes and grain taxes to the Rajput ruling class. Informal practices of "subinfeudation" (Pande 1982) further strengthened the exploitative character of the *jāgīrdari* system. Hereby, Jat and Gujar peasants, who managed larger tenancies, handed over parts of the land to untouchable castes in exchange for payments and tributes. This created a chain of hierarchical dependency where the burden of payment, labor, and production was routinely pushed onto Dalit agricultural laborers, who cultivated the least fertile plots. This vertical displacement of payment and responsibility resulted in degrading living conditions and financial destitution for most lower tenant farmers and agricultural laborers (Sharma 1990, 118; Sharma 1999), who often became subject to systems of caste bondage.

The exploitative practices of the *jāgīrdari* system gave rise to the Jat-led Shekhawati peasant revolts in the 1920s, which tried to disempower Rajput landholders (*jāgīrdars*). The peasant revolts are the reason for the limited influence the Rajput caste holds in Shekhawati today compared to other areas of Rajasthan. They also laid the foundation for the current agrarian power of Jats in Jhunjhunu, which was cemented through post-independence land reforms.

The peasant revolts unfolded in three phases between the 1920s and Indian independence in 1947. After a first logistical phase, which involved the founding of the Shekhawati Jat Sabha (Shekhawati Jat Council), the second phase of the movement (after 1930) saw a mass mobilization of Jats across northern India (Rawal 2015, 3). At this time, the modern state of Haryana, which borders on Jhunjhunu, emerged as one of the central sites of Jat resistance. During the peasant revolts Jats began to articulate demands for status parity with Rajputs: for example, they started adding the suffix "Singh" to Jat names, which had previously been a Rajput privilege (Datta 1999; Singh 1990). Across Shekhawati, peasant castes started to question the legitimacy of the land tenure system and devised slogans like "*thikānedāron ke zoolmon kā nash ho* (end the atrocities of the landlords)" (Singh 2014, 177).

During this period the Jat peasantry began to rely heavily on the support and collaboration of Dalit agricultural laborers, who backed the peas-

FIGURE 3. A typical Shekhawati village landscape at sunset.

ant struggle in hopes that the abolition of the *jāgīrdari* system would lead to land redistribution. However, they were disappointed. In the final phase of the revolts, which began in 1938 (Rawal 2015; Singh 1998; Singh 2003), the movement gradually came under the control of the Indian National Congress Party (INC) and changed in character and allegiance. The interests of poor Dalit peasants and tribal groups were overruled by those of a wealthier Jat peasantry (Omvedt 1980). In her analysis of the movements Hira Singh writes:

> The main slogan "Land to the Tiller," adopted . . . under the tactical and ideological guidance of the Indian National Congress, in effect excluded poor peasants, landless labourers and the entire group of service castes . . . as none of them were considered tillers. Those excluded from the movements . . . were ipso facto excluded from the land reform programmes in post-independence India. The beneficiaries were the class of better off tenants who were the vanguard of these movements, and having acquired a share in state power, used this to change property relations in the countryside. (Singh 2014, 179)

Therefore, the Shekhawati peasant movements largely profited the resident Jat community, which emerged as the engine of commercial agriculture.

In the decades after independence, the newly founded Rajasthan government implemented several laws aimed at land redistribution. The most important was the Rajasthan Jāgīr Lands Resumption (Validating) Act, 1957, in which the government officially resumed all rights on *jāgīr* lands and provided compensation to former owners that amounted to seven times the net income from the land (Rudolph and Rudolph 2011; Rawal 2015). Ownership (*khātiradāri*) of previous *jāgīr* lands passed on to those formerly employed as tenants.

In Shekhawati, most of these tenants were Jats who received large parcels of productive land. In contrast, Rajput elites retained control over substantial areas of so-called *khalsa* lands that had been under direct control of the central Rajput court (*darabāra*) during the colonial period in other parts of Rajasthan like Udaipur. In these areas Rajputs remain much more influential players in contemporary politics than in Shekhawati (chap. 3).

The opinion that Jats have now taken over Shekhawati and grabbed the lion's share of the land is widely shared among Dalit communities in Jhunjhunu. In my fieldwork village of Badrasar, Meghwals stressed that Jats were the winners of the land reforms (*Jāto ke liye thi land reforms*). Many felt betrayed. They argued that Jats had conveniently forgotten the support Dalits had provided during the peasant revolts and had tried to assume a de facto position as "rulers of the land" previously occupied by Rajputs.

A local Meghwal political leader (*netā*) in Badrasar village once told me: "Men like my grandfather participated in the peasant revolts. They marched alongside Jats and they thought there was respect. But Jats got more land and wanted to be on top. When Meghwals got educated they did not like it. Today many commit violence against us when we try to rise up." His words highlight the predominant dynamic behind caste atrocities in Jhunjhunu. Over the past five decades the original Meghwal beneficiaries of public sector affirmative action policies have amassed significant financial and social capital in Jhunjhunu. Former Meghwal government employees have reinvested their white-collar income in the professional development of their children. Pockets of Meghwals have used their capital to buy up land from an increasingly impoverished rural Rajput community as well as industrial plots and shops in towns. My own "fieldwork families" are proof of that: Avinesh's father owned a row of ten shops in a small town near Jhunjhunu city, which he rented out to shopkeepers from different castes. Similarly, Avinesh's father-in-law had bought over 200 *bigha* (32 ha) of farmland in his natal village. He leased this land out to resident Meghwal families to ensure the "progress (*vikas*)" of his caste brothers. Younger generations of Meghwals have used the educational and financial capital of their families to secure work in the private sector in Jaipur and Delhi.

Jats have become increasingly threatened by the growing socioeconomic strength of Jhunjhunu's Meghwal community. As in other parts of India, the reaction to this status anxiety has been violence (see Jodhka 2015; Jodhka and Manor 2017; Waghmore 2018). Avinesh once reflected, "Jats think everything is theirs (*saba kucha unka hai*), and that they should be able to do what they want but they are always afraid that Meghwals will learn to take their share. That is why atrocities happen."

The fact that more than half of the attacks against Megwhals in Jhunjhunu were perpetrated by Jats is, thus, no coincidence. It exposes that caste atrocities in India, and so-called hate crimes in the global North, share a fundamental DNA: they are messenger crimes (Perry 2001; Hall 2013), intended to reaffirm social hierarchies by etching them into the bodies of marginalized groups who dare to demand parity of participation (Fraser 1998).

OVERVIEW

I have divided this book into three parts. The first part (chaps. 1 and 2) is entitled "A Kaleidoscope of Imaginaries." It confronts the normative, bureaucratic vision of the Atrocities Act with the fractured sociolegal imaginaries that emerge around atrocity complaints in Rajasthan.

Chapter 1 discusses social genealogy, as well as the legislative features of the Atrocities Act, as a postcolonial example of culturally embedded hate crime law. Tracing the global legal discourses around mass atrocities and hate crime that shaped its formulation, the chapter explores the definitional and practical challenges facing the Atrocities Act. By situating the statute within India's wider landscape of special criminal laws and India's constitutional agenda, the chapter also discusses to what extent the social and legal contestations around the Atrocities Act are representative of wider issues in India's criminal legal system.

Chapter 2 then explores how the normative imaginary of the Atrocities Act becomes fractured when it is pulled into everyday negotiations around gender, politics, and professional activism. It traces how competing claims about the social purpose of the Atrocities Act shape the legal fate of caste crimes in Rajasthan. The chapter introduces the different stakeholders in atrocity complaints and explores the jurisdictional battle that unfolds among them. Following the story of Pinky, a teenage Meghwal girl who was raped by four upper-caste boys in her native village in Jhunjhunu district, the chapter shows how survivors can experience silencing at the hands of family, activists, and political leaders from their own communities, who treat atrocity cases as productive sites of power and want to imprint their vision of progress, honor, and justice onto the act. In this process new forms of intersectional, patriarchal violence and intracaste hierarchies are born. However, Pinky's story simultaneously highlights the complex interaction between survivors' own trauma and their legal agency in the aftermath of caste atrocities. The chapter asks who should be allowed to claim ownership over the "proper use" of hate crime laws.

Part 2 of the book (chaps. 3, 4, and 5) is called "When Atrocities Become Cases: Rewriting Law's Allegiance." It takes the reader into the arena of legal institutions and charts the obstacles that atrocity survivors face when attempting to turn their narrative of violence into legal cases. The three chapters trace how families, Dalit activists, and advocates try to overcome these obstacles and mobilize the Atrocities Act as a site for systematic and systemic legal transformation. By engaging in forms of positive sociality, stubborn resistance, and creative legal practice, they challenge the temporalities and evidentiary assumptions that define legal truth regimes. However, the chapters also highlight that ideas about how legal change should be achieved differ radically among these groups. This can produce new definitional conflicts of success and give rise to political polarization.

Chapter 3 takes us to the place where narratives of discrimination first encounter legal rule: the police station. The chapter explores the role of the Indian police in translating experiences of caste-based violence into official complaints under the Atrocities Act and illustrates the mundane and typical processes of conversion (Berg 2020) that police officers engage in to invalidate Dalit claims. By following Choti Lal Meghwal, an agricultural laborer, on his desperate journey to "get an atrocity case," the chapter analyzes the relationship between legal language, embodied inequality, and institutional translation. It illustrates how police verdicts often prevent Dalit complaints from entering the courts. Telling Choti Lal's story, the chapter explores wider problems within India's police structure and shows how police investigations can reinscribe the structural inequalities the Atrocities Act is meant to address.

Chapter 4 analyzes the character of juridical truth, by revealing how judicial actors in India actively construct both the Atrocities Act as a dangerous type of legislation and Dalits as unreliable legal narrators. The chapter explores a controversial 2018 judgment by the Indian Supreme Court, which dismissed the Atrocities Act as a vehicle for false accusations. It shows how local rumors that portray Dalits as abusers of the law are reproduced at various stages of the legal process and filter into the interpretation of individual cases as well as into national statistical data. Furthermore, the narratives in the chapter highlight that when Dalit complainants aim to rewrite legal truth regimes, they do so as a conscious response to local power structures and judicial biases. To regain control over a law they consider "theirs" and allow it to showcase the unique temporalities of discriminatory experience, complainants sometimes engage in acts of strategic disobedience that are meant to hold the Atrocities Act accountable to its spirit of anti-oppression.

Chapter 5 then takes the reader into the world of legal aid activism and examines the practice of out-of-court compromises (*rajināma*), which is popular among complainants and deeply disliked by human rights activist professionals. The chapter proposes that, despite activist discourses that lament the frequency of compromises as an indicator that the Atrocities Act is failing, atrocity survivors sometimes tactically use the threat of hate crime law as a negotiating ground for better compromises that provide an immediate sense of restitution and social leverage. The ability to achieve "better" compromises partially hinges on the emergence of strategic professional communities around the Atrocities Act. Survivors often tactically draw legal aid NGOs into their cases to signal to higher-caste perpetrators that they have new, powerful friends. This complicates anthropological debates around activist complicity and professional hierarchy. On the one hand, compromises unveil the Atrocities Act as a "jurisgenerative" site for the creation of new legal meanings, strategies, and publics (Baxi 1999; Cover 1983), which facilitates social change *outside* of the official legal arena. On the other hand, compromises can also weaken the credibility of the Atrocities Act and make hate crime legislation the target of further criticism. Hence, compromises raise new questions about the way success should be defined in the context of hate crime law.

The final section of the book (chaps. 6 and 7), entitled "Law at the Limits of Hate and Hope," moves away from the legal negotiations explored in part 2. Instead, it reveals the conditions under which the Atrocities Act can become either a barren landscape of disillusionment or a vibrant canvas of hopeful activity. The last two chapters bring the Atrocities Act to the limits and heights of its symbolic power. They show that, in the face of certain types of violence, hate crime laws can mean both nothing, and everything.

Chapter 6 introduces one of the most brutal caste atrocities in recent Rajasthani history: the Dangawas massacre in Nagaur district, which cost five Meghwals their lives. The chapter analyzes how, within the confines of Rajasthan's villages, some experiences of violence can render hate crime law an empty promise. The violence of Dangawas most clearly articulated the intention behind hate crimes: to send a message to historically marginalized groups that they will not be allowed to encroach on the space of dominant communities. Though the Atrocities Act was designed to bring justice in precisely such instances of intentional and extreme hate, the survivors of Dangawas ask what law can really do *in* their lives. They admit that the law seems "too far away" and cannot provide what they really need: to change the minds of their Jat attackers and protect Dalits from future suffering. The chapter draws on anthropological studies of transitional justice to highlight that sometimes hate crime law interferes with survivors' attempts to come to terms with loss and grief.

Chapter 7 finally puts the spotlight on the text of the Atrocities Act as a site for hope. It analyzes how engagement with the law in its textual form can give rise to new communities, which allow atrocity survivors to orient themselves in the world in a hopeful way. However, such hope is not a static fact but the result of stubborn labor in the wake of violence: through the cultivation of hopeful habits, families in Rajasthan who lost loved ones to atrocities were able to embark on a mission of *meliorism*: an attempt at comparatively bettering the oppressive world that harmed those they grieved. Teasing apart how markers of class and education shape engagement with the Atrocities Act, the chapter also explores the relationship between temporalities of hope, upward mobility, and legal engagement. Following the cases of two Meghwal women who lost family members to caste atrocities, the chapter shows that when people die, and the surviving families' faith in society is broken, hate crime law can sometimes become a symbol for, and a vision of, an improved world. This vision becomes intertwined with practices of faith that project a sacred promise onto the abstract nature of law.

The book ends with an epilogue, which takes the reader to a special public hearing on atrocity cases by India's National Human Rights Commission to reflect on the global potential of hate crime law to combat legacies of oppression. The book concludes that even though many activists and scholars believe that the Atrocities Act has failed, these chapters suggest that it has become a site for active labor towards social change and the birth of new social relations. On the one hand, these socialities have produced novel strategies of legal transformation and subversion. On the other hand, they have raised new questions about the accountability and goals of hate crime legislation.

PART I

A Kaleidoscope of Imaginaries

ONE

THE PREVENTION OF ATROCITIES ACT
A Social Genealogy

DEFINITIONAL COMPLEXITIES

In *Fragile Hope* I define India's Scheduled Castes/Scheduled Tribes (Prevention of) Atrocities Act (PoA) as a *culturally embedded postcolonial hate crime law*. I have chosen this categorization because the social and political dynamics around the Atrocities Act only begin to make sense when the act is analyzed through the lens of three different legislative categories: hate crime law, anticaste legislation, and Indian special criminal laws.

Even though the human rights and legal aid NGOs I worked with in Rajasthan, as well as organizational literature by bodies like the Commonwealth Foundation, colloquially refer to the Atrocities Act as an "antidiscrimination law" (CWF 2019)—a term that I also often adopted during my fieldwork—this designation is somewhat technically inaccurate. While the Atrocities Act indeed attempts to eradicate discrimination, in legal scholarship the phrase "antidiscrimination law" is generally reserved for statutes that deal with *civil* disputes between individuals to regulate discriminatory behavior in areas of employment or property (Kok 2008; Somek 2011).

The Atrocities Act is squarely a *criminal* law: it prosecutes caste violence as an offence against society. Therefore, the comparative legal literature has typically categorized the Atrocities Act as an Indian example of hate crime legislation (Myers and Radhakrishna 2018; Hota 2019), which punishes "manifestations of prejudice" against marginalized groups (Mason 2014, 293). The enhanced penalties the act specifies for criminal offences when they are committed against the historically oppressed Dalit and Adivasi communities (Guha 2019) are a typical, global feature of hate crime legislation (Jacobs and Potter 1998). The legislative framing of hate crime legislation is analytically potent in illuminating the procedural and substantive legal challenges atrocity complaints face in India. However, most importantly, the social life of the Atrocities Act provides a crucial ethnographic counterpoint to scholarly debates on hate crime law, which have predominantly focused on the global North.

Yet the concept of hate crime law must also be considered carefully in relation to the Atrocities Act. Its social genealogy reveals that the Atrocities Act was primarily inspired by international discourses around mass atrocity legislation in the 1970s and 1980s. Furthermore, the terminology of hate crimes is deeply steeped in the North American civil rights movement (Hall 2013; Bhat 2020a; Perry 2020) and can obscure the Indian history of civil liberties that inspired the act as well as distract from the unique cultural sensitivity which the law betrays (Naval 2004). The Atrocities Act is imbued with the socially transformative imaginary of the Indian constitution, which positioned a strong pro-equality and anti-oppression agenda at the heart of the postcolonial Indian state (Kannabiran 2012). Anticaste activists and advocates in Rajasthan always keenly reminded me of the inextricable link between the Atrocities Act and the aims of caste equality that were built into India's constitution by Dr. B. R. Ambedkar, chair of India's constitutional drafting committee, legal and political theorist, and the single most significant figure in the struggle against Dalit oppression.

Therefore the Atrocities Act is usually discussed as a distinctive type of anticaste legislation within India (Teltumbde 2008; Berg 2020; Waughray 2022). The designation "anticaste law" emphasizes the importance of the cultural context, from which the act was born, as well as the particular historical dynamics of discrimination it aims to combat. The Atrocities Act as an anticaste law represents an ambitious juridical rejection of Hindu caste hierarchies and untouchability (Berg 2020). The wording of the offences in the act delves deep into India's cultural landscape and historical psyche. It contours the blurry practices of untouchability and caste discrimination by detailing normalized, everyday ritual or symbolic acts of caste aggression and exclusion and punishing them as "atrocities." The cultural specificity of the offences outlined in the Atrocities Act has allowed the law to resonate with Dalit communities in India as a locally grown tool of anticaste resistance, which serves as a reminder that they must no longer accept suffering and humiliation as inevitable.

However, as a law, which tries to punish exceptional forms of violence against select social groups, the Atrocities Act also sits within the broader category of *Indian special criminal laws* in the modern Indian legal system (Sashittal 2023). Its status as a special criminal law, which tries to overrule general rules of criminal procedure, has been a source of public skepticism and resentment (Rao 2009).

Criminal law in India comprises three major acts. First, the Indian Penal Code (IPC) of 1860, which was introduced during British colonial rule.[1] The IPC constitutes a comprehensive code of all *substantive* aspects of criminal law in India. The distinction between substantive and procedural law is generally traced back to philosopher Jeremy Bentham (Malcai and Levine-Schnur 2014, 1). While the boundaries between the two categories are debated, substantive law generally refers to the "content of the rules" (Suresh 2023, 10). The IPC outlines the rights and duties of individuals and specifies what actions or offences represent a breach of these obligations. For example, section 375 of the IPC states that a man will have committed rape if he has sexual intercourse with a woman against her will and/or without her consent. The section defines *what* the criminal offence of rape is.

Meanwhile, the Code of Criminal Procedure (CrPC) of 1973 is India's main body of *procedural* law. This means it lays down the methods and means through which substantive law should be enforced. The CrPC spells out the administrative procedure that must apply to the enactment of the substantive rules specified in the IPC. To put it simply: if the IPC specifies *what* qualifies as a crime and sets corresponding punishments, the CrPC outlines *how* criminal investigations are to be conducted, how arrests can proceed, and how trials should be conducted. In this sense the CrPC is the structural engine of the IPC. Returning to the aforementioned example, section 164 (5A) of the CrPC specifies that in instances of rape, the victim's statement must be recorded by a judicial or metropolitan magistrate as soon as the police learn about the commission of the offence.

Finally, the Indian Evidence Act of 1872 sets out rules around the admissibility and relevance of evidence in criminal cases. It defines the framework of documentary and oral evidence, discusses the burden of proof in different types of law, and outlines what types of witness statements are admissible and under what circumstances.

In addition to these main acts, the Indian parliament has periodically passed "special" criminal statutes that supplement the general building blocks of criminal law. On a practical level, "special" criminal laws "create a distinct class of offences for certain acts" (Ambasta 2020, 3). According to section 41 of the IPC, they are laws that pertain only to a particular group, situation, or subject. The idea that certain categories of violence require exceptional or special legal responses and should be tried in special courts can be traced back to colonial India (McQuade 2021), when officers of the British Raj tried to suppress revolutionary activities among the native population through the introduction of special acts, procedures, and courts (see below).

Special criminal laws in postcolonial India have been primarily introduced for one of two reasons: first, to deal with crimes that are considered extraordinarily threatening to the state, like terrorism (Suresh 2023), and second, to ensure the protection of socially and economically weaker communities, who are at risk of special crimes that violate Articles 15 (nondiscrimination) and 16 (equality) of the Indian Constitution.

The character of the Atrocities Act as a special criminal law is significant. Special criminal protections are intended "to infuse criminal law with constitutional ideals of substantive equality by re-signifying previously stigmatized bodies as bearers of rights" (Baxi 2014, 284). Consequently, the special status of the Atrocities Act enabled the introduction of special courts for atrocity trials. It also sometimes allows the Atrocities Act to override procedural principles in the CrPC. Crucially, section (3) (2)(v) in chapter 2 of the Atrocities Act enhances punishments for IPC offences against a person or property that are punishable with a minimum of ten years' imprisonment, when they are committed against Dalits and Adivasis. Punishment for these offences is then increased to imprisonment for life and a fine. Meanwhile, section 3(2)(va) of the same chapter introduces a special "schedule" of select IPC offences, for which perpetrators incur an additional fine when they are committed against Dalits and Adivasis.[2]

Since the police are duty-bound to lodge any criminal complaint made by Dalits or Adivasis against a member not belonging to these communities under the Atrocities Act alongside the IPC, anyone accused of committing a casteist offence must theoretically expect to be convicted according to the more severe punishments specified in the Atrocities Act. This is no coincidence. When drafting the Atrocities Act, its authors thought that harsher penalties for seemingly ordinary crimes against Dalits and Adivasis were essential to nip in the bud the possibility of extreme, large-scale violence against these communities.

CASTE ATROCITIES: COMMUNICATIVE AGGRESSION

When I interviewed P. S. Krishnan, a bureaucrat who had been a central figure in the drafting of the Atrocities Act, at his house in January 2018, he explained that the name of the law was symbolically important: "When you look at the way the term has been used in India, 'atrocity' refers to a kind of violence that flows from the top of the social hierarchy to the bottom."

News of early post-independence mass violence against Dalits, such as the Ramanthapuram riots, which took place in the Indian state of Tamil Nadu in 1957,[3] and a later wave of Dalit-targeted violence in the 1970s, had convinced Mr. Krishnan—an employee of the Indian Administrative Service—that a special protection law for those at the bottom of India's caste and social hierarchy was needed (Krishnan 2018a; see also Devi 2017, 143, 135). He got a chance to make his vision a reality in 1987 when he was appointed Special Commissioner for Scheduled Castes under the Rajiv Gandhi government. "It was unbelievable the way Dalits were being slaughtered," he admitted to me during our interview in January 2018, "it wasn't just violence to get something. It was a statement about who was in power and a way to mark this power on Dalit bodies."

Mr. Krishnan's words resonate with sociological analyses, which have emphasized caste violence as a symbolic mode of aggression (Guru 2009) which brings to light deeply rooted societal notions of inferior personhood. Though it is not entirely clear how the term "atrocity" entered common parlance in India, scholars tend to agree that it "was used for the first time by the Commissioner of Scheduled Castes and Tribes—a special officer appointed under Article 338 (1) of the Constitution, as it originally stood—in his Annual Reports in relation to crimes against Scheduled Castes [SCs] and Scheduled Tribes [STs]" (Sankaran 2008, 128). In the 1970s, "atrocity" as a designator for violence against former untouchables slowly crept into the administrative language when the Office of the Commissioner for SCs and STs systematically started recording complaints of caste violence (Mendelson & Vicziany 1998). Mendelson and Vicziany propose that the phrase "caste atrocity" aimed to capture mounting acts of brutality in response to Dalit assertion. Soon the concept of the caste atrocity leapt off the administrative page into the world of media reporting to describe the specific mode of targeted and hierarchized violence that Dalit communities faced across the country on the basis of their identity (Mendelson & Vicziany 1998, 44). According to Pratiksha Baxi, the term was extended in the 1980s to denote crimes committed against Indian indigenous groups (Adivasis), who had equally been relegated to the social margins and were now demanding control over their traditional lands (Baxi 2014).

Global scholarship usually employs the term "atrocity" in relation to acts of mass violence. "Atrocity crimes" as a phrase to describe "unimaginably" brutal and extreme types of targeted aggression emerged in the aftermath of the Nazi Holocaust (Karstedt 2012, 384). Today, the term is used in international law to refer to large-scale political violence, including genocide, war crimes, crimes against humanity, and ethnic cleansing (Karstedt 2012, 384; Scheffer 2007). Atrocity crimes denote attacks that are enacted with the specific goal of decimating entire communities, which are considered simultaneously inferior and threatening by a socially powerful majority (Power 2002).

However, scholars of atrocity crimes have argued that such acts of extreme mass violence don't occur out of the blue. They are the result of a complex of historical and cultural processes (Mayans-Hermida and Hola

2023, 7), and the political construction of an ideological and emotional agenda that cultivates feelings of hostility or "hate" against specific groups (Alvarez 1999). The normalization of harm inflicted on these communities eventually escalates into unfathomable acts of large-scale brutality that seem disconnected from "normal" levels of violence. To describe the conditions under which atrocity crimes occur, Christian Gerlach developed the concept of "extremely violent societies." "Extremely violent societies" are social "formations" where diverse communities and different organs of the state actively participate in the production of hostility and the execution of physical violence against "various population groups" (Gerlach 2006, 1). He argues that in these societies mass violence is an activity that brings together social and political interest groups with a variety of concerns and motives.

As a nation which positioned the principle of nondiscrimination at the heart of its constitutional agenda, independent India does not neatly map onto Gerlach's notion of extremely violent societies. Nonetheless, scholars have asked whether the ideological systems of communalism and caste that have dominated India's history may systematically induce violence when they encounter other stimuli, such as "patriarchy, homophobia, or ethnic rivalry" (Chandhoke 2021, viii). In her recent study of Indian democracy, Neera Chandhoke goes as far as to ask "do 'we the people of India' have violence in our bones?" (Chandhoke 2021, vii).

Gerlarch's ideas also find new resonance in the current Indian political context, which has seen the systematic production of a government agenda of majoritarian Hindu nationalism (Chatterji, Hansen, and Jaffrelot 2019; Longkumer 2020). In an ethnographic analysis of the Gujarat pogrom of 2009, Moyukh Chatterjee argues that over the past two decades the country's Bharatiya Janata Party (BJP), which has been in power since 2014, has methodically engaged in the strategic composition of violence against minorities. The aim of this violence agenda has been the construction of a powerful Hindu majority population against the foil of minority populations, centrally the Muslim minority (Chatterjee 2023, 4). In India, violence has become a politically and socially "constitutive force" that produces new modes of (un-)belonging and secondary citizenship (Chatterjee 2023, 8–9).

While Chatterjee's analysis focuses on Hindu-Muslim relations, the idea that legal and political discourses and the routinization of everyday acts of aggression can turn certain groups into strategic targets of sociopolitical violence, is helpful in situating and analyzing the vision behind the Atrocities Act. When the term "atrocity" began to take center stage in Indian legal and political discourse in the 1970s and 1980s, it was meant to capture the idea that caste-based violence pursued a specific goal: to put Dalits, who resisted traditional caste roles and hierarchies, in their place, and to communicate upper-caste intolerance towards a potential shift in the hegemonic social order. Hence, caste atrocities have a communicative character.

It is at this juncture that the concept of the caste atrocity fully collides with scholarly theories on hate crimes. According to Barbara Perry, "hate crime . . . is a mechanism of power and oppression, intended to reaffirm the precarious hierarchies that characterize a given social order (Perry 2001, 10). Hence, hate crimes are often described as "messenger crimes" (Iganski 2001) intended to counteract political attempts to further "parity of participation" (Fraser 1998) and uphold the dominance of one community over another. Anthropologists have stressed that violent actions are often mobilized to affirm social orders (Sheper-Hughes 1992; Moore 1994; Eckert 2001; Eckert 2003; Whitehead 2004). Acts of harm committed by socially powerful groups against marginalized members of society, hence, reinforce ideas of supposedly "correct" social and political hierarchy (Das 1995; Eckert 2001; Goldstein 2003; Fuchs 2020b).

In this vein, so-called hate crimes imprint reminders of existing power differentials on the bodies and minds of those belonging to historically oppressed communities in order to enable the reproduction of oppression (Perry 2001). The element of systemic subjugation highlights the empirical and theoretical continuities between hate crimes and mass atrocities. Like mass atrocities, hate crimes are not isolated moments of aggression but the visible escalation of a deeper social process (Bowling 1993), which encompasses socially and historically diffuse dynamics of discrimination and prejudice.[4]

In recent decades, governments across the globe have begun enacting hate crime laws to signify their intolerance towards such oppressive acts of communicative violence (Perry and Alvi 2012). As Mohsin Bhat argues, in law the "hate crime concept simultaneously individualizes incidents of violence *and* places it in a social context, by illuminating the incident's harm on the victims, as well as the wider social harm. This emphasis directs institutional energies on identifying bias motivation in the individual legal case" (Bhat 2020b, 3).

Though not embedded in the vocabulary of hate but in the related language of atrocity, the contours of the Atrocities Act match that of a hate crime law: its ultimate purpose is to criminalize violent injuries that enable the conditions of oppression against Dalits and Adivasis. The term "caste atrocity" captures the essence of the hate crime by denoting the convergence of physical aggression and verbal humiliation (Guru 2009) that is intended to remind Dalits of their historical place at the bottom of the social hierarchy (Natrajan and Greenough 2009).

FROM UNTOUCHABILITY OFFENCES TO ATROCITY CRIMES

In its textual form, the Atrocities Act displays a remarkable historical and cultural sensitivity. The act embeds the concept of communicative violence in a particular set of social, economic cultural practices that are inextricably tied to the notion of untouchability. The actions that are classified as "atrocities" under the act include caste-specific forms of hostile communication or hate speech as well as a series of property- and access-related infringements, which have historically formed an integral part of the landscape of casteism.

The sensitivity and specificity of the act are the result of a longer process of legal evolution. The Atrocities Act is India's third statutory attempt to legally grasp and successfully punish caste-related violence. In line with Article 15 of the Indian constitution, which forbade discrimination based on caste, religion, race, sex, and birthplace, and Article 17, which abolished untouchability as a practice, the newly independent Indian government introduced the Untouchability Offences Act (UOA) in 1955. The UOA officially rendered the practice of untouchability a *cognizable* offence (Human Rights Watch [HRW] 1998, 182). This meant that in accusations of untouchability, police officers had the right to make an arrest without a warrant and could launch an investigation without waiting for permission from a court. The purpose of the UOA was to set up a legislative measure to "eradicat[e] pervasive discrimination practiced against Scheduled Caste members [and] . . . to enforce the abolition of untouchability under Article 17 of the Constitution" (HRW 1999, 182). However, public dissatisfaction with the act ran high. Many felt that the punishments it outlined were not severe enough.

Consequently, the UOA was amended in 1976 and henceforth became known as the Prevention of Civil Rights Act (PCR). The PCR made untouchability a serious, noncompoundable offence, which implied that cases involving accusations of untouchability could not be settled through out-of-court compromises (see chap. 5). One of the main objectives of the PCR was to counteract ritual practices that perpetuated untouchability, such as denying Dalit communities access to temples. It also specified extended periods of imprisonment for untouchability-related crimes (HRW 1999). However, the PCR failed to clearly define untouchability and neglected to penalize verbal expressions that conveyed discriminatory attitudes. Many lawmakers believed that commonsense sociocultural knowledge would allow officials to recognize untouchability when confronted with it. This meant that under the PCR "state officials charged with protecting untouchables [were given] great leeway in interpreting anti-Dalit crime" (Rao 2009, 174).

The PCR also failed to acknowledge that untouchability often entailed a violent dimension. Consequently, the Prevention of Atrocities Act was introduced in 1989, to prevent and punish *violent* practices against Dalit and Adivasis by differentiating caste atrocities from regular, non-caste-motivated crime. The new law created a set of special atrocity crimes that were not included in the IPC, while also extending the scope of penalties for some offences that were included in the IPC (Acharya and Acharya 2020). The introduction of the Atrocities Act was made possible by a resurgence of public concern with Indian civil liberties and fundamental constitutional rights. Following the 1975 Indian emergency, during which then Prime Minister Indira Gandhi suspended fundamental rights in the interest of majority satisfaction (Rubin 1987), the legislative upliftment of socioeconomically disadvantaged groups was reemphasized in Indian politics.

The initial version of the Atrocities Act included twenty-two offences as "atrocities." To gain parliamentary approval, several offences that the authors had wanted to include were initially left out. One example was the imposition of a social and economic boycott, a practice whereby upper castes often ostracized Dalits and Adivasis from the community if they demanded equal treatment. According to Mr. Krishnan, the passing of the Atrocities Act evoked mixed emotions among members of the drafting committee. On the one hand, there was concern that some parliamentarians were even calling this "weaker" version of the law dangerous. On the other hand, many felt that the ratification of the Atrocities Act as a law was an important practical and symbolic step in the fight against caste oppression. The Atrocities Act communicated government opposition to casteism and highlighted caste-based violence as illegitimate and illegal (Galanter 1989, 218). Signaling that aggression against India's former untouchables represented a violation of Indian constitutional ideals, the Atrocities Act, like all hate crime laws, marked the state's rejection of identity-based oppression (Perry and Alvi 2012).

However, the activists and lawmakers behind the act continued their efforts to make the Atrocities Act more potent. Twenty-six years later their work was rewarded. In 2015 the Atrocities Act was amended to include additional atrocity categories like the imposition of a social or economic boycott. Moreover, the amendment—which came into effect in January 2016—finally clearly delineated the duties of public servants in registering and investigating atrocity offences. Section 4 in chapter 2 of the 2015 Atrocities Amendment Act stipulates that public servants who, for example, neglect to accurately record witness statements are punishable with imprisonment up to one year. The amendment also outlined a comprehensive set of rights for victims and witnesses and introduced *exclusive* special courts for the speedy trial of atrocity cases in areas deemed high risk for violence against Dalits and Adivasis.

These new guidelines marked one of the most important differences between the Atrocities Act and its legislative predecessors: the Atrocities Act imposes *positive duties* on public officials, which imply a responsibility to resist and counteract caste violence through criminal law in line with India's constitutional vision. A complaint under the Atrocities Act can be registered by anyone who has information about a caste atrocity—a victim of a crime, a witness, or any other persons who are aware that a caste crime was committed. The offence is registered by the police in a First Information Report (FIR) and can be submitted to the police in writing or through an oral statement. Based on the information provided in the FIR the police then begin their investigation. Police officers may not refuse FIR registration of atrocity cases even if the reported incident took place outside their jurisdiction. In such cases, they are obligated to file the complaint and forward it to the concerned police station.

A POWERFUL TEXT
Pinpointing the Insidious

Today, the over thirty offences—or atrocities—listed under the Atrocities Act can roughly be divided into seven substantive categories (CHRI 2018): 1) General offences against the person (e.g., casteist insult or physical harm); 2) offences against the land or property of a SC/ST person (e.g., wrongful occupation of land belonging to SC/ST individuals); 3) employment-related offences (e.g., forcing an SC/ST individual to do manual scavenging); 4) offences against the household and sacred sites (e.g., damaging SC/ST houses of worship); 5) offences related to public resources (e.g., obstructing SC/ST members' access to wells); 6) electoral offences (e.g., forcing SC/ST individuals to vote for a particular candidate); and finally 7) offences against SC/ST women (e.g., sexual harassment of an SC/ST woman).

To be prosecuted under the act, these offences must be committed by anyone who is *not* a member of the Scheduled Castes or Scheduled Tribes against a person *belonging* to these communities (crimes committed by Dalits or Adivasis against other members of these groups do not fall under the jurisdiction of the act).

The Atrocities Act also specified that every complainant would be assigned a Special Public Prosecutor (SPP). SPPs are appointed by the state under the Code of Criminal Procedure, 1973. They are not part of the investigating agency (police) and represent an independent statutory authority. Advocates, who have been in practice for seven years or more, are eligible to act as SPPs. However, victims can elect to have a legal counsel of their choice assist the SPP. In Rajasthan, atrocity complainants were assigned an SPP by the state but usually chose to have the NGO advocates who supported their cases act as additional, independent legal advisers. Ironically, a regular task of these advisors was to petition the special SC/ST atrocity court to change the assigned Special Public Prosecutor because he/she displayed bias against Dalit narratives.

In Rajasthan, activists and advocates often emphasized the hopeful nature of the Atrocities Act as a legal document. Sonali, the women's activist whose family I stayed with in a village in Jhunjhunu district, enthused: "As a document this act is a thing of beauty! It tells you exactly what caste violence looks like in our villages . . . and has such strong punishments."

Sonali was not the only one to praise the Atrocities Act in its textual form. Even though the everyday life of the atrocity cases was usually defined by refusal and futility—police in Rajasthan regularly refused to file complaints under the act, while judicial magistrates and judges failed to acknowledge caste as a motivating force behind crimes—all stakeholders in atrocity cases agreed that the provisions and protections in the act outlined what a life free from violence and prejudice for Dalits and Adivasis should look like.

This insistence on the emblematic power of the legal text is analytically significant. While ethnographic studies frequently explore how formal law is practiced, experienced, vernacularized, and brought in conversation with alternative forms of dispute resolution (Moore 1993; Coutin 2000; Mattei and Nader 2008; Karandinos et al. 2014; Pia 2016), some anthropologists have drawn attention to the symbolic power of legal texts (Pirie 2019, 10). The ability of law-as-text to "invoke higher ideals and standards" (Pirie 2019, 5) can present an aspirational normative horizon which shapes people's everyday institutional engagements.

The social genealogy of the Atrocities Act shows that its authors were distinctly hopeful that law could play an important role in the creation of a more equal, less violent society. Thus, the text of the Atrocities Act carefully dissects historical and cultural practices of exclusion, oppression, untouchability, and humiliation. For example, chapter 2, section 3(1)(e) of the act details humiliating behaviors that have historically been exercised as part of the cultural complex of untouchability. It forbids anyone from forcing Dalits and Adivasis to remove clothes and moustaches, or from bullying members of these communities to paint their bodies and faces, stating that such involuntary actions are "derogatory to human dignity." These proscribed practices invoke clear notions of caste oppression in the Indian context. In many parts of Rajasthan, proudly wearing a moustache is still considered a symbol of status and masculinity, which has been seen as a privilege of the former Rajput ruling caste. Dalit men who grow moustaches are often beaten up and attacked by members of the local Rajput clans (Anjum 2022).

These examples highlight the lawmakers' intention to target a *cultural landscape* of structural violence built on, and around, habits of untouchability (Sarukkai 2009) which has been normalized and rendered invisible though the language of Hindu tradition (Muthukkaruppan 2017, 49). In January 2018, P. S. Krishnan told me: "When drafting this act, we didn't just want to say massacring Dalits is an atrocity. That is obvious! We wanted to criminalize all casteist actions that make massacres possible."

His words reflect the same theoretical insights that have driven scholarly analyses of mass atrocities: events of extreme group violence are the result of routine (micro)aggressions against minorities by powerful majority groups (Power 2002). These mundane, prejudice-laden social practices, which, as Benjamin Bowling points out, constitute the social evolution of hate crimes (Bowling 1993), ultimately result in a level of dehumanization that makes the most unfathomable brutality possible. To intercede in this process, the Atrocities Act aimed to stop culturally normalized acts of untouchability-related discrimination in their tracks. The goal behind the act was as simple as it was ambitious: to pull out casteism by the roots, by gradually eradicating the *social conditions of possibility* for large-scale caste aggression.

Spaces of Judicial Discretion

However, like all legal texts, the Atrocities Act provides much space for interpretation and institutional discretion. Echoing the challenges faced by other special criminal laws in India as well as hate crimes across the globe, the Atrocities Act contains interpretative lacunae that allow legal actors to render caste prejudice illegible. At the heart of this issue stands the dilemma of motive, which has haunted hate crime laws everywhere.

The question of how legal systems can prove hateful or discriminatory motivations behind crimes, or, as Alexander Somek calls it, "guilty minds" (2011, 6), has been widely contested among legal scholars and professionals (Brax 2016). In India, the authors of the Atrocities Act were aware of the complexities involved in substantiating casteism as a motive behind aggression against Dalits. This was partially because members of Indian law enforcement and judicial actors regularly dismissed the continued existence of caste bias in Indian society by denying that conditions of poverty were inextricably linked to the history of caste. This line of argumentation repeatedly reared its head during my time in Rajasthan. A sub-inspector of the Brahmin caste in Jhunjhunu expressed anger when I divulged that I was working on the Atrocities Act. He insisted that the act was a nonsensical piece of legislation because the real issue was not caste but economic inequality. "Anyone," he heatedly announced, "can get attacked because they are poor and weak (*kamazora aura garība*) not because Indians still believe in untouchability."

Aware of the systematic ways in which caste was usually argued out of offences against Dalits, Mr. Krishnan wanted to introduce a presumption of motive clause in atrocity cases (Khora 2016). This clause would stipulate that casteist motivations could be *presumed* by a judge if the accused knew the victim or their family. The presumption clause did not make it into the original version of the Atrocities Act for fear it would be interfere with parliamentary approval. However, in 2015 the clause finally became a reality, through the introduction of section 8(c) of chapter 2 of the Atrocities Amendment Act. This special section was "intended to combat any denial by perpetrators of knowledge of the victim's identity and hence that they should not be prosecuted under the [Atrocities Act]" (Waughray 2022, 81).

However, in practice the presumption clause is rarely applied by the police and often viewed skeptically by the judiciary (Mangubhai and Singh 2014). Historically, three dynamics have been at play here. First, courts have often inactivated the presumption clause by reintroducing considerations of causality. In 2022 the High Court in the state of Chhattisgarh argued that it was not enough for the prosecution to establish that the accused knew of a victim's Dalit or Adivasi identity but had to systematically prove that the attack occurred "because of" their caste status (Network LiveLaw News 2022). Second, there has been debate about the type of evidence required to prove the perpetrator's knowledge of the victim's caste status. For example, if the accused and the victim are from the same village, can one conclude beyond reasonable doubt that the victim's Dalit identity was known to their attacker? In response to this difficult question, courts have often dismissed atrocity cases where the accused did not explicitly demonstrate awareness of the victim's Dalit identity by engaging in caste insults (see, e.g., *Rajeshbhai Jesingbhai Dayara v. State of Gujarat*). Finally, courts have sometimes interpreted the rule that a crime must be committed *on the grounds of caste* to be prosecuted under the Atrocities Act in an extremely narrow way. Some judges have argued that *on the grounds of caste* really means "*only* on the ground of [caste]" (Kothari 2021) and that cases where other motives are involved should not be prosecuted under the Atrocities Act (see, e.g., *Hitesh Verma v. State of Uttarakhand & Anr.*). However, vulnerability to caste-based violence frequently goes hand in hand with other markers of marginality like gender or disability. Demanding that caste bias must be the only motive for an offence for the Atrocities Act to apply ignores the intersectional and cumulative nature of discrimination and inequality.[5]

Another complex area of judicial discretion has emerged around the issue of casteist hate speech. Sections 3(1)(r) and 3(1)(s) in chapter 2 of the Atrocities Act prohibit insult, intimidation, or verbal abuse against Dalits and Adivasis. However, the act only outlaws these practices if they occur "in public view." The question of how "public view" should be defined has repeatedly cropped up in atrocity cases (see, e.g., *Hitesh Verma v. State of Uttarakhand & Anr.*).

The above examples highlight that the Atrocities Act leaves ample room for legal actors to exercise modes of interpretive discretion that silence the aims of anti-caste legislation, specifically, and hate crime law more broadly. In India this has resulted in a public and judicial discourse which assumes that most complaints filed under the Atrocities Act are "false allegations." By the time I began my research in the summer of 2016, the Atrocities Act had become one of the country's most socially divisive laws (Carswell and de Neve 2015). Public discourse was rife with stories that painted the act as a vehicle for Dalits to exact vengeance against innocent higher castes (Carswell and de Neve 2015; Gorringe and Karthikeyan 2014), a perspective that remains dominant to this day (Legal Correspondent 2019; Rao 2019).

In 2018, just as my fieldwork was ending, the Indian Supreme Court declared the Atrocities Act a vehicle for fraudulent accusations and set out to dilute major provisions of the act (Fuchs 2018). Yet, the large-scale resistance that erupted in response to this dilution also reveals how atrocity survivors across India resist judicial interpretations that view the Atrocities Act as a socially dangerous policy. The survivors and activists in Rajasthan who inhabit these pages always remained determined to reclaim the Atrocities Act as their own in the face of these acts of silencing.

THE ATROCITIES ACT AS A "SPECIAL" CRIMINAL LAW

While the issue of proving casteist motives is distinct to the Atrocities Act, skepticism towards special criminal laws is common in India. Criminal laws introduced to address a special category of criminal offences to secure the rights of socially disadvantaged groups are regularly met with cynicism. Meanwhile complainants from socially weaker communities like women (Oza 2020), Dalits (Fuchs 2020c), or Muslims are often depicted as untrustworthy (Bhat 2020a).

In his ethnographic study of terror trials under India's Unlawful Activities (Prevention) Act (UAPA), Mayur Suresh highlights the fraught history of special criminal laws as a weapon for colonial control. He shows that the British Raj set up "special courts with special rules of evidence . . . in various colonial jurisdictions to deal with revolutionary violence" (Suresh 2023, 19). Here, special courts and rules of were set up with the intention of holding efficient trials that would make it easier to convict potential revolutionaries.

While these laws, thus, created no new substantive offences, they did alter general legal procedures. Some of the harshest critiques of special criminal laws come from within the legal profession. In 2020, Kunal Ambasta, Assistant Professor at India's National Law University, published an article in the NALSAR Student Law Review entitled "Designed for

Abuse." He argues that special criminal laws are not only practically unnecessary but indeed contrary to justice (Ambasta 2020). Ambasta's critique is both theoretical and practical. On a conceptual level he argues that the potential for fairness and justice inheres precisely in the generality of criminal law. He argues that special legal categories are often arbitrary since many of the offences outlined in special antiterrorism laws like UAPA or the Protection of Children from Sexual Offences Act, 2012 (POSCO) would also be punishable under general criminal codes (Ambasta 2020, 5). On a practical level, he maintains that the discourse of criminal exceptionality, which special laws generate, curtails basic rights of accused parties by overriding entitlements like bail or even the presumption of innocence.

Ethnographic work on special criminal laws in India tempers some of Ambasta's claims. In relation to the Unlawful Activities (Prevention) Act, India's main antiterror law, Suresh argues that, while terrorism cases indeed involve special evidentiary and procedural rules, they are also characterized by many of the same prosaic technicalities as other criminal trials (Suresh 2019b; 2023). He demonstrates that investigations and trials under special criminal laws are often discouragingly ordinary, bowing to the same documentary regimes and evidence rules that regulate general, criminal law.

However, both Ambasta's and Suresh's analyses focus on the risks that procedural and evidentiary "specialness" poses for accused parties. These scholars discuss UAPA, a terrorism law, which has often been mobilized politically to criminalize members of a marginalized Indian Muslim minority. Here the historically vulnerable group are the accused, the supposed perpetrators, the ones who have certain rights curtailed.

The Atrocities Act presents a reverse scenario: here the historically marginalized and politically vulnerable group are the complainants and victims—Dalits and Adivasis. Consequently, the concerns and challenges my interlocutors faced were also reversed. For many atrocity survivors, who had limited financial and social resources, the central legal problem was that the special substantive rules in the Atrocities Act that were meant to protect them were still largely governed by a general procedural and evidentiary framework. This framework was built on knowledge practices that were rooted in the normative assumptions and expectations of their historically and economically more powerful, higher-caste tormentors (comp. Derrida 1992). In other words, the legal landscape in which the Atrocities Act had been built often silenced its special aim to uplift marginalized groups through historically and culturally sensitive rules and categories of offences.

Conceptually, laws that specifically target hate attempt to counteract social and political inequalities (Hall 2013) by "differentiating" criminal law into subcategories (Blichner and Molander 2008, 42). However, the global criminological literature has shown that general evidential rules and processes of identifying, proving, and punishing often fail to grasp the special processual and cumulative character of identity-based violence (Walters, Owusu-Bempah, and Wiedlitzka 2018; Hardy and Chakraborti 2020). The technical and procedural ordinariness of atrocity investigations, hearings, and trials, and the repeated denial of casteist motives by police and judicial actors thus result in a discrepancy between Dalit experiences of exceptional or special violence and the ordinary manner in which the criminal system approached these experiences.

India's Dowry Prohibition Act of 1961, another extremely controversial special criminal law, which makes the giving and receiving of dowry illegal in order to protect women from violence at the hand of their own families, best illustrates this process. Indian feminist scholars have proposed that the Dowry Act not only obscured how dowry disputes are tied to everyday patriarchal processes and oppressive gender norms (Agnes 1992) but also gave rise to the myth of the "disgruntled wife" (Jaising 2014, 34), who files "false" cases for revenge. Indeed, work on India's newly established all-female police stations shows that rape claims by women are generally regarded as fabricated even by female police officers (Oza 2020).[6]

The parallels between the judicial and public debates around the Dowry Prohibition Act and the Atrocities Act are especially striking at the Supreme Court level. India's highest court has systematically pursued the "false case" narrative in relation to both laws. In 2017 the Supreme Court pointed to the high acquittal rate in dowry complaints to express concern that angry wives were misusing the dowry act to "frame their husbands and relatives" (Arora 2019). As I indicated above, the following year, in 2018, the court used a similar argument to curb key provisions of the Atrocities Act by claiming that Dalits and Adivasis were using the law to get special favors and blackmail upper castes.

CHALLENGING EXPECTATIONS

The skepticism leveled against the Atrocities Act as an anticaste law, a special criminal law, and a hate crime law shines the spotlight on the multiple and contrasting expectations that haunt the act. The act has a bold, socially transformative vision. However, it is precisely this vision which turns it into a battlefield of competing anxieties and hopes.

Seeing a law that was "meant to help Dalits" (Krishnan, Gurugram, pers. comm., January 2018) become paralyzed by the anti-Dalit biases of legal actors or upper-caste politicians led many of my interlocutors in Rajasthan to conclude that they had to find creative strategies to make it deliver on its promise. They regularly witnessed their claims rattle against the cage of general criminal evidence rules, which demanded documents and witness statements that historically marginalized groups like Dalits could rarely access. This convinced many that what needed reforming was not the Atrocities Act but legal institutions and the general criminal justice system, whose principles had been devised by historically privileged and powerful communities.

And so Meghwals in Rajasthan asked: Whose idea of generality or fairness do the rules of the legal system obey? Why can general evidentiary and procedural rules of criminal law not accommodate the truth regimes that govern lived discrimination? And why can we not rethink the foundational processes of criminal law in light of marginalized realities and resources?

My interlocutors didn't want *special* legal treatment. They wanted the Atrocities Act to become a catalyst for a more radical reimagining of supposedly fair general legal rules that still favored their upper-caste tormentors.

TWO

WHO OWNS THE LAW?
Politics and Intimacies of Atrocity Cases

WHEN PINKY WALKED TO COLLEGE

The broad, sandy road cuts straight across the village before opening onto a wide valley of yellow mustard fields, which glisten in the warm sunlight of the clear spring afternoon. The air is soft. Smells of hay and cardamom waft through the open car windows. Yet I can't help but feel that the gentle beauty of the day is mocking us.

My travel companion, Rajesh Meghwal, our driver, Chunni Lal, and I are making our way through Jhunjhunu, a district in the eastern corner of the Indian state of Rajasthan. Rajesh, whom I affectionately call *bhāiia* (brother), has become a good friend during my fieldwork in Rajasthan. I had met Rajesh's younger brother Avinesh Meghwal in Delhi, and he had invited me to stay with his family in Jhunjhunu town—the district capital—during my research. Deeply invested in the issue of caste atrocities and concerned for my personal safety, Rajesh *bhāiia* had soon begun accompanying me on interviews. But today's trip was especially emotionally challenging for him. We were driving to see Pinky Meghwal, a seventeen-year-old Dalit girl who, like Rajesh, belonged to the Meghwal *jāti* (subcaste). Two weeks prior, Pinky had been brutally gang-raped by four boys of the higher-ranking Jat caste in her home village of Bilaria. With the encouragement of a few respected Meghwal elders from Bilaria and the support of the three local caste associations—the Jhunjhunu Meghwal Association (Jhunjhunu Meghwal Samāj), the Jhunjhunu Association for Meghwal Assertion (Jhunjhunu Meghwal Sangharsh Samiti) and the Jhunjhunu Ambedkar Society—Pinky's father had registered an official complaint against the boys at the nearest police station (*thānā*) under the Atrocities Act. The decision surprised many villagers because Pinky's father was poor and held little influence in the community. But the brutality of the attack perpetrated against Pinky had shocked everyone because Jhunjhunu district was known for the upward mobility of its Dalit community.

As we drive along, Chunni Lal, who lives in Bilaria, tells me that since the incident Pinky's family has been swarmed by journalists, activists, police, and representatives of the Meghwal associations. "Of course, all of them have opinions," he sighs. We are now following a bumpy track through patchy fields. Finally, Chunni Lal stops the car. I see a small house in the distance. "That is Pinky's family's home," Chunni Lal explains: "they moved into their *chāni* (formerly a stable) to be closer to their field. It is also close to the road, so the daughters can catch the bus to college. But this place is far away from people. Only some Jats have big houses across the field. That's how these boys grabbed Pinky. They pulled her into a car . . ." Rajesh makes a gulping sound. The reality of what happened to a girl from his own community is hitting him hard.

As we get closer to Pinky's house, I spot a tent and two men wearing police uniforms. At least the family has been provided police protection. I can also see two elderly men in white, impeccably ironed *kurtā*s (long shirts) sitting in wobbly plastic chairs. A middle-aged man in a sleeveless shirt, carrying a rope and cut bundles of grass, is leaning against a nearby tree, listening to their conversation. "Ramram," Chunni Lal greets the men, "This is Sandhya-jī, she has come from London to work on caste atrocities. We are here to learn what happened to your daughter, Roshan Lal." Unsure whom to address I look around and meet the eye of the man carrying the grass bundles. The look he gives me is somewhere between weariness, hope, and resignation. He is the girl's father.

The situation is precarious. What happened to Pinky has become public knowledge. While everyone in Bilaria understands that the likelihood of the perpetrators being arrested rises as more public attention is paid to Pinky's story, such attention also brings discomfort and embarrassment. Pinky's name is now forever entangled with a whispered narrative of sex, crime, and indecency, matters that have the power to ruin any girl's reputation. Her father, Roshan Lal, knows that despite all efforts to prosecute the accused, despite all gestures of care, murmured questions about his daughter's respectability will now never be far from the surface. And so his face is etched with a demoralizing certainty: every supportive party and every legal win simultaneously means scandal and shame.

Roshan Lal ushers me inside the house, which is so small, it hardly deserves the designation. I take a moment to adjust my eyes to the darkness. At least fifteen women are squatting in the corners of the small, dimly lit space. In the farthest corner, tucked under a blanket on a *cārapāii* (woven bed), two young girls are huddled closely together. One is mindlessly swiping away on a phone screen; the other one looks at me apprehensively: she is Pinky. Roshan Lal murmurs a few words in the local Marwari dialect. Then he quickly exits, leaving me alone with the women, who seem in equal parts curious and suspicious. With typical directness, an older woman pulls me into a chair. "You are young," she says brusquely, "what are you here to do?" I smile, "I am not that young, Dādī-jī (grandma)," I tell her, "it's just dark and you are not wearing glasses." The joke breaks the tension. The women giggle. Even Pinky smiles a little.

By the time I met Pinky, I was no longer a novice at negotiating the complex social life of the Atrocities Act in Rajasthan. After several encounters with families like Pinky's, I had learned firsthand that there were no coherent accounts of violence that lay on the tongues of survivors and kin ready to be released (Das 2001). Women, especially, were rarely able or willing to talk about an incident of assault as brutal as the one Pinky had experienced. This reluctance was deeply woven into the social fabric of Rajasthan, a state still defined by clearly circumscribed and internalized expectations of feminine modesty, which, as in other areas of India, were policed by male family members (see Still 2011 on Andhra Pradesh). However, Pinky's silence also reflected the "fragmented" terrain of post-traumatic memory (Bedard-Gilligan, Zoellner, and Feeny 2017, 212). As her case unfolded, her fraught remembrance of events was increasingly molded, and suppressed, by the contested political and legal intimacies which engagement with the Atrocities Act engenders.

In Rajasthan, registering a complaint of caste-based violence against another member of the village community, especially against an economically high-status group like the Jats, was never a straightforward decision. Most importantly, it was never an individual decision. Debates about caste violence and its possible legal remedies extended beyond family, and even village, jurisdiction. Filing an atrocity compliant tore the narratives of violence from the hands of their experiential owners. This throws into question assumptions of private trauma and raises new questions about the limits of the individualized legal case format on which hate crime law relies.

During my first visit to Pinky's house, she herself told me little and I never pushed her. Instead, Pinky's friend, as well as her mother, father, and grandmother, later filled in some of the blanks. The four boys had taken Pinky to a field about five kilometers from Bilaria village and raped her one by one. Then they had "returned" her (*vāpasa kar dyia*) by shoving her out of the car in the same place they had grabbed her hours prior. Pinky somehow stumbled back home across the fields. When she arrived, only her father was present. Pinky initially didn't want to tell him what happened, but he saw her bruises and torn clothes. When her mother came home, Pinky broke down, sobbing against her mother's chest. Pinky's mother, Sundari Devi, said that she had never seen her husband so enraged. He immediately called the local Meghwal associations. Together, the next morning they went to the police and filed a First Information Report (FIR)—an initial complaint report—under the Atrocities Act.

This decision did not sit well with Sundari Devi, who was worried about the gossip a legal case would cause. She thought it would wreak havoc with Pinky's upcoming marriage. But Roshan Lal went ahead anyway. To his own surprise the police officers diligently registered his complaint. The FIR classified what had happened to Pinky as a case of kidnapping, abduction, and gang-rape under the Indian Penal Code.[1] In addition, the police applied three sections of the Atrocities Act, which specify aggravated punishments for sexual force used against a woman of the Scheduled Castes or Scheduled Tribes.[2] Due to Pinky's young age of seventeen, her case was also registered under the 2012 Protection of Children from Sexual Offences Act (POCSO) as aggravated penetrative assault.[3]

Roshan Lal had wanted to ensure that his daughter's case did not become one of the many neglected atrocity complaints in Rajasthan's police stations. Therefore, he phoned a man named Satyanarayan G. for support. G.-jī, as he was referred to, was one of the founders of the Jhunjhunu Association for Meghwal Assertion (Jhunjhunu Meghwal Sangharsh Samiti). He owned multiple housing developments and extensive landholdings. G.-jī promised Roshan Lal his full support. His promise would shape the fate of Pinky's case more than any other.

On the evening of my first visit to Pinky's house, G.-jī arrived, just as we were about to leave. Along with ten other important-looking gentlemen he strode purposefully towards a small assemblage of brightly colored plastic chairs—tall, grave, and clad entirely in white. As the men settled down noisily and received cups of steaming *cāya* (tea) from Pinky's mother, I scanned the crowd for her father. Finally, I found him. Half-hidden in the shade of his house, he observed the men: he knew that while the pain of the assault was his family's to bear, the way forward might not be theirs to pave. Rajesh *bhāiia* seemed to agree. He whispered in my ear: "You can't do law alone, but now everyone is swarming the place like bees. You don't know who might sting you."

WHO OWNS THE LAW?

Rajesh *bhāiia*'s words would prove prophetic. Tracing Pinky's story, I learnt that the social, cultural, and emotional life of the Atrocities Act begins long before narratives of caste violence ever encounter the police, let alone the courts. Pinky's story highlights that the outcome of atrocity cases is often decided outside state institutions in the hidden local arenas where memory, family, politics, and law meet. In these spaces ties of intimacy engender new structures of political kinship (Tenhunen 2003), legal care, and betrayal, turning community support into a double-edged sword.

The way Pinky's case unfolded shows that hate crime laws like the Atrocities Act are not neutral legal tools. In practice, they become socially fractured and contested in ways that pose urgent questions about legal ownership and accountability in the context of hate crimes. Pinky's narrative demands new reflections on the gendered manner in which hate crime laws are experienced, embodied, and interpreted. In Rajasthan, the legal and political engagements of Meghwal women produced hidden channels of agency that turned normative visions of legal success on their head (comp. Hirsch 1998).

The first chapter of this book traced the transformative vision that inspired the Atrocities Act. Fought into legislative existence by bureaucratic and activist voices, who aimed to infuse criminal law with the same democratic emphasis on nondiscrimination that inheres the Indian constitution, this chapter shows that the Atrocities Act represented something akin to Charles Taylor's concept of the social imaginary to its authors and supporters: it was meant to imprint factual realities of inequality onto criminal law by enabling legal categories to express "deeper normative notions" of a just society (Taylor 2004, 23). As Mr. Krishnan's words in the introduction revealed, the expectations placed on the Atrocities Act by its authors were characterized by normative cohesion: there was a specific manner in which successful cases under the Atrocities Act *should* be made to unfold, both in terms of procedural law—the technicalities, through which legal outcomes are administered and delivered—and its societal impact. Hence, the Atrocities Act represented a unique *sociolegal imaginary* upon its conception.

However, Pinky's case, which took many twists and turns, bursts this sociolegal imaginary wide open. It shows that the Atrocities Act is brought into the orbit of individual caste atrocities through various forms of "embodied" engagement (Griffiths 2001, 495), which are fueled by different fears and ambitions. Political scientists have argued that, in India, state and police violence is never a centralized effort but consists of disaggregated performances (Lokaneeta 2020) by different state actors (Jauregui 2016). Similarly, Pinky's experience shows that the "proper" implementation of the Atrocities Act is a highly politicized and gendered concept and endeavor.

Pinky's own interpretations give insight into the fact that caste atrocities involve synergetic, intersectional modes of oppression (Rege 2006; comp. Crenshaw 1989), which generate a legal experience that plays out differently through different bodies. In Rajasthan, the Atrocities Act enters a social field which is not only characterized by the brutality of caste but also by profound patriarchal violence (Baxi 2010; Baxi 2014). Hence, it must respond to layered realities of caste- and gender-based harm as well as the competing understandings of honor and agency among Meghwal women and men.

This process challenges theoretical work on caste, which has often stipulated a uniform "untouchable" body as the source of discrimination and subjugation (Guru and Sarukkai 2019; Muthukkaruppan 2017). It exposes how the already violated bodies of Dalit women are treated as blank slates of potential legal "casehood" by male relatives and advisers, who view a persistent and idealized engagement with the Atrocities Act as a path to assertion. Bodies like Pinky's become screens, onto which different visions of caste progress through law are projected and pitted against one another.

However, Pinky's experience also shows how Dalit women's interpretations of the law can actively resist this inscription and the new forms of intrasectional violence (Katri 2017) to which atrocity proceedings give rise. Pinky's story taught me that Meghwal women, like Pinky's mother, often rejected the linear, normative expectations of legal engagement their male relatives, as well as human rights activists and many "big men" in their community, tried to impose on them. Instead, they mobilized the new networks of sociality which atrocity cases created, to reinterpret the "proper" way to use the Atrocities Act in line with their own notions of a safe and honorable future. In Pinky's instance, her mother's acts of resistance ultimately undermined her official atrocity case and caused Pinky to turn "hostile" in court (Berti 2010): at her first official hearing in the special SC/ST court, she denied that the rape had ever happened.

However, it remained unclear how much agency Pinky herself had in shaping this strategy. Pinky struggled with the trauma of casteism and sexual violation, while trying to navigate her own ruptured memories. The familial and community disagreements around her legal case made it difficult to write her own narrative. The making and unmaking of her case was never truly her own.

Thus, Pinky's story posits urgent, yet frequently overlooked, questions that lie not only at the heart of controversies around law and caste in India, but face hate crime laws globally: Who are laws, which promise to punish bias and hate, ultimately for? Whose vision of justice should they champion? And how can they accommodate the reality that hate crimes, and hate crime laws, make different demands of different bodies?

Here I place Pinky's own experience at the center, by unpacking the stories she eventually told me over the course of many encounters, as well as the silences that always permeated her memory. Stepping into Pinky's shoes, this chapter introduces the different interest groups and moral stakeholders involved in the translation and management of her narrative, as it gradually became transformed into a legal case under the Atrocities Act. The gendered dimension of her experience meant that Pinky's story was particularly contested. Her identity as a young woman about to be married gave rise to nuanced concerns about honor and family status. Her legal journey was born out of, and ultimately ended due to, patriarchal concerns.

I explore these contestations by first tracing how Pinky's efforts to remember immediately became caught in a complex and intimate web of local Dalit politics. Meghwal associations, and individual Meghwal leaders, gradually inserted themselves into Pinky's home life and began to rewrite her story from the inside. In the South Asian literature, leaders, or so-called big men, have typically been referred to as *netā*s (Corbridge et al. 2012). They have variously been discussed as brokers, bosses, and gangsters (Michelutti et al. 2018). Under the banner of patronage, *netā*s mobilize feelings of helplessness produced by a complex, often intangible state (Shah 2009; Bear & Mathur 2015), to engage in various forms of clientelism, corruption, and solidarity. However, Pinky's case sheds light on a neglected aspect of *netā*-hood: the intimate bonds that *netā*s develop with the families of atrocity survivors can pit kin against kin and allow *netā*s to harvest the traumatic effects of violence to further agendas of political ascension.

Against this backdrop, the second part of the chapter then turns to analyze the fears and wishes of Pinky's innermost circle and of Pinky herself. I first consider the fears and hopes of Pinky's parents, who, along with Pinky, had most at stake in her case. Her parents had diametrically opposed views on the ongoing legal case, which were rooted in competing understandings of honor, and wove themselves into *netā* politics.

The final part of the chapter illustrates that in Rajasthan the desires of atrocity survivors, their families, and local Dalit *netā*s often violently clash with the aims of legal aid activists. While activists and NGOs are indispensable to translating experiences like Pinky's into "law" and a global language of human rights, they too are not neutral interpreters (Sharma and Kelly 2018). Instead, many considered atrocity complaints a platform to promote their own vision of the Atrocities Act as a legal vehicle for collective resistance.

Ultimately, Pinky's experience lays bare the most intimate life of the Atrocities Act and reveals how caste violence and its potential legal consequences emerge as (de-)construction sites for notions of gender, identity, and social responsibility (Cuno and Desai 2009), and as a battleground for different visions of legal success.

CASTE ASSOCIATIONS: A HELPING HAND?

When it came to Pinky's case, her mother and father never saw eye to eye. Though both were warmly concerned with Pinky's well-being, a rift gradually emerged between husband and wife after Pinky's attack. This rift mainly centered on her father's decision to call the local Meghwal associations for help and to embroil the family in a lengthy legal case, which, as it seemed at the time, held unusual promise for courtroom success.

Pinky's mother, Sundari Devi, believed that she was never allowed any input: "Pinky told us what happened and my husband [Roshan Lal] immediately calls the Meghwal men. Before I can do anything, everyone is at the police station and there are activists at our house. Then there is a protest for Pinky, and media, and nothing is in my hands."

It is easy to sympathize with Sundari Devi's feelings. Roshan Lal and members of the Jhunjhunu Meghwal Sangharsh Samiti (henceforth JMSS) got Pinky's case registered the day after the attack. Since another Meghwal girl named Kavita had been raped by two men of the Jat caste in a different part of Jhunjhunu two weeks before Pinky, the JMSS decided to act quickly. To put additional pressure on the police and reaffirm the idea that Dalits in Jhunjhunu had long overcome historical conditions of caste bondage, the JMSS staged a protest in front of the police headquarters in Jhunjhunu town a couple of days later. Over 300 men, and a handful of women, from different Dalit *jāti*s assembled for the occasion. Some upper-caste politicians were also present to express their solidarity (see fig. 4). Since Jhunjhunu has a Scheduled Caste (Dalit) population of almost 17%, upper-caste political aspirants were generally careful not to antagonize the Dalit voter bank, realizing that they would be hard-pressed to win a seat in the Vidhān Sabhā (State Legislative Assembly) if they openly disregarded Dalit concerns.

The spectacle drew attention. "*Jhunjhunu ke Dalit kamazora nahīn hain!*" the leader of the Jhunjhunu Ambedkar Society shouted, as the crowd broke out in cheers. "Jhunjhunu's Dalits are not weak! Meghwals have come a long way. We must remind those who touch our daughters. Once we fought alongside Jats against Rajput oppression but now they have forgotten. Justice for Pinky and Kavita. Our women are not their toys!"

He received a standing ovation as he articulated the insidious assumptions that underlay the attack on Pinky: that lower-caste women were sexually available to higher-caste men by status, and sexually willing by their very nature (Parry 2014).

However, his speech also hinted at the upward mobility and assertiveness of Jhunjhunu's Meghwal community. Though it seemed counterintuitive, I had learned that the high number of atrocity complaints registered by Meghwals in the district indicated their comparative social strength as a caste community. In Jhunjhunu, Meghwal complaints under the Atrocities Act were usually the ones marked by institutional longevity, public agitation, and reasonable representation in court, while cases filed by members of other Dalit communities (for example by members of the Khatik or Nayak *jāti*s) often received much less attention. This was largely the result of conscious efforts to grow and formalize local Meghwal caste organizations, which helped survivors productively engage legal institutions.

Contrary to the expectations evoked by the individualized case format of liberal law, effectively filing complaints under the Atrocities Act with the Indian police required family backing as well as local community and political support (Parry 2020, 466). In Jhunjhunu the Meghwal Samāj, the JMSS, and the Ambedkar Society were usually called upon to ensure

FIGURE 4. *Clockwise from top left corner*: A prominent JMSS member calls for urgent police action at a protest in front of the Jhunjhunu Police Collectorate after Pinky's attack; *Top right*: At the same protest, two members of the Jhunjhunu Ambedkar Society conduct a chant of assertive slogans (*Jhunjhunu ke Dalit kamazora nahīn hain*—"Jhunjhunu's Dalits are not weak"); *Bottom*: The Jhunjhunu Meghwal Samaj holds a meeting to discuss ongoing cases and local political developments.

that police listened to survivors' claims and registered atrocity complaints under the correct sections of the Atrocities Act and the IPC. The JMSS was particularly dedicated to this cause. JMSS leaders considered engagement with official law a sign of Meghwal educational and economic progress. They regularly corresponded with the local press about caste atrocities and helped organize mass protests (*āndolanas*) in response to incidents of caste violence. Though Meghwal associations claimed to defend the "whole Dalit community" in Jhunjhunu, they were most concerned with helping the members of their own Meghwal *jāti*. They represented crucial contact points for families, who had to navigate unfamiliar, nontransparent legal bureaucracies in the aftermath of caste atrocities.

Caste associations like the ones in Jhunjhunu represent a distinct feature of India's political and legal landscape. They have sometimes been described as a form of "traditional politics" which drive democratic engagement, though they stand apart from formal party-political structures (Rudolph and Rudolph 1960). Caste associations are voluntary organizations which limit membership to individuals who claim a "particular, ascriptive identity" (Harriss and Clark-Decès 2011, 392). However, membership in these associations is not granted simply based on one's *jāti* but is the result of a formal joining process (Rudolph and Rudolph 1960). Though no one ever stated this explicitly, in Jhunjhunu, membership in the Meghwal associations was generally deemed the privilege of upwardly mobile, educated Meghwal men.

Operating at the intersection of legal aid, party politics, and informal community service, the Jhunjhunu Meghwal associations thought of their work as *samāj seva* (social welfare) rather than politics. Avinesh, whose family I lived with in Jhunjhunu town, and whose father was a member of all three associations, referred to them as "civil society organizations." Similarly, activists in Jaipur and Jhunjhunu often interchangeably used the terms *samājwale* (community-people), "civil bodies," or *societywale* (society-people) to describe caste organizations.

Some scholars have suggested that the cellular nature of Indian society, which is hierarchically divided along religious, caste, and gender lines, makes it inimical to Western conceptions of civil society (Saberwal 2001), which presume that people publicly come together as equal rights-bearing citizens to address matters of common concern (Harriss and Clark-Decès 2011, 389).[4] However, others argue that caste associations represent a unique type of Indian civil society engagement. Carey Watt (2005) has proposed that India's vibrant associational culture emerged as a vernacular mode of civil society organizing, in conversation with the urban milieu of British colonial rule. In the Shekhawati region, the twentieth century saw the emergence of new social resistance movements among lower castes, triggered by the arrival of the Arya Samaj Hindu reform movement in the pre-independence era, and the movement for Dalit assertion, which began to expand during the 1930s.

In the late nineteenth century, the Arya Samaj Hindu reform movement gained popularity in the modern North Indian states of Haryana, Punjab, and Rajasthan (Datta 1997). Followers opposed traditional Brahmanical practices, which emphasized ritual purity (Pankaj 2016), and instead promoted social service work and educational activities as the pathway to social equality (Watt 2005). In Shekhawati, the Arya Samaj initially inspired peasant communities like the Jats to set up caste associations. The presence of the Arya Samaj was instrumental to the emergence of the Shekhawati Jat Sabha, which was founded in 1925 (Rawal 2015, 3). The Jat Sabha worked for the economic and social upliftment of Jats *within* the Hindu caste hierarchy, and became the base camp for the coordination of the regional peasant struggle in the first half of the twentieth century.

This emerging landscape of association-based politics in the region resonated with a wider movement of Dalit identity formation, self-assertion, and politicization which developed in the 1930s. This increasingly vocal transregional Dalit struggle, and the increasing power of Jat associations, also sparked a new determination among Dalit communities in Shekhawati to organize themselves. While the Meghwal associations that became involved in Pinky's case are more recent features of Jhunjhunu's social and political landscape, Avinesh's father and other association leaders suggested that the current Meghwal Samāj (Meghwal Association) was descended from earlier Meghwal organizations, which had played an important role in the peasant revolts against Rajput rule.

The trinity of Megwal associations which I encountered was founded by a group of upwardly mobile Meghwal men in the 1980s and 1990s. These men were educated, often retired, white-collar professionals, who had profited from India's affirmative action programs and worked in various government jobs. They had accumulated limited wealth and considered it their duty to use their resources for the upliftment of their caste community. The associations' leadership was determined to signal to the traditionally powerful Rajput and the now-landowning Jat castes that Jhunjhunu's Meghwals would no longer accept a place at the bottom of social, political, and economic life. Therefore, the exceptionally brutal attack on Pinky by a group of young Jat men, who believed they could rape a Meghwal girl without consequences, became a crucial moment of collective organizing.

FIGURE 5. All Meghwal associations and other Dalit communities assemble for a district-wide rally in honor of Dr. B. R. Ambedkar's birthday (*Ambedkar jayanti*) on April 14, 2017.

OF FAMILY AND HONOR

The day the associations organized the protest in front of the police collectorate to ensure police diligence in Pinky's case, they invited several journalists from the *Jhunjhunu Patrika* (Jhunjhunu Daily). A state-wide news program called *Khabhar Rajasthan* (News Rajasthan) was also present. The rally was effective. A few days afterwards, the Additional Superintendent of the Police, whose office was located inside the police headquarters, could be seen making his way across the fields to Pinky's house. The family was given police protection and, within the week, three of the four Jat boys were brought into the police station for questioning. Subsequently, they were presented to the magistrate under section 56 of the Code of Criminal Procedure (CrPC), which marked their official arrest. The fourth had absconded.

The police dutifully took Pinky to the judicial magistrate to give her statement. Magistrates are the lowest-ranking criminal judges in the Indian judicial hierarchy and are appointed by the High Court of a state to enforce the law in a specific town or district. The magistrate directly reports to the district judge (referred to as a sessions judge in criminal matters) and can oversee most court proceedings in the same way a judge would.[5] Section 164(5A) of the CrPC specifies that the investigating police officer in a rape matter must take the victim to give an official, confidential statement before the judicial magistrate as soon as possible after an initial complaint report—a First Information Report (FIR)—is filed.

After the arrests and Pinky's statement before the magistrate, human rights activists felt that her case was emerging as a textbook example of proper investigative procedure. "Pinky's case will be an example of how things should go!" my friend Sonali, a Jhunjhunu-born Dalit activist and the coordinator of AIDMAM Rajasthan told me. However, Pinky's mother was less pleased: "Everyone knows everything now. This case is going to ruin her honor (*ijjata*)!" Pinky's mother was particularly concerned about the effect the public nature of the case would have on Pinky's engagement. Pinky's marriage had recently been arranged to a respectable Meghwal family in the nearby town of Nawalgarh. But no one knew if the match could withstand the scandal that now surrounded her. The protests and the investigation, Pinky's mother thought, would dishonor Pinky more than even the rape itself.

Anthropological studies have highlighted that the honor of Dalit women is often perceived as a route to upward social mobility (Still 2011) and that North Indian brides are still expected to enter their marital home in "a state of honor" (Polit 2018, 287). However, honor can itself emerge as a gendered concept. For Meghwal men in Jhunjhunu, female honor often equaled public prestige. As K. Balagopal points out, the body of an Indian woman is thought to carry the honor of her entire community. Hence, when a woman's body is violated, her community is dishonored (Balagopal 1991, 2041).

During my fieldwork, Meghwal men strictly policed the honor of their wives, sisters, and daughters by trying to keep them inside the house, instructing them to veil their faces (*ghūṅghaṭa karanā*) and removing them from agricultural labor. Meghwal men whose wives and daughter did not "wander" (*ghūmanā*) were well regarded. Meanwhile, the Meghwal women I lived and spoke with tended to equate honor to sexual purity and respectability (Still 2011; Still 2017a,b; Basu 2015), which they deemed central to a happy marital life and the ability to perform motherly duties. When it came to Pinky's case, these familial and political ideals of female honor quickly became incompatible.

Following her assault, Pinky's family had to carefully weigh expectations of marital purity and their wish for public validation, prestige, and justice through law. For Pinky's mother, the rape itself had tarnished her daughter's image. However, as a Jat stronghold, Bilaria village was known for the power plays and brutal extravagances of this caste.

"In Bilaria," Pinky's grandmother used to say, "Jats do what they want when it comes to Meghwal women. The men scream that Jhunjhunu's Meghwals are not weak, but they forget that we women are still easy prey." Because of these conditions, Pinky's mother, Sundari Devi, didn't think the rape itself would *completely* destroy her daughter's respectability. Even though the protests had generated undesired limelight, she thought that the fact that the entire local Meghwal community backed Pinky's story was essential to proving her innocence.

However, she was convinced that an ongoing legal case would be disastrous: "No one wants a daughter-in-law involved in a public rape case," she said. "How can she be a good wife and mother, if she reminds every one of her sexual past?" For Sundari Devi, Pinky's respectability hinged on her ability to fulfill her traditional marital role, despite what had happened. Leaving the assault behind and focusing on her new responsibility as a future wife would (re-)establish her honor. Indeed, as the case dragged on, Pinky's fiancé's family grew restless. Pinky's future mother-in-law insisted that they still wanted Pinky as a daughter-in-law but only if her family dropped the case. She believed that being connected to a rape case under the Atrocities Act would ruin their name by turning Pinky into a sexualized political canvas.

Pinky's proximity to the realm of law created further complications of honor. According to Geeta, a female lawyer at the CDR in Jaipur, people in Rajasthan thought of law as a dirty business, unfitting for respectable women. The legal profession involved trickery and deal making, which were unbecoming for wives and mothers. As the months went by, Pinky's mother became adamant that Pinky's name could not remain embroiled in a legal dispute. "We got the first two installments of financial compensation under the Atrocities Act," she said. "JMSS has fought on our behalf and the Jat families are begging us to compromise out of court. They are scared and have promised not to touch our daughters again. We can move on now."

Section 357A of India's Code of Criminal Procedure (CrPC) stipulates that all state governments must institute and coordinate a victim compensation scheme in coordination with the Central Government.[6] Victims, their families, and dependents can apply to these schemes to receive compensation for injury and loss after a crime. If a case does not go to trial due to lack of evidence, compensation can still be provided (*Manohar Singh v. State of Rajasthan and Ors*).

According to the Rajasthan Victim Compensation Scheme of 2011, rape of a minor (a person under eighteen years) can be compensated with a maximum amount of 5 lakh (500,000) Indian Rupees (INR). Additionally, the Atrocities Act specifies that SC and ST women who have been sexually assaulted are due a compensatory payment of up to 2 lakh (200,000) INR. The first installment of compensation (25%) should be paid when the complaint is filed in a First Information Report. The second (50%) is due after the police conclude their investigation, file an official charge sheet (*challan*), and forward the case to the responsible court. The final installment must be paid if/when the accused is convicted (25%).

Pinky's family had already received the first installment of the compensation under the Atrocities Act, in the total amount of 150,000 INR (1.5 lakh). Three of the four accused boys had been arrested, taken into custody, and brought before a magistrate. For Sundari Devi it was enough to know how scared they had been after their arrest and knowing that they had a case pending against them: a case, which enjoyed great public support and could potentially result in significant financial loss and jail time.

However, her husband's understanding of the situation ran directly counter to her own. Roshan Lal, who only knew how to read and write a little, owned just one small field and some goats, and worked as an agricultural laborer, mostly for Jat farmers. He had educated his daughters to ensure they would have a better life than himself. While he had been scared to file an atrocity complaint, he was also tired of the humiliation that came with being a Meghwal without means. Now his and his daughter's honor was at stake. So he listened to "the big Meghwal men from his community (*apne samāj ke baḍe loga*)"—the leaders of the Meghwal associations—and decided to fight back through a law that was for "people like him." When he realized that the protest in front of the Police Collectorate had caused a spectacle powerful enough to make the Additional Superintendent of Police personally show up at his house, he was sure that following the atrocity case through to an official conviction for the perpetrators was the way forward. The day after the protest, he confided in me: "Jats think they can do anything. As a laborer (*mazadūra*) I get called names and sometimes the Jats don't pay me. But what they did to my daughter . . . it's enough! We have this law and the whole district has seen that the Meghwals of Jhunjhunu will fight back. Only when all boys are convicted, our family will have its honor back!"

Like his wife, Roshan Lal spoke of honor. And yet, his use of the term implied something more public. He wanted open validation of his daughter's and his own lived experience and the respect that comes with victory in a morally righteous court battle. Even though Indian women run the risk of losing respectability by engaging in public life, they can also acquire new forms of social esteem and admiration (Ciotti 2012, 158). Therefore,

Roshan Lal considered public validation after a courageous legal fight essential to the restoration of his family honor. Winning an atrocity case would force everyone to acknowledge that what happened to Pinky had been unjust. Rather than seeing a threat to personal modesty in the public and antagonistic nature of the law, he identified an opportunity for the reversal of the public humiliation which Dalits have historically suffered at the hands of higher castes (Guru 2009). By publicly punishing the Jat attackers, his family would gain pride and power.

The rift between husband and wife would determine Pinky's fate. Her parents' opposing perspectives engendered a complex series of legal entanglements that turned her case into a fruitful breeding ground for competing political and civil interests.

WHEN PINKY FORGETS

Five months after the protest in front of the police collectorate, Pinky's case—hitherto hailed as one of the rare instances where a conviction of upper-caste perpetrators was conceivable—was turned on its head. At the first official hearing of her case before the special SC/ST court, she turned "hostile" (Berti 2010): she told the magistrate she "made it all up," and that she had not been raped. The magistrate dismissed Pinky's case and acquitted the accused boys, but not before lecturing her on the dangers of inventing accusations against innocent men.

Afterwards, many Meghwals in Jhunjhunu were appalled: "You put your weight behind these cases," Avinesh's father confided in me, "and this girl makes it up. She made a joke out of us and the law." Miraculously, a video recording of the assault on one of the attackers' mobile phones, which had been confiscated by the police, also vanished.

But how was a case under the Atrocities Act so clear-cut and promising so drastically reversed? The answer to this question lies in the complex interaction between Pinky's own fragmented memories and the voices of her immediate family that had become entangled with local political agendas.

Over the course of my eighteen months in Jhunjhunu I grew close to Pinky, whose village, Bilaria, was not far away from Badrasar village, where I lived. And so I learned that Pinky always struggled with the fact that she couldn't remember the "correct" details of the attack and tell her story in a way the police officers wanted to hear it. The fractured memories that mark traumatic experience had turned her personal narrative into a barren land of legal evidence, which made her deeply anxious.

As we sat in her home one afternoon, drinking Pepsi, she admitted that her own mind scared her sometimes: "It's like I remember everything but then I also remember nothing, and everyone wants something. I don't know who to listen to."

Pinky's words resonate with studies of violence that have shown that moments of deep suffering are often partially or completely lost to the sufferer (Antze and Lambek 1996; Das 2006; Mulla 2014), since they are not encoded in the brain like everyday experiences (Welton-Mitchell, McIntosh, and DePrince 2013). What is more, moments of incomprehensible brutality can also curtail any desire for remembrance for the people living through them (Dale Scott 2004, 35). Hence, extreme violence often creates disorderly processes of forgetting for survivors.

While I am no medical professional, I always thought that Pinky displayed symptoms consistent with psychological trauma. A contested concept, "trauma" is often used to describe the amalgam of violent event and subsequent emotional and physiological responses of anxiety, anger, and memorial rupture (Fassin and Rechtmann 2009). Sometimes characterized as a form of experience that takes human beings to the edge of comprehension (Kirmayer, Lemelson, and Barad 2007), anthropologists have highlighted that trauma is a relational injury. It involves a loss of faith in the social world (Lester 2013) and is accompanied by a loss of words and coherent narratives (Das 2003; Tate 2007).

Pinky, as I knew her, was simultaneously plagued by her memories and terrified of what she might have forgotten. Above all, she desperately wanted to go home again: home to a feeling of youth, family, and community that had existed when she thought that the boys across the field, who assaulted her, were friends. She wanted to go back to careless days of college life and learning Bollywood dances off YouTube with her sister. She grieved the way she "used to be" (Smith 2016).

The painful loss of identity Pinky felt was accompanied by a tragic inability to make her suffering explicit to others. As her injury was transformed into a coherent, legally legible narrative in the First Information

Report her family had filed at the police station, she increasingly struggled with her memorial rupture. One police officer repeatedly told her that her story was incomplete when he conducted a follow-up interview at her house. If she couldn't remember so many details, he said, she might be lying.

In the realm of law, Pinky learned, memory and case narrative were expected to walk hand in hand, flawlessly unilinear, forming an impermeable block of testimony that could become evidence. Pinky's lack of voice was a lack of evidence.

Witnessing Pinky's struggle to remember and be a credible atrocity complainant was jarring. The lack of space she was given to grapple with the painful fragments of her memory, and to reintegrate her sense of self with her physical and psychological injuries, left Pinky's voice strangely absent from an atrocity case that supposedly was hers. One evening Sonali and I took her to get samosas in Jhunjhunu town, when she suddenly grabbed my arm: "I know that everyone is fighting this case for me. But I feel far away from it, like other people are making me into this scary story. I don't know what I think. I can't even really remember. My case is something everyone does things to, except for me."

Pinky's inability to feel close to her case made it easy for others to claim control over her narrative. The violence in her past became a cultural and political project for different civil supporters and stakeholders, who projected onto it their own ideologies of honor and caste progress as well as their vision of successful hate crime law. Finally, one member of the JMSS convinced Pinky to stand up in front of the Jhunjhunu judicial magistrate and announce that she had never been raped.

NETĀGIRI AND THE INTIMACY OF LEGAL POLITICS

In Jhunjhunu, members of the Meghwal associations, prominent local community leaders, were referred to as *netā*s. *Netā* figures are widespread across India and toe the line between informal and formal politics. Some are bureaucratic mediators or brokers (Gupta 2005), others are informal "big men" who employ performances of charity (*samāj seva*) to build support (Mines and Gourishankar 1990). Many engage in the art of "bossing" (Michelutti et al. 2018): a collection of social and political strategies that marry influence within political parties with subversive, even illegal, activities to establish new networks of power.

In Jhunjhunu, Meghwal *netā*s use the art of "bossing" and the threat of criminal proceedings under the Atrocities Act to innovate and promote Dalit political interests. However, Pinky's story highlights how "bossing" strategies can shape the legal interpretations and emotions of vulnerable atrocity survivors and their families. As certain Meghwal *netā*s established relationships of trust with Pinky's family, they created powerful intimacies which pulled Pinky's case into the realm of party-political agendas.

Some of the most prominent members of the Meghwal associations harbored political ambitions. Jhunjhunu's electoral constituency of Pilani had been reserved for a Scheduled Caste candidate and, as educated, professional leaders of their community, many Meghwal *netā*s were keen to secure the ticket for the 2018 Legislative Assembly elections. Avinesh's father, who was involved in the leadership of the Ambedkar Society, considered himself too old to "do politics." Nevertheless, he explained to me that the ambition among his association brothers to compete for a candidacy as an MLA—a Member of the Rajasthan Legislative Assembly—was the result of one goal: to get Dalit issues on the political agenda so that casteism could be tackled at all levels.

While different Meghwal *netā*s had different political affiliations, the three most popular figures in the JMSS and the Ambedkar Society were hoping to compete as candidates for the Indian National Congress (INC). This allegiance is reflective of Rajasthan's pre- and post-independence history, which was profoundly shaped by the INC (Jenkins and Manor 2017). However, data from the 2013 Rajasthan State Legislative Elections suggest that a growing number of Scheduled Caste candidates across the state were also running as BJP candidates (Special Statistics for EPW 2014).

Regardless of party-political sympathies, all representatives of the Meghwal associations considered themselves representatives of a pan-Indian Dalit movement. They envisioned the Atrocities Act as a powerful instrument in a struggle to impress Dalit visions of justice and equality onto India's political landscape. Turning their own political imaginaries of caste equality into "embodied . . . expressions" of legal counterpractice (Larsson 2017, 71), Meghwal *netā*s saw it as their duty to engage legal actors to register, investigate, and argue atrocity cases in line with Meghwal perceptions of events. They used associations like the JMSS to lend an air of institutional formality to their role as local mediators in atrocity cases. JMSS leaders were usually among the first to visit families affected by caste violence and to strategize about the best way to propel complaints under the Atrocities Act forward through targeted media engagements and repeated visits to police stations.

However, prominent Meghwal association members had to strike a critical balance: Positioned at the intersection of charitable service, legal aid, and party politics, they had to encourage people to utilize the Atrocities Act to socially strengthen the Meghwal presence, but also ensure that the local intercaste frictions generated by atrocity cases did not jeopardize their own political futures: futures which they considered to be vital for wider Meghwal progress.

*Netā*s were typically able to achieve this balance by blurring the lines between their role as knowledgeable legal advisor and intimate friend when engaging with survivors' families and shaping their cases at crucial junctures. Sometimes it meant convincing survivors to turn "hostile" by going back on their earlier claims in court—in order to ensure election support for Meghwal representatives down the line.

For Pinky, it was her family's involvement with JMSS leader Satyanarayan G. which ultimately determined the trajectory of her atrocity complaint. More than any other development I witnessed, the subsequent controversy about Satyanarayam G.'s intervention showed how, in everyday life, the sociolegal imaginary of the Atrocities Act fractures along gendered and political lines, and how local developments in atrocity cases could divide Meghwal communities.

Portrait of a Netā

Satyanarayan G. was an impressively tall man who wore impeccably ironed white shirts and trousers. G.-jī, as he was often referred to, was easily noticeable at every JMSS gathering. Towering half a foot over the crowd, he had an inimitable knack for photographic ubiquity. He owned a squeaky-clean Maruti Suzuki Dzire car and was happy to drive around other JMSS members and even activists at short notice. G.-jī's great-grandfather had been active in the Shekhawati peasant revolts. It was a point of pride with G.-jī that due to his ancestor's heroism no one thought of his family as Meghwal or Dalit anymore. While most Meghwals in Jhunjhunu own a little bit of land, the extent of property belonging to the G. family was unusual. G.-jī and his brothers owned sixty acres of well-irrigated fields which were maintained by Meghwal workers. They also ran a property brokerage.

In 2017, G.-jī was one of three Meghwal men in his town in Jhunjhunu district campaigning for a ticket from the Indian National Congress in Rajasthan's 2018 Vidhan Sabhā elections. For this purpose, he honed an image of respectability, abstaining from alcohol and sweets and maintaining good relations beyond the boundaries of his own caste. Many of his friends were Jats.

G.-jī was not entirely uncontroversial. Some Meghwal men who had been employed in government jobs, like Avinesh's father, viewed his real-estate dealings with suspicion. Still, as a Meghwal man of significant resources, he was usually one of the first to attend to atrocity survivors in the region. He was in touch with several independent activists and NGOs in Jaipur and informed them of any incidents of caste-based violence in Jhunjhunu district.

G.-jī appeared to hold Sonali, the human rights activist whose family I lived with for six months, in high regard. He was always keen to accompany her on her fact-finding missions. However, G.-jī's involvement in the lives of local atrocity survivors was much more intensive than Sonali's. Like many human rights activists, Sonali now worked and lived in the capital city of Jaipur. In contrast, G.-jī resided in Jhunjhunu and represented a trusted counselor from the local Meghwal community. He spoke to atrocity survivors regularly and was usually able to point to at least one common family relation. His vast personal network within the Jhunjhunu judiciary and law enforcement meant that he was often able to predict the next moves of police officials. This strengthened his reputation as a powerful counsel.

Pinky's father, Roshan Lal, had called G.-jī right after the assault. Over time, Pinky's entire family established a close bond with G.-jī, who frequently visited the family. He strategized with Roshan Lal and listened to Pinky's mother, Sundari Devi, as she expressed her concerns over the case. Because he was a married man from a devout family who had two beautiful daughters and a lovely, modest wife, Sundari Devi valued his opinion.

G.-jī's support initially helped Roshan Lal withstand pressure from the Jat attacker's families. A few weeks after the FIR had been filed and three out of the four Jat boys had been arrested, the boys' families sent a convoy to Pinky's father to threaten him into accepting an out-of-court settlement or compromise (*rajināma*). They told him he would no longer be able to find agricultural employment if he refused to take the deal and reminded him that he still owed some Jats money. Terrified, Roshan Lal called G.-jī. "Don't worry!" G.-jī told him, "if you don't want to compromise you should not. You can work on my brother's field, and you can use the compensation you will get to pay back your debts." Roshan Lal refused the settlement. Through his contacts in the police and some friends he had in Jaipur, G.-jī and the JMSS were able to expedite the first two compensation payments, which Pinky's family was due under the Atrocities Act. When I visited Pinky's home a few weeks later, construction of a new family home was in full swing. Roshan Lal proudly told me that he had put away money for Pinky's wedding. The Jats had not threatened him again. "G.-jī gave me good advice. He protects us," he beamed.

And so everyone was pleased with G.-jī at that time. During the months after the case registration G.-jī and Sonali often visited the family together. They befriended Pinky, her mother, sister, and grandmother. Due to G.-jī's local know-how and Sonali's networks to human rights organizations in Delhi and abroad, the two soon became known as a powerhouse team (*jodī*) for atrocity cases. G.-jī arranged for Pinky and her mother to come down to Jaipur for a workshop held to support victims of sexual assault, which Sonali organized. Sonali also invited Pinky to her family home in Badrasar village, where I too was staying. She asked Pinky to come along with us on fact-finding missions for other atrocities in hopes that Pinky might one day become an activist herself. G.-jī drove us everywhere.

Though Sonali and G.-jī worked hand in hand during this period, the latter grew much closer with the family due to his consistent presence. He even took Pinky and her sister shopping for gowns to wear to their cousin's wedding. Sonali fully trusted G.-ji to bring Pinky's case to a successful conclusion in court. She used to declare: "G.-ji and me will not allow Pinky's father to be bullied into compromising, we will make sure that these boys get convicted and the family gets justice and respect just like Roshan Lal wants."

But five months after Pinky's assault, Sonali received a shocking phone call from Anisha, a Shekhawati liaison of the Dalit Women's Forum. Anisha informed her that Pinky and her family had reached an out-of-court compromise (*rajināma*) with the Jat attackers' families. "It was a 40-lakh [4 million] Rupee compromise," Anisha told Sonali. "a few weeks ago, Pinky changed her testimony in court." Sonali was outraged. "What do you mean?" she screamed into the phone, "How is there a compromise? Compromises are not allowed in these cases! We should have won in court!"

Anisha's response turned Sonali's face to stone: "You remember this G. fellow?" she asked, "Well he has been in cahoots with the *pradhāna* (village leader) of Pinky's village, who is a Jat, and together they and Pinky's mother decided to compromise. They said this would be better for Pinky's marriage. Then G. and the *pradhāna* pocketed half the money. Pinky's family got the other half. So, when Pinky testified at the first hearing, she said she had made the whole thing up."

When Sonali tried to call G.-ji, he didn't pick up. Neither did Pinky. Pinky's number had been discontinued. Determined to get to the bottom of things, Sonali and I traveled to Bilaria only to run into Roshan Lal who seemed deeply uncomfortable. Upon Sonali's inquiry about what happened with Pinky's case he shrugged. "What can I say, my wife and G.-ji said that there was no point continuing the case because it would just go on forever and ruin Pinky's marriage . . . and the boys have been punished. My wife and G.-ji wanted to be done with it. We compromised. There is no point talking about it now." Pinky and her mother were nowhere to be seen.

G.-ji never got back in touch, which left Sonali heartbroken and disillusioned. I too was shocked by his actions. He had seemed like a good friend and ally. I later learned that Bilaria's Jat village leader (*pradhāna*), who had helped G.-jī arrange the compromise, had begun to support G.-jī's campaign for an INC ticket for the Vidhan Sabhā elections in 2018. So did the Jat families, whose sons had attacked Pinky.

Hostile Intimacies?

Unfortunately, Pinky's story is a common one. Sonali's outburst that "compromises are not allowed in these cases" refers to the fact that, technically, both rape and caste atrocities are "noncompoundable offences" under Indian law. This means that these crimes are considered such grave offences against society that, under section 320 of the CrPC, opposing parties are not allowed to come to an agreement or compromise outside of court. However, the sociolegal and ethnographic literature shows that many Indian rape and atrocity cases are, nonetheless, compromised. Compromises are unofficially enabled when witnesses and even survivors like Pinky deny their previous accusations during trial or "tone down" statements they had made previously to the police (Berti 2010, 236; Mehta 2016). In these cases, court records usually show that the judge has declared the witness "hostile" (Baxi 2014) and acquitted the accused. However, court records don't mention that the hostility of the witnesses is likely the result of an out-of-court compromise.

Courts rarely prosecute witnesses who turn hostile for perjury, although hostile witnesses do run that risk (Baxi 2014). In 2019, a court in Jhunjhunu sentenced a woman to one month in jail under section 193 of the Indian Penal Code (punishment for false evidence) for denying earlier claims that her minor daughter had been raped (Mehta 2019). However, in Pinky's case, G.-jī eliminated that risk. It turned out that G.-jī had personal connections to the magistrate in Pinky's case. He ensured that Pinky would not be charged with falsifying evidence and that her family would not be asked to return the compensation that had already been paid.

While G.-jī certainly became the villain of Sonali's story, as she accused him of selfish political strategizing and undermining the very foundations of a functioning legal system, others interpreted his actions more generously. "Why do you think he pushed for the compromise now?," a Meghwal notary and member of the Ambedkar Society asked me weeks after the news had broken. "Because now everyone wins!" The family, he explained, had already received some financial compensation and with the additional money from the compromise would be financially stable. Roshan Lal had shown strength by refusing compromises before, and the boys had been scared enough for everyone to understand that actions of the kind perpetrated against Pinky would not be permitted.

Pinky, the notary explained, had been getting overwhelmed by the idea of a long court process and found it hard to remember exactly what had happened. She wanted to move on. Her in-laws were willing to go ahead with the marriage if there was no ongoing case: "So, G.-jī got something out of the situation too, he arranged the compromise when it was good for him and good for them. Sure, he is a clever one, but Pinky and her family are happy. Only your activists from Jaipur are unhappy."

However, not everyone regarded G.-jī's action so charitably. Considering the scale of the protest in front of the police collectorate after Pinky's attack, many association members felt that Pinky's family and G.-jī had made fools of them: "After everything, this girl goes up there and says, oh it didn't happen," one member of the Meghwal Samāj vented: "This makes our entire movement (āndolana) seem like a lie. We got the police to act, and the media involved and now everyone thinks we are liars just trying to get compensation. This G.-jī and the girl and her whole family are criminals!"

Indeed, G.-jī's strategy reflects a certain willingness to subvert formal legal processes. One of the hallmarks of South Asian boss figures is their willingness to "transcend the law," feeding into popular narratives about the rogue social bandit who provides "local justice" and imbues institutional processes with his own moral code (Michelutti et al. 2018, 17). These analyses, perhaps, illuminate some of G.-jī's actions. Based on the support the Jat village leaders provided his MLA campaign, and the substantial sum of money he pocketed in the compromise, one can safely assume that self-interest played a part in his decision-making. What is more remarkable is the notary's claim that G.-jī encouraged the compromise at a juncture when he was able to reconcile his personal desires with his sense of obligation towards Pinky's family.

Here the disagreement between Pinky's mother and father regarding her legal case becomes relevant once more. While Pinky's mother was primarily concerned with the maintenance of a type of honor that hinges on female modesty, Pinky's father saw a case under the Atrocities Act as an opportunity to regain a different kind of honor, defined by social respect through public retribution. Pinky's father hoped a conviction under a law as harsh as the Atrocities Act would "speak for itself" and act as a future deterrent for sexual violence against "Meghwal daughters." If a formal court conviction was crucial to Roshan Lal's idea of honor, it was superfluous or even damaging to Sundari Devi's.

From what I later learned from Anisha, the local women's activist, it seemed that once the story of Pinky's assault began to fade from public consciousness and her own immediate sense of suffering became somewhat dulled by new experiences, daily concerns about her marriage and the family's livelihood took center stage once more. The last time I ever saw Pinky was right after her cousin's wedding. That day, it really had seemed that she was ready to move forward: "I cannot be *piḍita* Pinky (victim Pinky) forever. Thinking about it all hurts. I want to move on!"

A few weeks later G.-jī's compromise unfolded. I never got an opportunity to speak with him or Pinky again. However, the notary's interpretation, as well as Pinky's desire to escape the shadow of "the case," suggests that G.-jī may have been convinced that he was acting in accordance with a "local" moral code when he arranged the compromise, which aligned with the wishes of Pinky's mother and, maybe, even with Pinky's own wants. For a family like Pinky's, whose level of education and social mobility were limited and tied them to village life, settling with financial benefits, good marriage prospects, and with the satisfaction of knowing that the Jat boys had trembled before real legal consequences, could be seen as the best way forward.

One could interpret Pinky's mother's alliance with G.-jī as a refusal to let her husband and other Meghwal men dictate the "correct" way to justice at the cost of women's lives. The systematic way in which she cultivated her acquaintance with G.-jī may have been her effort to inscribe her vision of success onto the Atrocities Act and rip it out of the hands of professional civil society organizations and activists, who valued the movement (*āndolana*) more than the future of her unmarried daughter.

However, the outcome of Pinky's case always sat uncomfortably with me. Today I still wonder: Was the compromise G.-jī organized, seemingly with her mother's consent, a reflection of Sundari Devi's or even Pinky's agency? Or was it, simply, a most skillfully manipulative and harmful display of G.-jī's bossing skills?

THE ACTIVIST PARADOX: INDIVIDUAL CASES AND COMMUNITY UPLIFTMENT

For Sonali, it was doubtlessly the latter. She remained forever outraged by G.-jī's actions and never again believed in his good intentions. Only months after Pinky's case was concluded did I truly understand why. During a visit to the Jaipur High Court, Geeta, the female CDR lawyer I had befriended, gave me her take on the Atrocities Act: "Atrocity cases are exhausting because most of the time nothing works. But if you look at this law, it has so much strength. It is a sign that the world is changing for Dalits. So, I don't just see myself as a lawyer fighting the cases of individual families, I am a human rights activist defending this law."

Geeta's position illuminates the radical controversy between Sonali and G.-jī in relation to Pinky's case. Sonali saw herself as a human rights activist first and foremost and viewed the Atrocities Act as a tool for state-sanctioned, structural social change through law. The integrity and public reputation of this tool were paramount. The very existence of the Atrocities Act was a symbol for the righteousness of Dalit demands for a life free from violence, humiliation, and upper-caste sexual aggression. Hence, Sonali felt that its credibility as a legal document had to be safeguarded, and she expected atrocity complainants and Dalit politicians to use the act in accordance with its procedural, legal rules. While she sympathized with Pinky and was acutely aware of the gendered complexities that haunted stories like hers, Sonali thought that calling on the Atrocities Act for help implied a responsibility to clear legal and ethical guidelines. In her eyes, the help human rights activists had provided Pinky's family also obligated them to mobilize Pinky's tragedy for the creation of a better landscape of legal recognition for all Dalits. Undermining the Atrocities Act for a successful marriage and risking the reputation of the NGOs who had supported their cause was unforgivable.

I soon learned that the demand that survivors should "stick it out" put many human rights activists in Rajasthan at loggerheads with both survivors' families, who were concerned with their immediate circumstances, and with Megwhal *netā*s like G.-jī, who primarily conceived of the Atrocities Act as an instrument to cement Dalit political power. Pinky's story reveals that atrocity cases are sites where multiple, contradictory imaginaries of law, justice, and caste progress are generated.

One aspect of these contestations stands out in relation to the controversy between Sonali, G.-jī, and Pinky's mother. There resides an internal tension between personal suffering and community upliftment within the concept of hate crime legislation. Hate crime laws exist within a wider legal structure, which takes "the individual as the locus" (Das and Randeria 2015, 6) and aims to protect *marginalized communities* through *individual legal* cases. However, the focus of hate crime laws on the targeted punishment of singular crimes (Bhat 2020b) assumes that atrocity cases are merely about a dispute "between the named parties" (MacDermott 2018, 22). This assumption overlooks the reality that the harmed individuals in these lawsuits are targets of hate crimes only because they belong to a historically disadvantaged *collective*. Hence, the outcome of individual hate crime cases has ramification for others within this community.

Hence, social movements and NGOs that emphasize human rights and that envision more radical structural change in the name of historically oppressed communities (Eckert and Knöpfel 2020) often reject the idea that individual hate crime cases are just about the survivor. In atrocity cases, human rights NGOs and local activists frequently entered the picture as mediators (Mosse 2005; Merry 2006) who mobilized a variety of "social, political, and technical relationships" (Sharma and Kelly 2018, 309) to help translate stories of caste violence into the language of law. However, they didn't embark on this journey of mediation neutrally. Activists like Sonali and Geeta had a specific idea of the way cases like Pinky's should be fought. Pinky was meant to approach her case in a manner that acknowledged that the violence perpetrated against her body and her suffering was bigger than her. Her case was meant to leave behind a legacy that sharpened the tools of hate crime law for those women and men who would later suffer just like her.

This tension—between activist rationalities, which highlight a more distant future of structural social change, and the immediate needs and interpretations of vulnerable, rural communities—is well documented in the South Asian literature. As later chapters show, activist efforts to position styles of professional institutional engagement or certain modes of knowledge as the primary mechanism for the advancement of lower-caste communities can produce new forms of caste domination which bring activists face to face with the limits of their own ideologies (Cody 2013).

A FRACTURED IMAGINARY

Of all the cases I encountered, Pinky's story helps identify the different stakeholders in Indian atrocity cases most clearly. Her narrative exposes how the legal cases of the most vulnerable survivors of caste violence are often fought outside of courts, lawyers' chambers, and even police stations in the muddy arena of community politics, activism, and kinship relations. Pinky's case unveils the selective mobilization and silencing of voices various stakeholders engage in as they try to make a hate crime law—that problematically binds together histories of collective suffering and instances of individual violence—work in accordance with their own political, personal, and legal ambitions.

In this jurisdictional battle over the "right" way to use the Atrocities Act, gender inequalities within kinship networks come into sharp focus. Pinky, a young, unmarried girl, whose body is a projection screen for family status and whose life is envisioned in terms of future dependencies on men, got even less of a voice than most. Different visions of honor, anticaste politics, and legal progress are set against each other and painted onto her wounded body.

At the start of the chapter, I asked: *Who are hate crime laws for?* Pinky's violence was hers to bear, but the legal engagements to which it gave rise were never really her own. Thrown into a legal tug-of-war, her memory could not achieve the cohesiveness necessary to find meaning in her own court case. Rather than being counseled, she was instructed; her fate became public property, a figurehead for Dalit politics, a symbol for an idealized human rights struggle.

This highlights one of the central dilemmas with hate crime laws and other legal antidiscrimination measures: They set up historically oppressed groups as uniform recipients of law (Goldblatt 2015) and often neglect to address the intersectional ways in which discrimination and official law are *experienced* (Ajele and McGill 2020). In Rajasthan's atrocity cases, this gave rise to a kaleidoscope of ideas about "proper" legal labor, the goals of official justice, and definitions of legal success. These created battles of legal ownership which resulted in new inequalities and gendered agencies. As subsequent chapters lead us into the institutional arena of police and courts, these contestations become even more complex. The tension between professional imaginations of what the Atrocities Act "should" accomplish for a wider Dalit struggle, and the needs of individual survivors and families, rears its head again and again.

PART II

*When Atrocities Become Cases:
Rewriting Law's Allegiance*

THREE

THE CASE THAT COULD NOT BE
Police Translations at the Margins

HEADING SOUTH

In August 2017, as my first year of fieldwork was drawing to an end, I left Jhunjhunu for a month to travel to Rajasthan's southern district of Udaipur. Here I wanted to investigate a case I had been told about by a journalist called Raveen Meghwal, who lived in Udaipur and reported on caste atrocities across Rajasthan. I had met Raveen at an ActionAid event in Jaipur. During our first conversation he told me that the types of caste atrocities which haunted Dalit communities in southern Rajasthan differed from those in the Shekhawati region because the colonial and cultural history of the south had given rise to different economic dependencies and caste relations. "Caste hierarchies have changed less in Udaipur than they have in districts like Jhunjhunu because of the land patterns. You see this in the way the police respond to atrocities." He insisted that if I really wanted to see how traditional forms of caste power shaped police investigations under the Atrocities Act, I needed to come to Udaipur. When we spoke, Raveen continually referred to a case, which he had seen unfold five years prior in 2012. He called it "the case that could not be (*wo case jo case ban hī nahīn saka*)," and proposed that learning about the story behind it would show me how India's police force "makes or breaks atrocity cases."

The "case that could not be" belonged to a Meghwal laborer named Choti Lal who lived in the remote village of Libasha, forty kilometers southwest of Udaipur city. When Raveen and I first visited, we stayed with Choti Lal's family for a few days. Initially, Choti Lal and his wife were suspect of my presence. They had resigned their fight for a case under the Atrocities Act long ago and had no desire to relive the experience. Since I was neither a lawyer who could have analyzed their situation nor an activist or journalist like Raveen, they did not know what to make of me. The facts that the local *Mewari* dialect was different from the *Marwari* dialect I had learned to understand in Jhunjhunu, and that neither Choti Lal nor his wife was well versed in standard Hindi, did not help my case. Initially, Choti Lal remained reserved. As an illiterate laborer who had recently lived a life marked by humiliation and caste aggression, he was not quick to trust.

As so often during my fieldwork, it was not my credentials (the designation "anthropologist" never impressed anyone) but my ability to bond with the women of the household which allowed me to build a closer relationship with the family. Suman, Choti Lal's wife, enjoyed my company and liked to watch me play with her three-year-old granddaughter. I was the same age as her daughter-in-law Kavita, who spoke a little bit of Hindi, and Kavita translated for me when Suman's rapid chatter in Mewari went over my head. I accompanied the women on their chores, helped peel peas, and let them make fun of my inability to make round chapatis. I also did some English reading exercises with the neighborhood children. On the second evening over dinner, Suman and Choti Lal began to open up.

In June 2012, Choti Lal had filed a complaint under the Atrocities Act at the police station in the subdistrict (*tahasīla*) headquarters in a nearby town called Gogunda. The complaint concerned a recent disagreement between his family and the powerful upper-caste Rajput council in his native village of Libasha. Choti Lal had disobeyed Rajput orders relating to the construction of his house. Unlike Jhunjhunu, where former Rajput elites have lost much of their land and power, the Rajput community in Udaipur district has retained its control.[1] Therefore, Choti Lal's open defiance of the council had been a risky choice. The disagreement over the house had resulted in Choti Lal and his Meghwal peers in Libasha being ostracized from the village community. This action, which is popularly known as a "social boycott," was only implicitly outlawed under the original version of the Atrocities Act (previous to the amendment of 2015), which was in force when Choti Lal filed his atrocity complaint. The initial act only criminalized attempts to deny Scheduled Castes or Tribes customary rites of passage or access to water and common resources.[2] However, the police had dismissed Choti Lal's complaint by pointing out that the Rajputs had never openly prevented Meghwals from accessing village resources. "The police said that I never uttered the words 'social boycott' and that the Rajputs never directly said Meghwals are not allowed to go certain places and do things, and that therefore we don't have a case," Choti Lal explained. "Apparently for something to be declared an atrocity under the Atrocities Act you need to have the right words. But people like me don't have them! Still," he concluded with a shrug, "I should be grateful we got an investigation at all. People like us don't usually get an investigation or a case!" When I asked him what he meant, he shook his head, "I am uneducated, and my hands have seen hard work. I am not someone police officers believe."

Choti Lal's story, his resignation, and his reflection on his legal case, which hardly "was," and never truly "could have been," raised my curiosity about the unarticulated demands of speech and bodily performance that stand guard at the gates of hate crime law long before complainants ever set foot in a courthouse.

In India categorizations of crimes as caste atrocities rely on the interpretative engagements and performances of the institutional actors who are positioned at the meeting point of social and legal life: the Indian police, who act as the guardian of Indian criminal law. Since the mid-twentieth century, policing has gradually evolved into what Ong and Collier call a "global form" (Ong and Collier 2005)—a common sociolegal denominator established by governments with the explicit purpose of maintaining order through force (Bittner 1970). Nonetheless, police forces in different nation states have distinctive structures and legal responsibilities, operating within specific cultural frameworks of violence, law, and public harmony (Mutsaers 2019). In India, lower-level police forces stationed in districts and towns play a unique role within the legal system: they are responsible for translating stories of violence into official criminal complaints.

In Rajasthan, the act of registering a complaint under the Atrocities

Act at a local *thānā* (police station) is neither a mere formality nor a passive process of allowing police officers to categorize and investigate the "facts" of a case. Rather, survivors' encounter with the police is a "focal point" (Mutsaers 2019, 7) in the social life of the Atrocities Act, where everyday discrimination first encounters legal rule. The step of complaint registration is a make-or-break moment defined by intense political and social activity, which determines what types of arguments and interpretations are later (im-)possible in courtrooms.

Against this backdrop, Choti Lal's account brought into focus a central set of questions that haunt hate crime law in India: How do members of marginalized communities come to identify and name particular interactions as discriminatory? How does engagement with the police, the first set of legal actors that survivors encounter when mobilizing hate crime law, shape their own perceptions of events? And, which steps of institutional translation must the police conduct for acts of aggression against Dalits to be legally investigated as an "atrocity"?

Choti Lal's painful narrative grants new insight into these abstract questions by highlighting the intimate, embodied processes of interpretation and translation (Bear and Mathur 2015) that lead police to classify a crime as a hate crime within India's legal bureaucracy. His experience shows that survivors' ability to make caste discrimination legally legible is intimately bound up with their own embodied personhood and the social biases that have been mapped onto particular bodies. Analyzing Choti Lal's perception that familiarity with the "right" words determines who "gets" a case, this chapter zooms in on the way everyday interpretations and negotiations of police authority (Jauregui 2016) shape the fate of complaints under the Atrocities Act. By examining the acts of sociocultural translation, which police officers must complete for Dalit survivors of caste violence to become visible and legible to the judiciary as legitimate complainants, the chapter highlights how India's police produce and reconstitute (Garriot 2013) wider legal, social, and political understandings of hate crimes.

This chapter makes three main arguments: First, it shows that the Indian police are the most crucial sociolegal translators in atrocity cases: they hold the power to legally make or break incidents of caste violence as official atrocity crimes. Second, the chapter argues that this process of police translation is itself guided by a collective stock of assumptions about certain groups of people, or social types (Cicourel 1968), which police officers have developed over their lifetimes. Hence, survivors' embodied performances, which indicate class status, caste dependencies, levels of educational achievement, or gender, play a key role in determining if police officers deem certain stories of discrimination credible. Third, the chapter highlights that narratives, claims, and performances declared unreliable or unfounded by police are often those that fly in the face of a traditionally masculine authoritative habitus; a habitus that has been historically bound up with upper-caste and upper-class authority.

As the legal actors at the "edge of state and society" (Jauregui 2016, 22), the constables who worked at Rajasthan's police stations had to "name" (Felestiner, Abel, and Sarat 1980) specific actions of caste violence and translate them into offences under the Atrocities Act. However, the complex social and political networks police officers were embedded in, and the skeptical and patronizing attitudes towards Dalit complaints that permeate the police force, could often result in subtle refusals to engage in the acts of translation necessary to turn an experience of violence into an "atrocity offence" on paper. In this way police denied the violent experiences of men like Choti Lal entry to the judicial realm. These translational refusals often remained hidden behind strategic demands for particular verbal registers (Gal 2015) and legal aesthetics (Cabot 2013). Ironically, the socially patterned silences that mark incidents of caste violence as humiliating and severe in Rajasthan's villages were often what allowed law enforcement to turn a blind eye to caste atrocities. For survivors like Choti Lal, this engendered further trauma as well as self-blame.

CHOTI LAL'S TALE

In January 2012 Choti Lal and his wife had decided to build a concrete house (*pakkā makāna*) at the edge of the village, on a small parcel of land which had been in his family for three decades. Choti Lal was in good spirits. Tearing down his old clay home and erecting a stable concrete structure in its stead would make his family's life more comfortable. It would also show villagers that Choti Lal's family was climbing the social and financial ladder. Choti Lal's eldest son had been working as a concierge in a hotel in Gujarat's capital of Ahmedabad for almost ten years, while his grandson had gained employment in Mumbai. With their support the family had finally saved enough to finance the new home. Unfortunately, Choti Lal's happiness was quickly dimmed. A few weeks after he had started work on his new house, he was summoned to an assembly of the local Rajput council—an association of senior men who belonged to the most economically and politically powerful caste community in the area, and which had once constituted the official ruling elite of the Rajputana Agency. Though there was no formal rule to this effect, everyone knew that informally the Rajput council represented the village leadership committee. At the meeting, Choti Lal was told that he had made an immense blunder: he had built a balcony.

"We were so happy about our beautiful balcony," Suman, Choti Lal's wife told me, "you could sit, have tea and hang up laundry. But the Rajputs said that it had to go because trucks would no longer be able to use our road since the balcony was too low." She snorted derisively, "What nonsense, they just didn't want Dalits having a balcony in case we accidentally pollute them. We might empty a water bucket on someone from above and then they would be 'impure.' This was casteism (*jātibādi*)."

But, if one believes Khissak Lal Meghwal, a respected Meghwal *netā*

FIGURE 6. Choti Lal's house with the little balcony he wouldn't tear down.

in the village and manager at a cement company in nearby Gogunda town, the issue was never about a balcony. "Other Meghwals have balconies, and no one ever said anything. This is about power," he told me when we were having tea at Choti Lal's house. According to Khissak Lal, times were changing, and the fact that Choti Lal didn't ask permission from the Rajput council when he started construction on his house made the Rajputs feel like they were losing their historic status. So, they decided to set an example and demanded that Choti Lal tear down his balcony. After hearing the news Choti Lal petitioned the Rajput council for a hearing. However, he never received a response. So he went ahead with constructing the balcony.

Then things truly turned sour. One morning, Choti Lal headed out to a field owned by S. Jhalla, a wealthy Rajput who had employed him as a casual laborer for the past five years, only to be sent home. Except that he wasn't precisely sent home. "Jhalla-jī openly told me and the other Meghwals who work his fields that there is a new rule now, which says that no one is allowed to defecate on a field that isn't their own." My face must have shown confusion because Khissak Lal explained. "This was their way of initiating a social boycott and exiling Meghwals from village life."

At first this conclusion may appear bizarre. Yet, if we consider the history of Udaipur state, Choti Lal's claim begins to expose a particular logic. The modern district of Udaipur, where his home village of Libasha is located, is part of Rajasthan's Mewar region. Mewar is largely made up of hilly terrain and typically receives above average rainfall compared to other areas of the state. The lime-rich soil around Libasha village provides extremely favorable growing conditions for agricultural crops like wheat, barley, maize, and gram (Indian Council of Agricultural Research 2016). Consequently, as much as 80% of Udaipur's district population still resides rurally and relies heavily on agricultural work and subsistence farming (Census of India 2011; District Profile Udaipur).

Udaipur district also has a slightly different colonial history than the Shekhawati region, where Pinky's story in the previous chapter unfolded. While parts of Udaipur district were administered through the *jāgīrdari* system of land tenure, substantial areas of Udaipur are so-called former *khālsa* lands. Prior to Indian independence, the Rajput rulers of Mewar directly controlled vast stretches of fertile land. These lands, which fell under the direct control of the central kingly court (*darabāra*) of the Udaipur princely state, were known as *khālsa* lands and were often cultivated by lower castes and untouchable groups. *Khālsa* plots remained in Rajput ownership even after the post-independence land reforms, which aimed to redistribute agricultural land among different castes (Rudolph and Rudolph 2011).[3] When I met Choti Lal in 2017, seventy years after independence, Rajputs in Udaipur still maintained a firm grip on agricultural land compared to other districts of the state. Rajput families in Libasha made up a mere third of the village population but still controlled around 70% of fertile land. Meanwhile, Meghwals, who were almost equally represented in numbers, often had no land to their names or owned only very small plots. Most worked on Rajput properties as agricultural workers.

When explaining the logic behind the defecation ban, Khissak Lal and Choti Lal told me that Meghwal fields were far away from the village boundary, while Rajput lands are right at the edge of Libasha. When Meghwals like Choti Lal worked on Rajput fields, they were usually unable to walk the long road to their own properties when nature called. The new defecation rule, therefore, sent the implicit message that they

FIGURE 7. A field owned by wealthy local Rajput S. Jhalla that Choti Lal worked on before the boycott.

were no longer allowed to work on Rajput land and symbolically marked the community's ostracism (*bahāra kar denā*) from village life. From then on, Meghwals struggled to access basic services in the village: Landowners denied them employment, they were not allowed in the village shop, and they were prevented from using the main village well. Rajputs also chased them away from some smaller public wells, which were situated at the boundary of Rajput and Meghwal fields. Local medical practitioners refused to provide treatment. For a long time, Meghwals were also banned from the village temple dedicated to Ramdev Pir, a deity with deep cultural significance for Meghwals in Rajasthan.

POLICE VERDICTS: THE FIRST INFORMATION REPORT (FIR)

Choti Lal decided to act. He had heard about the Atrocities Act a few years earlier when a distant relative in Udaipur city had filed a hate speech complaint against his Rajput employer. His relative had told him that the complaint had scared his employer so much that he apologized and even promoted him. Choti Lal was impressed but he didn't want just an apology, he wanted a real case. "I wanted the Rajputs to see that Meghwals have the law on their side now, and that they can't just behave like thugs (*guṇḍās*) anymore. If you act like a criminal, the court will convict you like a criminal."

Choti Lal had felt nervous when he went to the Gogunda police station in 2012. He knew that much depended on the police report. In his experience the police could be unpredictable and were not usually favorably inclined towards men like him, who were poor, lower caste, and clearly looked the part. Yet the future of his life in the village depended on the police. The key to his fate was a seemingly mundane piece of paper, colloquially referred to as the FIR.

In Indian criminal law the First Information Report, or FIR, is the first written police record of a complaint, which is lodged by the victim of a cognizable offence (an offence where the police may arrest someone without a warrant under section 2c of the Code of Criminal Procedure—CrPC), or by someone on behalf of the victim. Police are duty-bound to file an FIR if a cognizable offence is reported to them.[4] Under section 154 of the CrPC, the FIR must include the complainant's personal details, the date and time of the supposed offence, the names of the accused, and the facts of the reported incident. Information may be relayed to the police in either written or oral form. The oral format allows people who lack literacy skills to register criminal complaints. However, the police must translate oral statements into an official written document and ask the complainant to sign the FIR. For people like Choti Lal, who cannot write, a thumb print may serve as a stand-in for a signature.

While the permission of oral statements facilitates initial access to the law for people regardless of education, a problem quickly arises: complainants like Choti Lal, who can't read, have no way of knowing what the police have actually written in the FIR and must rely on the help of others—NGOs, activists, literate relations—to ensure that their claims have been correctly represented in the FIR.

The FIR lays the foundation for the subsequent police investigation, which must be concluded within thirty days in atrocity cases. By law police must file *any* criminal complaint Dalits and Adivasis make against other castes under the Atrocities Act, alongside the Indian Penal Code. When registering an FIR, police officers are then required to complete a feat of abstraction: they must take the circumstances described by the complainant and decide how to legally code them by matching the reported incident with one or several of the offences included in the Atrocities Act. Hence, police officers make Dalit narratives legible to the law through a preliminary act of "categorical" translation (Bachmann-Medick 2013). Following the investigation, the superior officer in charge (who must hold the rank of Deputy Superintendent of Police or higher) has two options: he can submit a charge sheet to the district court or issue an alternative form called a Final Report.

While the submission of a charge sheet implies that the claims made in the FIR have—at least partially—been corroborated and that the issue is deemed serious enough to be subject to court proceedings, a Final Report (FR) essentially declares that a complaint is unsubstantiated and marks the conclusion of the matter (see chap. 4 for further information on Final Reports). Hence, the charge sheet acts as an administrative stamp of legitimacy for the victim, while an FR implies an invalidation of his/her account. This can be problematic, because most atrocity investigations I witnessed during my fieldwork were not overseen by a Deputy Superintendent of Police (DSP) or a higher-ranking official as the guidelines stipulate (comp. Teltumbde 2018a, 16). Though rarely analyzed in depth, the FIR thus effectively marks a "first line of (in-)justice delivery" (Khora 2014, 17).

While the FIR filing process is common to all Indian criminal cases, it is especially influential in questions of caste-based violence, which require a police officer to acknowledge often subtle, ongoing social issues of casteism and discrimination. At the police station a constable, of the Kumbhar potter case, whom Choti Lal described as diligent and sympathetic, lodged his complaint under the Atrocities Act. The resulting police report cited three sections of the original version of the Atrocities Act (previous to the amendment of 2015). It accused the thirteen Rajput men on Libasha's village council of humiliating Meghwals in public view (chap. 2, sec. 3(1)(x)), interfering with Meghwals' rights to enjoy any land, premises, and water (chap. 2, sec. 3(1)(v)), and blocking Meghwal access to common resources and places of public resort (chap. 2, sec. 3(1)(xiv)). The constable dutifully arrived in Libasha the next day to interview the accused Rajput men, as well as Choti Lal's family and further witnesses.

However, the tide soon turned. Under seemingly mysterious circumstances, which were later revealed to be the result of interference by a powerful local Rajput politician, the constable in charge, whom Choti Lal trusted, was transferred and a second, different, complaint was registered in Choti Lal's absence. The second FIR did not include sections 3(1)(xiv) and 3(1)(v), which specified the denial of "customary right of passage to a place of public resort" and the right to water and land use, and most accurately summarized the social and economic ostracism of the Meghwal community. Even though police officers are bound by law to supply a copy of the FIR to the complainant, Choti Lal received no copy and was not even informed that a new FIR had been filed. And so he remained unaware of these developments until a group of police officers appeared in Libasha village a couple of weeks later, allegedly to conduct a "proper investigation." However, they hardly spoke to Choti Lal and his family but spent most of their day interviewing the Rajput council. Soon after Choti Lal was told that the police were closing his case with a Final Report.

The report stated that there was no evidence to suggest the Rajputs had overtly denied Meghwals access to water wells or insinuated a social boycott. Consequently, Choti Lal's accusations were "false."

Fortunately for Choti Lal, he knew Raveen, the journalist who had brought me to Udaipur. Raveen had contacts to several NGOs across Rajasthan. With the support of the NGOs and independent activists, Libasha's Meghwal community successfully staged a sit-in protest (*dharanā*) in front of the police headquarters in Gogunda, and it garnered local media attention. The resulting bad publicity forced the police to reopen the investigation. In October 2012, the police formally filed a charge sheet in Choti Lal's case and forwarded their report to the special court for SC/ST atrocity cases in Udaipur. However, the police's assessment in the new charge sheet did not differ significantly from their statement in the original Final Report. They still argued that there was no evidence for a social boycott. Therefore, the court ultimately dismissed Choti Lal's case for "lack of evidence" in 2017, after leaving it pending for many years.

However, Choti Lal attributes the dismissal of his case to the way the police treated his testimony. "Read what the police say," Choti Lal challenged me in 2017, "their report says something like: 'the Rajputs never publicly pronounced a social boycott or said that Meghwals are not allowed to access lands or things in the village.' Of course, no one will tell you: 'You are not allowed to go use this shop, I am boycotting you!' But we still understand what certain statements or actions mean!" However, he also lamented his own inability to make himself understood. "These legal things are complicated," he sighed, "the Rajputs weren't obvious, but police also don't want to understand what it [a social boycott] looks like when you tell them. For something to be declared an atrocity you need the right words as they are in the act. If the words are not said, police can pretend it's not true."

One might file away Choti Lal's experience as a textbook instance of police corruption and political power play, a theme strikingly predominant in the current academic literature on the Atrocities Act (Nawsagaray 2018). Such analyses successfully highlight problematic fissures in an administrative structure that should ideally ensure equal opportunities based on constitutional values (Ambedkar 1989b [1936]). Yet Choti Lal's experience shows something much more insidious: Police officers in India can undermine complaints under the Atrocities Act through strategic refusals to translate marginalized experiences of discrimination, which are often narrated through local idioms, into the registers of law. This involves two simultaneous processes: First, police demands for specific language, or "the right words," as well as particular bodily performances, allow officers to cloak corrupt processes or personal (caste-) bias as a lack of available evidence. Second, police rejection of Dalit narratives and bodies then leads survivors like Choti Lal to internalize their own legal failure.

TRANSLATIONAL POLICING: LAW AND ACCOUNTABILITY AT THE EDGE OF THE STATE

When I discussed Choti Lal's story with Raveen, we quickly began to think of it in terms of translation. "You know it's like you coming here and being told about this case and Khissak Lal has to explain to you what the defecation ban means," Raveen reflected after we had said goodbye to Choti Lal. "But the thing is that Khissak Lal is *able to explain* the whole thing to you, and you *want to understand*. But that second group of police officers in Choti Lal's case, they weren't trying to understand, and Choti Lal struggled to explain!"

Choti Lal's story indicates a translational barrier between the normative universe enshrined in the linguistic registers of the law and the local cultural nuances that inhere in the metaphors which govern marginalized lifeworlds. This translational moment, which has the power to turn personal narratives of caste discrimination into a formal legal case, is guarded by India's field police force, which is simultaneously the most accessible and the most feared and brutal arm of the state for Meghwals in Rajasthan.

Legal theorists have argued that linguistic and legal rules create and maintain a specific set-up of reality (Agamben 1995). While language generates the very world it declares to describe, law creates the political and criminal categories it names through its own authoritative capacities of definition. The normative discourses and categories of state law reify and rewrite identities as they define them (Povinelli 2002). Hence, the categorizing force of the law not only bears productive power but also holds the potential for violence, as it can deny specific realities by refusing to "name" them (Agamben 1995, 31). Being denied entry to legal categories leaves people without social and political recognition.

Unfortunately, Choti Lal's experience shows that law's reliance on typified, linguistic categories of violence can obstruct attempts by marginalized groups to gain legal recognition for the harm done to them. Translating local registers of violence or exclusion like the defecation ban into an official language of offences or rights requires skilled mediators or translators (Merry 2006). In Indian atrocity complaints, these mediators are police officers who use the moment of translation to project their own worldviews onto the "rules," thereby essentially "[defining] the legal norms they are supposed to secure" (Dubois 2018, 39).

As intermediaries between courts and atrocity complainants, the Indian police have the crucial, and socially complex, task of rendering the distinct sociopolitical lifeworld of the village and the culturally cohesive arena of the law (Geertz 1983) mutually intelligible (Bachmann-Medick 2006). They must "classify" and "name" personal and contextually specific experiences of caste violence and convert them into the legally general atrocity offences (comp. Cheng 2017). In the process, the Indian police not only create the abstract legal categories they claim to work within, but determine whose bodies, cultural idioms, and claims will become legally legible and interpretable.

In Choti Lal's case, the discrepancy between the actions of the first police constable and the officers who led the second investigation unveils that the First Information Report is much more than an administrative document that captures information. Khissak Lal Meghwal told me that: "Through the FIR, the police make their own justice. People complain about Indian courts being slow and judges being upper caste. But really cases are decided at the police station by FIRs and FRs. Choti Lal says he wishes he had the right words to make the police understand but they do understand, they just don't want to admit it. Here they are too involved with Rajput politics. So, in atrocity complaints like this they want to keep Dalits silent."

Khissak Lal's statement powerfully highlights the role of local Indian police officers as active decision-makers in atrocity cases, and it mirrors what Kivanç Atak, in his work in Sweden, calls the "resentful reliance" of hate crime survivors on the police: the knowledge that, while police can make hate crime claims legible, their investigations often leave bias and discrimination undetected (Atak 2022). His analysis brings to light the complexities involved in having a field police force which is simultaneously accountable to the legal procedures of a distant state and also deeply embedded in local politics and interdependencies (Hornberger 2013). It also emphasizes the exceptional discretionary spaces of interpretation that police work involves in the context of hate crimes (Bhat, Bajaj, and Kumar 2020).

Globally, hate crime laws entrust the police with the special investigative "burden" of determining whether an offence is motivated by identity-based prejudice or whether it is a regular criminal offence (Boyd, Berk, and Hamner 1996, 831). As previously mentioned, the Atrocities Act instructs police to presume that any offence committed by higher castes against Dalits and Adivasis is caste-motivated if the perpetrators are aware of the victim's identity. However, unless there was obvious, public evidence of caste prejudice, police officers in Rajasthan were reluctant to "make a case" about caste.

Choti Lal was disheartened that the police officers in the second investigation had dismissed his complaint because the Rajputs neither used the phrase "social boycott" openly nor issued specific prohibitions about resources or public passage. "People don't tell you they are boycotting you, they aren't stupid," he told me. His dilemma resonates with the experiences of hate crime survivors beyond India. In 2017 a white man, who belonged to a Facebook group dedicated to Nazi ideology, stabbed a black man at the University of Maryland. However, the Maryland police hesitated to investigate the incident as a hate crime due to the absence of explicit racist statements by the perpetrator. In a frustrated tone, a reporting journalist had pointed out the futility of this argument: "many criminals are not going to be dumb enough to blurt out their exact motives in the course of committing a crime" (Lopez 2017), he concluded. Despite differences in Indian and North American policing structures, Choti Lal's words identify a parallel reluctance to classify offences as hate crimes. In 2018, scholar and activist Anand Teltumbde expressed similar frustrations almost verbatim. When adjudicating atrocity cases, he argued, police and judges seem to expect "that the perpetrator of an atrocity will shout aloud whilst in the midst of raping or murdering a Dalit that he is doing so because of the latter's caste!" (Teltumbde 2018a, 16).

These transcontinental similarities bring the role of the police in "translating" crimes into hate crimes into sharp focus. Choti Lal's experience of desperately fighting for a case under the Atrocities Act reveals that at Rajasthan's police stations requests for the "right words" can become a veneer for the arbitrary exercise of police authority, which is rooted in police officers' own prejudice. Toeing the line between community resources, criminal investigators, and guardians of state order, police officers navigate complex intimacies (Hornberger 2013) and political pressures (Caldeira 2002), alongside their own moral outlooks (Fassin 2013). Against the backdrop of these competing demands, police engagements with marginalized communities can themselves (re-)create local realities of discrimination (comp. Garriot 2013).

However, in India the issue of translation in atrocity cases is exacerbated by the lack of a vertical accountability structure within the police. India's police hierarchy is marked by a systematic disconnect between the high-level police bureaucracy and the regular field police force, which is considered the "face" of the police (Jauregui 2016).

In her ethnography of urban policing in North India, Beatrice Jauregui describes the four "lateral levels of recruitment" in the organizational hierarchy of the Indian police (Jauregui 2016, 21), which goes back to the colonial period. The highest level of recruitment (Class 1) is the Indian Police Service (IPS), whose officers are recruited on the basis of a competitive examination and are trained by the Central Government. Applicants tend to come from wealthier families, who could afford to send them to elite English-medium schools. Members of the Provincial Police Service (PPS) represent the second-highest level in the police hierarchy (Class 2); they are recruited and trained by state governments. Deputy Superintendents of Police (DSP), who are supposed to oversee investigations in atrocity complaints, are PPS officers. Levels 3 and 4 of the police hierarchy, which respectively comprise the ranks of inspector and constable, make up India's main field police force. They operate local police stations (*thāna*s) and have the most contact with local communities. These officers typically hail from lower-class or lower middle-class backgrounds and are educated in regional Indian language schools. Constables make up approximately 90% of India's total police force. Most only get promoted to the level of senior constable, and many never even reach the rank of Assistant Subinspector (Jauregui 2016, 21).

This means that there is little movement across the different ranks, and officers in the upper echelons of the police hierarchy usually have little knowledge about, and interest in, the everyday negotiations that take place at *thāna*s. In November 2016 a former Deputy Commissioner of Police—a Class 1 IPS police officer—in Jaipur told me that he had rarely ever set foot in a local *thāna*.[5] "But," he declared with absolute conviction, "our constables and inspectors follow the rules exactly. If they say a case is not about caste, there is no evidence for it and the accusation of caste atrocity is false. So, the guys at the station must file a Final Report (FR) (*jātibādi ki evidence nahīn hai to FR lagāni paḍati hai*)."

When I told Raveen about this conversation, he was furious: "This guy sits in his air-conditioned office far away from the *thāna* and is acting like proof (*sabūta*) of casteism is just flying around in the air. Casteism only becomes visible if you understand how people speak and what that means. Police must use knowledge of how casteism is shown in villages to make it something law can see. But most ignore what guys like Choti Lal, who are Meghwal and look poor, try to say. Then there is no atrocity case and that messes with victims' heads (*piḍiton ko pāgal banāta hai*)."

Raveen's words emphasize that police refusals to engage with local cultural idioms and practices allow them to "unsee" casteism and file FRs. This causes survivors like Choti Lal to doubt their own perceptions and abilities.

IDIOMATIC VIOLENCE: BODIES, WORDS, AND COLONIAL MASCULINITIES

Raveen's words also indicate another treacherous aspect of the translation process, in the context of atrocity complaints: when survivors speak through bodies and words that visibly betray their marginality, police tend to dismiss them as unreliable narrators.

In his exploration of colonial racism, Frantz Fanon argued that, globally, being black means inhabiting a historically "overdetermined" social space defined by the myth that blacks are "savages, brutes, illiterates" (Fanon 2008 [1967], 117). Similarly, Choti Lal learned that, at the police station, the prejudice he faced as a Dalit was compounded by his bodily and verbal presentation of poverty.

Fanon believed that in colonial Algeria the black body was a total social fact equated with certain physical attributes and intellectual potentialities. The immediate social signaling performed by black bodies was heightened by the difference in culturally and educationally determined speech patterns between blacks and whites, as the former were rarely fluent in standardized French, the supposed verbal manifestation of civilized lifestyles. The resulting feelings of inadequacy and marginalization that haunted black people in the former colonies and have arguably been perpetuated in modern nation states (Fanon 2008 [1967]) have often done even more damage than the initial acts of marginalization. They have convinced some black people of their inherent inferiority.

The parallel between caste oppression and structural racism is always a historically and phenomenologically imperfect one. However, institutional moments of legal aid-seeking throw certain colonial and experiential similarities between structural racism and caste discrimination into sharp focus (Wilkerson 2020). Choti Lal's case exposes that the historical depth of Dalit marginalization in all areas of social and economic life in India is also reflected by the Dalit body, not through color but through performance. As Choti Lal desperately tried to get his case registered, he learned that his bodily and verbal habitus of long-standing marginalization (Gorringe and Rafanell 2007) allowed police officers to ignore caste violence and reproduce casteist structures.

Aside from his position as an illiterate agricultural laborer without political connections or financial capital—the everyday socioeconomic hurdles members of marginalized groups face in legal contexts—Choti Lal's verbal register worked against him. When he went to the police station to file a complaint against the Rajputs—a step that required real courage—Choti Lal recounted his story to the best of his abilities in the local Mewari dialect, in which he had learned to think and filter his experience. While Choti Lal understood standard Hindi, he barely spoke it. In his conversations with me he often relied on Raveen, Khissak Lal, or his daughter-in-law Kavita.

The police officer who had initially filed his complaint had been sympathetic to Choti Lal's linguistic background. He was happy for Choti Lal to tell his story in Mewari. However, he said that his supervisor insisted that police officers themselves conducted interviews in Hindi or English because dialects would make them seem common. He would therefore ask questions in Hindi. Choti Lal appreciated the officer's transparency and sensitivity. He told me, "when I told the first officer about the defecation ban, he asked where my field was and then he understood that we were being boycotted."

Unfortunately, the second set of police officers that arrived in the village, after the original FIR had been discarded, were not so understanding. "Can't you speak Hindi?," one of them had apparently barked at Choti Lal. "I told them that I am sorry but that I am illiterate (*unpaḍh*)," Choti Lal recalled during my visit. Then he had quickly gone to fetch Khissak Lal to help translate. He could tell that his admission of illiteracy did not impress the police officers. He could also tell that they were incredulous and slightly disgusted when he told them of the defecation ban. A man who had never traveled beyond Udaipur and had largely avoided interactions with agents of the state, Choti Lal felt intimidated.

Fanon believed that the less masterful a black man's engagement with the French language was, the less likely he was to be perceived as human. For Choti Lal too, his inability to converse fluently in standard Hindi presented an obstacle in his quest for an atrocity case. Not only do the actions of the first and second police officer stand in sharp contrast, but Choti Lal's own demeanor and attitude shifted drastically when confronted with the demand to speak Hindi by two men who appeared stern, authoritative, and dismissive. If the first constable treated his narrative as a serious matter and Choti Lal as a legitimate complainant, the second officers' attitude reminded Choti Lal of his own socially inferior position at the very moment he was taking steps to claim his legal rights.

Their disgust at Choti Lal's mention of the defecation ban invokes historical—and yet still relevant—realities of traditional Dalit labor in manual scavenging. The ideas of pollution and unsanitary lifestyles that continue to be associated with this are used to treat Dalits as secondary citizens (Guru 2011; Saikia & Noklenyangla 2015). Moreover, I had learned during my time in Rajasthan that many police officers also viewed Dalits as a legally (over-)determined and overprotected community. As the original recipients of constitutional affirmative action programs in India (Galanter 1984; Deliege 1999) and targets of subsequent government safeguards, Dalit communities were often portrayed as pets of the state who received unfair legal advantages. "Dalits use this law for their own gain because they have special protection now," a police constable at the police station in Gogunda scoffed, when I asked him what he thought of the Atrocities Act, "I must be skeptical of their stories, casteism is not as widespread as Dalits pretend!"

Hence Choti Lal entered the police station as a man marked by an excess of prior social and legal categorization, which had rendered his body a projection screen for upper-caste resentment and doubt (Rao 2009). Happy to translate dialect into Hindi, metaphor into atrocity, the first constable implicitly asserted that the Atrocities Act was there for men like Choti Lal. Meanwhile, the second set of officers not only refused to engage with local metaphors but used their own verbal aggression to shed doubt on the very idea that someone like Choti Lal could make a legitimate legal claim against the Rajput council. In the second instance, acting the part of a "good complainant" was impossible for Choti Lal.

This impossibility was also rooted in a second aspect of Choti Lal's personhood: his body as a whole. His wife, Suman, told me that when the police officers visited their home, she had felt embarrassment. "They came in their uniforms looking like they walked out of a film, and we were in our working clothes. The officers were looking at my old sari and they asked Choti Lal to straighten his shirt. It made me feel ashamed (*sharma āti hai*)." Suman's shame at her clothing and Choti Lal's frequent use of the phrase "people like us" suggest that both knew that their physical performance told an unacceptable story of poverty, illiteracy, and marginalization, which would evoke police pity at best and disgust at worst.

Bodily experiences shape how we perceive and dwell in the world, and culturally rooted bodily routines play an important role in transmitting social messages (Ram and Houston 2015, 11–12; Jackson 1996). The way we use our bodies can trigger social stigmata by signaling membership in a specific class and racial group (e.g., Wade 2004), or in Choti Lal's context, a certain caste. Choti Lal was a slight man and looked older than his age of fifty. He had the air of someone who preferred to stay in the background. The hard, physical labor which he had performed all his life had caused him a back injury and he walked slightly bent over. He usually wore a loose-fitting shirt whose original white color had faded into grey. Khissak Lal Meghwal, who was more educated, nonetheless truly respected Choti Lal. "He is a hard worker, he never drinks, he got his daughter married into a good family. He never invested much in the education of his children, but he now realizes that was a mistake. He lives a small life, but he is a good man."

According to Khissak Lal, Choti Lal had filed the FIR because he honestly believed the facts were indisputable. He wanted his children to see that a better future was possible. Still, Khissak Lal remained unsurprised by the outcome of Choti Lal's efforts: "Choti Lal was always going to have trouble with the police. He doesn't know how to seem like a strong man," he said, "police only listen if you are strong."

Choti Lal's assertion that "people like [him]" usually do not "get" cases hints at the complicated web of disadvantage that has been woven around his family by an absence of education, a poor man's habitus, and a lack of overall socioeconomic capital (Bourdieu 1986). Language, taken as the complex whole of his verbal register and his bodily performance, became the ultimate signaler of this web, betraying Choti Lal when he most required its help. Speech exposed his educational disadvantage vis-à-vis the law, a cultural apparatus that is itself built on the categorizing power of language. Meanwhile, his clothing, posture, and laboring body all signaled his social vulnerability to the police, revealing that he inhabited the lower levels of the socioeconomic hierarchy. As gatekeepers of the Atrocities Act, the police thus dismissed Choti Lal's claims, only willing to engage seriously with those capable of producing the "right" words and the "right" body.

However, Khissak Lal's insistence that Choti Lal didn't know "how to seem like a strong man" also hinted as something else: Choti Lal failed to project the right type of masculine authority to the police. In police settings, gendered performances often signify status hierarchies or relations of power (Hinchy 2020, 1674). Choti Lal's habitus indicated weak manhood.

Khissak Lal thought that Choti Lal often "behaved like a woman": soft-spoken and "always asking for permission." His effeminate performance cast Choti Lal as a man that could not be respected in the eyes of a police force, whose professional identity is deeply tied to the use of force and violent performances of male dominance (Lokaneeta 2020). In many postcolonial nations, the exercise of power has historically been linked to performances of violent, male European authority (Salem and Larkins 2021, 87; also Parmar, Earle, and Phillips 2022; Parmar, Earle, and Phillips 2023). Similarly, Indian policing practices (re-)produce scripts that posit a particular type of masculinity, which is expressed through loud assertion and aggression, a precondition for police recognition (Sinha 1995). Choti Lal was quiet and careful, partially because of his caste status, partially because he had been through so much, and partially because he was simply a quiet man. He could not reproduce the appropriate masculine script and struggled to make the police listen.

When the police officers dismissed Choti Lal as a man whose language and body were not that of a credible legal complainant, they were ultimately punishing him for his own marginalization and his unfamiliarity with the milieu (Bourdieu 1977, 653) of law, from which he had historically been excluded. His speech and body were produced by exclusion, and in turn, they excluded him further.

HERMENEUTICS OF SILENCE

The Final Report that was filed in Choti Lal's case after the second FIR was registered in his absence presents a confusing picture. The police summary incoherently moves from the housing issue, to narrating broader intercaste disputes over water, to discussing the issue of the local temple of Ramdev Pir, a site the Meghwals had claimed to be banned from, before finally concluding there was no social boycott against the Meghwals. According to Raveen, messy police reports, which failed to paint a clear situational picture, were a hallmark of those atrocity complaints, which suffered from the interference of influential (Rajput) politicians in Udaipur district.

Human rights advocates at the CDR often argued that police officers at rural *thānā*s lacked "social and political education and could be bought with bribes" (Nairoth, pers. comm., May 2017). This claim finds resonance in other parts of North India. Lower-level police officers in Rajasthan's neighboring state of Uttar Pradesh often face pressure by superiors or upper-caste political actors to neglect certain complaints (Jauregui 2016), especially those of Dalit families (Faleiro 2021). In this way, established relations of caste power reinfuse police investigations with historical forms of bias, even when individual officers may be inclined to take complaints of caste discrimination seriously.

While some anthropologists have argued that corruption and bribery are fundamental to the bureaucratic and political structure of the Indian state (Gupta 2012), these practices can also further compound configurations of structural violence like casteism by teaching police officers that some types of cases should be habitually deprioritized. However, Choti Lal's story points to something even more sinister: invisible moments of police corruption can engender feedback loops of institutional weariness, self-doubt, and humiliation that convince communities who suffer discrimination that their ill-treatment is caused by their own inability to act the "right" way. This further reproduces their vulnerabilities (Fassin 2013).

In Choti Lal's case, police officers tried to hide the corrupt involvement of an influential, local Rajput politician in his complaint by claiming two things: They argued that, according to their records, the Rajputs had never openly restricted Meghwal access to resources. They also claimed that Choti Lal himself had never used the phrase "social boycott" to describe what happened to him. While Choti Lal acknowledges that the police officers' insistence on specific words represent a problematic unwillingness to contextualize the information he provided, he nonetheless internalized his failure to "get a case."

His wife, Suman, told me that Choti Lal's feeling of self-blame was exacerbated by the fact that for personal and social reasons he had found it hard to speak explicitly about the discrimination the Rajputs had inflicted on him. He was not alone in this. Many Meghwal atrocity survivors I met in Rajasthan's villages either avoided providing specifics of the brutality that they had experienced at the hands of upper castes or used metaphorical descriptions. I was usually told the most painful and humiliating details of caste atrocities after long periods of intimate acquaintance or friendship with survivors. In some cases I was never told details at all. According to Suman, Choti Lal had found it difficult to recount to the police exactly how the Rajputs had insulted him when he failed to comply with their instructions about the balcony, because the experience had been humiliating.

Reflecting on his assessment, one begins to understand that Choti Lal did not just lack knowledge of the right legal registers. He had additional personal and cultural reasons to evade the usage of those elusive "right words." As Pinky's story in the last chapter revealed, the very process of naming violence presents a challenge for survivors (Das 2003, 293). This challenge is heightened for those who not only face a long history of marginalization but have also endured recent, painful attacks on their livelihood that has shaken their sense of self-worth. Fear of humiliation made some of the most gruesome details of Choti Lal's experience unspeakable (comp. Ireland 1993).

Writers from Dalit backgrounds have marked moments of humiliation as an essential aspect of the untouchable experience. Ironically, the very language of rights that has provided Dalit communities with the tools to "overcome" historical circumstances marked by "fear" and resignation has simultaneously created additional "conditions for the production of humiliation" (Guru 2009, 5). A political and legal system which relies on the public articulation of traumatic incidents, or rights and atrocity talk, ultimately adds new dimensions of shame to these already hurtful experiences. If in earlier times untouchability was generally a familiar, personal burden for Dalits, human rights and state legal remedies now require them to explicitly share the ill-treatment they suffer with the wider world if they want justice.

Choti Lal's reluctance to repeat explicit casteist language used by the Rajputs may strike an outsider as ironic—how can someone expect to fight a successful criminal case without divulging all details of the crime in question? However, his actions betray an intelligent social sensitivity. Attempting to strike a balance between accurate description and the preservation of his sense of dignity vis-à-vis the police and his social reputation among non-Meghwals in the village, Choti Lal revealed as much to the police as he deemed essential. Meanwhile, he held back those particulars he thought damaging to his own sense of honor. "They called me a stupid animal, which is not allowed anymore, I know that," he told me on our last evening together, "but I didn't recount *every* insult the Rajputs directed at me to the police. It doesn't make me feel good and I fear it could make me look weak if other villagers hear!"

Walking the line between expression and protection, between mobilizing the law and not broadcasting his own social vulnerability, Choti Lal told the police as much as he thought he could afford. When he voiced a suspicion that he lacks the "right words," he was, thus, alluding to the fact that his agenda for social survival also partially silences him and prevents him from describing actions that can be classified as legal atrocities.

Paradoxically, the fact that the Rajput council also avoided the unambiguous verbalization of their discriminatory intentions worked to their legal advantage. Members of the Rajput council employed metaphorical expression to mask strategic power play. By announcing a defecation ban, they relied on the power of culturally embedded hermeneutic signaling to relay a powerful social message, while maintaining a safe distance from overt, verbal, and therefore legally legible acts of caste-based discrimination.

Choti Lal's problem partially arises from the fact that police translations bow to social and political hierarchies. The police are unwilling to translate the social meaning of the defecation idiom into sections of the Atrocities Act that can be listed in an FIR. This translational refusal obscures the blatant manner in which the strings pulled by the local Rajput politician shaped police engagement and reveals that the police are themselves embedded in complex "geograph[ies] of exchange" (Jauregui 2016) that determine whose stories are translated into the language of law with care and diligence. Choti Lal's story is simply declared as lacking in evidence, a verdict facilitated by the fact that it is not delivered with embodied authority. Yet the notion that he lacks "right words" is a normative judgment produced by the same political and legal universe Choti Lal is excluded from due to the intersectionality of lower class and lower-caste status that marks his existence.

A MUNDANE TALE OF "CONVERSION"?

Initially, I had gone to Udaipur to learn about Choti Lal's case because Raveen insisted that I would not be able to understand the landscape of caste violence in Rajasthan without learning about his story. At the end of my visit, I realized that Raveen's claim was valid, though perhaps not for the reasons he thought.

On the one hand, coming to Libasha highlighted the historical and political diversity of Rajasthan state more than any other journey I took during my fieldwork. The patterns of landownership in Udaipur district, and the impressive political influence of the Rajput clans, revealed a much deeper continuity with pre-independence patterns of property division and caste hierarchy than in Jhunjhunu district.

On the other hand, what was most striking about Choti Lal's "case that could not be" was that it was so utterly *typical* of the contestations that arise around the Atrocities Act everywhere in Rajasthan, and even across much of India. Activists from Delhi, Uttar Pradesh, and even the South Indian state of Tamil Nadu noted to me how representative Choti Lal's complaint trajectory was of the challenges facing atrocity survivors (interview, Ramesh Nathan, Coordinator of the National Dalit Movement for Justice, September 2017). Many scholars have argued that police corruption has created a situation of procedural legal paralysis for atrocity complainants (Nawsagaray 2018). As someone who got to know Choti Lal's circumstances intimately, I found it deeply troubling to learn how mundane his experience had been.

Choti Lal's futile hunt for a case shows that atrocity complaints declared unfounded or even "false" by the police are usually the result of complex processes of legal misrecognition that rely on discretionary translational spaces at the stage of FIR registration. These translational spaces obscure corrupt political processes and institutional biases. To show how translational refusals by the police shape legal accesses and recognition in caste atrocity cases is to acknowledge the unseen channels through which political power and deeply ingrained class and caste structures still operate in Indian law.

What is most striking about Choti Lal's experience is how easily the police officers in charge maintained an outward image of procedural correctness, while bowing to blatant political interference. To recognize how the police can obscure their own corrupt practices, while instilling in Choti Lal a sense of self-loathing for his failure to "get" an atrocity case, demands a deeper understanding of the ways caste hierarchies have shaped the bodily and verbal performances of marginalized communities. Choti Lal's habitus of social marginalization, which is also characterized by a lack of violent masculinity, betrays his lack of social power and flies in the face of what police consider the right legal aesthetics (Cabot 2013).

This brings to light how heavily hate crime laws like the Atrocities Act rely on the linguistic and cultural sensitivity and the translational goodwill of police officers, who must render experiences of discrimination legible to a legal system that is itself rooted in (colonial) histories of power (Sinha 1995).

I position his story here, at the start of this second, and central, part of the book, because of the unfortunate normalcy it represents despite all its nuance. Cases like Choti Lal's are what human rights organizations document all the time (Singh 2020). Scholars regularly recount stories of Dalit pain being batted away at the police station as officers try to convert the Atrocities Act (Berg 2020) into a legal tool which serves their own schema of social order (comp. Cicourel 1968; Zedner 2004).

Stories like Choti Lal's make it evident that Indian courts are not the (main) place where atrocity cases are made or unmade. They are shaped long before, at the institutional shores of local police work. However, in the current literature on the Atrocities Act, this is where the scholarly debate tends to end. Cases like Choti Lal's are cited as evidence that the Atrocities Act is toothless at best (Baxi 2014) and counterproductive at worst (Rao 2009).

However, the following chapters reveal that Choti Lal's story neither marks the ethnographic nor the analytical end point of the social life of the Atrocities Act. Instead, his typical case illustrates the starting point of legal engagement for many Dalit atrocity survivors, activists, and lawyers in Rajasthan. Choti Lal's situation was what most of my interlocutors expected to encounter in atrocity proceedings. Choti Lal's situation was also what they all agreed had to be strategically overcome.

FOUR

(RE-)WRITING LAW'S ALLEGIANCE?
Rumors, Deep Truths, and Strategic Disobedience

A CONTROVERSIAL JUDGMENT

On Tuesday, March 20, 2018, mere weeks after I had returned to London, the Indian Supreme Court passed a judgment that enraged everyone I knew in Rajasthan. A two-judge bench consisting of justices A. K. Goel and U. U. Lalit issued new guidelines to prevent what they deemed the "rampant misuse" of the Prevention of Atrocities Act (Times Press News 2019). In their verdict, which was passed in an appeal of *Dr. Subhash Kashinath Mahajan v. the State of Maharashtra*, the judges proclaimed that 15–16% of complaints filed under the Atrocities Act were fraudulent and that current complaint procedures provided no protection for higher castes, who were "falsely implicated" in caste atrocities. The bench concluded that the act made "itself readily available in the hands of . . . scheming complainants" who had ulterior motives (*Dr. Subhash Kashinath Mahajan v. the State of Maharashtra*, 2018).

Consequently, the Supreme Court curbed important provisions of the Atrocities Act. It introduced anticipatory bail into atrocity proceedings, which, under section 438(1) of India's Code of Criminal Procedure (CrPC), allows accused parties to seek bail in expectation of an arrest. The bench also declared that preliminary investigations would now have to be conducted before official complaints under the Atrocities Act could be filed with the police (Bajoria 2018). These amendments were a direct response to the appeal that formed the basis of the judgment. The previous year, the Mumbai High Court had denied anticipatory bail to the Technical Education Director in the Government of Maharashtra, Subhash Kashinath Mahajan, after the latter had been accused of casteism by an employee. Mahajan appealed the decision in the Supreme Court, which then suspended proceedings against him and decided to amend the Atrocities Act. In response to the judgment, protests broke out across India, resulting in the closure of public transport systems, schools, and shops. Many protesters were injured, and some died in police cross fire. Afraid to lose the support of Dalit and Adivasi voters, India's parliament passed the 2018 SC/ST Prevention of Atrocities Amendment Act on August 9, 2018, which largely restored the act to its former shape. However, the 2018 amendment added a new section (18A) that explicitly stipulated that a preliminary inquiry is not required to file a FIR under the Atrocities Act and stated that anticipatory bail *cannot* be sought in atrocity cases.[1]

In the days after the March judgment my WhatsApp kept buzzing constantly. The activists and lawyers I had worked with in Jaipur were deeply enraged by the Supreme Court's interpretations of the current legal landscape. Rohan, a Meghwal activist from Rajasthan's Bhilwara district, was most furious about the fact that the Supreme Court's conclusion was based on police statistics published by India's National Crimes Record Bureau (NCRB). "Always with these 'false cases,'" he ranted during a phone call, "If police say a complaint is 'false,' that doesn't mean that it is a lie. Police categorize complaints as false for many reasons." His sentiment was shared by Sonali, who also insisted that "false" atrocity cases were rare. However, she also pointed out something else: "Sometimes," she told me, "the truth courts want, isn't the *special* (*khāsa*) truth that defines Dalit lives. Casteism has a deep truth (*gehari*), sometimes law does not get that!"[2] Intriguingly, even higher-caste legal professionals were skeptical of the judgment. Advocate Sharma, a lawyer at the Jaipur High Court who belonged to the high-ranking Brahmin caste, found the judgment's simplistic use of the terms "true" and "false" dangerous. He thought it obscured the complexity of legal argumentation and was concerned that the Supreme Court was using emotionally loaded phrases like "scheming complainant."

This outrage was representative of the anger scholars were expressing across the country. In a scathing piece in India's journal *Economic and Political Weekly*, renowned academic and anticaste activist Anand Teltumbde went so far as to title the Supreme Court judgment itself a "Judicial Atrocity" (Teltumbde 2018a). Teltumbde called the persistent rhetoric of false cases a bogeyman: an illusion produced by shoddy police investigations. And he accused the court of emboldening perpetrators of caste violence.

My interlocutors' discomfort with the judgment's simplistic language of truth and falsity indicates that the Atrocities Act, as India's only hate crime law, has engendered new juridical and public controversies around truth. Anthropologists have extensively analyzed the difficulty individuals and communities face in converting lived realities of inequality and injustice into the abstracted and technical categories of official law (Merry 1990; Riles 2005; Latour 2010). However, the discourse around "false" atrocity cases in India reveals something more: it shows that the regime of truth (Foucault 1980), according to which Indian criminal law generally operates—the types of discourses, techniques, and bodies that make claims and narratives function as "true" within legal institutions (Lorenzini 2015)—is often incapable of grasping and recognizing true experiences of discrimination. Sonali pointed out that the "deep" truth of casteism is often overlooked by courts. Her words resonate with sociolegal scholarship, which has highlighted that racism and hate are cumulative experiences that unfold gradually over time (Bowling 1993) and are recounted through marginalized bodies that have historically held little credibility in legal settings (comp. Affolter 2021). Hence, these experiences are difficult to condense into the "flat" truth of law (Latour 2010), which takes a decontextualized (Cheng 2017) and largely ahistorical (Chowdhury 2017) snapshot of social interactions. By pouring narratives of discrimination into individualized legal cases (Bhat 2020b), law tries to establish their truth through institutionally sanctioned techniques and documents (Suresh 2023).

However, in Rajasthan, many Dalit communities were unable to access the relevant institutions and procure the documents that act as carriers of truth in courtrooms. Even when they did, juridical categories and technicalities of evidence often proved incapable of capturing the "deep" truth of caste discrimination that drives Dalit engagement with the Atrocities Act. This incompatibility regularly left Dalit claims unsubstantiated, giving rise to judicial and public discourses which portrayed Dalits as unreliable narrators. Anthropologists have shown that formal law can emerge as a site for the production and circulation of rumors—a form of "unauthenticated news . . . whose source can often not be determined" (Eckert 2012, 153). As rumors are passed on by listeners, they are brought in line with the "hopes, fears and worldview[s]" of the people who retell them (Scott 1990, 145). Their continuous circulation gives rise to predictions, which gradually constitute perceptions of reality at all institutional levels (Cody 2020, 484). This dynamic is reflected in the 2018 Supreme Court judgment which neglected to critically engage with two crucial questions: *What constitutes a "false" complaint, and who decides if an atrocity complaint is true or false?*

To make its argument about the prevalence of "false" atrocity cases, the Supreme Court verdict drew on statistics published by the National Crimes Record Bureau. The NCRB's annual *Crime in India* report uses police data on the number of atrocity complaints that are dismissed with a Final Report (FR) to calculate what percentage of atrocity cases are fraudulent. However, as Choti Lal's story showed, police categorizations of "false" complaints are not always based on objective or even thorough investigations. By failing to ask what makes an atrocity complaint false in the eyes of the police, and by dismissing Dalits and Adivasis as "scheming complainants," India's apex court portrayed the Atrocities Act as a law defined by a dual lack of credibility: On the one hand, it promoted the notion that as a *class of complainants* (McGuirk 2018), Dalits and Adivasis approach legal institutions with exaggerated tales of oppression. On the other, it entrenched the idea that on a *legislative level*, the Atrocities Act is a dangerous law, which perpetuates untruths (Rao 2009). Through this portrayal the Supreme Court institutionally sanctioned a rumor which upper castes in Rajasthan articulated daily: the story of the habitually lying, spiteful Dalit complainant.

In Rajasthan this rumor had two main consequences. First, as I will show through the story of Birendra—a Meghwal man, who embarked on a desperate odyssey to prove his father's murder—that rumor made it difficult for atrocity survivors to produce evidence for atrocity proceedings. This difficulty was constituted both at the level of legal documentation and at the level of institutional legibility (Fuchs 2020c). In India, paper files remain the main ingredient to a successful criminal case (Suresh 2019a, 3). Files construct authoritative transcripts of reality (Coutin 1995; Berti 2015), which become carriers of juridical truth in courtrooms (Kelly 2006; Latour 2010). Yet the ability to produce a persuasive legal file relies on complainants' access to institutional production points of evidence, such as police stations or hospitals. As Birendra's story will show, in Rajasthan access to these institutions is heavily determined by markers of upward class mobility and is controlled by upper-caste political and economic elites (Berg 2020). These elites shape public discourses on "moral deservingness" (Gottlieb, Filc, and Davidovitch 2012) in a way that negatively impacts the perceived credibility of Dalits as narrators of authentic legal claims.

Second, the popular discourse of "false" atrocity complaints also engendered new modes of legal disobedience in Rajasthan. Atrocity survivors, who had legal support networks or significant social and economic capital, took the realization that juridical truth regimes were stacked against them as a starting point for a multifaceted agenda of creative legal engagement. These survivors held on to a vision of the Atrocities Act as a law that was inherently accountable to the truth of Dalit oppression and emphasized its substantive goals defined by the "content of particular rules" (Suresh 2023, 10). Therefore, they used their atrocity cases as a platform to reimagine the procedural aspects of the Atrocities Act—how its substantive goals should be administered or achieved (Suresh 2023)—and strategically work towards a new legal truth regime that could capture what Sonali had called the "deep" truth of discrimination.

This chapter illustrates this second set of dynamics by discussing two cases. First, I narrate the story of Krishna Kumar Meghwal, a respected upwardly mobile advocate. His experience shows that Dalits with socioeconomic capital can sometimes find effective ways to make their stories of caste discrimination legible at police stations. However, his case also illustrates that, even then, upper-class markers of Meghwal economic mobility are often discredited and delegitimized in favor of dominant caste loyalties. In Krishna Kumar's case, this resulted in a moment of visceral anger and disillusionment, which upper-caste villagers later held against him.

Then the chapter follows Rahil, who filed an atrocity complaint that was declared "false" by most people in his village. However, upon closer inspection Rahil's complaint only appears false when viewed through a decontextualized, temporal framework of the immediate present (Özkan 2019). It reveals its truth against the backdrop of a deeper temporal horizon. It is this deeper truth, which defines experiences of discrimination, that Rahil wants the Atrocities Act to honor even if he knows that his case would never win in court. Like many Meghwals in Rajasthan, Rahil and his supporters felt that upper-caste economic power, and the ahistorical perspective of criminal law, had made the Atrocities Act complicit in caste violence. Therefore, they concluded that, if they wanted the act to be accountable to Meghwal realities of oppression, they had to subvert the temporalities of legal truth regimes.

Atrocity complaints like Krishna Kumar's and Rahil's represent an active challenge to an entire criminal legal edifice, which plays by the rules of communities who continue to practice violence with impunity (Chatterjee 2017). In Rajasthan, a state that has only seen scattered Dalit resistance movements, the strategic moments of disobedience Meghwals engaged in were a radical attempt to dismantle the feudal caste hierarchies that still held hate crime law hostage and prevented it from highlighting Dalit truths. These practices mirror what Kalpana Kannabiran has termed "insurgent constitutionalism" at the level of hate crime law. Kannabiran proposes that popular engagement with the Indian constitution is sometimes less about pursuing justice and more about demanding that injustice should end (Kannabiran 2012). The Indian constitution is above all an imaginary which positions the right to nondiscrimination so centrally that marginalized groups sometimes disobey laws which they consider at odds with constitutional values (Samaddar 2020). Similarly, Rahil's and Krishna Kumar's actions signify a moment of (strategic) disobedience, meant to hold the Atrocities Act accountable to its spirit of anti-oppression. It is an attempt to move Dalit bodies into legal spaces to dislodge the old caste allegiances of criminal law.[3]

A QUEST FOR EVIDENCE

In March 2017, I visited the village of Puranapura in Rajasthan's Jhunjhunu district with Randeep Meghwal, Avinesh's brother-in-law. Randeep, a well-connected young professional with a lower-level management job in one of the district's nationally owned copper mines, had a flexible work schedule and had taken interest in my work. Randeep's family was financially secure, educated, and had bought some tracts of agricultural land around their native village in Jhunjhunu, which they leased to a family of Meghwal farmers. His father supported the Communist Party of India and was actively involved in the Jhunjhunu Ambedkar Society. Randeep saw it as his mission to follow in his father's footsteps and to contribute to the upliftment of Jhunjhunu's Meghwal community. Like Avinesh's brother Rajesh, who came with me to Pinky's house, Randeep became a regular companion when I investigated atrocity cases in the district. He saw me as a younger sister and was fiercely protective of my safety.

In the spring of 2017, Randeep heard about a gruesome accusation of caste violence in Puranapura village, where one of his cousins lived. Economically and socially Puranapura was dominated by members of the Jat caste. Jats constituted the single largest caste group (approximately 600 individuals) in Puranapura and controlled almost 70% of fertile agricultural land. Puranapura also claimed a significant Dalit population of around 300 individuals, over half of which were Meghwals. Many Meghwals worked as agricultural laborers and had become increasingly dependent on Jat landowners, who controlled access to agricultural employment.

As in other parts of Jhunjhunu, Jat dominance in Puranapura had its origin in the peasant revolts against Rajput rule and against the system of *jāgīrdari* land tenure (see the introduction). The post-independence land reforms almost exclusively reallocated agricultural plots previously under Rajput control to the Jat peasants, who had formerly leased and "tilled" Rajput lands. This effectively established a new Jat agricultural regime in the region. Meghwals in Jhunjhunu, who benefited little from the land reforms, often worked on Jat lands and were left profoundly exposed to these new, and often exploitative, agricultural dependencies.

The power hierarchies engendered by this unequal agricultural landscape were deeply felt by the man I met in March 2017: Birendra Meghwal, son of the recently deceased Lakha Ram Meghwal. One morning in February 2016, Birendra got a phone call from a neighbor who told him that his father was lying dead on the field of his Jat employer L. Katheria. The news came in the aftermath of a contentious wage dispute between L. Katheria and Lakha Ram. Birendra and his brother rushed to the field, where they found their father's body. His face was swollen and bruised and covered in dried blood. Lakha Ram's trousers were on backwards. Birendra immediately phoned the police station. The officer on duty told him that someone would arrive as soon as possible. However, "as soon as possible" turned out to be twelve hours later. When three police officers finally arrived on site, they did not do much. They walked around the body once and told Birendra that they would take it along for investigation. Then Birendra heard nothing for ten days.

A Meghwal friend of Birendra's named Vivek worked for a Jat family whose house was next to Katheria's field. Vivek had heard screaming in the middle of the night Lakha Ram died. He had overheard Katheria verbally abuse someone, followed by strange cries. The next day when the news of Lakha Ram's death crept though the village, Vivek began to wonder if there was a connection. L. Katheria was nowhere to be found.

Armed with this knowledge, Birendra and his mother Rani Devi asked representatives of the CDR to help them file a First Information Report under the Atrocities Act. CDR lawyers told Birendra which sections of the Indian Penal Code should be applied in his father's case: IPC sections 120, 320, and 302, which would accuse L. Katheria of conspiracy, grievous hurt, and murder. They also told Birendra that the complaint should be filed under sections 3(1)(s) and 3(2)(v) of the Atrocities Act. The first section refers to verbal abuse by caste name in public view. The second enhances punishment for some of the aforementioned IPC offences when they are committed against a member of the Scheduled Castes and Scheduled Tribes. However, at the station, the police officer of the Rajput caste, who was supposed to fill out the FIR, seemed skeptical. He told Birendra that he was sorry for his loss but that accusing L. Katheria of murder was excessive. The officer was even more reluctant to register the complaint under the Atrocities Act. He told Birendra that, if anything criminal had happened to his father, it was because of a wage dispute, and had nothing to do with caste. After enlisting the help of two Jhunjhunu-based activists, Birendra finally managed to get his FIR registered a few days later. But the Rajput police officer was angry: "There is your FIR, you have managed to make everything about caste," he barked at Birendra.

The police told Birendra that Lakha Ram's body would be examined at the local hospital as part of the official investigation. However, two weeks later, Birendra was informed that the police investigation had shown his father's death to be of natural causes. Consequently, Lakha Ram's case was not forwarded to the courts and was closed with a Final Report (FR), which effectively declared it a "false case." With the help of the CDR, Birendra gained access to the police file. It contained a medical report from the local hospital, which stated that natural heart failure was the culprit behind Lakha Ram's sudden passing (fig. 8).

Birendra was sure that L. Katheria had something to do with his father's death, especially because of the ongoing conflict over wages. After seeing his father's bruised and bloody body, he also knew that the medical report was a lie. But he couldn't prove any of it. Vivek, who overheard the screaming in the fields, refused to testify at the police station. "Are you crazy?," he told Birendra, "Katheria has so much influence and money. I say something and my family finds *my* body in the fields!"

These days it is an open secret in Puranapura that L. Katheria paid the police to drop the investigation into Lakha Ram's case. However, Birendra believes that money wasn't even necessary. "Katheria's brother-in-law was a Member of the Legislative Assembly and is very rich and powerful. Police won't mess with that family."

Birendra has a veritable mountain of documents relating to his father's death. Copies of the FIR, photos of his father's body he took himself, the dubious medical report, newspaper clippings, a call for action circulated by a group of local activists regarding Lakha Ram's mysterious death. "Basically," Birendra laughs bitterly, "I have tons of evidence that I have no evidence! People say that Dalits don't know the law, but I know a lot. The problem is that the evidence judges want is the kind of proof a man like me can never get. Because proof (*sabūta*) is something only available to the right people (*sahī loga*)!"

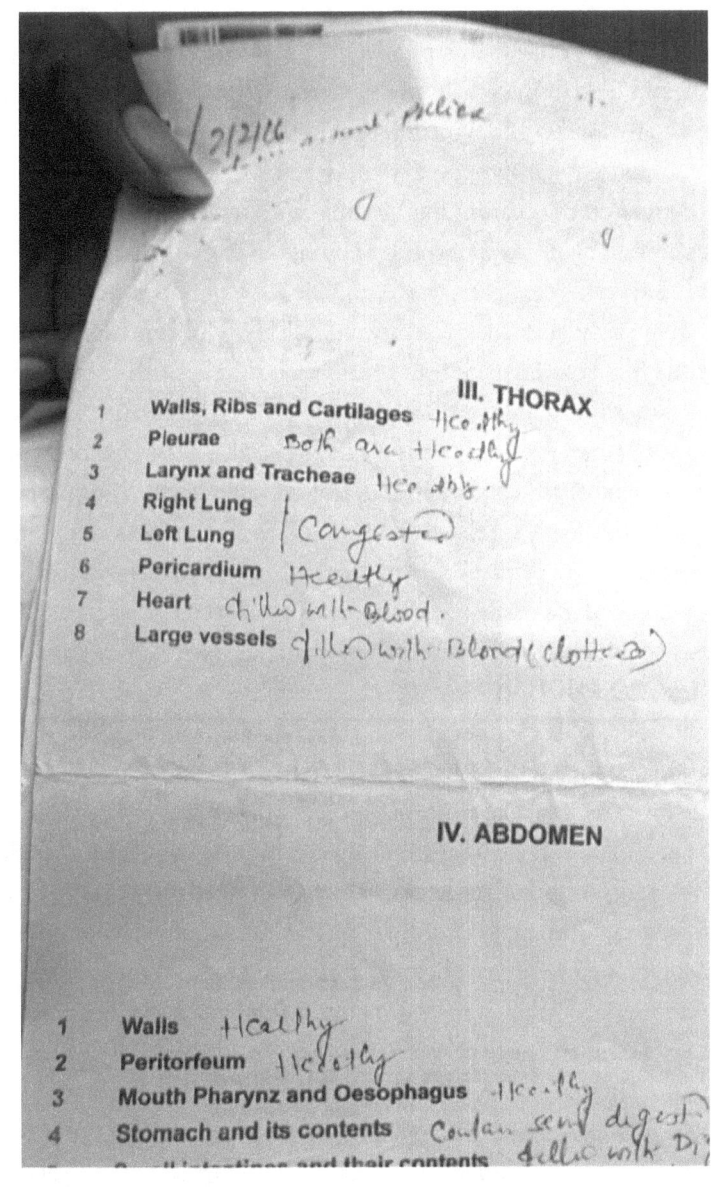

FIGURE 8. The medical report Birendra received upon his father's death: it states that Lakha Ram's heart was "filled with blood."

Lakha Ram's case is now one of the many "false cases" cited by the Indian Supreme Court. Yet Birendra's story highlights how survivors of caste atrocities in Rajasthan struggle to transform experiential realities of violence and discrimination into a legal transcript of a truth that will be recognized in courts: a convincing legal file.

Bruno Latour has proposed that, when assessing evidence in legal cases, "judges do not reason" but "grapple with a file that acts upon them" (Latour 2010, 192). He explains that to produce verdicts, legal professionals need to "harvest" files when they are "ripe" (Latour 2010, 82). This ripeness is defined by both the quantity and quality of information contained within the file. As Mayur Suresh's study of Indian terrorism trials shows, physical paper files remain the primary form of evidence in criminal proceedings in India. The "right" papers in the "right" technical order act as primary, official truth carriers in Indian criminal courts (Suresh 2019). A "ripe," thick file, with a First Information Report that lists claims which are corroborated by medical reports, autopsies, and witness statements as well as records of material and sometimes digital artefacts, are what judges regard as convincing evidence. A High Court Judge in Jaipur stressed the visual importance of a thick paper file during an interview. He told me: "As a general rule, if the file is thick, there is good evidence."

Unfortunately, as Birendra himself remarked, his father's file would never be given a chance to ripen because he himself was the "wrong" kind of person. This wrongness is primarily constituted by a lack of political influence and economic resources, which translated into a lack of legal credibility and, ultimately, a failure to secure institutional recognition. The documentary regime that validates stories as true in atrocity cases thus relies on the cooperation of institutions that function according to existing systems of dominant caste power (Teltumbde 2008; 2018a).

Furthermore, what Birendra was witnessing firsthand, and what Choti Lal too experienced (see previous chapter), was the *active destruction of potential evidence* by the accused parties. Katheria's family not only bribed the police officers to neglect and close the investigation but, as I later found out from a contact at the Jhunjhunu hospital, had also paid some money to the doctor in charge of postmortem medical reports. Cut off at the institutional production bases of "evidence," Birendra could never produce a ripe file that could be used to make technical legal arguments to speak truth to his father's story. As the wrong kind of person, all he could prove was that he had no proof. Meanwhile, Katheria was the "right" type of person.

Birendra's and Katheria's stories reflect what Dag Erik Berg has called the strategic "conversion" of anticaste legislation from policies aimed to destabilize higher-caste social and political control into laws which affirm it (2020). Yet this conversion relies not only on upper-caste political power but also on the way Indian legal actors have been conditioned to conflate class, caste, power, and the corresponding legal aesthetics (Cabot 2013) with ideas about complainants' credibility. Birendra's statement that people think Dalits don't know anything about the law indicates how Indian legal institutions engage with Dalit complainants as uninformed narrators, whose claims about discrimination are rooted in both ignorance and a desire for special treatment. When I asked the Rajput police officer in Jhunjhunu who had filed Birendra's complaint about the case, he responded skeptically: "He is illiterate and doesn't know how to behave, how much does he understand about this case? Dalits just say that everything in law is about caste. It isn't."

Like Choti Lal, Birendra had the appearance and demeanor of an illiterate, rural man. Along with his lack of political power and financial resources, the ever-present rumor that Dalits tried to make law about caste made it easy for the police to dismiss Birendra's legal claims.

Birendra's story highlights a central dynamic that feeds the rumors of "false" atrocity cases in India: the same social hierarchies and economic inequalities that give rise to hate crimes and motivate the introduction of hate crime legislation also hinder the ability of survivors to make their experiences legible within, and credible to, India's criminal truth regime. As one Jaipur High Court judge, also of India's highest-ranking Brahmin castes, stressed to me in August 2017: "*PoA atrocity complaints can only win in court by adhering to proper evidential procedure, using real evidence* like credible autopsy reports and credible witness statements" (emphasis mine).

Unfortunately, as Birendra and Choti Lal show us, *real* evidence is frequently unattainable for complainants in atrocity cases. The Supreme Court's dismissive, binary language of truth and falsity therefore displays not only ignorance towards the real dynamics that shape the production

FIGURE 9. Birendra's pile of unsorted documents and copies of the case report, obtained with help from the Centre for Dalit Rights, spread out on the floor.

of evidence for hate crimes but further fuels the rumors that negatively impact atrocity survivors like Birendra.

A *SARAPANCA* GOES TO COURT: BATTLES OF CASTE AND CLASS

Birendra's and Choti Lal's experiences of legal futility and failure are extremely typical in Rajasthan. They echo the existing literature on the Atrocities Act, which has highlighted the way atrocity complaints are undermined by the caste hierarchies the law is meant to change (Baxi 2014). However, as the next two examples show, many Meghwal survivors in Rajasthan were not willing to accept this state of affairs and actively fought to regain ownership of the act.

The next complainants I met showed that in some instances Dalits with extensive sociopolitical capital could successfully mobilize the Atrocities Act and make their stories of caste violence resonate as "true" in Indian courtrooms. However, their experience also showed that even then the credibility and moral deservingness (Gottlieb, Filc, and Davidovitch 2012) of Dalit atrocity complaints is often challenged. Markers of education and wealth can make well-connected, upwardly mobile Dalit families more institutionally palatable criminal complainants. However, their caste status as Dalits still produces ambiguous currents of legal truth production, as witnesses, police, and even local judges struggle to decide whether to obey traditional higher-caste allegiances or if new forms of Dalit political capital should outweigh these loyalties.

In April 2017, I was staying with Avinesh's in-laws and Randeep in their hometown called Copper. Copper is located in Jhunjhunu's southeastern subdistrict of Khetri and was built as a resident enclave for the employees of the local copper mine, which was run by a mining company called Hindustan Copper Limited (HCL). One day Randeep offered to take me to see Krishna Kumar Meghwal in nearby Jagta village, whom he described as "the Meghwal, who knows how to win a case!"

Jagta village was only twenty minutes away from Copper and one of the largest villages in Jhunjhunu district. Over the past fifty years some Meghwals in Jagta had achieved a level of prosperity through HCL's recruitment of local villagers in the 1970s and 1980s. However, economically Jagta still remains dominated by the Gujar community, a farming caste, which, like the Jats, acquired significant agricultural wealth in the aftermath of the post-independence land reforms in the 1950s and 1960s.

In 2016 Jagta was declared a reserved constituency. This meant that in the local village council elections the position of village head (*sarapanca*) had been reserved for a member of the Scheduled Castes (SC), or Dalit. This time the seat had specifically been allocated to a Dalit woman. The village elected Shrimati Radha Devi, the wife of Krishna Kumar Meghwal, a lawyer and the son of a police officer, who owned twelve hectares of land. Though Radha was now officially the *sarapanca*, Jagta's Meghwals all told me that effectively Krishna Kumar ran the village. This was not unusual. As Pinky's experience highlighted, patriarchal structures in Rajasthan are alive and well. This meant that even though local government seats had been reserved for women to increase their participation in village polities, it was usually their husbands (jokingly referred to as SP—*Sarapanca Pati*—Sapranch's Husband—in local circles)[4] who pulled the strings.

However, soon after the election Radha was attacked. She had walked home from the fields, when she was held back by Radhika, the local *ånganvādī* (kindergarten) worker and wife of Jagta resident Motu Lal Gujar. Radhika reportedly grabbed Radha's arm, pushed her against the wall of a building, and accused her of bribery. "You Chamar who grew up in the gutter (*nāli me baḍi hui tu Chamar*)," she screamed at Radha, "I will teach you how to be a *sarapanca* (*tujhe sarapancai karana sikhāungi*)." Radha returned home with bruises all over her back. Her husband, Krishna Kumar, immediately decided to file a complaint in her name under the Atrocities Act. At the police station he was seen promptly. Many of the officers remembered his father, one of the first Meghwals in the area to hold an inspector post in the nearby town. The complaint was registered under sections 354 (assault of a woman) and 504 (insult and breach of peace) of the Indian Penal Code. It was also filed under sections 3(1)(r) and 3(1)(s) of the Atrocities Act, which refer to intentional insult and humiliation, as well as public verbal abuse by caste name. The police carried out their investigation within a week, writing up a detailed report including witness statements that supported Radha's claims.

Krishna Kumar told me about his case while we were sitting in his impressive courtyard along with Randeep and a small group of local Meghwal and Gujar men. That day he was proud. Seated comfortably on a plastic-covered couch that had been brought outside for the occasion, Krishna Kumar, a tall, impeccably shaven man, felt assured of his victory. "My family has so much status (*ijata*). I know everything about the law (*kānūna ko khūba jānata hū mai*). My father had many police contacts, and my wife is the *sarapanca*. Didn't Radhika miscalculate?" I nodded, noting that Radha, his wife, in whose name the complaint had been registered, was quietly making tea in the background. Like Pinky, she seemed to be at the center of a legal battle she had little control over.

Yet, despite the model police investigation, the case quickly grew more complex. Motu Lal enlisted the help of an influential Gujar relative, who got the police to reopen the investigation into Radha's initial insult complaint under the Atrocities Act and produced his own witnesses who denied Radha's claim. Krishna Kumar doubled his efforts and ultimately convinced the local police to write another report which validated Radha's narrative. The details of this process were never revealed to me but in the end the police finally filed a charge sheet in Radha's complaint in the special atrocity court, so that court hearings could begin.

In May 2018, two years after the incident, the case was ultimately decided in Radha's favor and Radhika was sentenced to a fine of 1 lakh (100,000) Rupees. However, even though the Atrocities Act specifies that an attack on a Dalit woman should be punished with a minimum of six months in jail, no such sentence was issued. To this date Radha's is the only atrocity victory in court I have ever witnessed. Considering that some sources estimate Rajasthan's conviction rate under the Atrocities Act to be as low as 7% (Bairwa 2018), Radha's court victory is striking. Still, Krishna Kumar was saddened and dissatisfied: "Yes, we won but it should have been easier," he had told me: "Some Gujars, whom I considered friends, tried to help Motu Lal. Then the police started saying Radha was lying. I heard an officer say that Meghwals want attention. I guess caste still counts more than everything I have achieved."

Radha's story highlights how ingrained, horizontal caste loyalties and new forms of Dalit political capital can pull local and institutional support for atrocity cases in different directions and create competing currents of legal recognition and credibility. Krishna Kumar problematically forced a division of two kinds of influence: Professional accomplishment linked to class mobility versus historical legitimacy based in higher-caste status. Supporting Krishna Kumar's cause made pragmatic sense for many Gujars, but it came at a price in the eyes of others: the potential degradation of the Gujar community on the relative social hierarchy in favor of the traditionally "inferior" Meghwals.

Consequently, Radha's case had an afterlife. After Radhika's conviction, Motu Lal's son-in-law filed a counter-allegation at the police station accusing Krishna Kumar of raping his wife. The police dismissed the complaint, which was clearly fabricated since Krishna Kumar had been in Jaipur the day of the alleged assault. The police dismissal angered Motu Lal's family further. Some days later Motu Lal's son-in-law followed Krishna Kumar to his home and screamed at him, calling him a liar and a crook. In that moment Krishna Kumar snapped: he slapped Motu Lal's son-in-law. The next day Motu Lal's family filed a complaint of grievous hurt against Krishna Kumar. While the police dismissed this complaint as well, the entire village began gossiping about Krishna Kumar. Some villagers said that his actions made them doubt the truth of Radha's complaint. Krishna Kumar was haunted by his actions. When discussing the case, he told me: "I did slap Motu Lal Gujar's son-in-law and I know I shouldn't have, but I don't regret it. They tried to weaken my case and kept trying to turn the village against us even after the case was decided. But with the Atrocities Act the state (*sarakāra*) has given me a weapon to change caste-dynamics! I will not let it be weakened and I will not let them take this victory away. So, I slapped him in the service of truth (*meri piṭāii me saccāii hai*)!"

Krishna Kumar's and Radha's story showcases two aspects of legal truth production in atrocity cases, which have largely gone unrecognized by courts and which feed the public narrative of "false" cases: First, their case shows how caste and class do battle over the control of the investigative machinery that produces truth-carrying artefacts and documents for court. Second, their experience reveals that what the Supreme Court called the politics of "vengeance" is not an inherent or intentional part of the complaints Dalit survivors file under the Atrocities Act. Instead, microscopic acts of revenge can be the result of attempts by dominant castes to neutralize or convert (Berg 2020) the Atrocities Act and "take away" the rare legal victories Dalits achieve.

Krishna Kumar considered the Atrocities Act a special law, which was meant to protect Meghwals. When police officers, who were caught in a cross fire of legal claims and caste loyalty, hesitated to translate his wife's legitimate narratives of caste discrimination into documentary evidence, and Motu Lal tried to dilute his legitimate legal victory, a frustrated Krishna Kumar got caught up in his anger and in new micro-illegalities. These micro-illegalities then reinvigorated rumors that Radha's complaint might have been "false."

As the final story in this chapter shows, these rumors are further cemented by a third issue: legal categories and temporalities of truth are not equipped to grasp "deep" truths of discrimination.

WHEN TRUTH SPLITS: A "FALSE" CASE CAPTURES A VILLAGE

Deep Truth

In late October 2017 my own fieldwork village of Badrasar witnessed an uproar when four young men, two Meghwals and two Muslims, were unceremoniously arrested in a clash with Badrasar's wealthiest Jat landowner, Jataram. The boys were kept in unofficial custody. This meant that they were simply held by the police and not brought before a magistrate within twenty-four hours of the arrest as is required under section 56 of the Code of Criminal Procedure (CrPC). However, three weeks later all four boys were mysteriously released by the police and Jataram was strangely reluctant to discuss the matter.

According to the whispers I heard from Badrasar's Jat community, the situation was clear: Rahil Meghwal, the main accused, had registered a "false" atrocity case against Jataram to buy his freedom. However, Meghwals in Badrasar disagreed: Rahil had filed an atrocity case against Jataram, but the case had not been false at all. To gain some clarity, Sonali, whose family I lived with in Badrasar, suggested that we pay a visit to Bantu Meghwal, the lawyer who had advised Rahil in the dispute.

We learned that on the day of the arrest, Rahil and three of his friends had gone to one of the large wheat fields at the edge of Badrasar with some bottles of whiskey. The field belonged to Jataram Jat. The young men became intoxicated and began to disturb a family of the Kumbhar caste (traditionally potters) that had been employed by Jataram and lived in a house at the edge of the field. The tenants phoned Jataram who promptly made his way over on his motorbike. Jataram personally knew Rahil's father, whom he had aided in obtaining a work visa for Qatar seven years earlier. And so he targeted Rahil first. He shouted at him to get off his land and screamed Rahil was behaving like a "fallen man (*girā huā ādamī*)," disgracing his family. Rahil had long been resentful of the condescending way Jataram treated his father. He had also been angered by the fact that Jataram had a history of hurling casteist insults at his Meghwal agricultural laborers. Rahil also felt that the phrase "fallen man" alluded to ideas of untouchability and impurity. And so, drunk as he was, Rahil picked up a stone and threw it at Jataram, leaving him injured. Jataram's tenants promptly brought him to the hospital. After he was discharged, Jataram called the police. Within hours Rahil and the others were arrested and subsequently kept in custody at the police station. The police refused to provide further information to the boys' families, or to move forward with an official arrest or an investigation in the following weeks.

The situation soon proved detrimental for the boys' families, who relied on them for personal protection and income while their fathers worked abroad. Jataram, who harbored political ambitions, was well connected. Thus, the Meghwals in Badrasar village became worried. "Rahil and the others could have spent their entire lives in jail without interrogation," Sonali's neighbor, Bitu Aunty, told us, "something had to be done." Therefore, Rahil's lawyer, Bantu Meghwal, told him that if he wanted to walk free, he should file a complaint under the Atrocities Act and accuse Jataram of casteist insult. Jataram would be worried about his ability to secure Dalit votes in his upcoming run for a seat in Rajasthan's legislative assembly since he was competing with other Jat candidates, who were more popular with the resident Dalit voter bank. The plan worked. Bantu Meghwal got the local police to file a First Information Report (FIR) against Jataram. The officers initially refused to file the complaint, claiming that insult was a milder (noncognizable) offence, and that therefore they would not be able to register and investigate the matter without approval from the magistrate. But Bantu Meghwal, who had studied law in Jaipur, had extensive experience with atrocity complaints. He knew that all offences under the act were serious, cognizable offences. He also pointed out to the police that under chapter 2, section 4 of the Atrocities Act, public servants who displayed neglectful conduct in filing atrocity complaints could be punished with up to one year in jail.

Then the police finally registered Rahil's FIR. As in Radha's case, they applied sections 3(1)(r) and 3(1)(s) of chapter 2 of the Atrocities Act (intentional casteist insult with public humiliation). When Jataram got wind of this, he agreed to have the boys released if they apologized and withdrew their complaint. The boys agreed, and Rahil's complaint was dismissed as "falsely lodged" with a Final Report (FR).

So, was Rahil's complaint false, like Badrasar's Jats claimed? At first sight it might seem so. But upon closer investigation a different picture emerges, as Rahil's case brings to light the problem of "deep truth" in atrocity complaints.

Badrasar's Meghwal community was of two minds about Rahil's case. They thought Rahil drinking and hitting Jataram had been a criminal act. They also admitted that on the night in question Jataram had not used any *obvious* casteist insults when interacting with the boys. The term *"girā huā ādamī"* is not a phrase that exclusively invokes untouchability but is often used by locals to reprimand drunkards. However, Badrasar's Meghwals also felt that, in the context of Jataram's history of open hate speech towards Meghwals, the phrase had been casteist. They also thought that the extreme way Jataram yelled at Rahil was a symptom of oppressive caste hierarchies.

Sonali and I spoke to many Meghwals in the village who were convinced that two social dynamics were crucial to Rahil's claims. First they drew attention to the unequal sociopolitical relationship between Jataram and Rahil. In Badrasar, Jats make up around 50% of the village population and own approximately 60% of village plots. Jats have controlled the village *pancāyata* (council) for the past decade. Meanwhile, the Dalit community, which mainly identifies as Meghwal and makes up a quarter of the village population, only controls around 7% of agricultural land. Most depend financially on employment by Jats. Badrasar's Meghwals argued that this inequality in economic and political influence caused the boys to be held indefinitely at the police station after Rahil hit Jataram, while Jataram himself had always escaped consequences for his treatment of Meghwals. They proposed that this unequal playing field had to be considered when judging Rahil's complaint.

Second, Badrasar's Meghwals insisted that if one viewed Rahil's complaint against the backdrop of this historical horizon of local caste interactions, it was not fraudulent. Bitu Aunty summarized this idea succinctly: "If you just look at that evening, you can say Rahil's complaint is false, the words Jataram screamed were not clearly casteist. But Rahil is actually telling the truth. Jataram insults Meghwals all the time, calling them dirty animals, every week and nothing happens to him."

Sonali's mother further contextualized Rahil's actions: "You can debate whether *girā huā ādamī* is untouchability (*chhuāchūt*). But Jataram yelling at Rahil as extremely as he did, is casteism in itself (*jātibādi*). He would not have cursed out a young Jat boy who was drinking like he did Rahil."

These reflections highlight that a central issue when legally proving the validity of atrocity complaints is the cumulative and historically "deep," contextual, and additive nature of caste violence. Rahil's case splits the idea of truth into a present-focused, decontextualized form of juridical validity and a processual experiential type of veracity. Rahil's allegation is "false" only if one adopts a literal, socially abstracted reading of events, which operates according to a "presentist" (Özkan 2019, 319) temporal scale: if one sees only the "facts of the moment" and ignores a longer local history of caste interactions. However, if one widens the temporal scope, and contextualizes Rahil's claims within a history of prior interactions between Meghwals and Jataram, as well as within the Jat community itself, Rahil's complaint is true.

Reversing Legal Truth Regimes: Strategic Disobedience

Rahil's complaint reveals its truth value when horizontal-social as well as vertical-historical context is considered, because it operates according to the experiential truth logic of discrimination, which is processual, cumulative (Bowling 1993), and deeply contextual. Vertically, Rahil's truth emerges against the backdrop of a deeper past (Chowdhury 2017), which is characterized by harsh social, economic, and legal caste inequality. Horizontally, it shows itself in the context of a careful analysis of verbal exchanges between different castes in Badrasar. However, juridical truth is defined by a moment-focused case format, which relies for proof on a set of standardized, internally coherent procedures and files that abstract from context and history (Cheng 2017; Suresh 2023). Thus his claims appear legally false.

This insight in itself resonates with established anthropological analyses, which argue that the abstract categories of official law are often incapable of capturing nuanced social realities (Riles 2011). However, what is remarkable about Rahil's story is that his atrocity complaint helps him overcome local, casteist power structures, even if it is declared legally "false" and would have never succeeded in court.

Rahil's lawyer Bantu Meghwal thought of Rahil's actions as an act of strategic legal disobedience, which aimed to turn the Atrocities Act into a law that could actually help Dalits. He explained: "The Atrocities Act promises to fight for the truth of Dalits (*hamāri saccāii*). Police and courts are controlled by upper castes but this law is meant to change that and show that Dalits are still oppressed and insulted. We used the Atrocities Act to change caste power by making the complaint record the whole reality, not just that evening. We would not have won in court but, as you see, we still got this act to help us."

While these words could easily be disregarded as the justifications of a shrewd lawyer, Sonali's brother, Vikas, had a similar view. "When Meghwals are hurt every day by upper-caste violence and try to use the Atrocities Act, we are not believed. Jataram goes around and insults Dalits and the police don't want to hear it, but the moment one of us does something wrong, here come the police and Meghwal families fall into poverty. Two things happened here: Rahil made a mistake and hit Jataram. But Bantu and Rahil also took legal power back after being insulted by Jats for years. We used the Atrocities Act to make Jataram pay for his casteism. Isn't that what the act is meant to do?"

These words show that Rahil's and Bantu's attempt to unveil the "deep" truth of caste discrimination is also an effort to reverse a legal truth regime which contradicts the *substantive* aims of the Atrocities Act as a hate crime law. Vikas argues that legal actors refuse to see Dalits as credible complainants. Normalized casteist attitudes and violence do not strike higher castes' members as illegal or immoral even though they are, because the higher castes populate the police and judiciary. Hence, Bantu and Rahil mobilized the Atrocities Act to write a counter-transcript of truth, one that is accountable to marginalized Dalit realities.

Many Meghwals viewed Rahil's case as an attempt to dislodge traditional caste power from legal institutions and to make the Atrocities Act potent. By holding Jataram to account for his casteist habits through an atrocity complaint that was socially threatening but impotent in a courtroom, they succeed at chipping away at the field of power that has historically made criminal law the playing field of powerful upper castes.

Their actions can be seen as a type of insurgency against the structural inequities baked into the temporalities and social allegiances of India's criminal truth regime. Rahil's case shows that Dalits still disproportionately suffer at the hands of the police, while upper castes' offences are ignored. His case is meant to highlight that the way state institutions treat Dalit narratives goes against the spirit of the Atrocities Act, and that the regime of truth, within which the hate crime laws like the Atrocities Act are asked to function, fails to see the processual truth of lived discrimination.

INSTITUTIONAL PRODUCTIONS OF AN (IN-)CREDIBLE LAW

Bad Data

When I discussed Rahil's case with Geeta at the CDR in Jaipur, she was frustrated. On the one hand, she passionately argued that by "playing with the law according to their own rules," and disregarding how this could affect public perceptions of the Atrocities Act, people like Rahil were weakening the law (*kānūna ko kamazor banatein hai*). On the other hand, she also admitted that for Rahil or Birendra, playing by "the official rules of evidence and procedure" was almost impossible, because police and hospital personnel as well as lawyers and judges dismissed their stories as exaggerated and often took bribes from their attackers.

Geeta's reflections perfectly capture the vicious cycle of rumors which shape the assumptions and interpretive practices of legal actors in atrocity complaints. An interview I conducted with a notable police official of the Rajput caste at the Jaipur Police Commissionerate further highlighted the contradictions Geeta identified. The officer openly told me that he ignored most complaints Dalits filed under the Atrocities Act because they were attempts to get "special treatment." "Unless there is actually a massacre, the only thing that will make us [the police] pay attention to an atrocity complaint is media pressure."

His attitude was no outlier. Over the course of my fieldwork, police officers, court clerks, and judges repeatedly called the Atrocities Act a "dangerous, draconian law" riddled with "false complaints." These findings resonate with a 2015 study published by the Indian Ministry of Justice, which showed that many police officers thought of the Atrocities Act as a personal revenge tool for Dalits and Adivasis, while judges were hesitant to convict those accused under the act (Mangubhai and Singh 2014).

Ironically, the willingness of police to doubt Dalit statements, or to historically contextualize Dalit narratives, leads many officers to neglect thorough investigative practice. Therefore, most atrocity complaints are dismissed with a Final Report (FR) under section 173 of the Code of Criminal Procedure (CrPC). The CrPC specifies that Final Reports should be filed in three different instances: First, when there is a lack of evidence to prosecute the offences listed in the FIR; second, if the police conclude that no offence was committed; and third, if a complaint was "falsely" lodged." Yet, as Birendra's experience, at the start of this chapter, shows, the power dynamics that shape investigations in atrocity complaints make it all too easy for police to dismiss complaints for any of these reasons. In Rajasthan, police officers even habitually used the term "False Report" when referring to Final Reports (FRs) in atrocity cases.

FRs are an essential ingredient in the circulation of rumors that paint Dalits as vengeful abusers of the law. FR data recorded by police stations across India are passed on to India's National Crime Record Bureau, which then annually calculates what percentage of criminal complaints are legitimate or "true." These numbers are then published in the bureau's official *Crime in India* report. The fact that police officers in Rajasthan usually dismiss atrocity complaints with a Final Report thus directly impacts official crime statistics, which shape public, judicial, and political discourses around the Atrocities Act.

As the 2018 dictum by the Indian Supreme Court indicated, the discourse of false atrocity cases, which upper-caste politicians perpetuate during election campaigns and on social media platforms (Carswell and de Neve 2015), has filtered up from village police stations and district-level courts into the highest echelons of India's judiciary. The 2018 judgment in *Dr. Subhash Kashinath Mahajan v. the State of Maharashtra* relied on NCRB statistics when arguing that the Atrocities Act had become a vehicle for fraud (NCRB 2016). In the judgment, which builds on previous verdicts by High Courts in various Indian states, the judges drew on NCRB data to flatly map technical legal truth onto social reality by arguing that Dalits and Adivasis are "unscrupulous" and "concoct" allegations that are "nothing but false" in search of "personal vengeance." This allegedly results in "evil consequences" and "the misuse of law." These phrases convey imminent danger to justice and warn that the Atrocities Act is a "pawn" in the hands of Dalits and Adivasis.

While the court's concern for the protection of innocent parties may be rooted in good legal practice, the language of the verdict hardly conveys judicial neutrality. The Supreme Court presents atrocity complaints through the emotive lens of revenge and fraudulence as well as the moral language of good and evil. This reinforces popular assumptions about the (in-)credibility of Dalit and Adivasis as legal complainants.

In legal practice credibility is often defined as the "consistency of the witness's evidence with what is agreed or clearly shown by other evidence" (Glenn 2016, 2). Yet the Supreme Court judgment relies on police statistics that ignore how "other evidence" in legal files is shaped by the same structural inequality that forces Dalit and Adivasi engagement with hate crime law.

Intent, Motive, and Presumption

In Rajasthan, this issue was exacerbated by the fact that judges often had differing opinions about the way courts should evaluate a person's motivation to harm someone based on their caste: a question many judges referred to as *"casteist intent."* A Brahmin High Court judge in Jaipur once told me, "I must abide by the principle of *mens rea*, of criminal intent. If it's not clear that the intent to steal someone's land or even rape a woman is explicitly based on their identity as a Dalit, I will not apply the Atrocities Act. Then a landgrab is just a landgrab."

The judge's words indicate a problematic conflation of two principles of criminal law: intent (*mens rea*)—the targeted resolve to commit a crime—and motive—the reason behind the intention. The question of motive has long haunted hate crime legislation globally (Brax 2016). Critics of hate crime law have highlighted that attempts to prosecute bias amount to problematic attempts to read people's minds, which invites judges to imbue cases with their own worldviews (Candeub 1994, 2123).

Yet, in Rajasthan, judicial magistrates and sessions judges were often unaware that there was a technical distinction between intent and motive. Many used *mens rea* as a blanket term to dismiss Dalit complaints when faced with a lack of documents or statements that proved *conscious* caste bias by accused parties. In some ways, this is understandable, as intention is not clearly defined under the Indian Penal Code (Kaur 2020). However, as discussed in chapter 1 here, an amendment to the Atrocities Act, which became effective in 2016, aimed to mitigate this issue by adding a "presumption of offences clause" (sec. 8c, chap. 2). This section states that a court can presume casteist motive if the accused party was acquainted with the Dalit or Adivasi complainant and is aware of their caste membership (Waughray 2022). Still, legal professionals in Rajasthan often passionately rejected the premise of the clause. A court clerk at the special SC/ST court in Jhunjhunu frankly announced his disregard: "If I know that someone is a Dalit, that does not mean I am getting into a conflict with them *because* they are Dalit."

At the Supreme Court level judges have often followed a similar line of reasoning. In November 2020, more than two years after the end of my fieldwork, the Indian Supreme Court issued another judgment in *Hitesh Verma v. State of Uttarakhand & Anr.*, which challenged the presumption clause in cases of caste insult. The bench headed by Justice L. Nageswara Rao declared: "An offence under the SC/ST [Prevention of Atrocities] Act is not established merely on the fact that the informant is a member of Scheduled Caste unless there is an *intention to humiliate* a member of Scheduled Caste or Scheduled Tribe for the reason that the victim belongs to such caste" (Legal Correspondent 2020, emphasis mine). Taken together, the 2018 and the 2020 Supreme Court judgments on the Atrocities Act reveal a deep judicial skepticism towards the discrimination Dalit and Adivasi communities experience, the narratives they tell, and the truths they claim.

THE WAY FORWARD?

So, what really constitutes a "false" atrocity complaint? Rahil, Krishna Kumar, and Birendra's stories reveal that, despite its popularity in Indian public and judicial discourse, there is no uniform phenomenon of the "false case."

The phrase obscures the contested political, social, and financial pathways that lead Dalit narratives to be declared unsubstantiated by a police force, whose data act as a gatekeeper for all judicial arguments around caste atrocities. Moreover, it hides how the ability of Dalits to be recognized as legitimate complainants by the police hinges almost entirely on a type of credibility which associates political influence, demeanors of upward mobility, and financial capital with traditional higher-caste status. Thus, it hides fundamental differences between complaints like Birendra's that fail because of a lack of institutional access and cases like Rahil's, which involve strategic disobedience.

Ultimately, this highlights how juridical truth regimes, which rely on horizontal webs of institutionally sanctioned, interlinking evidence blocks (Latour 2010, Suresh 2019a, Suresh 2019b), must be critically reflected in the context of hate crime legislation. Anthropologists have argued that the self-referential nature of formal law neglects to describe a reality outside its own documents (Oorschot & Schinkel 2015) and produces temporal frameworks that fail to engage with deeper, complex pasts of political violence (Fuchs 2022). Yet laws that aim to protect marginalized communities can only do so if legal actors engage critically with the general documentary practices that produce legal evidence and the temporalities that shape judicial interpretations.

The gap between a moment-focused, "flat" legal truth (Latour 2010, 265), produced though technical processes performed by institutional actors who have not been systematically trained to interrogate their own structures of recognition, and the deep, cumulative, historical truth that characterizes discrimination as an experience creates new hiding spaces for the biases hate crime laws are meant to combat. In Rajasthan, the gap between juridical truth and experiential truths of discrimination has generated moments of strategic legal disobedience among Dalit communities. These strategies aim to chip away at the chokehold of higher-caste power and temporal presentism in which the Atrocities Act finds itself. Yet they are ambivalent forces in the fight against caste oppression.

On the one hand, cases like Rahil's create a vicious institutional cycle. Their aim to highlight the "deep" truth of caste discrimination through creative, legal engagements, can further feed the discourse of "false" cases. On the other hand, these strategic moments also represent a form of embodied, legal counterpractice (Larsson 2017; also Csordas 1994). Both Krishna Kumar's physical anger towards those who tried to take legal victory from his wife and Rahil's attempt to pull Jataram's history of casteism into his complaint are attempts to shift the baseline structure of legal power and to rewrite the social allegiance of criminal law. They can be seen as mirroring what Kalpana Kannabiran has termed the "insurgent imperative of the Indian constitution" on the level of hate crime law: to reject policies that contradict the value of nondiscrimination at the heart of India's foundational legal vision (Kannabiran 2012, 10).

The long-term social effects of strategic disobedience in atrocity complaints are difficult to predict. However, the intentionality behind cases like Rahil's is crucial to understanding the way hate crime laws are embraced by the people whom they are meant to protect. The stories in this chapter show that the social life of the Atrocities Act does not end with legal failures like Birendra's or Choti Lal's. Meghwals in Rajasthan don't always simply accept that the Atrocities Act is a law paralyzed by existing structures of caste power, unexamined institutional biases, and regimes of truth that struggle to capture the lived truth of discrimination.

Instead, many actively try to change this reality: They tirelessly fight to find *any* admissible evidence for their claims, they challenge established temporalities of juridical truth, and they physically move Dalit bodies into legal institutions that have historically been the purview of dominant castes.

This insight has global relevance. The battlefield of truth and credibility that defines the social life of the Atrocities Act mirrors issues facing hate crime and antidiscrimination laws across the world. In the United Kingdom, police regularly refuse to classify the complaints of racial and sexual minorities as hate crimes (Walters, Owusu-Bempah, and Wiedlitzka 2018), while in South Africa, court clerks consistently argue that complaints filed under the Promotion of Equality and Prevention of Unfair Discrimination Act, 2000 are not "truly" about discrimination (Kok 2008). This shows that historically oppressed communities often experience further violence at the hands of the legal system at the exact moment they stand up for their rights. If hate crime laws are here to stay, general processes of criminal truth production must be systematically interrogated in the context of these statutes.

FIVE

"YOU MUST NOT COMPROMISE!"
Contested Collectives and Complex Complicities

COMPROMISE OR BETRAYAL?

"You must promise," Mr. H. Nairoth demanded as he gazed sternly down at the elderly man sitting cross-legged on a woven bed (*cārapāii*) in the morning sunlight of a hot July day in 2017, "that you will not compromise, because when you compromise no one will take you seriously anymore." The skinny farmer, who went by the name Roop Singh Jatav, looked up at Mr. Nairoth. After a moment of hesitation, he nodded his head. "I promise (*main vādā karata hoon*), I will not compromise."

Mr. Nairoth was satisfied. "Good," he said, "let's head to the police station to talk to the DSP [Deputy Superintendent of Police] about this matter, maybe even the magistrate." With these words he gathered up his jacket and waved commandingly at the driver, who had been talking on his cell phone in the shade of a tree at the edge of the little housing plot. The other two members of his fact-finding team, an activist and mother of two named Nivedita Meghwal, and a young lawyer from a neighboring village peeled themselves out of their wobbly plastic chairs. Roop Singh too got to his feet and gestured at his wife and daughter-in law, who had been sewing in the shade of the narrow clay house and presumably listening to the conversation from underneath their veils (*ghūnghaṭas*). As the women rose, Mr. Nairoth smiled benevolently at them and strode off to the car. He had made his point; now he could get to work.

Mr. H. Nairoth was a Delhi qualified attorney and heir to the CDR, the Jaipur-based legal aid NGO in Jaipur that I had collaborated with throughout my fieldwork. His father—Mr. Nairoth Sr.—was also a lawyer and the current director of the CDR. A member of the Bairwa *jāti*, a Dalit community that was widespread in eastern and central parts of Rajasthan, Mr. Nairoth Sr. was a well-known figure in Rajasthan's small-scale Dalit movement. In 2004 he had founded his NGO and trained his son and son-in-law to follow in his footsteps. His son, Mr. H. Nairoth, proudly considered himself "an activist first and a lawyer second," and saw it as his personal mission to utilize the power of the law for the benefit of the Dalit movement (*āndolana*). The CDR dedicated many resources to the support of atrocity survivors who, as Mr. Nairoth put it, "bravely seek justice under the Atrocities Act."

Mr. H. Nairoth had inherited two principles from his father. The first was a firm belief in taking a professional approach to the continuing Dalit struggle. "Yes, we must go on marches and write poetry to make the public aware of what we still have to endure. But mainly, we must use good evidence and be professional, otherwise no one will take us seriously." His staunch faith in the "professional" method was only surpassed by his conviction that once treading the formal legal path, atrocity complainants should never settle or compromise out of court. Like his father, who had cochampioned the campaign to include caste oppression as a form of racial discrimination under international human rights law (see introduction), Mr. H. Nairoth was representative of an urban, upwardly mobile group of Dalit professionals who saw evidence-based approaches to human rights concerns around discrimination, as well as the cultivation of an expert legal persona, as the most effective way to pursue caste equality (Fuchs 2015). The widespread practice of "compromises" that dominated the legal landscape around the Atrocities Act and other special criminal laws in India was a thorn in Mr. H. Nairoth's eye: he deemed it a practice that undermined the credibility of Dalit litigants and endangered the reputation of the Atrocities Act. Individual atrocity cases were not individual matters for Mr. H. Nairoth. They were iterations of an ingrained landscape of structural Dalit oppression. Therefore he thought that every atrocity complaint had to be addressed through systematic, professional engagement with the Atrocities Act. If necessary, this engagement would last years, till finally a verdict was given by a judge; and even then he was always ready to appeal.

"If you compromise," Mr. Nairoth Sr. had told me the very first day I showed up at the NGO headquarters in Jaipur, "you are sending two messages to casteist people out there. One, you are saying that they need not worry about consequences of their crimes against Dalits because if they put enough pressure on victims, if they threaten or pay them, then the atrocity complaint will go away. So, they learn that they can keep committing violence without punishment. Secondly," he continued, "you are also teaching judges and the police that Dalit complaints are not believable. If police officers see Dalit witnesses change their testimonies in court because they have compromised, courts get the impression that Dalits are opportunistic and lie. Then, who will take atrocity cases seriously anymore?"

Therefore, the promise Mr. N. Nairoth had elicited from Roop Singh, that morning in July 2017, came as no surprise to any of the regular members of his fact-finding team. Nivedita, who exhibited some skepticism towards the Nairoth school of anticompromise, jokingly pointed out that it was his preferred method of concluding interviews. However, to Mr. Nairoth's dismay, merely two months after our visit, disappointing news reached the NGO headquarters in Jaipur: Roop Singh, like so many others, had broken his promise and compromised anyway. Now his FIR had been dismissed with a Final Report. Mr. H. Nairoth was furious. He condemned the cowardice of many of his caste brethren. Yet he also seemed unsurprised by the news. "This always happens," he declared, slamming a copy of Roop Singh's case folder on his desk, "always!"

Current data support Mr. Nairoth's claim that the incidence of so-called compromises (*rajināma*) is high in complaints filed under the Atrocities Act (Singh 2020). Among advocates and activists this is typically interpreted as a sign that the act has failed to provide true progress for Dalit communities (Nawsagaray 2018). In September 2018, P. S. Krishnan, one of the original authors of the Atrocities Act, drafted a letter to the chief minister of Madhya Pradesh, in which he declared that the police and powerful interest groups use "threat and coercion" to intimidate Dalits into dropping cases and compromising (Krishnan 2018b). Meanwhile, scholars view the frequent occurrence of compromises in atrocity cases as an indicator of corruption in the law enforcement machinery and of bullying by higher-caste interest groups (Teltumbde 2008; Khora 2014; Carswell and de Neve 2015; Thorat 2017). In the wider sociological and criminological literature on India, compromises after mass violence are typically presented as the result of a culture of impunity, which means that perpetrators are rarely "punished by the law of the land" (Mander 2012, 90).

These interpretations, as well as previous chapters, potently highlight how structural violence can make engagement with formal law seem laborious and futile. However, many of these studies have neglected to ask fundamental questions: *What actually is "a compromise"? And are there different kinds of compromises?*

As we already learned through Pinky's story, caste "atrocities," as well as some other serious crimes such as rape, are defined as *noncompoundable offences*. This means that legally these crimes cannot be resolved through mediation or out-of-court settlements. However, as we saw in Pinky's case, compromises happen frequently in both rape and atrocity cases. This is made possible through the "category of hostility" (Baxi 2010, 208), which denotes a process whereby witnesses or complainants later deny the facts that were recorded during the police investigation during a court hearing or trial (Berti and Tarabout 2012). When such denials occur, the witnesses involved are declared "hostile" by the court and the case is dismissed, allowing the adversarial parties to come to an informal agreement. Pratiksha Baxi argues that even though such settlements are not legally permitted, in rape or atrocity cases, courts use the category of hostility to "efface" these compromises from judgments and records (Baxi 2010, 209). In other words, compromises take place but are erased from legal transcripts. Hence, compromises represent a form of public secrecy (Baxi 2014). Judges know that compromises permeate social and political negotiations around noncompoundable offences but are aware that this pattern is difficult to counteract. The solution is to obscure compromises from the court record.

However, in Rajasthan, as in many other states, atrocity compromises don't just materialize at the trial or hearing stage. They are negotiated at various points in the legal process—sometimes even before a FIR is filed—and under drastically different conditions. Alongside the rumors of "false cases" discussed in the previous chapter, conversations around different kinds of compromises represented the other ubiquitous discourse around the Atrocities Act in my field sites. And much like the expression "false case," the term "compromise" ultimately obscures more than it reveals. "Compromise" is an umbrella concept, which groups together varied negotiations that are defined by distinct dynamics of gender, economics, and politics. What they have in common is that they are deeply at odds with normative understandings of a successful legal process, to which legal aid advocates like Mr. Nairoth adhere.

My fieldwork revealed that Mr. Nairoth's aversion to compromises is grounded in sound experience and logic: as in much of India, compromised atrocity complaints in Rajasthan are commonly the result of upper-caste threats, and they negatively impact judicial perceptions of the Atrocities Act. However, Nivedita's skepticism and the controversial turn taken by Pinky's case in Jhunjhunu force the question: Are there other reasons atrocity survivors like Roop Singh compromise? Is the willingness of atrocity survivors to drop complaints or turn hostile in court *only* a reflection of structural powerlessness and fatigue? Or can there sometimes be unspoken benefits to compromises?

This chapter unearths the sentiments around, and understanding of, the "atrocity compromise" in Rajasthan. It shows that analyses, which categorically represent compromises as a denial of justice for victims devoid of agency (Singh 2020), overlook the fact that all compromises are not created equal. Some rare compromises can provide real steps towards empowerment for atrocity survivors.

Despite the largely discouraging landscape of compromises in Rajasthan, there were instances when atrocity complainants strategically tried to craft what they called a "good compromise" (*acchā rajināma*), which aligned with their own social and financial priorities, to create incremental steps towards greater equality in their villages and neighborhoods. Drawing a clear distinction between compromises born from blackmail and compromises led by their own goals, these survivors argued that the latter could give them a sense of justice and hope which formal legal outcomes failed to provide. Roop Singh's story too exemplifies some of the visions and agencies that survivors articulated when considering a legal strategy. These agencies radically challenged Mr. Nairoth's normative idea of legal success.

The chapter advances three arguments. First, it shows that "good" compromises in atrocity cases radically challenge the distinction between formal legal justice and informal forms of dispute resolution. NGO professionals like Mr. Nairoth and Sonali often argued that compromises represented short-term relief, rather than a step towards real structural change, because they gave the Atrocities Act a bad name. They were convinced that compromising meant abandoning the potential transformative power of the act. However, these critiques miss something: rare "good" or "better" compromises do not imply a turn *away* from the Atrocities Act. Rather they are only possible *because* of it.

Professional legal aid advocates like Mr. Nairoth were often blind to the innovative ways in which atrocity survivors used the possibility of out-of-court compromises to jump-start social transformation from below. Many compromises were indeed the clear result of blackmail and only brought temporary relief. But others represented something I call "microagencies": a series of actions, which cumulatively and invisibly chip away at casteist structures. In this way the contours of "good" or "better" atrocity compromises can resemble the "just" settlements that anthropologists have described in Indian rape cases (Oza 2022). As in Pinky's case, rape settlements often defy understandings of justice as a formal, public process of inculpation, which result in incarceration (Oza 2022). Yet they are sometimes actively navigated and cocreated by rape victims, who insist that compromises represent a real sense of restitution. However, "good" compromises in atrocity cases are perhaps unique because they represent an active conversation with the Atrocities Act. In Rajasthan, the "better" atrocity compromises were made possible by the new networks of sociality, which the introduction of the Atrocities Act has opened up for Dalit atrocity survivors. This landscape of good compromises complicates previous ethnographic studies, which have posited that historically marginalized communities often shun state law in favor of informal settlements that allow for the preservation of social harmony and stability (Nader 1990; Shah 2007). "Better" atrocity compromises reveal a *symbiotic* relationship between formal law and alternative routes of dispute resolution as survivors integrate official filing procedures into locally specific methods of navigating oppression and humiliation. Atrocity complainants in Rajasthan, who thought they had compromised well, did not see themselves as turning away from the law. They thought that they had found a different approach to unleashing its power, through settlements negotiated soon after a First Information Report was filed.

The second argument the chapter makes is that the conflict over compromises, which often raged between legal aid advocates, activists, and atrocity complainants, arises from a disagreement about the type of collectivity which should be prioritized when seeking justice through hate crime laws. Activists like Sonali and Mr. Nairoth often argued that the Atrocities Act should be employed in service of a pan-Indian and somewhat abstracted Dalit community. Meanwhile, many survivors wanted to put the act in the service of a lived neighborhood community, which was the only home they knew, or had access to, even in the presence of oppressive structures (Baxi 2010). For people like Roop Singh, "better" compromises were appealing because they allowed them to rebuild a sense of belonging within a multicaste village community on *comparatively improved* terms. In Rajasthan, the true distinction between those who accepted some types of compromises and those who condemned all, was how they prioritized the collectives to which they belonged.

These opposing attitudes bring to light uncomfortable dynamics of complicity and new modes of intracaste violence. Professional NGO-based activists in Rajasthan often saw themselves as legal guides for Dalit victims of caste atrocities, who—in Mr. Nairoth's own words—were "socially and economically weak (*kamazora*)" and needed to be *taught* how to use the Atrocities Act to support the Dalit cause (*kānūnī bātein sikhāni paḍatein hain kamzora Dalito ko tāki ve āndolana ka saath de sake*). However, this paternalistic attitude, which was often heightened by educational and economic discrepancies between activists and survivors, could create new modes of silencing. Professional activists usually arrived at the sites of caste atrocities mere hours or days later to help families register complaints. However, they frequently failed to listen closely to the concerns and desires of the injured individuals and families, who were keenly concerned with their own hurts and futures. Instead, many activists tended to issue advice in the form of instructions, which were primarily concerned with the way a particular legal approach would reflect on the strength of the Dalit resistance movement (*āndolana*). By sidelining survivors' concerns in favor of a normative vision of legal success, activists sometimes unintentionally became complicit in harming the families they wanted to help. Their categorical rejection of compromises exposed families to further anxiety as well as moral pressure to be well-behaved complainants and perfect victims who complied with the demands of heroic activists.

At first sight, these insights seem to invoke an ethnographic literature on complicity, which shows that activist refusals to consider the grey zones of their own engagement can turn their well-meaning efforts into sites of harm that mirror political dynamics of oppression (Wright 2018). However, "good" or "better" compromises actually complicate this picture. In Rajasthan, atrocity survivors tended to strategically ignore activist instructions they didn't find useful. Some like Roop Singh even turned the tables and mobilized the professional performances of NGO advocates for their own use: to achieve a "better" compromise. Professional activists could open up new modes of sociality (Suresh 2023) and new publics (Baxi 1999), which helped survivors obtain small moments of agency and justice.

This leads to my final argument. As Pinky's story has already indicated, the conflict over compromises unearths a deeper definitional battle over legal success in hate crime cases. Activists and survivors agreed that the Atrocities Act was an important resource which could help create better futures for Dalit communities. Therefore, each group aimed to engage with the act in line with its own ideas of justice. However, they differed in their understanding of what a successful outcome of this engagement looked like. For many survivors, the promise of equality inherent in the Atrocities Act lay in its ability to create a sense of agency in the interstices of daily life: While many compromises in Rajasthan did indeed reflect a culture of upper-caste impunity (Mander 2012), the compromises survivors called "good" represented another strategy for social and legal transformation through hate crime law. Compromises could be a way of stamping survivors' visions of successful social change onto legal interactions and negotiations.

"Good" or "better" compromises served survivors by pulling hate crime law *out* of legal institutions that seemed foreign and inaccessible, away from legal actors who mocked them for their habitus and language, and *into* their everyday lives. There the threatening power of law could be used to attack the oppressive intercaste socialities that gave rise to caste violence in the first place.

ROOP SINGH: A SERIES OF COMPROMISES

In February 2017, I met Roop Singh. Roop Singh belonged to the Jatav *jāti*, which was the most populous Dalit community in his village. He had been born and raised in a village named Kotra, near the town of Karauli. Karauli is the capital of an eastern Rajasthani district of the same name. I had been invited on the fact-finding mission for Roop Singh's case by Mr. H. Nairoth and his team of CDR lawyers and activists, which had arranged to meet Roop Singh at a bus stop in Karauli town. When welcoming the team, Roop Singh looked decidedly and quite literally beaten. He was sporting two black eyes, a fresh head wound, and a lost tooth. He had further injuries on his back and stomach. Five days before our visit, Roop Singh and his family had suffered a brutal attack by a powerful local Jat clan, the third in a series of assaults that had begun one and a half years prior.

The initial altercation had occurred as early as October 2015. Five Jats had arrived at Roop Singh's house and slapped his wife after she had talked back to a Jat man called Raja Ram, who had been steadily encroaching on Roop Singh's fields. Roop Singh had phoned Pakka Lal Meghwal, who worked for the CDR. On the phone Pakka Lal had advised Roop Singh how to file a FIR accusing Raja Ram of touching and attacking a Dalit woman against her will under section 3(1)(w)(i) and 3(1)(w)(ii) of the Atrocities Act. However, before the FIR could be lodged, the NGO learned that the head of the village (*sarapanca*), a Brahmin named Rajesh Kumar, had successfully convinced Roop Singh not to file a complaint in exchange for a private apology from Raja Ram. Reportedly, Rajesh Kumar did not want his village to be known as one that was plagued by casteism. Roop Singh accepted the apology and did not file a complaint. He compromised.

However, one year later in 2016, Roop Singh went to his millet (*bājara*) field during the harvest season only to find that his grain had been cut down by Raja Ram's men. He was furious and feared for his family's livelihood. Roop Singh decided to stake a public claim to his land and temporarily abandon his paternal family home in the Jatav neighborhood of his village to build a new house on the contested field. Again, he thought about filing a complaint under the Atrocities Act but was convinced to compromise once again. Another private apology was issued under guidance of the same *sarapanca* and Raja Ram begrudgingly returned the stolen grain to Roop Singh.

The subsequent period of calm did not last long. In February 2017, matters escalated. While working in his field, Roop Singh accidentally damaged the electricity supply, which the surrounding farmers relied on to run their machinery. Raja Ram, who was driving by on his motorcycle, witnessed the mistake. He stopped Roop Singh and started to publicly insult him. "Who do you think you are that you can make decisions like that, you Jatav dog (*Jatav ka kuttā*)," he reportedly screamed at Roop Singh, "I will beat you up."[1] Roop Singh tried to ignore him. However, his calm attitude infuriated Raja Ram further, and he decided to make good on his threat.

Raja Ram, who hailed from a well-connected Jat family that owned sixty *bigha*s (approximatively fifteen hectares) of land, had many friends in the area. And so Raja Ram drove to Roop Singh's house with two other Jat men later that same afternoon. Together they overwhelmed Roop Singh and began beating him viciously. Terrified, Roop Singh darted into the house and locked himself and his daughter-in-law inside. Finally, Roop Singh had the smallest bit of luck: a Rajput man from the neighboring village happened to drive by on his motorbike and Raja Ram and his men fled the scene.

Frightened, Roop Singh and his wife decided to get help from Jaipur once and for all. They called Pakka Lal again. It was at this point that Mr. Nairoth's NGO decided to throw its entire weight behind Roop Singh. Pakka Lal traveled up to Karauli and together he and Roop Singh went to the police *thānā* to file an FIR. In the report they accused Raja Ram of casteist insult, verbal humiliation, and hate speech under sections 3(1)(r) and 3(1)(s) of the Atrocities Act as well as of grievous hurt under section 320 of the Indian Penal Code, which is punishable with seven years of imprisonment. Under section 3(2)(va) of the Atrocities Act, grievous hurt is also punishable with an additional fine. But a friend of Raja Ram's, who worked for the police, informed him of the complaint. Raja Ram was reportedly angrier than ever and Roop Singh feared for his safety, especially because the Rajput man who had witnessed the attack made it clear that he wanted no part of a court case and would not testify against Raja Ram.

Mr. Nairoth and Pakka Lal realized that they had to do more than simply register a complaint. They had to ensure Roop Singh was protected. And so our small fact-finding team headed up to Karauli to "give the police a talking to, and make sure Roop Singh's family was safe," as Mr. Nairoth put it. I learned that their decision to ask me along was also strategic. "Come and bring your camera," Nivedita said to me, "maybe if they see a white woman with a camera, the Jats and the police will think that they will get in some real media trouble."

If Raja Ram's relentless attacks on Roop Singh seemed nonsensical at first, his motivations became clear when we talked to Roop Singh's Jatav neighbors during our visit to Kotra village. It appeared that ten years prior, Roop Singh's brother Prem, a notorious drunk, had taken a loan in the amount of 80,000 Rupees from Raja Ram at an exorbitant interest rate. When he inevitably defaulted on the loan, Raja Ram took Prem's land, which, though limited in size, was near the village water pipeline and very fertile. Prem's piece of land directly bordered on Roop Singh's field, which was larger and even more productive. Raja Ram had then approached Roop Singh about the possibility of selling his field, but Roop Singh had refused. His land, he explained to Raja Ram, was the only financial security he could pass on to his own sons and he would never sell it. Soon after, Raja Ram began to bully him.

One of Roop Singh's main concerns was the fact that his family had not received any police protection. Section 15A(11)(h) of the Atrocities Act (chap. 4A)[2] specifies that the state is duty-bound to protect Dalit atrocity victims, who feel intimidated and harassed, from further violence. Raja

FIGURE 10. Roop Singh's fertile field.

Ram's family had blocked the road between Roop Singh's house in the fields and the family's old village home and had also threatened Roop Singh with further brutality if he continued to pursue the case. However, the local police had thus far ignored Roop Singh's repeated requests for protection.

On the day of our visit Roop Singh was confused and scared: "You say I should fight this case," he pleaded with Mr. Nairoth, "but no one in the village will testify against Raja Ram. And without police protection my family is in danger." Determined to help Roop Singh, Mr. Nairoth packed our whole team into the car and paid a visit to the police collectorate. There he loudly insisted on speaking to the Deputy Superintendent of Police (DSP). After initial reluctance he secured an impromptu meeting and obtained the required police protection. Well versed in legal jargon, he vehemently waved a paper copy of the FIR in front of the DSP's face, who seemed startled by Mr. Nairoth's eloquence and our entire team. But Mr. Nairoth was not done. The next stop was the district magistrate's office, which was in the same compound. Mr. Nairoth presented the facts of the case to the district magistrate and asked him to keep an eye on the police in this matter. To everyone's surprise the magistrate appeared sympathetic to Roop Singh's plight. He gave Mr. Nairoth his cell phone number so he could call if Roop Singh's complaint was neglected. As a final stop, Mr. Nairoth took us to visit a local journalist who was known to report on atrocity matters. He fed him the necessary information and asked him to keep following Roop Singh's case. At the end of the day Mr. Nairoth was proud and Roop Singh impressed. "See," Mr. Nairoth said to Roop Singh as we drove off, "this is how you work the law. No need to compromise now." Roop Singh agreed: "No sir, after all you have done, I will not."

Yet, six months later, Nivedita, the Dalit women's activist who had accompanied us to Karauli, and Mr. Nairoth informed me that Roop Singh had once again compromised. Only this time he had made specific demands: he wanted Raja Ram to issue a *public* apology in the village *chowk* (meeting place) in front of the whole village community, and he demanded 100,000 Rupees in financial compensation and a signed declaration from Raja Ram that he would leave him alone. Only then would he drop his complaint.

Nivedita seemed unsurprised by the compromise. "I don't know where Mr. Nairoth gets his ideas from," she told me in private when I visited her at home a few days after the news broke. "This family must live in the village, of course he compromised." Incredulous, I pushed the point: "But if he compromises every time how can he live in peace? Mr. Nairoth is right. It makes him seem weak."

Nivedita contemplated my comment before responding: "It depends how you define weak. He *is* weak in a way, but he has reasons to do this." I was dissatisfied with her answer. "What reasons?" I demanded. Nivedita shrugged, "Reasons like it's the only home he knows, and the only thing his family knows is to work the land, like his daughter-in-law will give birth there, like he knows that these kinds of fights will eventually go away, but a legal case stays for decades. Plus, he is smart, this is a better compromise than before."

I was confused. To me, history had simply repeated itself: another attack, another meaningless compromise. How could Nivedita think this one was different? Nivedita sensed my skepticism. Before this last compromise, she explained, it had all been private apologies and nothing else. Now Roop Singh had financial compensation that could change a lot in his life. Raja Ram also had to humiliate himself before the whole village by apologizing publicly and make a signed promise to the village council to stop harassing Roop Singh.

When I remained unconvinced, Nivedita smiled, "Also, you must not forget that Mr. Nairoth was really impressive at the police station. The police and the magistrate will remember our team, and the villagers will think Roop Singh has powerful friends."

I sat in silence for a while. Nivedita had touched on something that should have been obvious: in Roop Singh's life, justice was neither black-and-white nor could it be mapped onto the abstract ideas of legal resilience or weakness (*tākata ya kamazori*) that dominated the vocabulary of activists like Mr. Nairoth. Mr. Nairoth's line of logic seemed clear and sensible: stick to your guns, pursue your case, and strengthen the position of Dalit complainants and the Atrocities Act by refusing to give into demands to drop complaints and compromise. And yet, as Roop Singh's situation demonstrated, this method was neither necessarily realistic nor always desirable for many who had lived through atrocities. Mr. Nairoth's attitude partially reflected his unique positionality. His family was urban, upwardly mobile, and economically secure. They were no longer tethered to the same traditional caste and village dependencies as Roop Singh. Mr. Nairoth no longer inhabited a rural community that expected him to strictly adhere to a lower-caste role: if Mr. Nairoth felt threatened, he could leave.

According to Nivedita, the flow of power in compromise cases like Roop Singh's was messier than Mr. Nairoth made it out to be. As she further explained some of the dynamics behind the scenes, which Pakka Lal, the CDR advocate from Karauli, had relayed to her, Nivedita's perspective began to make more sense.

Roop Singh had been threatened by the Jats to not pursue an atrocity case. However, Nivedita told me something surprising: after hearing of Mr. Nairoth's visit to the police station and the magistrate, the Brahmin village head (*sarapanca*) and other Brahmins, Rajputs—and even some Jats—on the village council (*pancāyata*) had also threatened Raja Ram. The *pancāyata* members were concerned because the NGO's visit had been reported by a local news outlet and because ongoing atrocities and cases would eventually get real media attention. However, they did not want the eyes of the media, of the magistrate, or of any high-ranking police officers on the village, because the *sarapanca* and a few other council members had reportedly been involved in some rather shady real estate dealings. One council member had even previously had trouble with police over some unpaid fines. Meanwhile, the *sarapanca* worried that his village would be portrayed as a place dominated by cruel, old-fashioned forms of casteism that did not represent "modern," civilized India (Waghmore 2018). He was concerned that a legal case and Raja Ram's repeated aggression could cost him reelection. He would be perceived as a weak Brahmin leader, who could not keep a belligerent Jat in line, someone who ranked lower than himself in the caste hierarchy. Therefore, the *pancāyata* told Raja Ram that they would make his life difficult if he did not behave.

To Nivedita, these dynamics showed that power was not unilateral in Roop Singh's case: "Mr. Nairoth thinks it is simple: you compromise, and you are a weak Dalit. But that's not always true. Apologizing in front of the whole village, being bullied into it by the village head, it is humiliating for Raja Ram. So Jats don't have complete power, neither does the *sarapanca*. Of course, Roop Singh is the weakest. In a better world Dalits could file an FIR under this act and men like Raja Ram would go to jail. Then again in an ideal world, there would be no caste atrocities. For now, Roop Singh got a better compromise than before, because he filed an FIR under this act and gave us a chance to really get involved."

As someone who had seen Pinky's story unfold, it was initially difficult for me not to view Roop Singh as a mere victim of questionable political maneuvering (Ruud 2001). I saw a man with little social capital who was caught in a web of complex patronage relations (Piliavsky 2014) and had bowed to the threat of future violence articulated by Raja Ram's clan. I knew that families like Roop Singh's usually had few options to choose from in their pursuit of justice.

Yet Nivedita seemed to imply that despite this cruel set of circumstances, Roop Singh should be viewed as a man who had his own agency: a man who had cleverly mobilized the NGO's presence and made the most of his FIR. Time seemed to prove her right. A few weeks later Nivedita and I decided to visit Pakka Lal and his family in Karauli. The visit was also an excuse to drop in on Roop Singh's wife, Preity, who invited us for tea. As we chatted to Preity in the kitchen, I put my questions out in the open. "Why do you think your husband compromised before and why now?" I asked Preity, as Nivedita crouched on the comfortably cool kitchen floor. Preity hesitated. Finally, she spoke: "Before we had to because we were scared! Now Raja Ram's apology restores our honor (*ijzata*), and the fact that the *sarapanca* made him do so, also shows that he can't get away with everything. But mostly, you NGO people were here, and the police protected us because of you. Everyone has seen that this new law gives us different options now because it connects with big people from the city (*baḍe log*). We have shown how strong we Jatavs can be. This one was a good (*acchā*) compromise!"

Nivedita looked at me, raising her eyebrow. I knew what she was thinking: In the face of multiple expressions of power and threats, Roop Singh's decision to drop the case he registered had, in fact, been just that: a *decision*, not just hopeless surrender.

BETTER SETTLEMENTS?
Tactical Legal Engagements
Preity's and Nivedita's words highlight that there was more to Roop Singh's compromise than the public transcript (Scott 1990) of historical disadvantage and social weakness revealed. They suggest that, in the context of Roop Singh's compromise, power is both decentralized and multivalent. This betrays the existence of manipulative spaces for even the seemingly "weakest" and reflects what French philosopher Michel de Certeau has termed the tactical art of resistance (de Certeau 1984, 37). Marginalized individuals often display a type of "makeshift creativity" in navigating the social and institutional structures set up by socially powerful communities (de Certeau 1984, xiv). In their everyday lives marginalized individuals don't blindly obey the dominant order but resist it by manipulating its rules for their own use. Socially powerful communities "strategically" establish norms and institutions that regulate sociopolitical life in a way that benefits them (de Certeau 1984, 35–36). Meanwhile, "the weak" *tactically* maneuver these systems of power by subtly undermining their rules so that their own agencies can emerge (de Certeau 1984, 37). A product of contingency rather than design, the tactics of the "weak" rail against the strategies of the powerful, creating space for the "other" (Mitchell 2007, 99).

De Certeau's theories and categories only imperfectly map onto Roop Singh's case. The "powerful" elements in his story are not institutions but historically entrenched patterns of hierarchy and prejudice, and Nivedita tells us that the binary between the "powerful" and "weak" is too simplistic. Yet the concept of tactics encapsulates the essence of Roop Singh's final compromise as something that is both born out of structural disadvantage and real executive agency.

Roop Singh was a man who did not have the luxury to think about a long-term legal agenda for his atrocity complaint in terms of wider Dalit upliftment. However, his final compromise still represented a moment of choice and assertion. It took place at a juncture when bad publicity had caused the village leadership to resent Raja Ram. Most importantly, as his wife Preity suggested, the final compromise materialized when he had shown the village that he had powerful friends from the city, who had access to real legal resources and could create pressure on the police.

The final "better" compromise represented a meaningful step towards Roop Singh's vision of empowerment. It fulfilled what he considered to be the primary purpose of the Atrocities Act: to help people like himself make the best of a bad situation and allow him to improve his social and financial standing in a landscape of identity-based violence which was unlikely to drastically change in his lifetime. The public apologies he received bestowed on him a degree of honor (*ijzata*) that he could immediately *feel* and the financial settlement he received in the end improved his economic circumstances. While it is tempting to wave off his compromise as a poor stand-in for structural change, Nivedita and Preity asked me to acknowledge that Roop Singh himself felt more powerful now. He was still a Jatav and still poor, but he had signaled to the people in his village that he had more resources than they had assumed.

Living in the Village

The compromise allowed Roop Singh to develop *local* agency within his village rather than in relation to an abstracted, national Dalit struggle, which activists like Mr. Nairoth tended to emphasize. Roop Singh's wife Preity expressed a sentiment that many atrocity survivors in Rajasthan articulated: "We have to live in our village!" However, the Hindi expression "*apane gānva me hi to rehana*," which Preity used, can suggest more than just a forced situation. The expression "*rehana hai*" can equally indicate a sense of valued inevitability, which conveys the question: "What other than this life in our (*apana*) village could possibly be a life at all?"

Therefore, the "better" compromise may not just have been something Roop Singh agreed to in the absence of other options. For him it carried the potential for the birth of a new "ordinary'" sociality (Das 2006), within the most central collectivity in his life: his village community. Starkly aware of the continuing power differences between himself, the economically strong Jats, and the historically dominant Rajputs in the village, Roop Singh's compromise was also an attempt to rewrite these clear-cut caste roles within his community. Preity's words suggest that Roop Singh saw the combination of a public apology, financial compensation, and the visibility of outside NGO support for his case as a basis on which to renegotiate the contours of the village caste hierarchy. He was able to show that Jatavs were not just victims but true agents with ever more wide-ranging resources. Therefore, he considered his engagement with the Atrocities Act successful.

As the next chapter will show, the ordinary village intercaste collectivity remains existentially dangerous for Dalits. The community that they find in village life is a thin fabric stretched over a dormant volcano of potential caste violence. The ordinary is ambivalent, charged with both positive memories and the possibility of horrific hurt. Atrocity survivors in Rajasthan's villages all know that a true sense of positive village sociality can never be truly realized as long as casteist structures, mindsets, and prejudices persist and legal institutions remain controlled by the families and friends of their attackers.

Compromises like Roop Singh's are not the best solution in anyone's eyes. However, they represent a careful negotiation of what justice and agency survivors know is possible in their lives *right now*. "Better" compromises on the back of the Atrocities Act represent micro-assertions—a slightly better deal—which is meant to chip away at the caste-based power structures that enable men like Raja Ram to commit caste violence with impunity.

PROFESSIONAL COMMUNITIES

To an extent, the layered moments of subjugation and influence that define Roop Singh's compromise are not unique to the Atrocities Act. Anthropologists have highlighted similar dynamics in Indian rape cases. Detailing the story of Komal, a Dalit woman in Rajasthan's neighboring state of Haryana, Rupal Oza argues that compromises highlight the "production of agency in abjection" (Oza 2022, 7) rather than the absolute failure of the legal system. She shows that the abjection—the stigma, public revulsion, and social rejection—which experiences of rape and subsequent legal processes create for women are not a totalizing force. Women, Oza insists, actively navigate their rape cases. In the process they reforge their own subjectivities, making violence and law sites of incremental assertion. Compromises play an important part in the creation of this assertion. They "generate a script" (Oza 2022, 10) that allows women to narrate their own interpretation of events.

Similarly, Roop Singh subtly navigates his atrocity compromise in a way that creates moments of humiliation and subjugation for Raja Ram. The similarities between Oza's analyses and atrocity compromises like that of Roop Singh are perhaps particularly striking because Rajasthan and Haryana are neighboring North Indian states.

Nonetheless, there is something distinctive about atrocity compromises. As the first two chapters of this book revealed, the ambitious, socially transformative vision behind the law has turned the Atrocities Act into a fractured and contested sociolegal imaginary of success. Along with Pinky's case, Roop Singh's story illuminates how the act has given rise to new strategic communities, which have created complex channels of agency for survivors at the boundary of formal law and everyday life.

NGOs like Mr. Nairoth's CDR represent a professional collective dedicated entirely to making the Atrocities Act legally potent. They consist of financially secure legal professionals who are embedded in national and global networks of human rights advocacy (Fuchs 2015) and embody a new mode of legal sociality. This new professional sociality can be strategically harvested by atrocity survivors.

Legal texts, as Robert Cover has famously argued, are "jurisgenerative" (Cover 1983, 12)—they create new social meanings and legal interpretations, rather than simply communicating existing ones. As these new meanings circulate, new collectivities grow around them. Upendra Baxi has analyzed this process in relation to the social life of the Indian constitution. He describes the Indian constitution as an "ideological site" for the creation of a new public sphere of negotiation and discussion (Baxi 1999, 1188). Baxi proposes that the real power of the constitution lies in its ability to give rise to new debates and social convergences, which can shift existing social structures. More recently the notion of "jurisgenesis" has also been picked up by anthropologists, who study special criminal laws in India. In his discussion of criminal trials under the Unlawful Activities (Prevention Act) (UAPA), 1967, India's antiterror law, Mayur Suresh shows that the banal technicalities in terrorism trials create temporary interpretive communities. UAPA places the burden of proof on those accused of terrorism. Hence UAPA cases often play out during trials where the accused must produce evidence for their innocence. Previously unacquainted individuals accused of terrorism connect to share stories of police violation and engage in tactical interpretations of legal rules (Suresh 2023).

Roop Singh's story shows the emergence of similar strategic communities around the Atrocities Act. Yet while the interpretive communities in terrorism cases emerge to *defend* the accused, the new socialities that have grown around the Atrocities Act aim to *create* something. The Atrocities Act is the only special criminal law in India which is not simply *against* something but explicitly and *proactively aims to generate* a better, more equal society. The act tries to modify an entire structure of habitual prejudice, violence, and institutional neglect by punishing offenders who engage in normalized acts of casteism.

As Mr. Krishnan stressed when he told me about the evolution of the act during our January 2018 interview, "the goal of the 1989 Scheduled Castes/Scheduled Tribes Prevention of Atrocities Act is in its name: *prevention* rather than just punishment." With its hopeful agenda for social equality, the Atrocities Act perhaps resonates with the social vision of the constitution more than with the aims of other special criminal laws like UAPA.

Moreover, atrocity cases are mainly constituted during police investigations and *before* court hearings. Since the burden of proof is not reversed under the Atrocities Act, the responsibility of propelling a legal case forward and producing evidence for casteist violence rests firmly on the shoulders of atrocity survivors, who represent the more socially and economically disadvantaged legal party. Therefore, the new modes of juridical sociality the Atrocities Act has engendered are largely focused on the tactical management of the FIR filing stage and the strategic production of police reports. According to Preity, Roop Singh had been able to arrange a "better" or a "good" compromise because Mr. Nairoth's support had shown the police and the village leadership that he now had powerful new networks and friends. The third time he was attacked, he was able to stipulate conditions for the compromise because the CDR had changed the landscape of legal influence for him. Its representatives helped him register a complaint and then sent a team to produce media interest in his case and generate pressure on the police.

If survivors of caste-based violence in a rural, disconnected district like Karauli or remote areas of Jhunjhunu had previously been left to fight their fates in isolation, the proliferation of NGOs and caste associations like the Jhunjhunu Meghwal Sangarsh Samiti, which aim to support the Atrocities Act, have now created new tactical opportunities for survivors like Roop Singh. Caste associations and professional NGOs help incidents of caste atrocity along on their journey to become cases by debating events in village forums and pushing police officers to register complaints under specific sections of the Atrocities Act. The professional habitus many members of these organizations have, which is mirrored in the cars they drive and the suits and starched *kurta*s (long shirts) they wear, creates an impression of bureaucratic and political know-how and influence. This can be intimidating to village leaders and perpetrators like Raja Ram, who have historically acted with impunity.

In this context it becomes difficult for upper castes to "convert" the Atrocities Act to their advantage (Berg 2020). When survivors call in NGO support, the possibility of a lengthy legal battle becomes more likely. The financial burden and reputational costs of this process make compromises an attractive solution for accused parties even if they demand acts of public humiliation from them. As Sonali sarcastically commented when I told her Roop Singh's story: "It is easy to commit violence against

Dalits but dealing with an actual, public case under the Atrocities Act is not easy. It could go for years, cost you time and money and expose [you] as a primitive thug. So, perpetrators really want to compromise. I don't like compromises, but I guess if you are clever about it, atrocity victims can get *something* out of a compromise that involves the threat of an ongoing case."

Sonali pointed out something important: the Atrocities Act has slowly and selectively begun to change the *features* of compromises for Dalits in Rajasthan. Historically, the quest for formal, public forms of justice has often been the realm of upper castes in Rajasthan (Moore 1993). Meanwhile lower-caste families, women, and communities with little political and social capital typically pursued restitution through other types of settlements. However, the Atrocities Act has complicated this picture. As the vines of new strategic professional communities grow around the trunk of the Atrocities Act, survivors can tactically harvest the threat of formal law in informal ways.

By calling on NGO employees who "knew the law," had media connections, and could impress the police and the magistrate with educated legal terminologies and, perhaps, even the strategic presence of a foreigner, Roop Singh was able to procure a "better" settlement. Despite Mr. Nairoth's belief in his own authority, Roop Singh had also tactically mobilized Mr. Nairoth and the entire NGO presence to secure the best possible compromise deal. His story shows that survivors can sometimes alter the landscape of compromises in a way that has real benefits for them by deploying the new strategic, professional communities around the Atrocities Act.

Through the grapevine, Pakka Lal, the CDR lawyer who had been brought up in Karauli, heard that Raja Ram had been intimidated by the way Mr. Nairoth had made heads and tails with the local police officers and gotten Roop Singh police protection. He also had been scared by the white lady with a camera and the big Jeep. He was shocked that Roop Singh had "big friends."

As I write these words in the summer of 2023, six years after I accompanied Mr. Nairoth to Karauli, Roop Singh has never been attacked again. He used the money from the settlement to send his granddaughter to school. She is one of the few Jatav girls in the village—and even in the wider district of Karauli, where female literacy is low—who may move outside the village one day.

COMPLICATING ACTIVIST COMPLICITY

Roop Singh's case shows that "better" atrocity compromises in Rajasthan don't represent a rejection or betrayal of the Atrocities Act but are only possible *because* of it. In a state like Rajasthan, which has only a fractured landscape of Dalit political resistance (Bhatia 2006, Rawat 2017), the Atrocities Act has become a productive site for legal knowledge exchange as well as community-building across district and class boundaries, which helps survivors tactically navigate their experiences long before cases encounter courts.

When I introduced Roop Singh and Mr. Nairoth, it seemed as if their relationship was marked by a clear hierarchy: the educated, professional Mr. Nairoth clearly instructed Roop Singh how to use the act. However, the importance of strategic NGO communities and caste associations in propelling atrocity complaints forward complicates this picture.

Anthropological studies have argued that professional activism often reproduces dynamics of oppression (Wright 2018) and creates intrasectional forms of violence (Katri 2017). Similarly, the normative ideas of proper legal engagement, which activists like Mr. Nairoth preach to survivors, along with their authoritative habitus, bring class differentials within Rajasthan's Dalit communities into stark focus. Mr. Nairoth once told me: "If you file, you fight! Any legal proceeding under the Atrocities Act should serve our [Dalit] struggle (*sangharsha*) and when you file a complaint you become an ambassador for the movement (*āndolana*)."

For him, the Atrocities Act was a symbol for the advancement of the collective national Dalit struggle against casteist oppression. However, his mantra glossed over significant differences in access, time, and financial capital between himself and many of the atrocity survivors he considered *kamazora* (weak). Through his loud insistence that they were all part of the same Dalit struggle (*sangharsha*), he actively obscured the existential dangers and challenges a protracted court case poses for many survivors, who remain embedded in rural structures of agricultural dependency. Most problematically, his idea that every complainant was an ambassador of the Atrocities Act rendered the individual suffering of families marginal.

On the one hand, these dynamics are reminiscent of ethnographies that detail activist complicity in other contexts defined by structural inequality. In her discussion of radical left Israeli activists who align themselves with the Palestinian cause, Fiona Wright (2018), for example, argues that activists' unwillingness to recognize the moral grey zones of their work makes them complicit in structures that "other" Palestinians. Yet these ethnographies have primarily studied activist groups that belong to a different community than the people for whom they advocate.

Usually, activists in these accounts hail from more socially and politically influential groups, such as Israelis or white South Africans who opposed Apartheid politics (Sanders 2002). In this context complicity translates into a reproduction of existing political hierarchies, which stands in direct contrast with assurances of allyship. Activists like Mr. Nairoth, who identify as Dalit just as do most the atrocity survivors they work with, are of a different kind. Their work can reinforce other structures of oppression, such as classism or patriarchy, while activists enthusiastically rattle the cages of caste oppression.

However, Roop Singh's "good" atrocity compromise shows that survivors, who may seem weak on the surface, challenge activist authority and the new patriarchal and classist injuries it can create, by ignoring activist advice. On the surface Roop Singh appears to be obedient to Mr. Nairoth's instruction not to compromise. However, it later becomes clear that he mobilized the NGO presence to get his complaint filed and send a clear message to Raja Ram that he is no longer helpless and alone.

Roop Singh's case, hence, highlights that the new socialities the Atrocities Act gives rise to are deeply ambivalent. Productive of new intracaste hierarchies on the one hand, they also hold the seeds for effective tactical legal engagements. These engagements can result in surprising power reversals between professional activists and the atrocity survivors they deem "weak."

In this light, the term "good" or "better" compromise gains a new meaning: it not only implies a beneficial negotiation with upper-caste perpetrators but also an empowerment of survivors vis-à-vis upwardly mobile Dalit professionals, who claim to know what legal success is and want to decide how survivors and their families should engage with hate crime law.

WHAT MAKES A LAW SUCCESSFUL?

The conundrum of the compromise cannot be wrapped up in a pretty bow. So-called better compromises can, at once, be seen as a sign of the Atrocities Act's success and of its failure; an indicator that the law cannot deliver on its promises or as evidence that it already does.

On the one hand, "better" atrocity compromises have opened small spaces of agency for survivors that chip away at deeply entrenched structures of caste power. Roop Singh's creative rendering of the Atrocities Act shows how so-called alternative routes of local dispute resolution are being actively transformed in conversation with the Atrocities Act. In Rajasthan, compromises that can be considered "good" or "better" are profoundly dependent on the existence of the Atrocities Act, which looms threateningly over higher-caste communities (Carswell and de Neve 2015). This highlights how state laws influence the way justice is navigated outside legal institutions (Moore 1973). "Good" atrocity compromises also reveal something even more radical. They show that the Atrocities Act has not simply become vernacularized in Rajasthan (Levitt and Merry 2009) but has emerged as one of the most expansive sites of social and political negotiation. Hence, the biggest success the Atrocities Act can claim to date may well be its emergence as the backbone of "better" compromises.

On the other hand, the Supreme Court's declaration in the previous chapter that the Atrocities Act is regularly misused also shows that Mr. Nairoth and other professional activists and advocates are right to be skeptical of compromises. Mr. Saxena, a prominent criminal defense lawyer in Jaipur and the son of a former Rajasthan High Court judge, succinctly summarized the issue during an interview in January 2017. "The problem is," he said, "that by compromising you are actually handing people who do hold on to a casteist mindset a gun to shoot you with!" According to Mr. Saxena the prevalence of compromises delivered a perfect point of attack for those claiming intentional blackmail and extortion of upper castes by Dalits. "If people see that Dalits are filing cases and then withdrawing them after getting money or a public apology, people won't take atrocity complaints seriously. I get why someone would compromise, I am a lawyer and I have no illusions that our criminal system is working well. But when it comes to cases under the SC/ST [Atrocities Act], complainants who compromise neglect their social responsibility. When they compromise, they are weakening the reputation of a law that was made to protect them."

Pinky's story, which ended in a compromise no one ever saw coming, supports assumptions like Mr. Saxena's. In February 2018, a month after Pinky's compromise had unfolded, Avinesh's family in Jhunjhunu continued to debate her case with severe anger. Avinesh's older brother, Rajesh, who had accompanied me on my initial visit to Pinky's house, felt that Pinky had dragged the name of Jhunjhunu's Megwhal associations through the mud. "Who will listen to Meghwals ever again?" he asked.

His frustration captures a fundamental truth that neither Mr. Nairoth nor Mr. Saxena managed to express with such clarity: in a world where everyone constantly looks for reasons to deny realities of caste violence, there may be detrimental consequences to repurposing hate crime law for the creation of micro-agencies on the ground.

When Mr. Nairoth makes men like Roop Singh promise not to compromise, when Mr. Saxena cautions against compromises, or when Rajesh expresses anger at Pinky, they are all motivated by the same fear: that compromises will generate further judicial and public biases towards the Atrocities Act.

Globally, hate crime laws have often engendered violent backlash towards the minorities they aim to protect (Dixon and Ray 2007) as well as judicial skepticism towards claims of hate (Walters, Owusu-Bempah, and Wiedlitzka 2018). Considering the long-standing resistance many caste groups in India have levied against the country's affirmative action program, which is meant to economically uplift Dalits and Adivasis (Lerche and Shah 2018), the rise of atrocity compromises may fuel discourses that portray Dalits as coddled, untruthful pets of the state.

The social life of the Atrocities Act in Rajasthan unveils that the conundrum of the compromise represents one of those rare battles where both sides are unquestionably right about something and unquestionably blind to something else. Before I left Rajasthan in 2018, Nivedita confided in me: "After filing an FIR and bringing in our NGO to really scare these Jats, Roop Singh has had peace. His wife called me the other day and said that after we came, other Jatav Dalits in their village started filing atrocity cases because they think that if they all start doing it, then the Jats will have to buckle eventually. I want to ask Mr. Nairoth, how is that not success?"

Unknowingly, Nivedita asked the question that would come to stand at the center of this book: What makes a hate crime law successful and who gets to decide? The Atrocities Act and its culture of compromises give contradictory answers. In Rajasthan, the act lives and breathes in extralegal spaces, creating agencies for survivors that go unacknowledged. Success and transformation through hate crime law may, thus, look different from what legal professionals expect. But this reality also creates new problems.

PART III

Law at the Limits of Hate and Hope

SIX

FIELDS OF MASSACRE
A "Hollow" Law?

AN "EXEMPLARY" ATROCITY

As I ducked out of the blazing sunlight and entered the small cement house located by an inconspicuous dusty road in Dangawas village, the home seemed strangely silent. A group of women were sitting on the kitchen floor, *ghūnghaṭas* (veils) covering their faces. I felt uneasy. Over two years earlier, in May 2015, this family had fallen victim to one of the most brutal caste atrocities in recent Indian history. In an escalated land dispute that resulted in a mob attack perpetrated by members of the locally dominant Jat caste, five Dalits lost their lives and many more were seriously injured. That day Ratna Ram Meghwal was killed, and his family lost any semblance of security or belonging they might have had. Even now, years after the attack, police officers still sometimes stood guard at their door. As of 2023, the family's court case, which had become Rajasthan's banner case for the Atrocities Act, is still ongoing.

The events of Dangawas took place long before I set out on my fieldwork in Rajasthan. Dangawas, which is a small village located in the central Nagaur district of Rajasthan, was two days by road from my main fieldwork site in Jhunjhunu, although some locals still considered the eastern corner of Nagaur part of the Shekhawati region. Yet, whenever I mentioned my research to Meghwal families in Jhunjhunu, they immediately told me about the "Dangawas massacre." In Rajasthan, I soon learned, the meaning of the Atrocities Act *was* Dangawas. Due to extensive media coverage, the large-scale involvement of activists and the Central Bureau of Investigation (CBI)—India's highest and most powerful investigative agency for domestic crimes—Dangawas had grown synonymous with the continuing reality of caste-based violence. The Dangawas massacre was perhaps the one incident that allowed Dalits across Rajasthan to defend the existence of the Atrocities Act in the face of repeated political and legal challenges to its existence. Yet media coverage of Dangawas often seemed strangely incomplete: local television reports spoke of arrests, NGO reports lamented the casteism at the heart of Indian society, and newspapers offered details of the CBI investigation. However, the voices of the Dangawas survivors were mostly absent.

Even though the Atrocities Act was introduced to punish and prevent incidents of cruel caste aggression precisely like Dangawas, it is also Dangawas that exposed the shortcomings of hate crime legislation most urgently. The aftermath of Dangawas unveils that cases under the Atrocities Act can keep families, who have been deeply injured, trapped in a post-traumatic moment, without offering a meaningful sense of justice and healing. The social and legal afterlife of the Dangawas massacre shines a harsh spotlight on everything that formal law *cannot* give people: restitution, defined by a sense of repair and the return of irreplaceable networks, goods, and sentiments, which have been lost (Fay and James 2008).

In September 2017 I gathered the courage to visit Dangawas, along with Advocate Gaurav, an independent lawyer from the nearby city of Ajmer, who had followed the family's story intimately. I knew that Ratna Ram's surviving family in Dangawas had grown tired of the perpetual stream of journalists and activists. I wanted to respect that but also knew I could not entirely ignore Dangawas if I wanted to understand the possibilities and limits of the Atrocities Act in Rajasthan. When I met Advocate Gaurav at an activist gathering in Jaipur and learned that he was close with the family, I asked him whether he would accompany me to the village. He agreed but insisted we should not stay with Ratna Ram Meghwal's family overnight. "If people see a white lady hanging out in the family home for longer, the Jats will think they are getting a foreign lawyer or something and that could be dangerous," he explained.

Of all the survivors I encountered in Rajasthan, Ratna Ram Meghwal's remaining family were perhaps least optimistic about the possibility of achieving any form of justice through law. The exceptional violence they had experienced made them acutely aware that their identity as Meghwals had turned them into eternal targets of brutality. Law, they thought, could do little to change social prejudice and oppression. It would not bring back the people they had lost or help them unsee what they had seen: that their neighbors were willing to murder them.

What many seemed to want was a life without fear. The day I first visited Dangawas, Anu, one of Ratna Ram's surviving female relatives, told me: "A world . . . where I have space to live and work on my land in peace (*apani zamīna para shānti se jīne ke lyie jagaha ho*), and no one attacks me for it. And where Jats must accept that Meghwals have a right to own land just as much as they do. That's what justice means to me."

By invoking the idea of land (*zamīna*) as a symbol for a just life in which Meghwals are allowed physical and social space (*jagaha*)—the space to claim ownership and navigate village life without fear of violence—she rooted her idea of equality deep in Dangawas's scorched earth. While Anu and other Meghwals in Dangawas thought that the potential for official state punishment for the perpetrators, which the Atrocities Act offered, was important, they also felt that law missed the point. Another Meghwal woman told me: "These legal things (*kānūnī cīza*) are far away. I must live here in my village and as long as Jats think they have right to rule Meghwals, no law will prevent these incidents. Punishment is important but what do you do about castcist mindsets (*soca*)? This act can't help me forget that my neighbors want to kill me because they think my land is theirs."

At first glance the skepticism towards the potential of official justice inherent in the Atrocities Act, which many Meghwals in Dangawas expressed, as well as their restrained appeals to being *given peace*, were perplexing. They ran counter to the open and assertive claim to rightful land ownership and equality before law that had cost the deceased Ratna Ram Meghwal his life. Though the dispute over Ratna Ram's plot of land had been simmering for decades, it had been his overt decision to build a house on the disputed plot and to move his family there which caused the explosive eruption of Jat anger that would come to be known as the Dangawas massacre. During a group interview, several Meghwal men in Dangawas told me that Ratna Ram had no longer wanted to negotiate with the Jats over land he *knew* to be his. He believed that it was time for the Jats to accept that the heart of modern India beat to the drum of equality and that they were no longer superior. By claiming his due in such a forceful manner, Ratna Ram had crossed an unspoken line within Rajasthan's social structure, which still bows to traditional caste hierarchies (Bhatia 2006; Vyas, Acharya, and Singh 2007; Rawat 2017). His assertion threatened not only the family of Chinma Ram Jat, which was laying claim to his land, but the status of the entire Jat community in Dangawas and Nagaur district. And so the Jats made him pay.

These dynamics echo accounts of other mass atrocities against Dalits, like the Khairlanji massacre in Maharashtra. In Khairlanji four members of a Dalit family of the Mahar *jāti* were brutally murdered by a mob of the dominant Kunabi-Maratha caste in 2006. Like the Dangawas incident, the Khairlanji murders were the result of a deep-seated fear of Dalit defiance among higher-caste communities, who saw their own status waning (Teltumbde 2008, Teltumbde 2011). The Khairlanji murders were not simply a brutal attempt to "teach assertive Dalits a lesson, but also [a way] to flaunt how openly [the Kunabi-Marathas] could afford to do it." Similarly, the violence of Dangawas was a public statement by the local Jat community that traditional caste hierarchies and dominant caste rule were above and beyond state law (Jaoul 2008, 1).

Moreover, the Dangawas massacre reflects the same emotional challenges that characterized the Khairlanji killings: Under the layers of media coverage and behind the ongoing court hearings that portray Dangawas as a textbook atrocity case, the search for restitution and assertion among the Meghwals in the village had become fragile. When I visited the village, many Meghwal survivors were haunted by a deep terror of repeated violence. The Jat violence in May 2015 and Ratna Ram's death had reminded the Meghwal survivors that it was existentially dangerous to claim what Jats were unwilling to grant (comp. Waghmore 2018). Caught in grief and terror, survivors found it difficult to imagine "fighting again," even as activists and lawyers championed their cause.

So-called hate crimes are unique in the type of pain and trauma they inflict (Iganski and Lagou 2014; Hardy and Chakraborti 2020). They are messenger crimes (Perry 2001; Hall 2013), intended to reaffirm traditional social hierarchies by brutally etching them into the bodies of stigmatized groups that are daring enough to demand "parity of participation" (Fraser 1998). Hate crimes imprint a message of hostility on the bodies of those deemed "other" or "less than" when they demand equality. This imprint is highly visible and deeply intentional. It is meant to serve as a reminder to historically oppressed groups to always carry an awareness of their own inferiority and never again challenge the established social order. Forced to carry traces of their own subordination through life, hate crime survivors experience a type of trauma that reverberates through their communities. Their visible pain warns everyone who shares their identity that assertion can bring death (Perry and Alvi 2012).

In Dangawas this trauma was evident. In my memory Dangawas stands out as a barren desert of hopeful practice in Rajasthan: a place where fear still hung in the air and the shock of having one's call for equality met with murder still defined survivor's perspectives and debates about law and the future.

Therefore, this chapter leaves public representations, debates, and media coverage of the Dangawas massacre by the wayside. Instead, it focuses on the family members and immediate survivors who had to come to terms with a deeply disrupted life in a village that has become purgatory: a home that hurt unimaginably. The chapter offers an analysis after the fact, in an attempt to understand how oppressed communities conceptualize desires for restoration when threats of further violence still loom.

In doing so, it responds to an aspect of hate crimes only sparsely discussed in the current literature: the temporal suspension of hope. The ever-present threat of death and suffering, which is inextricably bound up with marginalized identities, can leave families who have lived through hate crimes frozen in time. They are unable to heal within the community that harmed them and still denies them real space in society even though it remains the only home they have ever known. Simultaneously, they find themselves incapable of locating meaning in the legal tools at their disposal, which seemingly cannot change the conditions that make hate crimes possible. This analysis draws inspiration from scholarship on transitional justice, which has argued that formal legal processes can hinder organic pathways to healing after violence. Anthropologists have emphasized that government efforts to provide redress to victims after large-scale human rights violations often impose external rhythms and bureaucratic processes on victimized communities at a time of mourning (Ferrándiz and Robben 2015, 11). They highlight that legal attempts to punish or foster reconciliation following mass violence can sideline local ways of grieving and truth-telling (Hinton 2010, Wagner 2010).

Extending these arguments, this chapter proposes that the highly publicized atrocities of Dangawas confounded local ways of coming to terms with the violence. The overtly antagonistic nature of the ongoing legal case, which starkly divided the village into hunters and hunted, murderers and victims, confused survivors' already complex desires. On the one hand, Ratna Ram's family held on to profound rage and grief, which engendered a hunger for resistance, revenge, and justice through public, official courtroom punishment of the perpetrators. On the other hand, they also wished for a livable village. "The law is out there but we have to live here," they often said. Ratna Ram Meghwal's surviving family members wanted justice in the structural sense of evening the playing field of caste power, but they also wanted affective restoration and a change in upper-caste mindsets, which would shield them from future violence.

In anthropological literature, the term "restitution" has typically been used in the context of government-led efforts to return land, territory, and property to communities that were forcibly dispossessed (Fay and James 2008; Fairweather 2006). This is usually predicated upon the liberal concept of an individual who can be "unburdened" of past violence (Trouillot 2000, 179). Moving beyond the property framework, this chapter uses the term "restitution" to capture Dangawas survivors' craving for social transformation after a type of brutality which not only aimed to dispossess them of their land but meant to keep them forever confined to the bottom of the social hierarchy. In Dangawas the desire for repair or peace was not simply a sign of resignation or a wish for a return to a previous status quo that had been built in patterns of caste discrimination. It was characterized by an open demand for a *better* kind of sociality, which would prevent atrocities like the 2015 massacre in the future. For Dangawas Meghwals, restitution could only partially be achieved by winning a legal case. It also needed to come from within the village and the land, from a change of casteist biases in the form of space to freely farm, own property, and live.

The case under the Atrocities Act brought to court in the name of Dangawas survivors has disappointed them on all fronts. It has neither allowed for organic grief nor has it, thus far, brought a real sense of justice through official punishment. It certainly has not changed casteist attitudes. For the Meghwals I spoke to (many of whom were women), the ongoing legal case has become a reminder of everyone who has been lost and of the painful fact that Dangawas village will never be a safe home for Meghwals, as the possibility of upper-caste violence is always lurking. This realization was particularly agonizing, because many Meghwals in Dangawas were convinced that the Atrocities Act was a "good law" that *should* give Dalits a voice in exceptionally cruel circumstances. In the face of their own trauma, the inefficacy of the act created additional grief.[1]

THE DANGAWAS MASSACRE

"It was like a hoard of angry beasts storming our land," one Meghwal woman told me when I visited Dangawas in 2017, "I saw them coming and I knew we were going to die!" Her words hung in the air as the other women in the room nodded silently. Some of them had been present at the attack and had come out alive but seriously injured. Following the altercation, Meghwal survivors not only had to deal with loss, physical pain, the destruction of their land, the fear of further brutality, and the stress of an ongoing court case, but also with practical household issues since many women had been injured in the attack. May 14, 2015, brought about a complete rupture in the already precarious lives of Dangawas Meghwals and made them feel like hunted prey.

The Dangawas massacre represented the culmination of a longstanding land dispute between Ratna Ram Meghwal and the family of Chinma Ram Jat. The attack transpired at the exact moment when the chips of state law seemed to fall in favor of Ratna Ram Meghwal. The violence was meant to send an "immediate message" to him as he dared to challenge the established hierarchies: an intention, which—as Claudia Card (2004) proposes—lies at the conceptual heart of caste atrocities. According to Bhanwar Meghwanshi (2015), who wrote the first widely circulated report on the Dangawas massacre, the controversy had been festering for over two decades. For Meghwanshi, what happened in 2015 represented the boiling point of a long-simmering Jat anger rooted in anxieties over a waning status monopoly.

Historical accounts of the Nagaur region confirm Meghwanshi's claim. The influence of Jat landowners, which dates back decades, even centuries (Nagaur District Gazetteer 1975; Sisson 1969), is unparalleled in the district and has long determined political outcomes and economic formations (Shanmugaratnam 1996; Bharadwaj 2012).[2] Meghwanshi emphasizes that while over 50% of the land that belongs to Dalits in Nagaur is correctly registered in their names, most of these plots have unofficially been occupied by Jats and other castes as the result of mortgaging deals (Meghwanshi 2015). Given the fact that section 42(b) of the Rajasthan Tenancy Act of 1955—which applies still today—states that anyone who is not a member of the Scheduled Castes (or Tribes) is not permitted to buy or mortgage land from a member of these groups, this situation is particularly concerning. It highlights that Dangawas and its home district of Nagaur are a historical nest of barely questioned Jat power that has put local Dalit groups on the defensive in all areas of life. Therefore even some Dalit MLAs (Members of Legislative Assembly) from Nagaur were fearful to openly express their support for Ratna Ram's family after the massacre.

The twenty-three *bigha* (approx. 3.5 ha) plot at the root of the Dangawas bloodshed had originally been acquired by Ratna Ram Meghwal's ancestor, Basta Ram Meghwal. However, in 1998 a man named Chinma Ram Jat claimed title to the plot, stating that the property had been sold to him in 1964. This claim is intentionally misleading. In 1964 Basta Ram's family had briefly mortgaged the land to Chinma Ram's father in exchange for a loan in the amount of 1500 Rupees. However, according to Ratna Ram Meghwal's family, the debt was short-lived: "The biggest lie the Jats tell is that we sold the land. We only took out a loan that we repaid. But they wanted to keep the land and since then we have been fighting."

With both parties insisting on their version of events, the conflict came to hinge on a single piece of paper: the sales deed. The Indian newspaper *Frontline* reported that in 1998 "Chinma Ram Jat claimed title to the property . . . on the grounds that he and his ancestors had held possession of the land for the past thirty-five years." However, Chinma Ram did not submit any documentary evidence to the nearby district court in Merta town to prove his ownership (Rajalakshmi 2015). Therefore his claim was rejected shortly before his death in 2007. Soon after, Chinma Ram's sons, Kana Ram Jat and Oma Ram Jat, who would later be named as two of the main accused in the First Information Report for the Dangawas killings, produced a sales deed claiming that the land had been sold to their father by Ratna Ram's predecessor Ghisa Ram (Rajalakshmi 2015). Then they filed a complaint with the Merta revenue court.

Dangawas Meghwals argue that the sales deed submitted by the Jats was a forgery. If the paper had been real, they point out, Chinma Ram would have produced it in the first court case. Therefore, Ratna Ram Meghwal's sons, Munna Ram and Krishna Ram, quickly filed a counterclaim to Kana Ram and Oma Ram's case at the Merta revenue court. In it they first questioned the authenticity of the sales deed and then proposed that any sale of the land to Chinma Ram Jat would have been void anyway per the 1955 Rajasthan Tenancy Act. Unfortunately, the situation remained in limbo as the revenue court stayed proceedings in the matter.

In early 2015 Ratna Ram Meghwal decided to make his right to the plot in question explicit. He took possession of the contested land and started construction of a proper cement house (*pakkā makāna*) on the premises. This assertive move was perceived as an unforgivable expression of defiance against the caste hierarchy. Many Jats felt they had to respond. Combined with the degrading experience of losing the official court case in 2007, Chinma Ram Jat's family had experienced a moment of deep social humiliation. "They felt forgotten by the law," an independent lawyer who was helping Ratna Ram's surviving family with the atrocity case told me, "then Ratna Ram goes and starts building that house. The world as Jats knew it was ending."

In April 2015 Chinma Ram Jat's sons aggressively forced their way onto the contested plot with a JCB tractor, dug up the valuable *Prosopis cineraria* (*khejri*) trees, and began excavating a pond.[3] Even though Ratna Ram

Meghwal reported these events at the police station in Merta, the authorities remained unresponsive. After a village *pancāyata* (council) meeting on May 10, 2015, which was scheduled in Ratna Ram's absence, a delegation of Jats submitted a memorandum to the Subdivision Officer, the Deputy Superintendent of the Police (DSP), and the District Collector. The document stated that the Jat community of Dangawas wanted help in evacuating Ratna Ram from the contested plot. Should the police fail to comply with the request, Jats would take justice "into their own hands" (Meghwanshi 2015, 7). Although the Jat delegation gave the police a week to respond, mere days later, on May 14, a mob of approximately 250 Jats pushed onto the disputed plot with motorcycles, weapons, and tractors. In one of the most cruel acts conceivable, the mob surrounded Ratna Ram's house, set it and the surrounding field on fire, mutilated several Meghwal women, and then proceeded to crush two Meghwals underneath their tractors (Meghwanshi 2015; Husain 2015). Ratna Ram Meghwal was one of two Meghwal men to lose their lives to the tractor attack. Three more Dalits died during later medical treatments, while a dozen others were admitted to the hospital with severe injuries.

Even though the Merta police station is located merely five kilometers from Dangawas, the police arrived on site far too late. In his report on

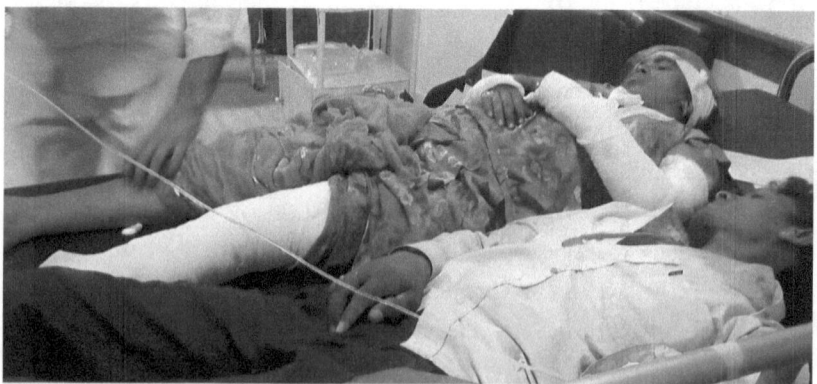

FIGURE 11. Two Meghwals who were injured during the Dangawas massacre. Source: Photo taken by Bhanwar Meghwanshi; originally published by *Scroll India* on May 22, 2015. Reprinted with permission.

the attack, Bhanwar Meghwanshi recalls the words of one Govind Ram Meghwal, who managed to escape without physical harm: "If the police had arrived on time, my family members would be alive today." This statement betrays unspoken skepticism about the police's neutrality. As the representatives of the state most deeply embedded in local negotiations and interactions (Hornberger 2013; Jauregui 2016), police punctuality or tardiness were read as signposts for the true social sentiments of the state.

The brutality of Dangawas quickly drew attention from media, NGOs, and human rights groups across the state. The Dangawas Meghwal community and activists from across Rajasthan staged a sit-in protest (*dharanā*) outside the Jawaharlal Nehru Hospital in Merta. They submitted a letter with eighteen demands to the state government: among other things, they wanted adequate compensation, the arrest of all culprits, and an inquiry by the Criminal Bureau of Investigation (HT Correspondent Ajmer 2015). While some of these demands were met, many were not. The Government of Rajasthan handed over the case to the Central Bureau of Investigation (CBI) in June 2015. The CBI filed a charge sheet against thirty-six Jats under sections 3(1)(v), 3(1)(x) of the preamended version of the Atrocities Act—wrongful land dispossession and intentional insult of a member of the Scheduled Castes or Tribes—as well as sections 307, 436, 147, 149, 447, 323, and 325 of the Indian Penal Code, accusing the named Jats of attempted murder, explosive mischief, unlawful assembly, criminal trespass, and (grievous) hurt. The CBI also issued arrest warrants for all accused (Times News Network 2016).

When I visited Dangawas in 2017, I was told that sixteen of the accused Jats had been arrested. In December 2019, the *Times of India* reported that the CBI had offered rewards of up to 50,000 Indian Rupees for deliverance of each of the remaining accused who had still not been arrested (Times News Network 2019). The trial of the case began in the Merta court in January 2018 and is still ongoing.

Despite these legally encouraging developments, I learned during my brief stint in Dangawas that, on an intimate level, survivors were most concerned with the circumstances that made the violence of Dangawas possible. "Ratna Ram didn't think something like murder would happen," a male Meghwal neighbor of the family told me. However, in the aftermath of the massacre, many of Ratna Ram's remaining relatives began to feel that he miscalculated. Hence, they grappled with a difficult question: How could their experience of violence, justice, and the revenge they desired be reconciled with the only life they had access to: their life in Dangawas village?

"How can we make sure that this kind of thing doesn't happen again?," one of the Meghwal women in the village asked me the evening of our first visit. "That's what we are most concerned about. Living in the village without more violence (*hinsā*)," another Meghwal man told me. "This law [the Atrocities Act] is good, but law is far away. Maybe now Jats won't do anything again but sometimes cases get forgotten. The law cannot bring my people [Meghwals] a feeling of justice from the inside (*andara se*). We still live in a divided and dangerous village."

The Atrocities Act, he seemed to say, is a protective and hopefully preventative measure, since Jats too have felt the consequences of their actions. However, it ultimately hovers above the lives of the Dangawas survivors and can neither bring a true feeling of justice nor a real promise that society will change.

LAND AS A CASTED CANVAS
Carving out a Space for Meghwals

When I accompanied some Meghwal men from Dangawas to the Merta district court to consult with their case lawyer, one man who was injured during the attack, Nanu Lal Meghwal, gave a deeply emotional speech: "It is when we demand our rights and our land, then the Jats kill us. They won't budge from their place. They want to own the village, and now we must fight through the law."[4]

His legal counsel agreed. "He is right," he told me as we discussed the details of the charge sheet later, "the Jats don't think the Meghwals have a right to that land . . . or any other."

Nanu Lal's words underline the retributive tendencies inherent in the attack of May 2015.[5] However, they also hint at deeper disagreements between Meghwals and Jats about the meaning of social order and space that lie at the heart of caste atrocities and of hate crimes more widely. Nanu Lal attributes the violence to the unwillingness of the Dangawas Jat community to give up physical land, but also symbolic social space and economic security. The Jat attack, initiated by an economically powerful family, unearths deep Jat anxieties about ceding privilege by allowing Meghwals entry into a socioeconomic and agricultural arena they consider exclusively their own. Jat violence marks a refusal to move aside and accept the reality of legal transformation to the established caste hierarchy.

Anu, one of Ratna Ram's surviving female relatives, had earlier articulated her wish for "space (*jagaha*) to live." In Hindi "space" (*jagaha*) demarcates a physical area as well as a metaphorical sphere of being. The lengths to which Ratna Ram Meghwal had gone to claim his land suggest that land is not only economically crucial for Meghwals, but that in Rajasthan Meghwal conceptions of belonging are rooted in the notion that land grants security by enabling participation (Fraser 1998) in the social arena. Land represents economic security as well as status and voice in the community. "In Jhunjhunu at least Dalits have a little bit of land," Sonali told me when we discussed the Dangawas massacre, "this means that the earth our villages are built on is ours as well. If we had no land like Dalits in other areas, we wouldn't be a real part of the village."

For Anu, the autonomy of owning and cultivating land, of passing it on to the next generation without threat, signifies freedom and social equality. Yet Nanu Lal's appraisal of the dynamics behind the Dangawas massacre highlight the danger of Meghwals demanding their rights to land. Insisting on land is perceived as provocative by those who have historically been disproportionately entitled to the economic value and societal power it represents. As a unique type of property that cannot be circulated (Hann 1998), land mirrors systems of social dominance and becomes a battleground on which demands to reconfigure class, caste, and gender hierarchies play out (see Whitehead 1984; Mondal 2021).

In Dalit struggles for recognition, land as economic resource and meaningful physical space has played a central role (Lerche and Shah 2018).[6] Indian agricultural land reflects and produces power relations by putting a bright spotlight on social roles: Who works the land and who commands those who do? "We work on Jat land, and so often it seems to me that by doing that we are taking part in our own oppression," Nanu Lal grimly admitted to me at the Merta district court. His words emphasize that land and its practices show who has the power to impose their claims, memories, and imaginations on social space (Lefebvre 1991; Christie 2013). The reworking of material land relations can, hence, bring about meaningful alternatives to the dominant social structure (Harvey 2006).

The contested plot in Dangawas had emerged as a highly "casted" space prior to the massacre: Ratna Ram's claim to the land reflected the potential transformation of caste hierarchies in the agricultural landscape. By simultaneously asserting his land rights through legal proceedings (his land title claim) and through physical action (constructing a house), Ratna Ram Meghwal acted doubly audaciously in the eyes of the local Jat population. His efforts to openly claim ownership over land represented a de facto social revolution. The ensuing panic found its outlet in absolute brutality.

Jat Order: Preserving the Status Quo

In the aftermath of the Dangawas massacre, *Scroll India* reported that a noteworthy section of the Jat community in Rajasthan expressed support for the attackers. Some vocal Jats proposed that Meghwals had in recent years become "emboldened by reservations and the 1989 Prevention of Atrocities Act." One noted that Dalits "should not forget their place in society" (Meghwanshi 2015).

As I combed through newspaper reports on Dangawas, it became obvious that Jat opinions on the massacre resonated with accounts of caste atrocities in different parts of India. In the southern state of Tamil Nadu, dominant Gounder landowners, who resemble Nagaur's Jats in terms of status, have also expressed concern that the Arunthatyiar (Dalit) community they used to rely on for agricultural labor was increasingly "pampered by the state." Many believe that Arunthatyiars use the Atrocities Act to take advantage of Gounder employers (Carswell and de Neve 2015, 1113). Moreover, research has shown that perpetrators of caste atrocities rarely express feelings of guilt. Instead, most consider their actions a necessary response to Dalit attempts to subvert what they view as the correct social and economic order. Dominant caste communities often argue that Dalits are coddled by state law and express the opinion that the high castes are the real victims of a state that gives preferential treatment to Scheduled Castes and Tribes (Lal 2023). Together these analyses suggest that an event that was a murderous massacre for the Meghwals of Dangawas was conceptualized as a moment of self-defense by many Jats in Nagaur: a determined decision to combat what they saw as problematic reversals in the social hierarchy. Chinma Ram's sons' declaration that they would take justice "into their own hands" indicates their conviction that the law is setting a problematic benchmark by granting the Meghwals something Jats are not ready to give up.

When a legal system doesn't reflect the desires and values of certain groups, members of these communities often feel betrayed by the state. This frequently results in a desire to take the law into their "own hands" (Abrahams 1998; Goldstein 2003). Taking the law into one's own hands is a "communicative act" (Goldstein 2003, 25), a critique of what society is becoming. The communicative intent is also common to hate crimes. Scholars and policy makers have struggled to find a definition of hate crime which covers the varied modes of violence, bias, and antagonism that socially marginalized communities face when they try to claim greater social and political space. However, one common ingredient in all hate crimes is the perpetrator's motivation to keep marginalized communities in their place by communicating that attempts to transgress established social hierarchies will have violent consequences (Chakraborti and Garland 2013; Walters 2022).

Sending a message vis-à-vis "proper" caste hierarchies is precisely what the historically dominant Jat community hoped to do in Dangawas. The mob attack and subsequent killings were attempts to undercut state laws that were meant to change structures of historical inequality. Chinma Ram Jat's family, accustomed to caste impunity in a context where their own social and agricultural power was well established, saw Ratna Ram Meghwal's actions as defying the "correct" social order. Hence, both Dalit and Jat understandings of the Dangawas massacre, while radically divergent in their experiential dimensions, are based in the recognition that the plot of land represents much more than its agricultural yield or financial value. It is a field of war on which competing understandings of social order are battled out.

For Ratna Ram Meghwal and his remaining family, the plot is a symbol of what must be changed and gained if Meghwals are to live in peace and finally have their space. For the Jats, the plot of land represents a novel status precarity that must be combatted.

The history of the princely state of Jodhpur further illuminates the reasons behind Jat status anxieties. In Jodhpur state, which formerly encompassed what is now known as Nagaur district, resistance against Rajput rule and land tenure systems started in the 1920s and was led by the Jat community. However, the history of Nagaur's Jats is not only one of opposition against Rajput supremacy but also one that speaks of desires for upward caste mobility or even Sanskritization—the emulation of upper-caste customs (see Srinivas 1952). Jats founded an independent peasant organization, the Marwar Kisan Sabha, in 1946 to reform and purify their caste community (Sisson 1969, 948) through opportunities in nontraditional employment and access to Western education. While this helped Jats to challenge dominant elites of the Rajput caste by establishing economic and political power, the community's social reputation and claims to ritual purity with respect to the higher castes like Rajputs and Brahmins, remain precarious. The prospect of ceding space to Meghwals and potentially showing weakness was, therefore, seen as politically risky.

In Nagaur, Jats and other dominant castes often tried to mobilize the history of Rajasthan's land reforms to justify violence against Meghwals. In May of 2017 I secured an interview with Mr. X, a high ranking, upper-caste police officer in Jaipur, who had been stationed in Nagaur during the Dangawas massacre. When I asked him to share his thoughts on the Dangawas incident Mr. X seemed annoyed. "Of course, the actual attack was bad. But, in my opinion, it was simply an unfortunate escalation of a land ownership dispute that was much more complicated than the Meghwals claim. The family actually tilling the land since the 1960s, was that of Chinma Ram Jat. The land reforms specified that land was to be redistributed to the tillers. So, the Jats have claims too."

Similar sentiments were expressed by a Jat High Court lawyer in Jaipur who had relatives in Nagaur. He was not sympathetic to what he called the "casteist narrative (*jātibadi wāli kahāni*)." He told me that the Merta revenue court had obviously not been paying attention to the precedents set by the land reforms that promised land to those who tilled it when it failed to take the Jat claims seriously.

The argument put forth by Mr. X and the Jat lawyer is deeply contentious. The state of Rajasthan officially came into being on April 7, 1949. The newly formed state government was committed to the abolition of all *jāgīrdari* land tenure practices (see introduction). In 1952 the Rajasthan government introduced the Rajasthan Land Reforms and Resumption of Jagirs Act, which was the first direct step towards land redistribution (Iyer 1995; Rawal 2015). The Resumption Act gave the state permission to repossess and redistribute *jāgir* lands "upon providing compensation to the former *jāgirdars* (landowners)" (Kumar 2001, 266).[7] Then in 1955 the Rajasthan Tenancy Act was introduced to facilitate the redistribution effort and provide "a unified law to deal with land tenure." The act specified that "from then forward land belonging to members of the Scheduled Castes or Tribes could only be sold and bought by other members of the Scheduled Castes/Tribes" (Shanmugaratnam 1996, 170). Two years later, in December 1957, the Rajasthan government officially resumed all rights on *jāgir* lands for redistribution, providing compensation to former owners that amounted to seven times the net income from the land (Rudolph and Rudolph 2011; Rawal 2015).

However, Dalit gains from these land redistribution schemes were limited. This first phase of the Indian land reforms directed against established systems of intermediary land tenures (like *jāgīrdari* and *zamindari* models in Rajasthan) questionably invoked tilling rights as the main axis of redistribution. Critics of this reform model have pointed out that the slogan "Land to the Tiller" excluded "poor peasants, landless laborers and the entire group of service castes subsumed . . . as none of them were considered tillers" (Singh 2014, 179).

According to this policy, only those who had been *tenants*, and not those who had been cultivating the lands as *wage workers*, were considered tillers (Chattopadhyay 1975). Tenants were usually members of the Other Backward Castes, like Jats, who employed Dalit wage laborers under exploitative conditions. A report by *ActionAid India* entitled "Land to the Tiller" (2016) specified that "inferior tenants, for example, sharecroppers, tenants at will, contract farmers, and those engaged in cultivating *khudkasht* (personal cultivation)" effectively lost access to land in the reform policies (Trivedi 2016, 2). For Rajasthan, the report also stresses the issue of "concealed tenancies." Even when agricultural land was transferred to lower-caste communities like Dalits and successfully registered in their names, much of that land was still not being cultivated by these communities. Informal contracts, mortgages, or refusals to accept repayment for mortgaged land, as in Dangawas, were only some of the ways in which former landowners like Rajputs or politically dominant Jat groups retained de facto control of land.

Given this historical backdrop it becomes evident that by evoking tilling rights in favor of the Jat perpetrators, Mr. X and the Jat High Court lawyer are skillfully manipulating the narrative of Dangawas. Their reference to the "Land to the Tiller" motto is intended to turn the Dangawas massacre from a story of brutal caste-based violence into one of competing, legally valid land claims, one of which is simply ignored by a state that has stylized itself as the protector of Dalits. In this narrative Ratna Ram Meghwal infringed on a space that may have rightfully belonged to the Jats.

In an analysis of the Karamchedu massacre in Andhra Pradesh, where six Dalits were killed at the hands of the agriculturally dominant *Kamma* caste, Dag Erik Berg has argued that caste hierarchies and violence against Dalits often intensify when "landowning peasant castes [emerge] as a dominant and politically powerful caste" (Berg 2014, 384). This analysis finds reflection in the expression of Jat solidarity in the aftermath of the Dangawas clash and the perception that Dalits had come to display unacceptable audacity.

These sentiments mirror the dynamics at the heart of hate crimes: socially dominant communities consider assertive action by members of historically stigmatized groups an infringement on their own economic and political space and resort to violence to counter this assertion. These acts of violence are intended to—quite literally—put the traditionally inferior community back in its place.

RECONNECTION, SPACE, AND VIOLENT BOUNDARIES

During our visit to Dangawas, Advocate Gaurav from Ajmer, who had introduced me to Ratna Ram's family, arranged for some Meghwal men who had survived the events of May 14 to assemble at the deceased Ratna

Ram's house. For hours we listened to their stories and their fears. At one point an older Meghwal man, who had been sitting silently on the sidelines, spoke up: "We want to live in peace and without fear on our land (*shānti se aura binā ḍara apani zamīna para jīna hai*), but for that we need people's thoughts (*soca*) to change. If the thoughts of Jats don't change, violence will happen when we demand our rights. Of course, we want justice under the law (*kānūna se hama nayā cāhate hain*) but the law does not live in the village."

Another man nodded. "He is right," he said, "What can law do about the fact that every hour I fear my neighbor will murder me?" The men's words powerfully unearthed that moments of profound violence, and the trauma that follows, can temporarily alter how survivors assert themselves, and to what extent they can imagine possibilities of justice and recognition in a ruptured social world (Das 2006; Lester 2013).

For the Meghwals of Dangawas, the continued possibility of murder at the hands of their Jat neighbors exposed the emptiness of the very concept of community. Analyses of mass violence have highlighted that the question of how people can kill their own neighbors, which often gets posed after massacres, makes a fatal category mistake: it equivocates physical proximity with shared respect and sociality (Belleau 2022, 3). The Meghwal men of Dangawas had been shocked into this realization by the events of May 14, 2015. They knew that as long as casteist mindsets prevailed, there was no true village community in Dangawas. What mattered was the hierarchy of caste.

Caste atrocities are usually the direct result of Dalits refusing to accept the parameters of freedom and partial inclusion awarded to them within the framework set up by upper-caste Hindus (Jodkha 2015, 63–64; Waghmore 2018). At first sight, the growing representation of Dalits in white-collar jobs, as well as laws like the Atrocities Act, may give the impression that caste hierarchies are indeed waning in India (Kaviraj 2000; Gupta 2004; Waghmore 2018). However, increasing numbers of caste atrocities reveal that the caste model of visible hierarchy, based on purity and exclusion, has simply been replaced with a more subtle one. Dalit access to new educational opportunities within the modern state and capitalist market, and the increasing levels of "caste competition" (Waghmore 2018, 113) which follow, have not resulted in greater caste-based equality. Instead, historically dominant castes now see themselves as graciously granting Dalits a modicum of space in society.

However, when Dalits claim more than the resources and space higher-caste groups are content to politely cede, the latter react with violence. Violence is the boundary marker that tells Dalits: "We have given you this much, don't take more!" The thin veneer of "politesse" that is suspended over caste relations in contemporary India is itself "a form of atrocity that violates [Dalit] rights" (Waghmore 2018, 135).

Before the violence of May 14, 2015, Ratna Ram Meghwal openly rejected a system which demanded that he operate within a Jat-approved social framework and hierarchy. Filing a case in the revenue court, taking up his father's battle for land, and confidently building his house on the plot, he was not concerned with village peace or Jat discontent. He wanted a more radical social transformation for himself and his community. His assertiveness was brutally countered. Now, Ratna Ram's open demand for equal rights has given way to a painful insight among his surviving relatives: Along with assertion, Jat minds would also have to be decasted. Otherwise, the fields of massacre would spread.

LEGAL BAND-AIDS: PUNISHMENT AND HOLLOW JUSTICE

Despite the hovering shadow of their atrocity case, I hardly ever heard Meghwal survivors in Dangawas speak of law. One afternoon I sat in the kitchen with some of the women as they made chapatis. I was watching entranced as Anu produced one perfectly round chapati after another at record speed, when she said something that jolted me back to reality: "I know you are doing research on this act," she began, "and I think that's important . . . but all this talk about courts and CBI investigations. I often feel far away from it. Tell me, how will this law give me a better life?"

I felt uneasy. Anu's words reminded me of Pinky, who had repeatedly been distressed by the fact that "her" case under the Atrocities Act was far removed from her own experience: though registered in her name, the case became something everyone was engaging with and acting upon—other than herself. It dawned on me then that Satyanarayan G.'s compromise, as cruel it had been for activists and her father, and as problematic as it had been in terms of the power dynamics it represented, may have been a true relief for her. It had allowed her to return to the concerns that dominated her daily life and had, at least, given her some comparatively better opportunities by enabling her marriage.

This brings the limitations of hate crime law as a response to extreme violence into sharp focus. In Dangawas, the Atrocities Act, and even the idea of official, public justice, emerge as a hollow promise because ordinary social life is fragile or even dangerous. In Dangawas, the family that was lost would never return, and the well of prejudice that was at the root of the massacre was unlikely to dry out.

This resonates with scholarly arguments which have pinpointed the problematic assumptions at the heart of transitional justice efforts. "Transitional justice," a term that came to prominence in the 1990s (Teitel 2000, Teitel 2008), aimed to capture the potential of human rights regimes and international law to redress historical acts of violent injustice (Hinton 2010) and produce deeper democratic transformations (Mani 2008). Globally, transitional justice has encompassed the establishment of international war tribunals as well as the introduction of national commissions to hear and compensate those who were harmed by oppressive regimes (one famous example is the Truth and Reconciliation Commission in South Africa). However, anthropologists have argued that the emphasis on justice and reconciliation glosses over the tensions and frictions that bureaucratic efforts to change the future by repairing the past can create in communities (Tsing 2005; also Wagner 2010). Alexander Hinton argues that transitional justice bureaucracies often fail to interrogate whether "universalist assumptions about the benefits of justice accord with what people think on the ground" (Hinton 2010, 5). The abstracted modes of top-down justice delivery that transitional justice bureaucracies introduce to equalize the playing field of history can ring hollow for survivors of massacres and their kin and interfere with local ways of coming to terms with a brutal past (Ferrándiz and Robben 2015).

Dangawas reveals that many of these critiques are also valid in the context of hate crime law. The Atrocities Act was indeed "far away," as many survivors claimed. On the one hand, it could not engage the language through which the Meghwal survivors of Dangawas expressed their understanding of oppression: the metaphor of space and land. On the other hand, it failed to capture what survivors saw to be essential for restitution: a change of mind and the creation of a decasted sociality.

Dangawas survivors wanted restitution: to reclaim their physical world—their neighborhood, their village—as well as their symbolic space in society, but on terms that were acceptable to them. More than just negotiating formal justice, characterized by court convictions, they tied their search for restitution to the landscape of economic and social interaction they inhabited (comp. Satterlee 2006, 71). Many of the Dangawas survivors focused on the notions of "land" and "space" to convey their understanding of restitution and justice. They wanted land, the physical and metaphorical space, which signifies economic security and belonging. Land signifies the right to take up social space equal to other caste communities, which is essential to a life defined by an absence of violence. At the same time, Anu's repeated evocation of peace springs from a continuing post-traumatic experience of constant dread and fear, even after the actual moment of brutality has long passed. One of the women who had been injured during the attack told me: "There were always insults and casteism, but it was still my village. Now it's different. We have no space and no home (*na jagaha na ghara*). Sometimes it feels like nothing can be ok again (*kabhī kabhī aisā lagata hai jaisā kucha ṭīka nahīn ho sakata hai*)."

The sadness, fear, and disillusionment of the Dangawas survivors capture the inability of law to address the root causes of violence, even when hate crime law has been devised precisely to stop violent prejudice in its tracks (Marks 2011). Once again, the notion of "space" (*jagaha*) captures an understanding of restitution, which treats claims for redistribution (economic restructuring) and recognition (cultural and symbolic change) as equally valid dimensions (Fraser 1998).

This idea of restitution is set up in opposition to the justice-as-punishment option offered by the Atrocities Act. Punishment is vertical, top-down justice through formal institutions, while *jagaha* represents a social landscape of justice anchored in land and people: justice that comes from within and is inextricably linked to the notion of equality.

As the memory of violence hung heavily over Dangawas, the Atrocities

Act with its promise of validation by a distant state bureaucracy simply missed the point. As Dangawas survivors mapped their suffering onto the world around them, they had to reconcile the recent memories of violence with a sense of loss over a home that had never existed. Punishment of the perpetrators through the Atrocities Act was a necessary element in their quest for justice and equality, but it was also a mere band-aid, which could never rip out the roots of caste-based violence.

BETWEEN ASSERTION AND RESIGNATION
When I left Dangawas last in September 2017, I felt like a curtain had been lifted: like I had stepped out of a frozen scenery back into a moving world. In some ways, the sense of paralysis that hung over Dangawas was the result of the continued grief and undigested trauma with which the Meghwal community was still coming to terms. However, it also highlighted the internally contradictory nature of the Atrocities Act and of hate crime legislation more widely.

The massacre of Dangawas fit the definition of a hate crime neatly. Yet, ironically, it seemed that it was precisely this type of violence the Atrocities Act was least able to handle or challenge. When trying to fight and prevent the types of massacres that had inspired P. S. Krishnan to draft the Atrocities Act as a law that would counter violence that flows from "the top of the social hierarchy to the bottom" (Krishnan, pers. comm., January 2018), the law stumbled. Casteism or other forms of prejudice and structural oppression are always woven into the social, cultural, and historical landscapes of their homelands. These beliefs, attitudes, and practices have become part of everyday actions (MacMullan 2009), mindsets, and interactions (Guru and Sarukkai 2019). Hence, hate crimes are not incidents but processes (Bowling 1993) that represent the boiling point of normalized social hierarchies and biases (Botha and Kok 2019). For Dangawas' Meghwals, who were still embedded in these hierarchies and biases, the Atrocities Act shot through their world like a sharp arrow that missed the mark. Punishment and deterrence, the two motivations at the heart of the act, were unable to reconfigure social relations; therefore the law left them exposed to further harm.

"Punishment is a tricky thing," Advocate Gaurav said to me when we sat on the bus returning to Ajmer. "Part of me wants to see all these Jats hanged, and I think we really need to win this case in court because that sends a message to people like them. It says: you can't go around committing crimes like this against Dalits anymore. But then again . . . punishment . . . Does it really make dominant castes not want to commit these crimes or does it just make them angrier? I don't doubt that punishment is necessary. But I wonder if it is enough . . . !"

In Rajasthan's public discourse, an avalanche of newspaper reports, activist demonstrations, the CBI investigation, and the ongoing court case have turned Dangawas into an exemplar of the caste atrocity. In this context, the Atrocities Act has emerged as a necessary means to address the cruelty of Dangawas. But my own time in Dangawas left me wondering about the social impact of hate crime law: What did the Atrocities Act really mean in survivors' lives? How did it touch them?

I learned that, in the face of sheer brutality, the Atrocities Act itself was pushed to the limits of meaning. As the expression of a slow-moving, impersonal, bureaucratic state apparatus, which, as the Dangawas survivors repeatedly highlighted, was "far away," the ongoing case under the Atrocities Act could not give the Meghwals of Dangawas the sense of safety they needed. Moreover, the court case, which hung over the village as an eternal reminder of the extreme forms of rejection and oppression Meghwals were subjected to, was in some ways experienced as an obstacle to restitution by the survivors of the massacre. They sometimes perceived it as an external force which directed the social developments in the village and shaped their own grieving process without being able to provide anything socially meaningful.

In the face of the most extreme hate, the Atrocities Act fell silent. Dangawas shows that hate crime laws—even ones that are usually actively negotiated by marginalized groups—often fail to hit at the antagonistic mindsets and normalized hierarchies which lie at the core of caste violence. They can create new pathways to resistance, new agencies in- and outside of court, and even new hope, but they cannot immediately grant stigmatized communities a life with rights and without fear. The Meghwals of Dangawas knew this, and so the Atrocities Act hovered across their landscape like an empty promise.

The Dangawas I encountered was neither an emblem for Dalit assertion nor a marker of resignation in the face of caste oppression (Fuchs 2020a). What lay behind the overreported and politically overdetermined moment of the Dangawas massacre was a group of people still trying to come to terms with their own suffering (Purohit 2018) in a village that was still largely in the grips of their attackers: people who lived in the shadow of violence, from which state officials could have protected them and chose not to. Their words force us to acknowledge that, like transitional justice efforts, hate crime laws can at times be powerless, and even counterproductive, in the face of the most inhuman violence (Hinton 2010).

After the initial attack *Frontline* reported: "Dangawas will never be the same anymore. . . . . The general feeling is that one had to abide by what the 'village' wanted, which is a euphemism for the dominant community. 'Had Ratnaram succeeded in his objective of securing titular possession of the land, he would have opened a Pandora's box,' said a lawyer on condition of anonymity" (Rajalakshmi 2015).

Still, the ongoing legal case, the arrest of many of the perpetrators, a continuing outpouring of public support, and the passage of time have given some of the surviving Meghwals a sense of potentiality: a vision of the day they will rise up once more to challenge and resist. When I said goodbye to Anu, she told me: "One day, we can fight again! But we must get ok on the inside first and find a way to think about the next steps. . . . Maybe law can help with that?"[8]

As the next chapter will show, law can indeed sometimes help with that. The promises of the Atrocities Act may have rung hollow in Dangawas but, under different conditions, the promises of hate crime law can become saturated with meaning.

SEVEN

HABITS OF HOPEFULNESS
Legal Labors for a Better Future

AUNTY-JĪ WAS OFTEN FRUSTRATED with lawyers. "The thing about lawyers is," she declared one day, as she forcefully placed a plate of biscuits in front of her tenant, who was completing a law degree in Jaipur, "they always tell you not to get your hopes up. How stupid! The reason I get a lawyer is because I want to hope. If I didn't hope, I would not fight a case. Lawyers need to understand that it is their job to help us hope." With those words she quickly wiped her eyes with the corner of her sari. The tenant stared at the floor.

I had been observing the scene from the balcony along with Sonali, who also rented a room from Aunty-jī. We had expected an entertaining interlude, since lecturing her younger tenants under the pretense of tea and biscuits was one of Aunty-jī's preferred past times. But today there was nothing humorous about her rant and we all knew why. One year ago, in January 2016, Aunty-jī's youngest son, Ragu, a promising young doctor, had committed suicide after being tortured by five members of the Brahmin caste. His case was still pending in court.

At the very beginning of this book (Scene 1), I briefly introduced Aunty-jī. I recounted how she lost Ragu, who had fallen in love with a young Brahmin girl called Karishma at university. The two had married in secret but when Karishma's family got wind of the marriage, her father told Karishma that she had destroyed the family honor by marrying the lowest type of man there was: "a damn dirty Dalit (*gandā Chamar, sāla*)." He disowned Karishma, and she went to live with her new husband and Aunty-jī in Jaipur. Karishma suffered deeply from the loss of her family and always prayed for reconciliation. I met her in December of 2015, when I first came to Rajasthan with my mother, who had worked in India for many years. As Karishma watched Aunty-jī prepare lunch and chat to my mother she teared up. "It is so nice you are here with your mummy," she said, "I miss my mother. She doesn't talk to me anymore!"

Months later when I had returned to my university in the United Kingdom and Karishma was pregnant, it appeared that her wish to be reunited with her mother would come true. Karishma's family contacted her and Ragu and invited them to Delhi. But, as I revealed at the start of the book, the invitation was a trap. When the couple arrived at Karishma's family home, Ragu was tortured and kidnapped by Karishma's brothers, who left him in a sewage canal (*nālī*) near Gurugram. His father came to his aid and brought him to a hospital in Jaipur. But Ragu was heartbroken when Karishma asked for a divorce. The day after Ragu was released from the hospital, he threw himself under an approaching train. He left behind a letter for his brother. Ragu wrote: "I have been made to feel like I am nothing and my love is a burden, and that will never change. This is not the life I want."

After Ragu's suicide, Aunty-jī's family was devastated. They no longer slept, and Ragu's brother feverishly reread Ragu's letter for nights on end. Quickly, their sadness turned into anger. "Ragu was a happy man," Uncle-jī, Aunty-jī's husband, often said, "He just wanted to be a good husband and they made him feel like he wasn't worth it. Even if it was technically suicide, this was murder, murder because of caste."

The disgust and violence Karishma's family had expressed were difficult to bear for Ragu's parents, who belonged to a small group of urban and upwardly mobile Meghwals in Rajasthan. Though raised in relative poverty in a village in Rajasthan's eastern Dausa district, Aunty-jī and Uncle-jī had moved to Jaipur after getting married at eighteen. For three decades they built an impressive life. Uncle-jī worked himself up to a managerial position in one of Jaipur's better-known hotels, which he held until retirement in 2015. His job allowed his family to steadily climb up the socioeconomic ladder and acquire many material and habitual markers of Indian middle-class status, such as education and discretionary income (Donner 2011). The family constructed a big four-story house in a nice neighborhood and rented out the bottom two flats. They sent their sons to good, private schools, and went on family holidays to South India. Ragu's older brother, Ramesh, completed a degree in engineering and held a prestigious government job in the city of Ajmer. Meanwhile, Ragu studied medicine and worked at a hospital in Jaipur. When I first met the family in December 2015 and told them about my research topic, Uncle-jī expressed his approval. He thought it was important for someone to do research on the "weak" (*kamazora*) sections of the Meghwal community who still suffered from caste discrimination. "Families like ours are different," I remember him telling me, "No one even realizes we are Dalits. The atrocities that you are talking about happen to people who are uneducated and live in villages."

When I returned eight months later, Ragu was dead and Uncle-jī's world had fallen apart. Ragu's torture had shown him that his move up the class ladder had not changed how his caste status was perceived by upper-caste families. Uncle-jī had become a disillusioned man, haunted by grief. He admitted to me: "Now I realize that to others we are always untouchables regardless of how educated my children are. People won't say it, but deep inside it's all still there."

The family decided to not let Ragu's fate be forgotten and registered a complaint against Karishma's father and brothers in February 2016. In the First Information Report (FIR) the complaint was recorded under sections 354 (grievous hurt) and 362 (abduction) of the IPC. Moreover, Ragu's parents insisted on the addition of IPC section 306 (abetment of suicide) which accused Karishma's family of instigating or compelling Ragu to take his own life. Finally, the complaint was registered under the Atrocities Act citing hate speech under sections 3(1)(r), 3(1)(s). Sections 3(2)(v) and 3(2)(va) of the Atrocities Act were also applied to enhance punishments for IPC sections 354 and 362. Ragu's brother hoped that there could be justice for Ragu even after death, and that his story would show the world that Meghwals would fight for justice . Aunty-jī concurred: "We have hope and faith (*ummīda aura vishvāsa*) that this isn't the end of Ragu's story. That's what this Atrocities Act is for—to make things better!"

TOWARDS LEGAL MELIORISM

I return to Aunty-jī's story in this final chapter for two reasons. First, because her grief, as well as her stubborn determination, was a journey that I experienced most intimately. Aunty-jī was not a woman I sought out in the context of my research, and I never interviewed her formally. Aunty-jī was my friend first and foremost. I had met her upon my initial visit to Jaipur because she was Sonali's landlady. Back then she was a content woman, who loved to laugh and stuff me with *puri*s (fried bread). When I returned, Aunty-jī's laughter seemed to have died with Ragu. Although she always insisted on hoping, her story still haunts me today. It is one of the reasons I wrote this book. Ragu's fate and his family's grief are living proof that caste atrocities are deep wounds, which families carry with them for the rest of their lives.

However, there is a second reason I discuss Aunty-jī's experience here, at the end of the book. Her family's search for justice illustrates an exceedingly rare lived experience of hate crime law: an experience which indicates that, in the face of a tragedy like Ragu's, the Atrocities Act can remain an important, hopeful resource for survivors. Considering the monstrousness of Ragu's final days, and the habitual institutional obstacles that are laid in the path of atrocity complainants, Aunty-jī's insistence on hope was surprising. Aunty-jī was a woman who, like the survivors of Dangawas, had lost all faith in the social structures she inhabited. Hence I expected the law to ring hollow in her ears. Yet her story ultimately unveiled the flipside of Dangawas. Following the most unimaginable of losses, the text of the Atrocities Act can sometimes become a pathway to hopeful practice: this hopefulness grows out of the new modes of collective legal laboring, which the Atrocities Act engenders as a normative, authoritative document. Though the language of hope Aunty-jī used was imbued with religious undertones, this hopefulness was also deeply pragmatic at its core; it was driven by the idea that even if things can never be good, they can be made comparatively *better* through consistent, determined effort (Fiala 2019).

The voices of Dangawas prove that experiences of brutal, targeted violence can cause an utter loss of faith in the grammar of ordinary sociality (Das 2006, 7). They cast doubt on the potential of hate crime law to bring a sense of restitution. Meanwhile, Pinky's story showed us in chapter 2 how violent performances can become a productive site of power for those who claim to speak on behalf of survivors (Das 1995, 2001; Brass 1997). Other chapters have highlighted how the Atrocities Act has given rise to new subversive practices, political and economic micro-agencies, and even strategic attempts to rewrite legal truth regimes. While hope latently exists in all these cases, any explicit reference to *hope in the law* has been markedly absent in these tales of negotiation. In contrast, hope was the crucial ingredient in Aunty-jī's experience of the Atrocities Act. As she stated so confidently, atrocity survivors file and fight cases because they hope that the world can be different.

Therefore, this last chapter analyzes the Atrocities Act as a site of something I call the *meliorist hope complex*: a cluster of practices, attitudes, and imaginaries which give rise to a belief that the future can bring meaningful justice through persistent engagement with hate crime law. I explore the conditions under which the "hard cash" (Habermas 2010, 345) of formal law can emerge as a meaningful horizon of future possibility, and for sustained positive emotions (Abrams & Keren 2007) in the aftermath of caste atrocities. However, in the context of these hate crimes, hope cannot be understood as a self-explanatory ethnographic fact or even as uniform emotion or practice. Anthropologists have often discussed hope as an indispensable ingredient of social life. Yet they have often frequently underexplored the links between how people act or hopefully position themselves in the world and the conditions that shape their disposition to do so. Hope in anthropological studies is typically shown to be crucial to agency "as it complicates the relationship between what people do and the circumstances that constrain them" (Kavedžija 2016, 2) and represents a "reorientation of knowledge" towards a future goal (Miyazaki 2006, 149).

Here hope is an expression of what Arjun Appadurai calls "the capacity to aspire" (Appadurai 2013, 179). However, these analyses largely neglect to analyze how the capacity to hope or aspire is shaped by circumstances and experiences of oppression. Just as the sociolegal imaginary of hate crime law becomes fractured through political and gender-based negotiations, hope emerges as a disaggregated orientation and practice in the context of caste atrocities. As Laurence Ralph argues, diverse social conditions result in different kinds of "dreams," "aspirations," and "strategies for social change" (Ralph 2014, 6–7). Similarly, there exists no single understanding or exercise of hope among atrocity survivors. The different social and economic conditions in which survivors are embedded give rise to varied forms of hopefulness and anticipatory orientations, which steer their strategic engagement with the Atrocities Act.

This chapter compares two journeys of hope: Aunty-jī's and that of a young Dalit woman called Anisha. Anisha belonged to the Balai sub-caste (*jāti*), which in some parts of Rajasthan and Madhya Pradesh is synonymous with the Meghwal *jāti* (Snodgrass 2006). Her family lived in a village in Rajasthan's Sikar district, which borders on Jhunjhunu and is also part of the Shekhawati region. Anisha lost her two younger sisters to suicide after they were sexually assaulted by two boys of the dominant Rajput caste in their village.

Aunty-jī's and Anisha's ways of hoping bore important similarities. Both women and their families articulated a similar, quasi-religious belief in the Atrocities Act as a textual horizon of justice and a better future. Anisha's and Aunty-jī's hopeful practice abstracted the Atrocities Act as a visionary written document from the day-to-day institutional failures of individual atrocity cases. They conceived of the act as a normative, and even sacred, manuscript, which functioned as an almost supernatural symbol of a better and more caste-equal society—a society as it "should be." This belief in the Atrocities Act as an "authoritative text" (Pirie 2013, 146) was rooted in the profound disillusionment with the ordinary social environments both women lived through. Their family members had committed suicide after being violated by intimate family and village relations. This inspired an unrelenting faith in both women; faith in the Atrocities Act as a law, which uniquely existed to protect Dalits. For Aunty-jī and Anisha, holding onto their legal cases was a way of orienting themselves towards a better future (Bryant and Knight 2019), which was still a distant dream but would eventually unfold if they followed the right legal path.

However, their hope in the potential of the Atrocities Act to bring about this better future was neither static fact nor blind or passive idealism. Rather, it was the source of a stubborn resolve to improve official mechanisms of justice delivery. Both women worked for their legal cases with gritty determination to gradually transform a barren landscape of caste violence, police corruption, and judicial bias into a world where justice for their loved ones was possible. Hope, for Anisha and Aunty-jī, lay in the act of laboring itself. The Atrocities Act became an active site for the creation of hopeful habits, which were sustained by the belief that they owed it to the people they had lost to "push beyond dark times" (Shade 2001, 7). Their hope was defined neither by an idea of continuous progress nor by its utopian end point. Rather, it captured something pragmatist philosophers like John Dewey have referred to as *meliorism*: "the belief that the specific conditions, which exist at one moment, . . . may be bettered" through persistent, targeted action (Dewey 1963, 178). The Atrocities Act was the platform on which Aunty-jī and Anisha embarked on a journey to transform the world that had harmed their loved ones and to make it comparatively better. The act-as-text served as a constant reminder that a better world *should* be possible, and that Dalit communities had the right to insist on steadily reshaping their environment until it fell in line with the vision of an equal society. However, most importantly, the Atrocities Act became an arena that allowed for the creation of new communities that made this more equal society appear within reach.

Yet, despite their shared hopeful labor, Anisha's and Aunty-jī's differences in upward mobility and social environment also gave rise to distinct modes of hoping. These differences translated into variations in the longevity of their legal cases and the temporal orientations of their legal engagements. While Aunty-jī and her family are pursuing Ragu's case until this day, Anisha and her family eventually dropped their complaint under the Atrocities Act. This illustrates the role of socioeconomic circumstances in the development of hope (Jakimov 2016). For many rural families in India, who remain enmeshed in traditional agricultural work and lack significant financial resources, hope is defined by its fragility: it amounts to a practice of hesitantly looking towards a future that is always threatening to vanish. For Anisha, hopeful legal labor was shaped by harsh realities of village dependency, which eventually caused her family to abandon its case. Like the Meghwals of Dangawas, Anisha knew that, in the present and near future, any hope for official justice had to be negotiated within the family's village environment.

This temporal orientation stood in stark contrast to Aunty-jī's framework of hope, which was forever fixed on a distant future horizon. This shows that distinct temporal articulations of hope can reflect differences in power and indicate unequal social relationship. Anisha's and Aunty-jī's stories tell us that, despite its many failures, its meaninglessness in the face of abject brutality, and the questions it raises about legal regimes of truth, the Atrocities Act has become a crucial pillar of aspirational engagement in Rajasthan. The act offers a bureaucratically grounded reference point for hope, which allows many survivors to cultivate new habits of resistance, not despite its character as a formal law, but because of it.

TREACHEROUS SOCIALITIES
Aunty-jī

At the time of Ragu's passing, Aunty-jī had been Sonali's landlady for four years. Throughout this time the women had become close friends. Sonali had a twelve-year-old daughter, Nisha, who had come to regard Aunty-jī as motherly figure in her own right. Sonali's husband suffered from ill health and could not work. Therefore Nisha often stayed behind with Aunty-jī and took care of her father when Sonali was called out on fact-finding missions in her function as the Rajasthan state coordinator of the All India Dalit Women's Forum (AIDMAM). Before taking over as AIDMAM coordinator, Sonali had worked for the Centre for Dalit Rights (CDR) in Jaipur, and she still maintained good relationships with many former colleagues.

Over the years of knowing Sonali, Aunty-jī had been introduced into the NGO and activist circles in Rajasthan. So it was no surprise when, after Ragu's death, she turned to Sonali and the CDR—Mr. Nairoth's legal aid NGO in Jaipur—to help her advance her legal case. She spent hours in the CDR office strategizing with NGO advocates, while Uncle-jī routinely attended capacity building workshops held by the NGO. At these events he presented Ragu's story to other survivors who were considering filing a complaint. As time went on Sonali started to invite Aunty-jī along on fact-finding missions.

Initially, I worried that witnessing the suffering of other families and discussing atrocity cases would make it even harder for Aunty-jī to come to terms with Ragu's fate. But Sonali firmly rejected my worries. "This is good for Aunty-jī," she resolutely stated, "she can see how much good work is being done for people like her. She is a strong woman and this is helping her fight!" It seemed that despite the multiple ways in which Aunty-jī and Sonali tended to disagree about Ragu's case—who it was for and what it should mean—they agreed on this one point. One evening, when Sonali and I were discussing another case in her room, Aunty-jī joined us. As she watched Sonali strategize, she suddenly smiled: "It is good to be part of this group of people who are helping," she said, "especially when you have seen what people can do to you because you are still just an untouchable to them."

Her statement betrayed a radical disillusionment with the Indian social hierarchy and the prevailing casteist mindsets (*soca*) of higher-caste communities. Much like Avinesh's father in Jhunjhunu, who once proudly declared that "Meghwals in Jhunjhunu were moving from caste to class" (*Jhunjhunu mein hama Meghwal loga to caste se class mein cale jārahe hain*), Uncle-jī and Aunty-jī had believed that caste prejudice could be overridden by a middle-class habitus and economic progress. It was only the torture Ragu's own in-laws had inflicted on him which had thrown the flashing boundary lines of caste into stark focus. Aunty-jī and Uncle-jī had learned firsthand that violent acts can function as symbolic performances of power that convey wider social messages (Das 1995), and that caste atrocities are intended to reaffirm historical hierarchies of social power. However, as Aunty-jī's journey reveals, the deep disillusionment with ordinary social structures that accompanies experiences of hateful violence also gives rise to new needs, meanings, and aspirations (Peteet 1994; Schmidt & Schröder 2001).

Like all hate crimes, Ragu's torture was intended to send a message (Iganski 2001): that marriage between a Dalit and a Brahmin was still unfathomable, and that Dalits who dared to ignore this rule would be punished. Ragu committed suicide because he knew that—try as he might—he would never be able to overcome what Dalit student Rohith Vemula famously called the "fatal accident of [his] birth" before he also took his own life (Wire Staff 2019). Aunty-jī and Uncle-jī often said that witnessing the active destruction of their son's spirit and life had made them feel betrayed by society and people (*samāja aur loga*). The definitiveness of Ragu's death marked a complete break from the life they knew before and from the way they had positioned themselves in the world. It created a piercing realization that the society they had thought they were part of was a treacherous veneer. Their experience reflects the sentiments of poets and writers from Dalit backgrounds, who have described their communities and villages to be places that live a "double existence" (Sukirtharani 2012). They are sites of belonging, but also sites of suffering and oppression where Dalits are only selectively included and always at risk of rejection and harm (Thorat and Newman 2007, 4122). Some writers have described the neighborhoods they grew up in as a simultaneous source of tender memories and surreptitious hurt, emphasizing that this dual existence has carved caves of pain into their hearts (Lanjewar 1992).

However, unlike Pinky, Roop Singh, or the Meghwals of Dangawas, whose economic and social existence remained tied to the very village community that had brought them harm, Aunty-jī's and Uncle-jī's urban life and financial resources allowed them to find and build new, meaningful social networks. After Ragu's death, Aunty-jī's family sought new communities that could support their central goal: to avenge Ragu's death and convict his tormentors under the Atrocities Act. Aunty-jī's involvement with Sonali's work and the CDR in Jaipur made her feel like she belonged to a *better*, determined, and purposeful community, which could help families like hers by legally fighting prejudice. One day, as we were folding her saris, Aunty-jī told me: "Working with Sonali gives me hope, but this law [the Atrocities Act] also gives me hope (*ummīda*) that the world can be better." As an upwardly mobile urban woman, Aunty-jī found positive sociality in what Mayur Suresh has called the life of legal strategies and "technicalities" (Suresh 2023). By actively laboring for a good case outcome for Ragu and by inserting herself in a professional legal aid community, she was able to imagine that the tyranny of caste might one day fade.

Anisha

There was something in the Atrocities Act in its pure, written form that Aunty-jī always returned to when she spoke of hope (*ummīda*). And she spoke of hope often. The first time I met her after Ragu's death, I noticed a booklet on her coffee table. In bold black letters the cover declared: "The 1989 Scheduled Castes/Scheduled Tribes Prevention of Atrocities Act as amended in 2015." Aunty-jī caught me deciphering the title and smiled. "I always keep it near me," she said, "there is something beautiful about this law, the way it is written."

Her confession did not strike me as important at the time and I soon forgot about the interaction. It was only three months later, when Anisha, a young woman of the Balai *jāti* from the Sikar district, shared an uncannily similar sentiment that I began to consider the importance of Aunty-jī's words. In April 1017, Sonali and I were staying with her parents in Badrasar village, in Jhunjhunu, when she got a phone call from a former colleague at the CDR. The colleague told her about a recent incident involving two young Dalit girls in the district of Sikar, which borders on Jhunjhunu. Like Jhunjhunu, Sikar is part of the Shekhawati region. Based on Sonali's knowledge of the area and her work on gender issues, her colleague asked whether she would be willing to collaborate with the CDR and follow up on the case. Sonali agreed and so we caught the bus from Jhunjhunu to Sikar the next morning.

With a literacy rate of 72% Sikar is known as one of the most educationally advanced areas of Rajasthan state. The Dalit family, which we were due to visit, still lived in a village near Sikar town, where they owned and tended some land. However, they had recently made strides towards a more urbanized lifestyle. The family had five children: two sons and three daughters. The eldest son had moved to Sikar town to find employment as an accountant, while the younger son, Ramesh, was attending college to study engineering in Sikar. Anisha, the eldest daughter, worked as a teacher in another nearby town. Anisha had two younger sisters, Meena and Radha, who went to a high school in a neighboring village.

However, just as the family seemed to be looking towards a more financially promising future, they were hit with a devastating loss. Meena and Radha, who were sixteen and fourteen years of age, committed suicide after being brutally assaulted and raped by two boys of the dominant Rajput caste in the village within the confines of their own home. The girls knew the two Rajput boys from school. According to a neighbor, the girls' parents had been working in their field one day, when the boys came to the house and asked Radha and Meena for some tea. Suspecting no harm, the girls had agreed and invited the boys inside.

Soon after, their brother, Ramesh, had spontaneously returned home from college. When he entered the house, he found his young sisters struggling and pleading with their attackers. Utterly enraged he had grabbed a cricket bat and started attacking the boys. He chased them out of the house, and down the road until he eventually lost sight of them. Shaken, he turned around and went back home. However, when he got there Meena and Radha had disappeared. He called his sister Anisha, his older brother, and his parents and told them what had passed. Together, the family searched all afternoon, but the girls were nowhere to be found. Then, in the evening Anisha's phone rang. It was an officer from the local police station who asked her to identify the bodies of two girls. The girls were Radha and Meena, who had thrown themselves onto the train tracks.

When Sonali and I arrived at Anisha's house in April 2017, the brutality and tragedy of the story had drawn a large crowd. At least twenty activists from four different Rajasthani NGOs had made an appearance, along with the members of the village council (*pancāyata*) and the leadership of a local Balai caste association. As far as I could see they were all men. Together they were devising a strategy to ensure that the complaint the family was planning to register would be filed under the right sections of the IPC and the Atrocities Act and would subsequently be properly investigated by the police. Part of this strategy was to drum up media publicity around the incident. However, Sonali was uninterested in the meeting of big men. She wanted to speak to the girls' mother and their sister Anisha. After greeting Anisha's father and some of the other activists, we went inside the kitchen where Anisha and her mother sat, being consoled by other Balai women. When Sonali introduced herself, Anisha started sobbing. She cried for a long time, while her mother wept silently. Eventually she wiped her eyes with her mother's *dupatta* (scarf) and looked at us as she spoke: "Why do these things always happen to our [Dalit] girls? It's never Rajput or Jat girls in this village and still they say, oh, it is not about caste. It is about caste because people still believe Dalit girls are toys (*khilaunā*). All we can do is hope and believe that god gave us this law, this SC/ST [Atrocities] Act, so we can do something to find justice (*nyāya*) for my sisters."

As Sonali comforted the young woman and her mother, I was reminded of Aunty-jī. Anisha, too, had invoked the Atrocities Act as a platform for hope in a situation marked by extreme personal loss and a sense of social breakdown. Like Ragu, her sisters were no more. Like Ragu, her sisters had chosen to end their own lives after living through something that had ruptured their minds and bodies irreparably. Just like Pinky, they were terrified that in addition to bearing that pain they would have to live with the shame of no longer being considered respectable women. After the shock of being violated, the young girls had been unable to imagine a happy future for themselves. Seemingly, even death had been preferable to living as both outcasts and "fallen" women.

For Anisha and her family, Meena's and Radha's suicide brought not only unbearable suffering but a social disillusionment similar to the one Aunty-jī had faced. On the advice of local activists, Anisha's family decided to file a case under IPC sections 354 (assault or criminal force to woman with intent to outrage her modesty) and 306 (abetment of suicide). Moreover, the case was registered under section 3(w)(i) of the Atrocities Act (nonconsensual touching of a Dalit or Adivasi woman) and section 3(2)(va), which increases the punishment for offences under IPC section 354 when the assault is perpetrated against a Dalit or Adivasi woman. However, the other caste communities in the village turned against Anisha's family when they heard of the complaint. The dominant Rajput clan in the village was especially outraged that two of their own were being prosecuted under this "draconian" law. A delegation of Rajputs arrived at Anisha's family home shortly after Meena's and Radha's suicide and tried to threaten Anisha's father into dropping the case. But he stood his ground. "They are saying that our girls only killed themselves because they threw away their honor by getting involved with these boys and were discovered by their brother," he told Sonali and me when we followed up with the family a few weeks after the initial activist gathering. "They say my daughters were flirting. It is a lie! We must stick with this case to prove that our children were good and innocent. I know it is difficult. But I believe that *god* gave us this law for a reason!" He pointed at the paper copy of the Atrocities Act that was poking out of Sonali's bag and looked at her intently: " I hope and believe that this paper (*kāgaza*) has power (*dhama*) and will help us!"

These repeated appeals to hope, faith, and trust in a divine plan was curious to me in the context of everything I had learned about the social life of the Atrocities Act. In a country where entire Bollywood film franchises had been built on a widely shared disillusionment with the criminal legal system (I refer the reader to Jolly LLB), trust (*vishvāsa*) in the potential reckoning power of a single, politically divisive statute was astounding. It was Sonali who helped me understand the situation better. "If you lose faith in your village and your people (*gānva aura loga*)," she reflected on the way home, "you must find something else. A law like this is written and can't betray you the way people can! Look at Aunty-jī, she also keeps a little booklet of this act on her table."

I thought about her comparison. Anisha and Aunty-jī had much in common: They both grieved for people who were forever lost as the result of the violence Dalit communities continued to face, and they both actively labored for the restoration of their honor. And perhaps most importantly they appeared to conceptualize their quest for justice in relation to an almost sacred notion of law-as-text, which was bound up with wider, culturally situated, religious beliefs and Hindu practices.

HOPE-AS-TEXT

The attention Aunty-jī's and Anisha's families paid to the Atrocities Act as a "good" textual document, associated with ideas of divine intervention, exposes how the normative imaginary of hate crime law can resonate with local and personal ways of hoping and believing. This resonance exists even in, or perhaps because of, the absence of a criminal system that functions fairly for Dalits.

In studies of law, anthropologists have often given precedence to lived practice and steered away from textual engagements (Pirie 2013, 15; see also Abel 1995). This may be because the interpretation of legal texts and rules has historically been the realm of legal theorists, or because anthropological sensibilities are attuned to questions of experience and social negotiation, as showcased by the first part of this book. However, the role of the Atrocities Act as a document of entitlements and rights, which survivors and their communities can refer to, is significant.

In chapter 4 we saw how Meghwals in Jhunjhunu are attempting to enact procedural legal change through subversive institutional engagements, with the aim of holding criminal law accountable to the substantive vision of caste equality that is outlined in the *text* of the Atrocities Act. Meanwhile, chapter 5 traced how the Atrocities Act has emerged as a site for the construction of new strategic legal communities, who labor for the better implementation of the provisions and procedures of the act. While my interlocutors always acknowledged the impermanence of the Atrocities Act as a document that had been amended and could be subject to further change, the text itself, nonetheless, carried what Jonathan Parry has termed the "prestige" of the written word (Parry 1985, 207): the notion that texts expose a unique form of normative authority. Activists like Mr. Nairoth even regarded the Atrocities Act in its written form as an authentic representation of a just path to equality.

As Aunty-jī and Anisha show us, the perceived prestige of law-as-text could become an essential ingredient of hopeful practice for atrocity survivors in Rajasthan. For both, there is something almost "sacred" about the Atrocities Act, as it enshrines the possibility of future "good" and the idea that a higher power is watching over them. Here, the text of hate crime law represents a symbolic bridge between a life defined by oppression and imperfect institutional realities, and an idealized horizon of future justice.

The symbolic significance of the written legal text as a site of hope must be seen in the cultural context of Rajasthan, a state where many Meghwals and members of other Dalit communities remain devout Hindus and continue to be deeply embedded in Hindu practices. As I highlighted in the introduction, the Meghwal community in Rajasthan has actively attempted to position and reinvent itself as a ritually pure community *within* in the context of the Hindu caste system (Mullard 2010) rather than rejecting Hinduism completely. In this way Meghwals in Rajasthan stand in stark contrast to some Dalit communities in other parts of India that have converted to Buddhism in line with Ambedkarite ideals.

Aunty-jī and Anisha both strongly identified as Hindu. During the time I spent with Sonali, I came to know Aunty-jī as a woman who embraced daily religious routines. Even though she rejected the idea and practice of untouchability and deeply wished for caste equality, she never felt the need to abandon Hindu cosmology entirely. She had a little private shrine (*mandira*) in her living room that remained covered during the day, where she primarily worshiped the female mother goddess (*mātā*) in various incarnations. In particular, Aunty-jī prayed to Kalka Mātā, who is widely understood to represent a form of the goddess Kali and whose temples can be found across the state with prominent sites near Jaipur and in Sikar.

When Aunty-jī felt the pain of Ragu's loss particularly strongly she prayed to *mātā* to give her strength (*tākata*) and bring justice for her son. Her shrine also contained a large painting of Hanuman, whom she considered the god of righteous battles and who is often said to represent "power and devotion" in popular Hinduism (Lutgendorf 1997, 314). Aunty-jī prayed to Hanuman because she believed he aids those who fight the good fight, those who have a just cause.

Anisha too often turned to religion in the aftermath of her sisters' deaths. Like Aunty-jī, Anisha used her prayers to ask for specific legal outcomes. She prayed to Kalka Mātā for the conviction of the boys who harmed her sisters. She told me that the day their complaint under the Atrocities Act had been registered at the police station, she and her mother went to the *Mātā Mandir* (mother goddess temple) in their village to perform a ritual (*pūjā*). "She is a mother and will help us make this case strong. As Papa-jī (father) said, god gave us this law for a reason," Anisha declared. Her belief in the Atrocities Act as a law for Dalits was intimately bound up with her faith in a higher power, a transcendental being who had a cosmological plan beyond her immediate human comprehension.

The Hindu identity of women like Aunty-jī and Anisha is important: First, notions of divine moral order are systematically mapped onto legal codes in Hindu texts. Patrick Olivelle has argued that the very distinction between morality and law can be called into question in ancient Indian texts (Olivelle 2011). Instead, the entire realm of discourse and experience, which is demarcated through distinct terms like "law," "duty," and "social obligation" in modern scholarly discourse, is encompassed by the Sanskrit notion of *dharma* (Olivelle 2011, 25). Olivelle stresses that what liberal traditions tend to identify with the "legal" realm, namely a situation where law equals a system of rules governed by a state, which comes with a delightfully impervious set of formal administrative guidelines, is not a universally applicable concept. In Rajasthan this understanding of law fails to capture the lived experiences of authority, or the beliefs about order and justice, which have arisen around Hindu traditions of thought and practice.

The idea of written text as both law and guiding moral code, which outlines a clear path to a more just world, resonates strongly with my interlocutors' understanding of the Atrocities Act. To many of them, it was a law *for Dalits*, which had been introduced with the purpose of delineating a bureaucratic route to a society where oppression was not tolerated. Hate crime law in its documentary form thus comes to represent the basis for purposeful practice. When Aunty-jī or Anisha and her father refer to the Atrocities Act as a source of hope, given to them by god (*bhagavāna*), they invoke deeper Hindu discourses of legal texts as sites which depict moral order. Since their social world has proven to be unreliable, volatile, and dangerous, law-as-text materializes as a fixed horizon of belief and anticipation which is woven into existing cosmologies and religious practices.

Both families knew legal processes to be unpredictable and contingent on the biases and passions of institutional actors. They were under no illusion that fighting a case would be a simple feat. But the Atrocities Act as a little, inconspicuous, written booklet, which they could hold, read, and carry, still represented evidence for the wrongs that were done to them. It made their unjust suffering "explicit and public" (Pirie 2013, 145) and helped generate sentiments of defiance.

According to Jack Goody, the production of written texts allows societies to come to terms with the past by producing different futures (comp. Goody 1986, 154). Goody argues that written legislation is one of the central ways in which these new futures are imagined and created. While Aunty-jī and Anisha's faith in the Atrocities Act as a document of deep normative significance for Dalit futures echoes this argument, it also highlights something more. It shows how legal texts can become sites for the continued production of hopeful habits and attitudes through active legal labor.

"UMMĪDA KE ĀDATEIN": HOPEFUL HABITS
Aunty-jī

As Ragu's case was submitted to the special SC/ST court in Jaipur, Aunty-jī developed some new habits. Every morning she would read the newspapers, something she had never cared to do until Ragu's death. She would scour the *Rajasthan Patrika* with a black marker in hand, in search of stories that reminded her of Ragu's. When she found something, she noted down the details in a black-and-white college notebook. Then she would seek out Sonali to discuss the details of the incident: How was the reported incident similar to what happened to Ragu? How was it different? Would Sonali go out to fact-find in this incident? Finally, she would pull out her copy of the Atrocities Act and would try to match possible sections to the incident. Aunty-jī had no formal legal training, but with Sonali's help she tried to engage in legal labor: she tried for Ragu.

Then once a week Aunty-jī and Uncle-jī would put the notebook and their copy of the Atrocities Act in a bag and take an *autorikshaw* over to the CDR where they met with one of the advocates, and sometimes even Mr. Nairoth. They would get updates on Ragu's case and ask the team about the other incidents. They inquired whether the CDR had sent a team to investigate new attacks against Dalits, if the family was filing a complaint, and whether the case had similarities to Ragu's. The team was used to these visits and did not mind. "If everyone fought as hard as Aunty-jī," Mr. Nairoth used to say, "we would be much further along." The truth was that Aunty-jī's and Uncle-jī's presence was also helpful to Mr. Nairoth. The two conformed to his vision of proper atrocity complainants, who were applying the law in "the right way." Moreover, they were financially resourceful and had connections, which were sometimes helpful in other cases. And so he was happy to meet them every week to pour over a copy of the Atrocities Act, and sometimes the Indian Penal Code or the Code of Criminal Procedure (CrPC) and discuss sections, previous cases, and possible future cases.

Once a month, Aunty-jī also joined Sonali in her office. Sonali had an open-door policy. Women who had been harassed by higher-caste men would often come to her office with their families to discuss their legal and nonlegal options. Aunty-jī would sit and listen to distraught young girls and mothers, while Sonali interviewed their male relatives in another room. While she always insisted that she was not an activist and that Ragu's case was only about Ragu, she liked to comfort these women. She would tell them about Ragu and she found meaning in the shared grief they could experience. But especially, she felt that she could tell them about the importance of the Atrocities Act and encourage them to hope as well.

One day, shortly before I was due to return to the United Kingdom, Aunty-jī and I had tea. Taking sips in a pensive manner she told me: "I see mothers crying with their daughters, and it reminds me what I am fighting for, for Ragu, my son! Sometimes I tell them about our case, and I show them the sections we filed. It feels good to know that there are people who understand, and who feel understood by me, and who are fighting too. Looking at this law and looking at their faces . . . It gives me hope."

In the years I knew Aunty-jī, she often used one term to describe the pattern of her life after Ragu's death. That term was "*har roja ki ādatein*." In Hindi, the expression *har roja* means "everyday" or "always," while the word *ādat* translates to "habit." Translated, the phrase thus means "everyday habits." She always told me that her new daily habits helped keep her hope (*ummīda*) alive that Ragu would one day get official and public justice. Therefore, Aunty-jī came to think of her routine around Ragu's case—her newspaper clippings, her visits to the CDR, and her involvement with Sonali's work—as new daily habits of hope.

Anthropologists have described hope as the root of agency, as it captures the emotions that allow people to act even in the face of constraining circumstances (Kavedžija 2016). This idea finds resonance in pragmatist theories, which see hope as the source of self-growth and determination. In his study "Habits of Hope," Patrick Shade writes that "hope functions to energize and sustain the self as it reconstructs itself in the teeth of trying circumstances" (Shade 2001, 13). However, Shade argues that this kind of energizing hope is not an emotional state. Rather, it is the result of hope-directed activities that are pursued to successfully reach what John Dewey has called the "end-in-view." The end-in-view is a purpose or aim, which is formed into a living plan (Dewey 1958, 101), and depends for its actualization on new habits: repetitive actions that develop in response to, and in interaction with, people's social and natural environment and eventually become automatic. According to Shade, habits of hope are those which "function to support and nurture" their commitment to an end-in-view, such as persistence, courage, or resourcefulness (Shade 2001, 25).

The notion of hopeful habits that arise in conversation with one's social environment and circumstances resonates powerfully with Aunty-jī's new routines. For her, Ragu's case and the possibility of a court conviction for Karishma's family had become the end-in-view, which she pursued through determined, persistent activities. The text of the Atrocities Act, which she carried with her and studied, acted as a reminder of her end-in-view and as a resource for its steady pursuit. Meanwhile, her engagement with the CDR and the women Sonali worked with became a source of courage. She found herself in the role of counselor and comforting mother to people who had suffered like her. Aunty-jī was not a blind optimist, but she was also not a pessimist. She was a *meliorist*, who thought that by helping she could make the world, at least comparatively, better. That's what she thought she owed Ragu.

Anisha

Though I never got to know Anisha as well as Aunty-jī, later visits to Sikar revealed that her family also developed new routinized activities as their daughters' case progressed: activities, which relied heavily on the idea that the Atrocities Act would be a pathway to justice for Meena and Radha. Every morning Anisha and her mother prayed to Kalka Mātā and other deities. Like Aunty-jī they had a little shrine, which they furnished with little statues and pictures of various Hindu gods. Most of them were female deities like Durga and Sarasvati. Anisha's mother always said that female gods would understand the pain of a mother better. They too had a paper copy of the Atrocities Act, which a local activist had given them. Anisha and her mother had laid the act in front of their shrine. It was opened at the page that listed section 3(w)(i), which had been registered in their First Information Report.

Anisha, and her eldest brother, the accountant, also began to regularly meet up with other local Balai families who had registered complaints under the Atrocities Act. Once every few weeks, Anisha took the bus to Sikar town, where she was picked up by her brother. Together they went to a meeting, which was usually held at the house of an independent activist. There they discussed cases, exchanged information about good lawyers in town, and kept track of each other. Men and women did so separately and so Anisha and her brother were usually in different rooms having different conversations. But on their way home they would share their information and discuss.

Anisha found relief and hope in these meetings: "In my village the Rajputs are so strong that we can't really talk about the case, they all want us to drop it. But at these meetings I can talk about Meena and Radha and we can plan how to move forward. And my brother and I, we can really discuss. It makes me feel like there is hope as long as I keep going."

Neither Anisha nor her brother liked being involved with the legal system. They thought it was corrupt and slow and did not favor Dalit families like them. But somehow the regular activity of discussing their case with members of their own community, who had also experienced loss and violence, helped them hope. The sense of determined effort, enacted by both Anisha's and Aunty-jī's families against the backdrop of the Atrocities Act, represented a kind of angry resolve to overcome their desperate circumstances. The new forms of sociality that had slowly evolved in tandem with the law, allowed them to reorient themselves hopefully in the world. However, they were also realistic. They did not believe in a perfect social utopia, in a quick resolution of their cases or even in the idea that winning in court would mean that caste structures had changed.

Just like Aunty-jī, what they did believe was that their efforts could make things "better": better for their lost ones, who would have their honor restored, better for the families who were living through similarly hard circumstances. Anisha actively hoped, because she wanted to believe that a world could exist where girls like Meena and Radha would not have to suffer so terribly that they felt compelled to take their own lives.

This emphasis on creating better justice, a better community, and better legal outcomes is crucial because it shows that the hopeful habits and orientations both families cultivated while fighting their cases were not based in passive faith or blind idealism. Anisha, Aunty-jī, and everyone around them understood the reality of the criminal legal system; they knew that their cases had little chance of success and that the road to official justice was long and likely impossible. But the families were hopeful because they were actively working for a possibility of justice, which was rooted in the meliorist conviction that social and legal conditions for Dalits could be improved through efforts exerted by their own communities. They were hopeful because at the very least they were laboring for justice.

TEMPORALITIES AND ECONOMICS OF HOPE
Precarious Legal Horizons

For all their similarities, Aunty-jī's and Anisha's hopes ultimately took different directions. While Aunty-jī and her husband are fighting Ragu's case till this day, Anisha's family eventually compromised. Still, the compromise turned out to be an unusual one. Anisha and her family refused the financial settlement the Rajput clan had offered them for dropping their atrocity case. But they had demanded something else: If the boys made a public declaration at the next meeting of the village council (*pancāyata*) and admitted that they had harmed their daughters, they would drop the case. The NGOs would stop talking to the media and writing reports. If not, they would continue until the boys were called to trial.

The Rajput family knew that it was unlikely that the boys would ever get convicted. As previous chapters have shown, there are a myriad of ways in which police, defense lawyers, and state bureaucrats can create what Moyukh Chatterjee has called the "impunity effect," a process whereby legal data is collected and interpreted in ways that creates technical inconsistencies and undermines the claims of minorities and vulnerable groups (Chatterjee 2017, 127). However, to manipulate legal procedures in this way requires influence and, usually, money. The Rajput boys' families were not wealthy or hugely influential. They belonged to a growing group of Rajput families in Rajasthan's Shekhawati area who had consistently sold off land and other assets since the post-independence land reforms. Both Meghwals and Jats in Shekhawati often presented the narrative that as members of the Rajputana Agency's elite ruling class, Rajput families had failed to adjust to the economic demands of post-independence India. While other caste communities had actively embarked on a mission of education or agricultural development, many Rajput families had failed to insert themselves into productive economic activities. To make money they had sold land and were now often left with little financial capital.

While I was unable to collect extensive survey data on household income and land ownership in Sikar and Jhunjhunu, conversations with different caste groups in Anisha's village and an in-depth survey in my own fieldwork village of Badrasar seem to corroborate these claims. Many Rajput families appeared to be less well-off than either Jats or the Bania trader castes in the region. Claims about Rajput financial precarity were certainly true of the families of Meena's and Radha's attackers. "Old caste arrogance and nothing else," Sonali often said when following up on the girls' case. She was convinced that one of the main reasons the Rajput boys raped Radha and Meena was to feel powerful again in a village where their power was waning.

"But they are stupid because they don't have the money to pay for the legal consequences," Sonali scoffed when she called to inform me about the compromise in Radha's and Meena's case. "Unfortunately, Anisha's family doesn't have it either," she sighed. At the time the compromise unfolded I had already returned to London, so I never got to hear the story from Anisha herself. What I know now came from Sonali, who herself got the information from a colleague in Sikar. But reportedly the Rajput boys did as they were asked. "Apparently one of them said: 'it is because of us that these girls committed suicide (*in laḍakīon ne hamāri vajaha se suicide kiya*),'" Sonali told me over the phone. She seemed torn over the situation. On the one hand, she understood the relief this admission would bring for Anisha's parents, who wanted the world to know that their daughters had been innocent and honorable. On the other hand, she couldn't help but feel that Anisha's family had given up.

I too found it difficult to not see the compromise as a cheap stand-in for justice, especially remembering how hard Anisha's mother had prayed and how determinedly Anisha and her brother had strategized with other atrocity survivors. However, I too was inclined to agree with Sonali, that the public admission at the village council meeting had at least given the family some sense of restitution. Anisha's story ultimately unveiled how much the socioeconomic horizon, the context within which hopeful habits are cultivated after caste atrocities, matters.

Anisha's family had one foot in the village and one foot in urban life. Like Aunty-jī, they were educated and striving for financial independence and security. Yet, like Roop Singh in chapter 5, they were not yet economically independent and were still tied into the treacherous networks of sociality which defined their village. Fighting an atrocity case long-term required the privilege and the ability to project oneself into a distant future of court conviction, which might come in two, five, or ten years. It required resourcefulness as well as material resources. Aunty-jī had this privilege; Anisha's family did not. Yet Anisha never stopped believing that things could get better. According to Sonali, Anisha and her brother still go to the meetings in Sikar town to connect with other survivors. Their hopeful habits have not died with the compromise.

The Amnesia of Legal Hopefulness

Comparing Anisha's story and Aunty-jī's shines the spotlight on the way economic circumstances give rise to particular temporalities of legal hope. Hopeful habits exist in all communities, but hopeful activity directed at the deliverance of hate crime law requires a particular nexus of "spatio-temporal relations" (Bear 2016, 494). It demands not only financial resources but also an environment characterized by social independence. Anisha's family still lived in a village, and although they owned some land it was not enough to sustain them. Anisha's father sometimes worked for a wealthy Jat in his village to make extra income.

These social dependencies are perhaps most important when considering the pursuit of a lengthy, antagonistic legal case. This is evidenced by Aunty-jī, a woman who lives in an urban environment and whose family income is fully severed from any caste relations. She can afford to set an extreme temporal end point for Ragu's case: the end of her and her husband's own lives. But even then, she always said, Ragu's brother would keep fighting.

Sonali used to say that she thought Aunty-jī only breathed for future justice and never fully lived in the present. The moment Ragu died, her identity had turned towards the future, vibrating to a new frequency of anticipatory determination (see Heidegger 2008 [1962]) that could see nothing but the need to bring justice for her son. Aunty-jī was driven by what she always referred to as a singular hope and faith or trust (*ummīda aura vishvāsa*) that Ragu's case would be decided in their favor. Her hopeful habits were radically oriented towards a faraway horizon and towards the Atrocities Act as the central tool to both punish and restore.

Aunty-jī is still convinced that one day Ragu will get justice. Yet she has no clear timeline. She simply keeps going. In 2017 she found out that her former daughter-in-law, Karishma, had filed a counter-case against herself and her husband under the Indian Anti-Dowry Act of 1961, claiming Ragu's family had attempted to extort her. However, she was not scared but emboldened. "How dare they," she said, eyes coldly fixed on the court notice. "Now we will absolutely not give up our case."

It seemed that Aunty-jī's powerful determination to bring about victory in court came with a degree of factual amnesia. "It's like she forgets everything that is difficult about this case," Sonali ruminated one day, as Aunty-jī dug her way through a pile of police reports. "In a way that is good because she won't stop fighting, but for me personally it is a bit scary to see." I had to agree. For Aunty-jī, cultivating hopefulness seemed to mean forgetting: forgetting about the long and expensive road a court case would mean, forgetting about the stories she had heard from me and Sonali about Dalits who desperately searched for evidence and never found it, forgetting about her own financial limitations and the fact that India's judiciary did not have the best track record with atrocity cases: it meant forgetting about the limits of law.

In a study of kinship and migration in Langkawi in Southeast Asia, Janet Carsten (1965) proposes that forgetting cannot simply be equated with loss but can represent a way to allow for positive, future-oriented social labor and a new sense of belonging. Similarly, for Aunty-jī forgetting setbacks in Ragu's case allowed her to keep engaging in hopeful activities. It allowed her to keep working towards her end-in-view, which was justice for Ragu. To echo the words of philosopher Ernst Bloch, hope for Aunty-jī knew neither remembrance nor fear (comp. Bloch 1986).

Ragu's case, which has been in the works for over seven years now, has cost the family a small fortune. In 2018, the case was dismissed by the Jaipur special court for atrocity cases; a year later, an appeal processed by the Jaipur High Court was equally unsuccessful. Meanwhile, the dowry case filed by Karishma's family is being handled by well-known and successful lawyers. Her family is better connected and financially stronger. Still Aunty-jī's husband is currently working with the CDR, hoping to petition the Supreme Court to overrule previous judgments on Ragu's case. Even activists like Sonali are doubtful that Ragu will get justice in court, but Aunty-jī still hopes.

Imagining Alternative Worlds
The stories in this chapter suggest that hate crime laws like the Atrocities Act can become sites for the imagination and construction of new legal and social practices. In Rajasthan, the text of the Atrocities Act can serve as a platform for the birth of new socialities and hopeful orientations even in the face of a legal system which fails survivors.

If Aunty-jī and Anisha teach us anything, it is that in the context of hate crimes and the legal engagements they engender, hope is neither static nor uniform. In Rajasthan, atrocity survivors did not *have* hope but were actively involved in efforts of *hoping and bettering*. It was the cultivation of new persistent habits of community building, research, and demand-making that produced a sense of possibility. In the context of the Atrocities Act, hope was actively under construction and always infused with a meliorist sense of betterment. Hoping was an activity, not a passive state. The aim of hoping was the steady creation of *improved* conditions for Dalit communities, so that one day the text of the Atrocities Act might be translated into institutional legal realities.

Their stories also highlight that modes of legal hopefulness that evolve in the wake of profoundly violent attacks on marginalized identities, are the result of economically and socially situated social imaginaries (Taylor 2004): imaginaries that have formed against the backdrop of certain types of injury (Ralph 2014) and the intangible complex of perceived possibilities, motivations, and limitations that shape survivors' horizon of anticipation (Bryant and Knight 2019). The economic conditions, values, and anxieties that shape Dalit imaginaries in Rajasthan influence how atrocity survivors hope, what they hope for, and where their hope is oriented in time and space.

However, what is perhaps most important to note at the end of a book which has told stories of unimaginable brutality and loss, and repeatedly foregrounded the limits of hate crime laws, is that people *do* hope. Survivors pull the Atrocities Act, a dry bureaucratic document, into their practices of faith and into their creation of community and turn it into a site of courage. Aunty-jī, Anisha, and many others cultivate new habits of hope in dialogue with the Atrocities Act, which they weave like garlands around the textual pillar of the law, infusing it with new meaning, slowly growing its capacity to make things better.

EPILOGUE

NEW DIRECTIONS

ON JANUARY 18, 2018, I arrived at the Rajasthan State Institute for Public Administration in Jaipur, flanked by Sonali, Surya Chand—the state coordinator of the Human Rights Law Network—Mr. H. Nairoth Jr., and three advocates from the ActionAid office in Jaipur. Everyone had come for the same purpose: Over the next two days the National Human Rights Commission (NHRC) of India would hold an open hearing on "various issues relating to atrocities and problems faced by Scheduled Castes & Scheduled Tribes," presided over by the chairperson of the commission, Mr. Justice H. L. Dattu (former Chief Justice of India), as well as NHRC members Justice Pinaki Chandra Ghose and Justice D. Murugesan. Complainants, activists, and legal counsels had arrived from across the state to voice their grievances and hold state authorities, and especially the police, accountable for neglectful and compromised investigations in atrocity cases. Over the two days the three benches heard 169 cases. They called for further reports in 108 cases. In the remaining cases, the bench instructed the authorities in charge to take further action or issue compensatory payments to the victims (National Human Rights Commission 2018). "Finally," Mr. Nairoth beamed, "the police are held to account and people can feel justice!"

Everyone around him shared his joy. As I learned over the next forty-eight hours, activist dreams came true at NHRC hearings. "See Sandhya-jī," advocate Surya Chand explained over lunch, "we spend all our time chasing up on atrocity investigations, being dismissed by police and now they are all here to be judged by the former Chief Justice of India. The police become so small in these hearings (*choṭe ho jāte hain*). I always tell complainants who are hopeless, to come for the NHRC open hearing if their case is being presented. Because judges are more easily convinced if they see the people behind the files, but also because seeing the police officers who threatened them or neglected their cases reprimanded like schoolboys gives many a feeling of justice and new strength (*dhama*) to fight!"

A few hours later I found myself privy to one of these rare, affective moments of justice. I had come to watch Sonali present a case that involved the abetted suicide of a thirty-year-old Dalit gang-rape victim before Judge Dattu's bench. The father-in-law of the victim had traveled all the way from the distant Barmer district to attend the hearing. When I entered, the room was packed. Sonali's reputation as a fierce presenter and the intersectional nature of the case as a matter of both caste and gender-based violence had drawn many activists to the hearing.

As I pushed into the back of the room and squeezed into a window seat next to Nivedita—the activist whom I knew from Roop Singh's case—Sonali walked up to the bench. The deceased woman's father-in-law followed behind her, while three police officers, who had been summoned from Barmer district, positioned themselves to her right, also facing the bench. Justice Dattu was leaning back in his chair in a rather relaxed manner. Loud and confident Sonali began her story: The deceased victim, she told the bench, had been at home by herself on July 22, 2017, when two Rajput men forcibly entered her house and raped her. Afterwards they threatened to hurt her family if she breathed word of the attack. Despite the threats, the victim's father-in-law contacted the local police station and registered a case against the men. However, the police failed to properly investigate the incident or to provide a police escort. Escalating threats from the accused caused the victim to take her own life on September 12, 2017 (Joseph 2018). After protests before the Block Office in the nearby town of Chohatan, the victim's father-in-law filed a second FIR against the men, citing "abetment of suicide." Once again, the police failed to take any action. Sonali concluded by stating that the deceased woman's husband and children were suffering deeply and had not received any compensation.

When she had ended, Justice Dattu straightened up in his chair. "Is this true?" he asked the police officers who stood quietly next to Sonali, "Why didn't you investigate?" From my vantage point at the back of the room it was difficult to hear the response. The highest-ranking officer present, who had overseen the investigation, mumbled something about "not knowing how serious it was," and stared at the floor. "Look at this man," Justice Dattu directed him, pointing at the victim's father-in-law: an elderly man in a worn-out jacket and a cap. "This is a weak (*kamazora*) man, and you are taking advantage of it." The police officers continued to stare at the floor, but Dattu was not finished. "Is this what you call justice in this state?" he thundered to the delight of Nivedita, who was sitting next to me. "Get me your DGP!" The room gasped. DGP was short for Director General of Police, the highest-ranking position in the state's police force. The DGP of Rajasthan was stationed in Jaipur. Chatter broke out immediately: "Sir, the DGP has meetings," one officer pleaded. "I don't care," bellowed Dattu, "get me your DGP or I will write a report to the central government and summon him to Delhi!" After a moment, two police officers hastened outside.

Two anticipation-filled hours later the DGP arrived. Flanked by six police officers, he marched into the building, chased by local journalists. Justice Dattu did not scold him the way he had his inferior officers. Nonetheless, he was clear in his instructions. The DGP was to act against the negligent police officers in the Barmer case and submit a follow-up report to the commission. Justice Dattu also commanded the DGP to sit down with Sonali to discuss the case. If he failed to do so, he would be summoned to Delhi.

Afterwards Sonali beamed with pride! Activists and NGO representatives who were usually critical of each other were huddled together laughing and drinking tea as the DGP walked back to his Jeep. The father-in-law of the deceased woman sat quietly in the corner. I walked over to

FIGURE 12. A sign directing people to the open hearing on atrocities in Jaipur, held by India's National Human Rights Commission in 2018.

FIGURE 13. A group of police officers wait in the courtyard of the Rajasthan State Institute of Public Administration for their case numbers to be called.

sit next to him. "Are you ok?" I asked him. He nodded. "We won't get her back, but today . . . I have seen justice and that has changed me (*nyāya dekha me ne aura abh me badalā hua ādamī hu*)!"

A MOMENT OUT OF TIME

The NHRC hearing, which I attended at the very end of my fieldwork, was the singular instance during my time in Rajasthan where I witnessed activists, atrocity complainants, and their families agree that an institutional process had unfolded according to their vision of justice and had brought a distinct feeling of resolution. They left the NHRC hearing "changed from the inside." At the NHRC hearing the Atrocities Act was successful according to everyone's standards.

In part this was due to the reputation and structure of the NHRC itself. India's National Human Rights Commission was established through the Protection of Human Rights Act of 1993 as a "proclaimed independent governmental body charged with ensuring that every individual's rights are statutorily protected by the state." The NHRC has a wide mandate and has the right to conduct investigations, depose witnesses, ask to evaluate evidence, and issue recommendations to the government. It can even ask the central government of India to directly enforce some of its recommendations (Krishnan 2004, 542).

NGO activists in Jaipur often thought of the NHRC as a body that was "better than the courts." Surya Chand always told me that after the 2002 Gujarat riots, which saw the torture of thousands of Muslims at the hands of Hindu mobs, it had been the NHRC that tried to hold the state government to account. The commission had called out the police for not acting adequately and failing to prevent the violence. But for many atrocity complainants who were unfamiliar with this history, it was the structure of the NHRC hearing which gave them hope. The NHRC is typically chaired by a former Chief Justice of India—in this case Justice Dattu. For the father-in-law of the deceased Barmer victim, this was significant. "If a small man (*choṭā ādamī*) like me can be heard by a Chief Justice of India and see him reprimand (*ḍānṭanā*) the police on my behalf, then there is hope," he told me after the hearing.

Even though I was painfully aware that Justice Dattu's performance had likely been just that—a performance—and I knew that NHRC recommendations are often not enforced, I could not help being moved. Witnessing Sonali's unbridled joy, I wanted to rejoice myself. Like the activists around me I suddenly felt a sense of faith that formal systems of law could deliver all the social transformation that marginalized communities in India hoped for. The expressive, spectacular, and near ritualized nature of the event seemed to have generated a unique moment of emotional catharsis. Even though the theatrical aspect of legal trials and hearings is often decried as a manifestation of its implicit foundation in hegemonic systems of power, sometimes it is precisely this performativity that allows for the externalization of conflict and can bring a felt sense of resolution (Peters 2008, 180–81). The NHRC trial combined this cathartic performativity with a structural power reversal, which—in the vein of anthropological theories of ritual—brought institutional accountability (e.g., Turner 1969) and indicated a temporal rupture, a moment "out of time" (Sabea 2013).

In this moment survivors, who had been habitually ignored by police officers, had their suffering openly acknowledged. They even held the power to hurt the institutional players who typically acted with impunity. Here, both activist hopes for assertion and survivors' longing for a moment of justice that could be immediately felt and would restore their sense of honor coincided. Justice Dattu's confrontation with the DGP publicly strengthened the perception that somewhere in India's legal landscape there might just be seeds of institutional accountability: that maybe one day atrocity survivors would not have to go to absurd lengths to get the ear of a judge, or labor extensively to bring legal procedures in line with their truths. They would be taken at their word in a courtroom by a man as powerful as Justice Dattu.

At the same time, the intense emotions the NHRC hearing evoked were ultimately an indicator of the deep disappointment atrocity survivors, activists, and lawyers felt with the everyday workings of India's legal system and with the institutional implementation of a law that had promised them profound social change. The moment of agreement the NHRC hearing generated also brought into sharp focus how the expectations different stakeholders articulate vis-à-vis the Atrocities Act diverge most of the time.

THE ATROCITIES ACT: CONTESTED PROJECTS OF LEGAL MELIORISM

Throughout this book the voices of my interlocutors have highlighted two crucial experiences of the Atrocities Act. On the one hand, their stories and case trajectories have shown that the Atrocities Act is a law which has been jurisgenerative as well as generative of new affects and socialities. Over the past decades new interpretations of legal transformation, and new strategic communities, have grown around the Atrocities Act in Rajasthan. Varied forms of engagement with the act and with the new communities represent a project of *meliorism* for many stakeholders: a determined attempt to improve the legal landscape and social conditions for Dalits. On the other hand, the ability of the Atrocities Act to inspire different visions of the future, of law, and of justice has also given rise to new forms of inter- and intrasectional violence.

Embodied Legal Counter-Practice

During my fieldwork Mr. Krishnan and many others repeatedly stressed that the hope of preventing and ending violent caste prejudice had always stood at the heart of the Atrocities Act. Through an ambitious agenda of punishment, the lawmakers behind the act hoped to create a future where caste violence was no longer a feature of sociopolitical life in India. As a result of this aim, the Atrocities Act is a law that is plentifully imagined and creatively engaged among Dalit communities in Rajasthan—and especially the Meghwal groups I worked with most closely. What these engagements share is that they demand more than the "proper" implementation of the act according to bureaucratic ideals.

The survivors, whose cases I followed in Rajasthan, were aware that India's legal system habitually fails lower-caste and lower-class communities. They knew about police corruption and judicial bias, they knew that upper-caste perpetrators strategically filed counter-cases, and they knew that their complaints could be turned against them (Berg 2020). Despite that, many engaged with the Atrocities Act because they believed it should be "their" weapon to gradually transform conditions of oppression.

However, this is where agreement ended. For some of my interlocutors—usually, but not exclusively, upwardly mobile, professional Dalit men—the act represented an opportunity to actively move Dalit bodies into legal spaces and to force a shift in the operations of the criminal legal system. Here, one of the core issues at stake was that of legal temporality—as illustrated by Rahil's case in chapter 4. Rahil's conflict with Jataram reveals that hate is a process that is difficult to capture within the snapshot of a single legal case. Throughout my fieldwork, atrocity survivors struggled with the temporal dissonance between the present-focused format of legal cases and their own methods of identifying and naming casteism, which relied on a processual, historical perspective. For survivors, families, and even activists, casteist motives could not be measured in *one moment* or a singular incident. They argued that any interaction had to be evaluated within a deeper local past to reveal its casteist character. This reflects Benjamin Bowling's argument that hate and racial victimization are both social processes, not events (Bowling 1993). Therefore, many felt that legal truth regimes had to be rethought radically, to allow the Atrocities Act to reveal Dalit truths of discrimination. This call for changing legal evidence regimes also crystallized in discourses around the dominance of the paper file as a carrier of truth (Suresh 2019a): a file that was produced by institutions over which Dalits in Rajasthan still have little influence.

Consequently, some survivors, advocates, and activists tried to make the Atrocities Act potent by creatively rewriting legal strategies and redefining legal frameworks. They did not want the Atrocities Act to stand apart as a special criminal law that made promises of social change but could not deliver them. What they wanted was for the entire legal system to make space for the practices and artefacts available to Dalits in their pursuit of proof and truth. They wanted the Atrocities Act to perform in line with its aims of antidiscrimination and India's constitutional vision of equality (Kannabiran 2012).

In Rajasthan, a state where Dalit political mobilization has been fractured, this type of embodied legal practice may perhaps be especially prominent. For the communities I worked with, the Atrocities Act provided a legal foundation, on which to structure a new resistance. However, despite legal scholarship, which has decried India's special criminal laws like the Atrocities Act as statutes that necessarily infringe on the rights of the accused and are a platform for "false" cases, the ultimate goal Dalit communities in Rajasthan were pursuing *wasn't legal exceptionalism*. They simply wanted to have the *same* access to, and credibility within, legal institutions as the upper castes, whose presence and demands had shaped Indian law.

Ownership

This resistance was plagued by questions about legal ownership and purpose. Perhaps above all, the families I spoke to demanded to know whose dreams, whose truth, and whose future were at stake in atrocity cases. "Tell me whose truth the Atrocities Act is for!" Birendra, who had desperately been searching for proof of his father's murder, asked me. "Tell me who it is for, because how Meghwals like me suffer has been inscribed in history, you find it in every poem, song, and village. Our suffering is what this law should change!" Similarly, Pinky once commented, "Sometimes I don't know if this legal case is for me, the Meghwal associations, or for Sonali."

Birendra's and Pinky's exclamations hit at the heart of the social and political contestations that haunt the Atrocities Act. While Birendra is asking if the purpose he ascribes to the act aligns with its formal legal vision, Pinky points out that the act has turned her experience of both sexual and caste-based violence into a stage for the social and political goals of others. Pinky's statement is reminiscent of the interaction between Aunty-jī and Sonali at the start of the book. As Sonali tried to turn Ragu's case into an advocacy platform for the Dalit movement, Aunty-jī reminded her that, for her, it was about her son Ragu, and Ragu alone.

The stories in this book show that these battles of ownership often intensify along gendered lines. Previous sociological and legal analyses of the Atrocities Act have often paid little attention to how experiences of the legal process, as well as the political negotiations around the act, play out differently through different bodies (a notable exception is Pratiksha Baxi's work). Similarly, there has been little scholarly discussion of the new forms of intragroup violence atrocity cases produce. Pinky's statement shows that the radical championing of the Atrocities Act as an anticaste weapon often comes at the cost of women's voices and needs, thus further entrenching patriarchal structures. This is also reflected in experiences like Choti Lal's and Roop Singh's, men who fail to perform the type of assertive, professional masculinity that has currency within legal institutions and within activist and political circles. However, the way their case narratives unfold also shows that women and male survivors, who cannot engage in classic masculine performances, don't simply allow agency to be taken from them by their better educated counterparts or more upwardly mobile men. They develop their own subversive strategies to pull the law into their lives and make it deliver on their notion of justice. These strategies often rely on the controversial practice of out-of-court compromises.

In some ways these battles of ownership are unique to India, a country whose history of transformative constitutionalism and judicial activism has often resulted in exceptional levels of legal activity. As the Atrocities Act emerges as a site for strategic resistance in Rajasthan, it generates new interpretations of legal procedure, official justice, and equality. However, these battles of ownership also highlight a gap in the global discourse around hate crime law, in scholarship, and at the level of applied practice.

Sociolegal scholars have proposed that comprehensive, *civil antidiscrimination laws* are built on a vision of social transformation (Kok 2008). By addressing racial or gendered attitudes in hiring processes, rental markets, or other areas of the marketplace, comprehensive antidiscrimination laws try to iron out the wrinkles of everyday discrimination. Yet, *hate crime laws* like the Atrocities Act appear to have a double function: to punish past acts of identity-based violence and prevent future ones. Primarily reliant on the idea of enhanced punishments for criminal offences against certain groups, the sociolegal debates around hate crime legislation have focused on the question of "how": How does one prove a prejudicial mindset in court (Brax 2016)? How might one profile perpetrators of bias crimes (McDevitt, Levin, and Bennett 2002; Walters, Brown, and Wiedlitzka 2016)?

The debate has neglected to explore the questions around meaning and experiential jurisdiction which Birendra is so urgently posing: Focused on the "how" of court procedures, the criminological debate has overlooked the "what" and "who" of hate crime legislation: *What do hate crime laws achieve socially and politically? What new interpretations of law, politics, and equality do they generate? And who gets the ultimate say in the interpretation of their societal aims?*

Amplitudes of Legal Success

What does it mean for the Atrocities Act to be successful? The only thing the social life of the act makes clear beyond the shadow of a doubt is that there can be no definitive answer to this query. The answer depends as much on the kind of violence at stake as it does on the social positionality of survivors and the types of hopeful habits they can cultivate.

What becomes evident in this book is that the success of hate crime laws may look differently than legal practitioners, bureaucrats, and even scholars expect. The outcome of the same atrocity case can represent soaring heights of agency to one person *within* Rajasthan's Dalit communities, while appearing like an abysmal failure to another. Pinky taught us that ideas about the success of the Atrocities Act can even diverge radically within the same family. The successes of the Atrocities Act are not scalar! They neither trickle down into communities from legal institutions, nor do they waft up into courts and judicial mindsets as the result of broadly consensual community action. They are amplitudinal. Across Rajasthan's villages and institutions, they reverberate at frequencies that are at the same time glaringly loud for some and inaudible to others.

Hence, attempts to evaluate the transformative potential of hate crime laws must pay attention to the dialectical and mutually constitutive character of legal implementation and social change (e.g., Moore 1973). If we equate the transformative potential of the Atrocities Act with a high conviction rate, or with the absence of corrupt and negligent behaviors in law enforcement, or even with a landscape where most complainants don't "give up" on their case, it is easy to conclude that the Atrocities Act has failed. If we equate the success of the law with an immediate, felt sense of justice and healing among survivors of caste atrocities, then the Atrocities Act is largely ineffective.

However, if we look at the more nuanced shifts the act has produced in Rajasthan—the new micro-agencies it has birthed (chap. 5), the subtle local reversals in social and legal power it has generated (chap. 4), the habits of hopefulness and forms of resilience it has given rise to beyond courtrooms (chap. 7)—the chapters in this book bear witness to how the Atrocities Act has seeped invisibly into established systems of caste oppression.

In short, we might find that hate crime laws are not immediately effective in their legal form within legal institutions. The initial "success" of this type of legislation may well lie in the projection screen it represents for the new, competing visions of equality, agency, and hope, and for the anticipation it generates. The initial success of the Atrocities Act may be the result of its emergence as a site for new communities and hopeful habits. However, most importantly, the Act's immediate potential for the promotion of an anticaste agenda may reside in the opportunities it provides Dalit communities to employ legal provisions in the service of their own social visions of justice. The Atrocities Act has engendered a profound awareness among Meghwal communities in Rajasthan that they have the rights and tools to demand real structural change from a legal system that has historically pushed their communities to the sidelines and often even replicated oppressive structures. In Rajasthan, the Atrocities Act gave rise to a systematic desire to correct deep (legal) power differentials through creative forms of legal engagements and strategic disobedience.

However, as previous scholars have highlighted, these demands may lead to further political and judicial polarizations around the Atrocities Act and could permanently mark Dalits and Adivasis as outsiders, injured bodies (Rao 2009), or unreliable legal narrators. Survivors' attempts to remake formal law in accordance with their own realities and possibilities is also deeply threatening for legal actors. It confronts them with the fact that official law is not an eternally valid structure but a historically specific cultural assemblage (Vissman 2008). By calling for change to evidentiary formats and general criminal procedures, Dalit engagements with the Atrocities Act bring legal institutions face to face with their own ephemerality.

And yet, discourses that emphasize the danger of these antagonisms miss half the picture. In combination with the threat of punishment (Carswell and de Neve 2015), the "good" or "better" compromises, deals, and compensations the Atrocities Act gives rise to in Rajasthan, as well as the new modes of sociality and imaginaries it generates for survivors, have the power to slowly chip away at entrenched discriminatory structures. This process, which still predominantly happens outside of courtrooms, may eventually contribute to the type of grassroots social transformation necessary to generate effective institutional reform in police, courts, and the law.

GLOBAL QUESTIONS OF HATE AND LAW

What can these reflections on the Atrocities Act as a postcolonial form of culturally attuned hate crime law tell us about the relevance and challenges of this kind of legislation? Even though this book can only hope to be a starting point for any such conversation, there are three ways in which the analyses presented here help move the conversation forward.

Colonial Continuations and the Importance of Context

First, the previous reflections showcase that the disproportionate focus on the global North in scholarly debates on hate crime legislation has hindered deeper insight into the ways (colonial) historical conditions shape engagement with, and the social impact of, hate crime laws. Conflicts around the implementation of the Atrocities Act in India can, to some extent, be traced back to the fact that the institutions of the state in charge of applying the act remain deeply rooted in colonial systems of thought. The colonial government not only introduced new, and often antagonistic, categories of social and legal identity (Dirks 1987) but also reshaped legal and political institutions in line with these categories (Mbembe 2001; Mamdani 2003; Chatterjee 2001; Berti and Bordia 2015). Thus, postcolonial law has often been accused of continuing the repressive legacies of colonial law and even innovating the social power differentials encoded in legal categories, such as caste or religion.

In relation to the Atrocities Act, the obvious example of this sticky colonial hangover is the police. The structures, ranks, investigation procedures, and administration of India's police force is a continuance of the British Imperial Police, which was set up between 1860 and 1861 with the explicit purpose of strengthening the empire's grasp on its crown colony. The origins of India's police force as an instrument of control, characterized by a profound "antipeople" agenda, has significantly shaped the training of Indian police officers, many of whom display profound skepticism towards the narratives of India's most marginalized (Rai 2020).

Similarly, the three pillars of modern Indian criminal law—the Indian Evidence Act, the Indian Penal Code, and the Indian Code of Criminal Procedure—are updated versions of the original codes issued under the British colonial government. Thus, the fundamental structure of Indian criminal law still has roots in British colonial policies. This can generate problematic legal definitions. For example, under the Atrocities Act, verbal insults—or hate speech in the widest sense—against Dalits and Adivasi only count as an atrocity if they are committed "in public view." This focus on the public impact of violence rather than on the inherent harm of caste insults grows out of colonial concerns around public order and the control of indigenous populations considered irrational and unruly (Nair 2018). However, in the modern Indian context and the current political climate, which is shaped by a government-led antiminority agenda, it is questionable whether the "public view" approach to caste insults sufficiently protects Dalit and Adivasi communities, especially because the term "public" not only remains ill-defined in law, but it also is a socially blurry concept in Rajasthan's villages, where homes are in close proximity, often have open courtyards, and where neighbors and extended family habitually walk in unannounced. Given framings like this, it is perhaps unsurprising that atrocity survivors and activists in Rajasthan thought the evidentiary categories of Indian criminal law, as well as procedures of Indian policing, inadequate.

These observations highlight that trying to analyze the success of hate crime laws by studying them without deeper historicization or cultural contextualization may not yield profound insight into the structures that prevent marginalized groups from getting justice. Scholars must pay attention to the deeper historical processes that have shaped modern constellations of policing and criminal practice, which determine how hate crime laws are experienced.

Constitutional Visions: Why People Engage with Hate Crime Laws
This leads to my second point. By failing to consistently analyze hate crime laws in postcolonial nations like India—countries that have only recently emerged as independent democracies—scholars have missed an opportunity to understand how constitutional frameworks shape the conception and experience of hate and antidiscrimination measures.

India gained independence in 1947. Its constitution, which placed the principle of equality, freedom, and nondiscrimination at the heart of its vision for democratic India, was formulated as late as 1950. The social life of the Atrocities Act in Rajasthan highlights how the constitutional agenda of antidiscrimination, and the insurgent imperatives it invoked for historically marginalized groups (Kannabiran 2012), define the engagement of Dalit communities with the Atrocities Act: as a special criminal law, they try to hold it accountable to the eradication of systems of structural inequality.

Many of my interlocutors filed complaints because they considered the Atrocities Act "their" law, seeing it as a policy that could change their social realities as well as the legal system; they filed because the text of the Atrocities Act emphasized their historical suffering as well as their entitlements; and they filed because the act was threatening enough to upper castes to grant them a better standing in local negotiations.

To summarize, the willingness of Dalit—and especially Meghwal—communities and individuals in Rajasthan to engage with the legal system was a result of the vision of a brighter social future the Atrocities Act communicated to them, as a law that emphasized the prevention of violent casteist harms. This vision was tightly bound up with a broader Indian discourse of social equality and transformation that resonates in affirmative action policies and finds its roots in the Indian constitution. As caste organizations like JMSS in Jhunjhunu and NGOs like the CDR in Jaipur position the Atrocities Act at the center of their mission to fight caste oppression, they unveil new imaginaries and social networks for survivors.

Therefore, a systematic study of hate crime laws in other postcolonial, or recently independent, nation states will help scholars better understand how constitutional imaginaries and other foundational legal principles shape the social production of hate crime laws and other antidiscrimination policies.

Technicalities and Colonial Comparisons

This brings me to my final point. Moving the scholarly lens around hate crime law to the postcolony also allows for new technical legal insights. In 2000 South Africa introduced the Promotion of Equality and Prevention of Unfair Discrimination Act. Though this Equality Act falls firmly into the category of civil antidiscrimination laws, there are distinct parallels between its structure and that of the Atrocities Act in India.

The Equality Act was introduced to uphold and further the central principles of equality and human dignity outlined in the South African Constitution (Grant 2007; Krüger 2011) and sets out positive state duties for the advancement of a more equal society. Among others, the act prohibits "unfair discrimination on the basis of race, gender, sex, [and] ethnic and social origin." The South African government established special equality courts under the act and specified that clerks and judges in these courts had to undergo special training. In a procedural sense the Equality Act is even more radical than the Atrocities Act: it places the burden of proof on the shoulders of the defendant.

Yet, despite these measures, data from most equality courts suggest that only a handful of complaints are brought to equality courts annually (Botha and Kok 2019) and that only roughly one-third of complaints of unfair discrimination are decided in favor of the complainant.

The parallels and differences between the social life of the Equality Act in South Africa and the Atrocities Act in India pose urgent questions about the way legal technicalities encourage or discourage engagement with state-led antidiscrimination and antihate measures. Why does there seem to be comparatively more engagement with the Atrocities Act in India? In South Africa complaints under the Equality Act are directly filed with a court clerk rather than the police. In what ways is this procedural difference relevant to the discrepancies in legal engagement between the two countries, if at all? In Rajasthan, Dalit activists like Sonali often claimed that the burden of proof in atrocity complaints should be reversed. This is the case for the Equality Act in South Africa. How does this reversal shape case outcomes? And in what ways has South Africa's unique history of independence and constitutional genesis shaped the way communities engage or do not engage with legal protection measures?

These questions show that examining legal protections against discrimination and hate in postcolonial nations can be a source for fruitful comparative analysis. These comparisons would allow scholars to understand the operations, demands, and experiences of such laws in deeply contextual ways.

FRAGILE HOPE

This book proposes that both expanding debates around hate crime law beyond the global North and drawing on detailed ethnographic insights from postcolonial nation states are paramount if scholars and practitioners want to understand the possibilities and social dynamics of hate crime law: what it means, what imaginations it inspires, and how it demands the expansion of legal formats. Perhaps most importantly, it can help scholars to decolonize their own taken-for-granted assumptions about the structure of formal law and its limits.

During my time in Rajasthan, I heard the Atrocities Act condemned as useless, as a tool for false accusations and blackmail, and as a form of toothless "paper justice." Yet I also heard it called something to believe in, a strong aid for negotiation, and something to build a movement (*āndolana*) around. The performances around the act are multiple, multifaceted, and deeply rooted in local perspectives on, and frameworks of, law, caste, and community.

To evaluate the success of the Atrocities Act can, therefore, never be a straightforward task. As I journeyed alongside atrocity cases, I slowly came to understand that to isolate the socially transformative effects of hate crime laws, "their success or failure," I had to look beyond spaces and interactions associated with formal legal institutions. Anthropologists have argued that, at its most basic level, law is a "distinctive manner of imagining the real" (Geertz 1983, 167). However, hate crime laws like the Atrocities Act tell us something slightly different. For communities that have long been marginalized, they can represent a distinctive way of imagining the future, and of coming to terms with a violent past, without forgetting it.

In the context of caste atrocities, the painful labor of overcoming suffering and trauma, finding effective pathways to felt restitution, and maintaining or repairing local social relations often firmly falls on the shoulders of survivors. Meanwhile, judgments about the success of the Atrocities Act and the "right" way to engage with it are set by institutional and civil society actors who are rarely personally affected by caste violence. The latter usually live, see, and pass judgment at a safe distance.

This book shows that those affected by caste atrocities in Rajasthan are no longer ready to accept this hierarchy. Aunty-jī, Roop Singh, Pinky, and many others demanded agency over the public and judicial parameters and conceptions of success in atrocity cases. They wanted ownership over "their" law and over the possibilities that it could bring them and their communities. With a deep meliorist spirit, they struggle every day to change social and legal outcomes from the ground up. The people in this book demand to be equal participants in a public conversation around legal success. After all, the Atrocities Act is ultimately about *their* future.

APPENDIX

The Scheduled Castes and the Scheduled Tribes (Prevention of Atrocities) Act, 1989
No. 33 of 1989
(As amended in 2015)

THE SCHEDULED CASTES AND THE SCHEDULED TRIBES (PREVENTION OF ATROCITIES) ACT, 1989[1,2]

ARRANGEMENT OF SECTIONS

SECTIONS

CHAPTER I
PRELIMINARY

1. Short title, extent and commencement.
2. Definitions.

CHAPTER II
OFFENCES OF ATROCITIES

3. Punishments for offences atrocities.
4. Punishment for neglect of duties.
5. Enhanced punishment subsequent conviction.
6. Application of certain provisions of the Indian Penal Code.
7. Forfeiture of property of certain persons.
8. Presumption as to offences.
9. Conferment of powers.

CHAPTER III
EXTERNMENT

10. Removal of person likely to commit offence.
11. Procedure on failure of person to remove himself from area and enter thereon after removal.
12. Taking measurements and photographs, etc., of persons against whom order under section 10 is made.
13. Penalty for non compliance of order under section 10.

CHAPTER IV
SPECIAL COURTS

14. Special Court and Exclusive Special Court.
14A. Appeals.
15. Special Public Prosecutor and Exclusive Public Prosecutor.

---

1. Downloaded by author from *India Codes: Digital Repository of all Central and State Acts* and converted from PDF to a text file (https://www.indiacode.nic.in/handle/123456789/1920?view_type=search&sam_handle=123456789/1362).

2. As amended per the SC/ST (Prevention of Atrocities) Amendment Act, 2015 (No.1 of 2016).

CHAPTER IVA
RIGHTS OF VICTIMS AND WITNESSES
15A. Rights of victims and witnesses.

CHAPTER V
MISCELLANEOUS
16. Power of State Government to impose collective fine.
17. Preventive action to be taken by the law and order machinery.
18. Section 438 of the Code not to apply to persons committing an offence under the Act. 18A. No enquiry or approval required.
19. Section 360 of the Code or the provisions of the Probation of Offenders Act not to apply to persons guilty of an offence under the Act.
20. Act to override other laws.
21. Duty of Government to ensure effective implementation of the Act.
22. Protection of action taken in good faith.
23. Power to make rules.

THE SCHEDULE

THE SCHEDULED CASTES AND THE SCHEDULED TRIBES (PREVENTION OF ATROCITIES) ACT, 1989

ACT NO. 33 OF 1989

[11*th September*, 1989.]

An Act to prevent the commission of offences of atrocities against the members of the Scheduled Castes and the Scheduled Tribes, to provide for[1][Special Courts and the Exclusive Special Courts] for the trial of such offences and for the relief and rehabilitation of the victims of such offences and for matters connected therewith or incidental thereto.

BE it enacted by Parliament in the Fortieth Year of the Republic of India as follows:—

CHAPTER I
PRELIMINARY

1. Short title, extent and commencement.—(*1*) This Act may be called the Scheduled Castes and the Scheduled Tribes (Prevention of Atrocities) Act, 1989.

(*2*) It extends to the whole of India[2]***.

(*3*) It shall come into force on such date[3] as the Central Government may, by notification in the Official Gazette, appoint.

2. Definitions.—(*1*) In this Act, unless the context otherwise requires,—

(*a*) "atrocity" means an offence punishable under section 3;

(*b*) "Code" means the Code of Criminal Procedure, 1973 (2 of 1974);

[4][(*bb*) "dependent" means the spouse, children, parents, brother and sister of the victim, who are dependent wholly or mainly on such victim for his support and maintenance;

(*bc*) "economic boycott" means–

(*i*) a refusal to deal with, work for hire or do business with other person; or

---

1. Subs. by Act 1 of 2016, s. 2, for "Special Courts" (w.e.f. 26-1-2016).

2. The words "except the State of Jammu & Kashmir" omitted by Act 34 of 2019, s. 95 and the Fifth Schedule (w.e.f. 31-10-2019).

3. 30th January, 1990, *vide* notification No. S.O. 106(E), dated 29th January, 1990, *See* Gazette of India, Extraordinary, Part II, sec. 3(*ii*).

4. Ins. by Act 1 of 2016, s. 3 (w.e.f. 26-1-2016).

(*ii*) to deny opportunities including access to services or contractual opportunities for rendering service for consideration; or

(*iii*) to refuse to do anything on the terms on which things would be commonly done in the ordinary course of business; or

(*iv*) to abstain from the professional or business relations that one would maintain with other person;

(*bd*) "Exclusive Special Court" means the Exclusive Special Court established under sub-section (*1*) of section 14 exclusively to try the offences under this Act;

(*be*) "forest rights" shall have the meaning assigned to it in sub-section (*1*) of section 3 of the Scheduled Tribes and Other Traditional Forest Dwellers (Recognition of Forest Rights) Act, 2006 (2 of 2007);

(*bf*) "manual scavenger" shall have the meaning assigned to it in clause(*g*) of sub-section (*1*) of section 2 of the Prohibition of Employment as Manual Scavengers and their Rehabilitation Act, 2013 (25 of 2013);

(*bg*) "public servant" means a public servant as defined under section 21of the Indian Penal Code (45 of 1860), as well as any other person deemed to be a public servant under any other law for the time being in force and includes any person acting in his official capacity under the Central Government or the State Government, as the case may be;]

(*c*) "Scheduled Castes and Scheduled Tribes" shall have the meanings assigned to them respectively under clause (24) and clause (25) of article 366 of the Constitution;

(*d*) "Special Court" means a Court of Session specified as a Special Court in section 14;

(*e*) "Special Public Prosecutor" means a Public Prosecutor specified as a Special Public Prosecutor or an advocate referred to in section 15;

[1][(*ea*) "Schedule" means the Schedule appended to this Act;

(*eb*) "social boycott" means a refusal to permit a person to render to other person or receive from him any customary service or to abstain from social relations that one would maintain with other person or to isolate him from others;

(*ec*) "victim" means any individual who falls within the definition of the "Scheduled Castes and Scheduled Tribes" under clause (*c*) of sub-section

---

1. Ins. by Act 1 of 2016, s. 3 (w.e.f. 26-1-2016).

(*1*) of section 2, and who has suffered or experienced physical, mental, psychological, emotional or monetary harm or harm to his property as a result of the commission of any offence under this Act and includes his relatives, legal guardian and legal heirs;

(*ed*) "witness" means any person who is acquainted with the facts and circumstances, or is in possession of any information or has knowledge necessary for the purpose of investigation, inquiry or trial of any crime involving an offence under this Act, and who is or may be required to give information or make a statement or produce any document during investigation, inquiry or trial of such case and includes a victim of such offence;]

[1][(*f*) the words and expressions used but not defined in this Act and defined in the Indian Penal Code (45 of 1860), the Indian Evidence Act, 1872 (1 of 1872) or the Code of Criminal Procedure, 1973 (2 of 1974), as the case may be, shall be deemed to have the meanings respectively assigned to them in those enactments.]

(*2*) Any reference in this Act to any enactment or any provision thereof shall, in relation to an area in which such enactment or such provision is not in force, be construed as a reference to the corresponding law, if any, in force in that area.

CHAPTER II
OFFENCES OF ATROCITIES

3. Punishments for offences atrocities.—[2][(*1*) Whoever, not being a member of a Scheduled Caste or a Scheduled Tribe,—

(*a*) puts any inedible or obnoxious substance into the mouth of a member of a Scheduled Caste or a Scheduled Tribe or forces such member to drink or eat such inedible or obnoxious substance;

(*b*) dumps excreta, sewage, carcasses or any other obnoxious substance in premises, or at the entrance of the premises, occupied by a member of a Scheduled Caste or a Scheduled Tribe;

(*c*) with intent to cause injury, insult or annoyance to any member of a Scheduled Caste or a Scheduled Tribe, dumps excreta, waste matter, carcasses or any other obnoxious substance in his neighbourhood;

---

1. Subs. by s. 3, *ibid.*, for clause (*f*) (w.e.f. 26-1-2016).
2. Subs. by s. 4, *ibid.*, for sub-section (*1*) (w.e.f. 26-1-2016).

(*d*) garlands with footwear or parades naked or semi-naked a member of a Scheduled Caste or a Scheduled Tribe;

(*e*) forcibly commits on a member of a Scheduled Caste or a Scheduled Tribe any act, such as removing clothes from the person, forcible tonsuring of head, removing moustaches, painting face or body or any other similar act, which is derogatory to human dignity;

(*f*) wrongfully occupies or cultivates any land, owned by, or in the possession of or allotted to, or notified by any competent authority to be allotted to, a member of a Scheduled Caste or a Scheduled Tribe, or gets such land transferred;

(*g*) wrongfully dispossesses a member of a Scheduled Caste or a Scheduled Tribe from his land or premises or interferes with the enjoyment of his rights, including forest rights, over any land or premises or water or irrigation facilities or destroys the crops or takes away the produce therefrom.

Explanation.—For the purposes of clause (*f*) and this clause, the expression "wrongfully" includes—

(*A*) against the person's will;

(*B*) without the person's consent;

(*C*) with the person's consent, where such consent has been obtained by putting the person, or any other person in whom the person is interested in fear of death or of hurt; or

(*D*) fabricating records of such land;

(*h*) makes a member of a Scheduled Caste or a Scheduled Tribe to do "*begar*" or other forms of forced or bonded labour other than any compulsory service for public purposes imposed by the Government;

(*i*) compels a member of a Scheduled Caste or a Scheduled Tribe to dispose or carry human or animal carcasses, or to dig graves;

(*j*) makes a member of a Scheduled Caste or a Scheduled Tribe to do manual scavenging or employs or permits the employment of such member for such purpose;

(*k*) performs, or promotes dedicating a Scheduled Caste or a Scheduled Tribe woman to a deity, idol, object of worship, temple, or other religious institution as a *devadasi* or any other similar practice or permits aforementioned acts;

(*l*) forces or intimidates or prevents a member of a Scheduled Caste or a Scheduled Tribe—

(*A*) not to vote or to vote for a particular candidate or to vote in a manner other than that provided by law;

(*B*) not to file a nomination as a candidate or to withdraw such nomination; or

(*C*) not to propose or second the nomination of a member of a Scheduled Caste or a Scheduled Tribe as a candidate in any election;

(*m*) forces or intimidates or obstructs a member of a Scheduled Caste or a Scheduled Tribe, who is a member or a Chairperson or a holder of any other office of a Panchayat under Part IX of the Constitution or a Municipality under Part IXA of the Constitution, from performing their normal duties and functions;

(*n*) after the poll, causes hurt or grievous hurt or assault or imposes or threatens to impose social or economic boycott upon a member of a Scheduled Caste or a Scheduled Tribe or prevents from availing benefits of any public service which is due to him;

(*o*) commits any offence under this Act against a member of a Scheduled Caste or a Scheduled Tribe for having voted or not having voted for a particular candidate or for having voted in a manner provided by law;

(*p*) institutes false, malicious or vexatious suit or criminal or other legal proceedings against a member of a Scheduled Caste or a Scheduled Tribe;

(*q*) gives any false or frivolous information to any public servant and thereby causes such public servant to use his lawful power to the injury or annoyance of a member of a Scheduled Caste or a Scheduled Tribe;

(*r*) intentionally insults or intimidates with intent to humiliate a member of a Scheduled Caste or a Scheduled Tribe in any place within public view;

(*s*) abuses any member of a Scheduled Caste or a Scheduled Tribe by caste name in any place within public view;

(*t*) destroys, damages or defiles any object generally known to beheld sacred or in high esteem by members of the Scheduled Castes or the Scheduled Tribes.

Explanation.—For the purposes of this clause, the expression "object" means and includes statue, photograph and portrait;

(*u*) by words either written or spoken or by signs or by visible representation or otherwise promotes or attempts to promote feelings of enmity, hatred or ill-will against members of the Scheduled Castes or the Scheduled Tribes;

(*v*) by words either written or spoken or by any other means disrespects any late person held in high esteem by members of the Scheduled Castes or the Scheduled Tribes;

(*w*) (*i*) intentionally touches a woman belonging to a Scheduled Caste or a Scheduled Tribe, knowing that she belongs to a Scheduled Caste or a Scheduled Tribe, when such act of touching is of a sexual nature and is without the recipient's consent;

(*ii*) uses words, acts or gestures of a sexual nature towards a woman belonging to a Scheduled Caste or a Scheduled Tribe, knowing that she belongs to a Scheduled Caste or a Scheduled Tribe.

Explanation.—For the purposes of sub-clause (*i*), the expression "consent" means an unequivocal voluntary agreement when the person by words, gestures, or any form of non-verbal communication, communicates willingness to participate in the specific act:

Provided that a woman belonging to a Scheduled Caste or a Scheduled Tribe who does not offer physical resistance to any act of a sexual nature is not by reason only of that fact, is to be regarded as consenting to the sexual activity:

Provided further that a woman's sexual history, including with the offender shall not imply consent or mitigate the offence;

(*x*) corrupts or fouls the water of any spring, reservoir or any other source ordinarily used by members of the Scheduled Castes or the Scheduled Tribes so as to render it less fit for the purpose for which it is ordinarily used;

(*y*) denies a member of a Scheduled Caste or a Scheduled Tribe any customary right of passage to a place of public resort or obstructs such member so as to prevent him from using or having access to a place of public resort to which other members of public or any other section thereof have a right to use or access to;

(*z*) forces or causes a member of a Scheduled Caste or a Scheduled Tribe to leave his house, village or other place of residence:

Provided that nothing contained in this clause shall apply to any action taken in discharge of a public duty;

(*za*) obstructs or prevents a member of a Scheduled Caste or a Scheduled Tribe in any manner with regard to—

(*A*) using common property resources of an area, or burial or cremation ground equally with others or using any river, stream, spring, well, tank, cistern, water-tap or other watering place, or any bathing *ghat*, any public conveyance, any road, or passage;

(*B*) mounting or riding bicycles or motor cycles or wearing footwear or new clothes in public places or taking out wedding procession, or mounting a horse or any other vehicle during wedding processions;

(*C*) entering any place of worship which is open to the public or other persons professing the same religion or taking part in, or taking out, any religious, social or cultural processions including *jatra*s;

(*D*) entering any educational institution, hospital, dispensary, primary health centre, shop or place of public entertainment or any other public place; or using any utensils or articles meant for public use in any place open to the public; or

(*E*) practicing any profession or the carrying on of any occupation, trade or business or employment in any job which other members of the public, or any section thereof, have a right to use or have access to;

(*zb*) causes physical harm or mental agony of a member of a Scheduled Caste or a Scheduled Tribe on the allegation of practicing witchcraft or being a witch; or

(*zc*) imposes or threatens a social or economic boycott of any person or a family or a group belonging to a Scheduled Caste or a Scheduled Tribe, shall be punishable with imprisonment for a term which shall not be less than six months but which may extend to five years and with fine.]

(*2*) Whoever, not being a member of a Scheduled Caste or a Scheduled Tribe,—

(*i*) gives or fabricates false evidence intending thereby to cause, or knowing it to be likely that he will thereby cause, any member of a Scheduled Caste or a Scheduled Tribe to be convicted of an offence which is capital by the law for the time being in force shall be punished with imprisonment for life and with fine; and if an innocent member of a Scheduled Caste or a Scheduled Tribe be convicted and executed in consequence of such false or fabricated evidence, the person who gives or fabricates such false evidence, shall be punished with death;

(*ii*) gives or fabricates false evidence intending thereby to cause, or knowing it to be likely that he will thereby cause, any member of a Scheduled Caste or a Scheduled Tribe to be convicted of an offence which is not capital but punishable with imprisonment for a term of seven years or upwards, shall be punishable with imprisonment for a term which shall not be less than six months but which may extend to seven years or upwards and with fine;

(*iii*) commits mischief by fire or any explosive substance intending to cause or knowing it to be likely that he will thereby cause damage to any property belonging to a member of a Scheduled Caste or a Scheduled Tribe, shall be punishable with imprisonment for a term which shall not be less than six months but which may extend to seven years and with fine;

(*iv*) commits mischief by fire or any explosive substance intending to cause or knowing it to be likely that he will thereby cause destruction of any building which is ordinarily used as a place of worship or as a place for human dwelling or as a place for custody of the property by a member of a Scheduled Caste or a Scheduled Tribe, shall be punishable with imprisonment for life and with fine;

(*v*) commits any offence under the Indian Penal Code (45 of 1860) punishable with imprisonment for a term of ten years or more against a person or property [1][knowing that such person is a member of a Scheduled Caste or a Scheduled Tribe or such property belongs to such member], shall be punishable with imprisonment for life and with fine;

[2][(*va*) commits any offence specified in the Schedule, against a person or property, knowing that such person is a member of a Scheduled Caste or a Scheduled Tribe or such property belongs to such member, shall be punishable with such punishment as specified under the Indian Penal Code (45 of 1860) for such offences and shall also be liable to fine;]

(*vi*) knowingly or having reason to believe that an offence has been committed under this Chapter, causes any evidence of the commission of that offence to disappear with the intention of screening the offender from legal punishment, or with that intention gives any information respecting the offence which he knows or believes to be false, shall be punishable with the punishment provided for that offence; or

(*vii*) being a public servant, commits any offence under this section, shall be punishable with imprisonment for a term which shall not be less than one year but which may extend to the punishment provided for that offence.

---

1. Subs. by Act 1 of 2016, s. 4, for "on the ground that such person is a member of a Scheduled Caste or a Scheduled Tribe or such property belongs to such member" (w.e.f. 26-1-2016).

2. Ins. by s. 4, *ibid*. (w.e.f. 26-1-2016).

[4. **Punishment for neglect of duties.**—(*1*) Whoever, being a public servant but not being a member of a Scheduled Caste or a Scheduled Tribe, willfully neglects his duties required to be performed by him under this Act and the rules made thereunder, shall be punishable with imprisonment for a term which shall not be less than six months but which may extend to one year.

(*2*) The duties of public servant referred to in sub-section (*1*) shall include—

(*a*) to read out to an informant the information given orally, and reduced to writing by the officer in charge of the police station, before taking the signature of the informant;

(*b*) to register a complaint or a First Information Report under this Act and other relevant provisions and to register it under appropriate sections of this Act;

(*c*) to furnish a copy of the information so recorded forthwith to thein formant;

(*d*) to record the statement of the victims or witnesses;

(*e*) to conduct the investigation and file charge sheet in the Special Court or the Exclusive Special Court within a period of sixty days, and to explain the delay if any, in writing;

(*f*) to correctly prepare, frame and translate any document or electronic record;

(*g*) to perform any other duty specified in this Act or the rules made thereunder:

Provided that the charges in this regard against the public servant shall be booked on the recommendation of an administrative enquiry.

(*3*) The cognizance in respect of any dereliction of duty referred to in sub-section (*2*) by a public servant shall be taken by the Special Court or the Exclusive Special Court and shall give direction for penal proceedings against such public servant.]

5. Enhanced punishment subsequent conviction.—Whoever, having already been convicted of an offence under this Chapter is convicted for the second offence or any offence subsequent to the second offence, shall be punishable with imprisonment for a term which shall not be less than one year but which may extend to the punishment provided for that offence.

---

1. Subs. by Act 1 of 2016, s. 5, for section 4 (w.e.f. 26-1-2016).

6. Application of certain provisions of the Indian Penal Code.— Subject to the other provisions of this Act, the provisions of section 34, Chapter III, Chapter IV, Chapter V, Chapter VA, section 149 and Chapter XXIII of the Indian Penal Code (45 of 1860), shall, so far as may be, apply for the purposes of this Act as they apply for the purposes of the Indian Penal Code.

7. Forfeiture of property of certain persons.—(*1*) Where a person has been convicted of any offence punishable under this Chapter, the Special Court may, in addition to awarding any punishment, by order in writing, declare that any property, movable or immovable or both, belonging to the person, which has been used for the commission of that offence, shall stand forfeited to Government.

(*2*) Where any person is accused of any offence under this Chapter, it shall be open to the Special Court trying him to pass an order that all or any of the properties, movable or immovable or both, belonging to him, shall, during the period of such trial, be attached, and where such trial ends in conviction, the property so attached shall be liable to forfeiture to the extent it is required for the purpose of realisation of any fine imposed under this Chapter.

8. Presumption as to offences.—In a prosecution for an offence under this Chapter, if it is proved that—

(*a*) the accused rendered [1][any financial assistance in relation to the offences committed by a person accused of], or reasonably suspected of, committing, an offence under this Chapter, the Special Court shall presume, unless the contrary is proved, that such person had abetted the offence;

(*b*) a group of persons committed an offence under this Chapter and if it is proved that the offence committed was a sequel to any existing dispute regarding land or any other matter, it shall be presumed that the offence was committed in furtherance of the common intention or in prosecution of the common object;

[2][(*c*) the accused was having personal knowledge of the victim or his family, the Court shall presume that the accused was aware of the caste or tribal identity of the victim, unless the contrary is proved.]

---

1. Subs. by Act 1 of 2016, s. 6, for "any financial assistance to a person accused of" (w.e.f. 26-1-2016).

2. Ins. by s. 6, *ibid.* (w.e.f. 26-1-2016).

9. Conferment of powers.—(*1*) Notwithstanding anything contained in the Code or in any other provision of this Act, the State Government may, if it considers it necessary or expedient so to do,—

(*a*) for the prevention of and for coping with any offence under this Act, or

(*b*) for any case or class or group of cases under this Act,

in any district or part thereof, confer, by notification in the Official Gazette, on any officer of the State Government, the powers exercisable by a police officer under the Code in such district or part thereof or, as the case may be, for such case or class or group of cases, and in particular, the powers of arrest, investigation and prosecution of persons before any Special Court.

(*2*) All officers of police and all other officers of Government shall assist the officer referred to in sub-section (*1*) in the execution of the provisions of this Act or any rule, scheme or order made thereunder.

(*3*) The provisions of the Code shall, so far as may be, apply to the exercise of the powers by an officer under sub-section (*1*).

CHAPTER III
EXTERNMENT

10. Removal of person likely to commit offence.—(*1*) Where the Special Court is satisfied, upon a complaint or a police report that a person is likely to commit an offence under Chapter II of this Act in any area included in 'Scheduled Areas' or 'tribal areas', as referred to in article 244 of the Constitution, [1][or any area identified under the provisions of clause (*vii*) of sub-section (*2*) of section 21], it may, by order in writing, direct such person to remove himself beyond the limits of such area, by such route and within such time as may be specified in the order, and not to return to that area from which he was directed to remove himself for such period, not exceeding [2][three years], as may be specified in the order.

(*2*) The Special Court shall, along with the order under sub-section (*1*), communicate to the person directed under that sub-section the grounds on which such order has been made.

(*3*) The Special Court may revoke or modify the order made under sub-section (*1*), for the reasons to be recorded in writing, on the representation

---

1. Ins. by s. 7, *ibid.* (w.e.f. 26-1-2016).

2. Subs. by s. 7, *ibid.*, for "two years" (w.e.f. 26-1-2016).

made by the person against whom such order has been made or by any other person on his behalf within thirty days from the date of the order.

11. Procedure on failure of person to remove himself from area and enter thereon after removal.—(*1*) If a person to whom a direction has been issued under section 10 to remove himself from any area—

(*a*) fails to remove himself as directed; or

(*b*) having so removed himself enters such area within the period specified in the order,

otherwise than with the permission in writing of the Special Court under sub-section (*2*), the Special Court may cause him to be arrested and removed in police custody to such place outside such area as the Special Court may specify.

(*2*) The Special Court may, by order in writing, permit any person in respect of whom an order under section 10 has been made, to return to the area from which he was directed to remove himself for such temporary period and subject to such conditions as may be specified in such order and may require him to execute a bond with or without surety for the due observation of the conditions imposed.

(*3*) The Special Court may at any time revoke any such permission.

(*4*) Any person who, with such permission, returns to the area from which he was directed to remove himself shall observe the conditions imposed, and at the expiry of the temporary period for which he was permitted to return, or on the revocation of such permission before the expiry of such temporary period, shall remove himself outside such area and shall not return thereto within the unexpired portion specified under section 10 without a fresh permission.

(*5*) If a person fails to observe any of the conditions imposed or to remove himself accordingly or having so removed himself enters or returns to such area without fresh permission the Special Court may cause him to be arrested and removed in police custody to such place outside such area as the Special Court may specify.

12. Taking measurements and photographs, etc., of persons against whom order under section 10 is made.—(*1*) Every person against whom an order has been made under section 10 shall, if so required by the Special Court, allow his measurements and photographs to be taken by a police officer.

(*2*) If any person referred to in sub-section (*1*), when required to allow his measurements or photographs to be taken, resists or refuses to allow the taking of such measurements or photographs, it shall be lawful to use all necessary means to secure the taking thereof.

(*3*) Resistance to or refusal to allow the taking of measurements or photographs under sub-section (*2*) shall be deemed to be an offence under section 186 of the Indian Penal Code (45 of 1860).

(*4*) Where an order under section 10 is revoked, all measurements and photographs (including negatives) taken under sub-section (*2*) shall be destroyed or made over to the person against whom such order is made.

13. Penalty for noncompliance of order under section 10.—Any person contravening an order of the Special Court made under section 10 shall be punishable with imprisonment for a term which may extend to one year and with fine.

CHAPTER IV
SPECIAL COURTS

[1][**14.** **Special Court and Exclusive Special Court.**—(*1*) For the purpose of providing for speedy trial, the State Government shall, with the concurrence of the Chief Justice of the High Court, by notification in the Official Gazette, establish an Exclusive Special Court for one or more Districts:

Provided that in Districts where less number of cases under this Act is recorded, the State Government shall, with the concurrence of the Chief Justice of the High Court, by notification in the Official Gazette, specify for such Districts, the Court of Session to be a Special Court to try the offences under this Act:

Provided further that the Courts so established or specified shall have power to directly take cognizance of offences under this Act.

(*2*) It shall be the duty of the State Government to establish adequate number of Courts to ensure that cases under this Act are disposed of within a period of two months, as far as possible.

(*3*) In every trial in the Special Court or the Exclusive Special Court, the proceedings shall be continued from day-to-day until all the witnesses in attendance have been examined, unless the Special Court or the Exclu-

---

1. Subs. by Act 1 of 2016, s. 8, for section 14 (w.e.f. 26-1-2016).

sive Special Court finds the adjournment of the same beyond the following day to be necessary for reasons to be recorded in writing:

Provided that when the trial relates to an offence under this Act, the trial shall, as far as possible, be completed within a period of two months from the date of filing of the charge sheet.]

[1][**14A. Appeals.**—(*1*) Notwithstanding anything contained in the Code of Criminal Procedure,1973 (2 of 1974), an appeal shall lie, from any judgment, sentence or order, not being an interlocutory order, of a Special Court or an Exclusive Special Court, to the High Court both on facts and on law.

(*2*) Notwithstanding anything contained in sub-section (*3*) of section 378 of the Code of Criminal Procedure, 1973 (2 of 1974), an appeal shall lie to the High Court against an order of the Special Court or the Exclusive Special Court granting or refusing bail.

(*3*) Notwithstanding anything contained in any other law for the time being in force, every appeal under this section shall be preferred within a period of ninety days from the date of the judgment, sentence or order appealed from:

Provided that the High Court may entertain an appeal after the expiry of the said period of ninety days if it is satisfied that the appellant had sufficient cause for not preferring the appeal within the period of ninety days:

Provided further that no appeal shall be entertained after the expiry of the period of one hundred and eighty days.

(*4*) Every appeal preferred under sub-section (*1*) shall, as far as possible, be disposed of within a period of three months from the date of admission of the appeal.]

[2][**15. Special Public Prosecutor and Exclusive Public Prosecutor.**—(*1*) For every Special Court, the State Government shall, by notification in the Official Gazette, specify a Public Prosecutor or appoint an advocate who has been in practice as an advocate for not less than seven years, as a Special Public Prosecutor for the purpose of conducting cases in that Court.

(*2*) For every Exclusive Special Court, the State Government shall, by notification in the Official Gazette, specify an Exclusive Special Public Prosecutor or appoint an advocate who has been in practice as an advocate

---

1. Ins. by Act1 of 2016, s. 9 (w.e.f. 26-1-2016).

2. Subs. by s.10, *ibid.*, for section 15 (w.e.f. 26-1-2016).

for not less than seven years, as an Exclusive Special Public Prosecutor for the purpose of conducting cases in that Court.]

¹[CHAPTER IVA
RIGHTS OF VICTIMS AND WITNESSES

15A. Rights of victims and witnesses.—(*1*) It shall be the duty and responsibility of the State to make arrangements for the protection of victims, their dependents, and witnesses against any kind of intimidation or coercion or inducement or violence or threats of violence.

(*2*) A victim shall be treated with fairness, respect and dignity and with due regard to any special need that arises because of the victim's age or gender or educational disadvantage or poverty.

(*3*) A victim or his dependent shall have the right to reasonable, accurate, and timely notice of any Court proceeding including any bail proceeding and the Special Public Prosecutor or the State Government shall inform the victim about any proceedings under this Act.

(*4*) A victim or his dependent shall have the right to apply to the Special Court or the Exclusive Special Court, as the case may be, to summon parties for production of any documents or material, witnesses or examine the persons present.

(*5*) A victim or his dependent shall be entitled to be heard at any proceeding under this Act in respect of bail, discharge, release, parole, conviction or sentence of an accused or any connected proceedings or arguments and file written submission on conviction, acquittal or sentencing.

(*6*) Notwithstanding anything contained in the Code of Criminal Procedure,1973 (2 of 1974), the Special Court or the Exclusive Special Court trying a case under this Act shall provide to a victim, his dependent, informant or witnesses—

    (*a*) the complete protection to secure the ends of justice;

    (*b*) the travelling and maintenance expenses during investigation, inquiry and trial;

    (*c*) the social-economic rehabilitation during investigation, inquiry and trial; and

    (*d*) relocation.

---

1. Ins. by Act 1 of 2016, s. 11 (w.e.f. 26-1-2016).

(7) The State shall inform the concerned Special Court or the Exclusive Special Court about the protection provided to any victim or his dependent, informant or witnesses and such Court shall periodically review the protection being offered and pass appropriate orders.

(8) Without prejudice to the generality of the provisions of sub-section (6), the concerned Special Court or the Exclusive Special Court may, on an application made by a victim or his dependent, informant or witness in any proceedings before it or by the Special Public Prosecutor in relation to such victim, informant or witness or on its own motion, take such measures including—

(a) concealing the names and addresses of the witnesses in its orders or judgments or in any records of the case accessible to the public;

(b) issuing directions for non-disclosure of the identity and addresses of the witnesses;

(c) take immediate action in respect of any complaint relating to harassment of a victim, informant or witness and on the same day, if necessary, pass appropriate orders for protection:

Provided that inquiry or investigation into the complaint received under clause (c) shall be tried separately from the main case by such Court and concluded within a period of two months from the date of receipt of the complaint:

Provided further that where the complaint under clause (c) is against any public servant, the Court shall restrain such public servant from interfering with the victim, informant or witness, as the case may be, in any matter related or unrelated to the pending case, except with the permission of the Court.

(9) It shall be the duty of the Investigating Officer and the Station House Officer to record the complaint of victim, informant or witnesses against any kind of intimidation, coercion or inducement or violence or threats of violence, whether given orally or in writing, and a photocopy of the First Information Report shall be immediately given to them at free of cost.

(10) All proceedings relating to offences under this Act shall be video recorded.

(11) It shall be the duty of the concerned State to specify an appropriate scheme to ensure implementation of the following rights and entitlements of victims and witnesses in accessing justice so as—

(*a*) to provide a copy of the recorded First Information Report at free of cost;

(*b*) to provide immediate relief in cash or in kind to atrocity victims or their dependents;

(*c*) to provide necessary protection to the atrocity victims or their dependents, and witnesses;

(*d*) to provide relief in respect of death or injury or damage to property;

(*e*) to arrange food or water or clothing or shelter or medical aid or transport facilities or daily allowances to victims;

(*f*) to provide the maintenance expenses to the atrocity victims and their dependents;

(*g*) to provide the information about the rights of atrocity victims at the time of making complaints and registering the First Information Report;

(*h*) to provide the protection to atrocity victims or their dependents and witnesses from intimidation and harassment;

(*i*) to provide the information to atrocity victims or their dependents or associated organisations or individuals, on the status of investigation and charge sheet and to provide copy of the charge sheet at free of cost;

(*j*) to take necessary precautions at the time of medical examination;

(*k*) to provide information to atrocity victims or their dependents or associated organisations or individuals, regarding the relief amount;

(*l*) to provide information to atrocity victims or their dependents or associated organisations or individuals, in advance about the dates and place of investigation and trial;

(*m*) to give adequate briefing on the case and preparation for trial to atrocity victims or their dependents or associated organisations or individuals and to provide the legal aid for the said purpose;

(*n*) to execute the rights of atrocity victims or their dependents or associated organisations or individuals at every stage of the proceedings under this Act and to provide the necessary assistance for the execution of the rights.

(*12*) It shall be the right of the atrocity victims or their dependents, to take assistance from the Non- Government Organisations, social workers or advocates.]

CHAPTER V
Miscellaneous

16. Power of State Government to impose collective fine.—The provisions of section 10A of the Protection of Civil Rights Act, 1955 (22 of 1955) shall, so far as may be, apply for the purposes of imposition and realisation of collective fine and for all other matters connected therewith under this Act.

17. Preventive action to be taken by the law and order machinery.—(*1*) A District Magistrate or a Sub-divisional Magistrate or any other Executive Magistrate or any police officer not below the rank of a Deputy Superintendent of Police may, on receiving information and after such inquiry as he may think necessary, has reason to believe that a person or a group of persons not belonging to the Scheduled Castes or the Scheduled Tribes, residing in or frequenting any place within the local limits of his jurisdiction is likely to commit an offence or has threatened to commit any offence under this Act and is of the opinion that there is sufficient ground for proceeding, declare such an area to be an area prone to atrocities and take necessary action for keeping the peace and good behaviour and maintenance of public order and tranquility and may take preventive action.

(*2*) The provisions of Chapters VIII, X and XI of the Code shall, so far as may be, apply for the purposes of sub-section (*1*).

(*3*) The State Government may, by notification in the Official Gazette, make one or more schemes specifying the manner in which the officers referred to in sub-section (*1*) shall take appropriate action specified in such scheme or schemes to prevent atrocities and to restore the feeling of security amongst the members of the Scheduled Castes and the Scheduled Tribes.

18. Section 438 of the Code not to apply to persons committing an offence under the Act.— Nothing in section 438 of the Code shall apply in relation to any case involving the arrest of any person on an accusation of having committed an offence under this Act.

¹[**18A. No enquiry or approval required.**—(*1*) For the purposes of this Act,—

(*a*) preliminary enquiry shall not be required for registration of a First Information Report against any person; or

---

1. Ins. by Act 27 of 2018, s. 2 (w.e.f. 20-8-2018).

(*b*) the investigating officer shall not require approval for the arrest, if necessary, of any person, against whom an accusation of having committed an offence under this Act has been made and no procedure other than that provided under this Act or the Code shall apply.

(*2*) The provisions of section 438 of the Code shall not apply to a case under this Act, notwithstanding any judgment or order or direction of any Court.]

19. Section 360 of the Code or the provisions of the Probation of Offenders Act not to apply to persons guilty of an offence under the Act.—The provisions of section 360 of the Code and the provisions of the Probation of Offenders Act, 1958 (20 of 1958) shall not apply to any person above the age of eighteen years who is found guilty of having committed an offence under this Act.

20. Act to override other laws.—Save as otherwise provided in this Act, the provisions of this Act shall have effect notwithstanding anything inconsistent therewith contained in any other law for the time being in force or any custom or usage or any instrument having effect by virtue of any such law.

21. Duty of Government to ensure effective implementation of the Act.—(*1*) Subject to such rules as the Central Government may make in this behalf, the State Government shall take such measures as may be necessary for the effective implementation of this Act.

(*2*) In particular, and without prejudice to the generality of the foregoing provisions, such measures may include,—

(*i*) the provision for adequate facilities, including legal aid, to the persons subjected to atrocities to enable them to avail themselves of justice;

(*ii*) the provision for travelling and maintenance expenses to witnesses, including the victims of atrocities, during investigation and trial of offences under this Act;

(*iii*) the provision for the economic and social rehabilitation of the victims of the atrocities;

(*iv*) the appointment of officers for initiating or exercising supervision over prosecutions for the contravention of the provisions of this Act;

(v) the setting up of committees at such appropriate levels as the State Government may think fit to assist that Government in formulation or implementation of such measures;

(vi) provision for a periodic survey of the working of the provisions of this Act with a view to suggesting measures for the better implementation of the provision of this Act;

(vii) the identification of the areas where the members of the Scheduled Castes and the Scheduled Tribes are likely to be subjected to atrocities and adoption of such measures so as to ensure safety for such members.

(3) The Central Government shall take such steps as may be necessary to co-ordinate the measures taken by the State Governments under subsection (1).

(4) The Central Government shall, every year, place on the table of each House of Parliament a report on the measures taken by itself and by the State Governments in pursuance of the provisions of this section.

22. Protection of action taken in good faith.—No suit, prosecution or other legal proceedings shall lie against the Central Government or against the State Government or any officer or authority of Government or any other person for anything which is in good faith done or intended to be done under this Act.

23. Power to make rules.—(1) The Central Government may, by notification in the Official Gazette, make rules for carrying out the purposes of this Act.

(2) Every rule made under this Act shall be laid, as soon as may be after it is made, before each House of Parliament, while it is in session for a total period of thirty days which may be comprised in one session or in two or more successive sessions, and if, before the expiry of the session immediately following the session or the successive sessions aforesaid, both Houses agree in making any modification in the rule or both Houses agree that the rule should not be made, the rule shall thereafter have effect only in such modified form or be of no effect, as the case may be; so, however, that any such modification or annulment shall be without prejudice to the validity of anything previously done under that rule.

[THE SCHEDULE

[*See* section 3(2)(*va*)]

Section under the Indian Penal Code	Name of offence and punishment
120A	Definition of criminal conspiracy.
120B	Punishment of criminal conspiracy.
141	Unlawful assembly.
142	Being member of unlawful assembly.
143	Punishment for unlawful assembly.
144	Joining unlawful assembly armed with deadly weapon.
145	Joining or continuing in unlawful assembly, knowing it has been commanded to disperse.
146	Rioting.
147	Punishment for rioting.
148	Rioting, armed with deadly weapon.
217	Public servant disobeying direction of law with intent to save person from punishment or property from forfeiture.
319	Hurt.
320	Grievous hurt.
323	Punishment for voluntarily causing hurt.
324	Voluntarily causing hurt by dangerous weapons or means.
325	Punishment for voluntarily causing grievous hurt.
326B	Voluntarily throwing or attempting to throw acid.
332	Voluntarily causing hurt to deter public servant from his duty.
341	Punishment for wrongful restraint.
354	Assault or criminal force to woman with intent to outrage her modesty.
354A	Sexual harassment and punishment for sexual harassment.

---

1. Ins. by Act 1 of 2016, s. 12 (w.e.f. 26-1-2016).

Section under the Indian Penal Code	Name of offence and punishment
354B	Assault or use of criminal force to woman with intent to disrobe.
354C	Voyeurism.
354D	Stalking.
359	Kidnapping.
363	Punishment for kidnapping
365	Kidnapping or abducting with intent secretly and wrongfully to confine person.
376B	Sexual intercourse by husband upon his wife during separation.
376C	Sexual intercourse by a person in authority.
447	Punishment for criminal trespass.
506	Punishment for criminal intimidation.
509	Word, gesture or act intended to insult the modesty of a woman.]

GLOSSARY

AIDMAM: All India Dalit Mahila Manch (All India Dalit Women's Forum).

Charge sheet (*challan*): a report submitted by the police to the concerned magistrate once a police investigation is concluded and has yielded sufficient evidence to prosecute the accused.

CBI: Central Bureau of Investigation, India's main investigative agency for domestic crimes.

CDR: Centre for Dalit Rights (Dalit Adhikar Kendre), a Jaipur-based legal aid NGO.

Cognizable Offence: Defined by section 2c of the IPC as any offence for which the police are authorized to start an investigation and make an arrest.

CrPC: The Indian Code of Criminal Procedure, 1973, which outlines the procedures in criminal cases.

DGP: Director General of Police, the highest-ranking police officer in Indian States and Union Territories.

DSP: Deputy Superintendent of Police, a senior officer in the Indian police force and typically the head of the police force in a subdivision of a district. The DSP oversees investigations under the Atrocities Act.

(Exclusive) Special Court: For the speedy trial of cases under the Atrocities Act, all state governments in districts with high rates of atrocity complaints must set up an exclusive special court. In other districts, the state designates a sessions court as a special atrocity court.

FIR: First Information Report, the first written police record of a complaint lodged by the victim of a cognizable offence, or by someone on behalf of the victim.

FR (Closure Report): Final Report, a report filed by police to conclude an investigation under section 173 of the CrPC. Police file a closure report—colloquially FR—if they find insufficient evidence to file a charge sheet.

IPC: The Indian Penal Code, 1860. India's main criminal legislation.

JMSS: Jhunjhunu Meghwal Sangarsh Samiti (Jhunjhunu Association for Meghwal Assertion).

Magistrate: The lowest-ranking criminal court judge in India's judicial hierarchy. Magistrates (also referred to as metropolitan magistrates in cities designated as metropolitan areas) preside over magistrate courts—the lowest criminal courts in a district. While their powers are not equivalent to those of judges, they can conduct trials for lesser offences and deal with all motions concerning arrest and evidence prior to trials.

NCDHR: National Campaign on Dalit Human Rights.

NHRC: National Human Rights Commission of India, a statutory body responsible for the protection and promotion of Human Rights in India.

Noncompoundable Offence: crimes considered so grave that they cannot be settled or compromised (compounded) outside of court.

PoA: The Scheduled Castes/Scheduled Tribes (Prevention of Atrocities) Act, 1989.

SC: Scheduled Caste.

Sessions Court: The highest criminal trial court at the district level. It is presided over by a sessions judge (or a metropolitan sessions judge in metropolitan areas).

SP: Superintendent of Police, a senior rank in India's police service. The SP is usually the head of the police force in a district and ranks above the DSP.

SPP: Special Public Prosecutor, a lawyer appointed by the state government under the CrPC. SPPs represent an independent statutory authority.

ST: Scheduled Tribe.

NOTES

Preface

1. In transliterating Hindi to English, I have followed the Collins Hindi-English dictionary standards for romanization.

Introduction

1. *Jī* is a gender-neutral honorific used in Hindi.

2. *Chamar*, which is an official designation for a specific Dalit community (*jati*), is now also often used as an derogatory term to insult Dalits.

3. Dalits and Adivasis are referred to as Scheduled Castes (SCs) and Scheduled Tribes (STs), respectively, under Articles 341 and 342 of the Indian Constitution. A complete list of SCs and STs was compiled via two orders: the Constitution (Scheduled Castes) Order, 1950, and the Constitution (Scheduled Tribes) Order, 1950. The lists have been amended several times.

4. P. S. Krishnan passed away in November 2019 at the age of eighty-seven.

5. These commitments are laid out in the Preamble of the Indian Constitution.

6. The central issue of social equality is enshrined in a trifecta of constitutional articles in part 3 of the Indian constitution (Fundamental Rights of Citizens): Article 14 guarantees the right to equality, Article 15 outlaws discrimination on the basis of caste, religion, gender, sex, or place of birth, and Article 17 abolishes untouchability.

7. Maharati is a language spoken in the Indian state of Maharashtra.

8. Seats for SCs and STs were also proportionally reserved in all state legislative assemblies and in the lower house of parliament (*Lok Sabha*). The 1990s saw the implementation of SC/ST quotas in public sector promotions (Desai and Kulkarni 2008). In 1992 the 73rd and 74th Amendment Acts of the Indian Constitution reserved one-third of all seats in *panchayats* (village assemblies) and local urban governing bodies for women.

9. The report was issued by the Mandal Commission, which was set up in 1979 by the Janata Party government. Its mandate was to identify India's educationally and socially backward classes.

10. India's reservation policies have contended with a wide range of problems. Kriti Kapila argues that "the criteria for SC/ST and OBC status [rely] on contentious colonial classifications" (Kapila 2008, 6; also Cohn 1987). Others claim that reservations only benefit already upwardly mobile sections within SC/ST or OBC communities (Nayyar 2011), Some fear that the positive quota system will keep caste distinctions alive (Béteille 1992, 225).

11. Affirmative action policies only represent one aspect of a constantly evolving

arena of Dalit politics and assertion (Thorat 2002; Guru and Sarukkai 2012; Thorat and Sabharwal 2014; Jodhka 2015; Teltumbde 2018b; Waghmore 2018). Wide-scale mobilization (Juergensmeyer 1982; Gooptu 1993; Omvedt 1994, 1995; Rodrigues 2002) has continued alongside the creation of a particular arena of Dalit party politics (Pai 2002; Jaffrelot 2003; Gorringe 2005) and new economic pathways through social welfare programs (Hasan 2011; Carswell & de Neve 2014). Alternative religious discourses are also sometimes used by Dalits as a tool for upward mobility, claiming rights, and the generation of self-worth (Kapadia 1995; Beltz 2005; Mosse 2012; M. Fuchs 2019).

12. One notable exception is the work of Gadd et al. (2011), which relied on in-depth interviews with perpetrators of hate crime in the United Kingdom.

13. Meliorism as a concept finds its roots in pragmatist philosophy, which was one of the major theoretical strands that shaped the thought and writings of B. R. Ambedkar. John Dewey, perhaps the most towering figure in pragmatism theory, was a professor at Columbia University where Ambedkar studied and was the teacher who impressed Ambedkar the most (M. Fuchs 2019, 369). As I am submitting this book, a new historical treatise has just been published by philosopher Scott Stroud, which explores Ambedkar's time studying at Columbia and pragmatist themes of reconstruction and meliorism in his writings (2023).

14. "Harijan" translates as "People of God" and was introduced by Mahatma Gandhi to name the "untouchables."

15. Except the region of Ajmer-Merwara, which was ceded entirely to the British. Ajmer-Merwara became Ajmer state in 1950 and merged into the state of Rajasthan in 1956. The borders of Rajasthan were set in their current form by the State Reorganisation Act of 1956.

16. In select areas of Jodhpur state, the Jat peasantry had a more dominant position (Sisson 1969).

17. The Socio Economic and Caste Census 2011 (SECC) collected data on single caste affiliations for the first time since 1931. To date these data have not been officially released.

18. While the percentage of Scheduled Castes (SCs) who work in agriculture in Jhunjhunu doesn't deviate significantly from the overall figure, the proportion of SCs classified as agricultural laborers (ratio of cultivators to laborers 2:1) is much higher than the percentage of laborers among the overall population (ratio 7:1).

19. This number is higher than even the most generous official estimates of their population share. Meghwals in Jhunjhunu consistently claimed that they account for about 40% to 50% of Dalit groups in the district.

20. Atrocity complaints by Dalits of the Nayak *jāti* amount to 10% of all police registrations, those of Khatiks come to 4%, while Bairwa and Raigar complaints make up merely 2% each. Meanwhile Meenas, one of the rare ST communities in Jhunjhunu (under 2% of the district population), are also disproportionately represented in the police statistics. Their complaints constitute 12% of total PoA case registrations in Jhunjhunu.

21. Six other atrocity incidents also involved locally influential OBC castes, such as Gujars and Yadavs, and only two complaints were lodged against Rajputs, whose influence in the region has waned since independence.

22. With 2,491,551 million, Chamars are the second-largest SC group in Rajasthan.

23. The 1991 Census of India estimates the total Meghwal population in Rajasthan at

over one million (Shyamlal 2006, 21), while census data from 2001 mention Meghwals as the second-largest SC community in Rajasthan or (21% of the total SC population). Finally, the 2011 Census of India lists Meghwals as the most numerous SC group in the state.

24. Meghwals are also referred to as Meghbhanghi, Meghwanshi, or Megh.

25. For references on lower-caste assertion under British rule, see Aloysius 1998.

26. For information on Bhangis, Raigar, Chamars, see Shyamlal 2006.

27. The formation of the Bairwa *jāti* followed a similar pattern to that of the Meghwal *jāti*. Members of the Chamar caste from different North Indian regions united under the new Bairwa name in 1944 and adopted a written constitution (Shyamlal 2006, 11).

28. For comparison, see Rao (2002) on the writing of Khatik caste histories in Bhopal. Khatiks aimed to redefine themselves as a "heritage group that people feel proud of" (Rao 2002, 348).

29. Ramdev is also known as one of the five Pirs or "equestrian heroes" (Crooke 1968 [1896], 1:206). By the seventeenth century, Ramdev had come to prominence as a lower-caste deity, "whose followers were dominantly the untouchable dhedhs [now called Meghwals]" (Dhali 2011). Folkloric songs suggest that Ramdev, the son of a king, had a particularly strong bond with the members of the untouchable castes that his father employed (Khan 1997). Jordan Mullard encountered different versions of this story during her fieldwork in Rajasthan's Bikaner district. In one version Ramdev's mother could not bear a son. Therefore, her husband, the king, demanded that the next family in the kingdom to have a son should exchange him for one of his daughters. The next son to be born was from a Meghwal family. Therefore, Ramdev himself was a Meghwal. Another version of the story emphasizes the loving relationship between Ramdev and his adoptive Meghwal sister (*dharm-bahan*) Dali Bai (Mullard 2010, 237–38; cf. Khan 1997, 68). During my fieldwork I heard both versions of the story.

30. Sikar follows closely at 71.91%, while Jaipur has an even higher literacy rate of 75.51%. The district of Kota has the highest literacy rate in Rajasthan (*Statistical Handbook of Jhunjhunu 2020*).

31. The so-called *jāgīrdar* (holder of land) acted as an intermediary between the agricultural tenants, who tilled the soil, and the owners of the land, namely the state, or rather its Rajput gentry (Udaipur District Gazetteer 1979, 73). The *jāgīrdar* had to be paid tribute by the tenant. In turn, the *jāgīrdar* paid tribute to the Rajput gentry. But the amount the *jāgīrdar* paid was usually less than what he extracted from his tenants. The *jāgīrdari* system prevailed in 60% of contemporary Rajasthan (Central Press, Government of Rajasthan 1959).

Chapter 1: The Prevention of Atrocities Act

1. In December 2023 during the final editing stage of this book India ratified the Bharatiya Nyaya Sanhita Bill, 2023, to replace the Indian Penal Code.

2. Section 20 of the Atrocities Act states: "save as otherwise provided in this Act, the provisions of this Act shall have effect notwithstanding anything inconsistent therewith contained in any other law for the time being in force, or any custom or usage or any instrument having effect by virtue of any such law."

3. The Ramanathapuram riots are the subject of a recently published book by K. A. Manikumar (2017).

4. For a genealogy of the hate crime concept, see Jacobs and Potter 1998; Hall 2013; Chakraborti and Garland 2013.

5. In 2021 a two-judge bench headed by D. Y. Chandrachud recognized the issue of intersectionality in caste violence. In *Patan Jamal Vali v. State of Andhra Pradesh*—a case that involved the rape of a Dalit girl with visual impairments—the bench explicitly acknowledged that caste violence is often intersectional. Justice Chandrachud argued in his judgment that courts must understand how "social inequalities function in a cumulative fashion" (*Patan Jamal Vali v. State of Andhra Pradesh*).

6. The skepticism leveled against complaints filed by both Dalits and women partially finds its roots in colonial policies, which considered native witnesses unreliable (Oza 2020, 108) and savage (Bej, Sonavane, and Bokil 2021). Colonial courts systematically doubted women's stories and often expressed tacit support for upper castes accused of demeaning action towards Dalits (Galanter 1969).

Chapter 2: Who Owns the Law?

1. Sections 363, 366, 354, 375, and 376G of the Indian Penal Code.
2. Sections 3(1)(w)(i), 3(1)(w)(ii), and 3(2)(va) of the Atrocities Act as amended in 2015.
3. Section 6 of the Protection of Children from Sexual Offences Act, 2012.
4. Partha Chatterjee proposed that civil society engagement in India has been limited to middle-class involvement in public matters, while rural and economically weaker classes constitute a field of "political society" where citizens demand specific service from state institutions (P. Chatterjee 2001, 178).
5. Judicial magistrates cannot issue grave sentences like lifetime imprisonment.
6. Section 357A was added to the CrPC in 2008.

Chapter 3: The Case That Could Not Be

1. In Libasha and many other villages, the Rajput council is an unofficial political body and advisory council (*pancāyata*) that presides over village matters. The Rajput men on the council still retain authority over the rights and choices of the lower-caste groups.
2. The amended version of the act, which was introduced in 2015, three years after Choti Lal's case, actually includes "social and economic boycott" as a separate offence under chap. 2, sec. 3(1)(zc).
3. Rajput landowners employed several tactics to hold on to their land. Some families set up a company which technically owned the land, though the family retained ownership in practice. Sometimes, landowners only nominally transferred some land to their laborers.
4. If the police refuse to file an FIR, complainants can approach the Deputy Superintendent of Police (DSP) to investigate the matter. If this is unsuccessful, they can also enlist a lawyer to submit a request to the magistrate, asking him/her to direct the police to file the FIR. However, this route is time-consuming and costly and is usually not an option for atrocity complainants.
5. A Deputy Commissioner of Police is also referred to as a Superintendent of Police.

Chapter 4: (Re-)writing Law's Allegiance?

1. Advocates upset with the reversal of the verdict asked the Supreme Court to stay the amendments. A Supreme Court bench consisting of justices Arun Mishra and U. U. Lait heard the petitions in May 2019. The bench upheld the amendment act for the time being. However, in February 2020, a three-judge Supreme Court bench in *Prathvi Raj Chauhan v. Union of India* indicated that anticipatory bail may be granted when "no prima facie case could be made out" (Times Press News, October 3, 2019).

2. In Hindi: "Judge loga bhī na, hameshā 'false case' chīlate hain. Saccāii ke alaga alaga cehare hote hain. Aura kabhī kabhī court walī saccāii hamare saccāii se alaga hai. Dalito ki jindagī ki eka khāsa saccāii hai aura court mei je samajhānā mushkila hai. False cases mei bhī aksara saccāii dikhati hai."

3. Parts of this chapter have been published in the *Journal of the Royal Anthropological Institute* under the title "Counter-Truths and Incredible Laws: Caste Atrocities, False Cases, and the Limits of Hate Crime Legislation in North India."

4. The term is a word play on Superintendent of Police, a position that is also abbreviated as SP.

Chapter 5: "You Must Not Compromise!"

1. Upper-caste Hindus have often used animal comparisons to insult Dalits. Dogs especially are often associated with dirt and impurity (see Doniger 2014).

2. This is the Atrocities Act as per the amendment of 2015; see appendix.

Chapter 6: Fields of Massacre

1. Parts of this chapter have been published in *Contemporary South Asia* under the title "'Give Me the Space to Live': Trauma, Casted Land, and the Search for Restitution among the Meghwal Survivors of the Dangawas Massacre."

2. According to the *Indian Express*, "Nagaur is one of the two seats in North India that was won by the Congress even in its abysmal performance in 1977 thanks to its Jat sympathizers" (Dutta 2015).

3. Khejri trees can survive in extremely dry climates and be used for fodder. They often indicate low-lying water reservoirs.

4. In Hindi: "Hama apanā haq jab bhī mangānte hai, tabhī apanī zamīna se vo bhagādete hai, tabhī mār dete hai. Jagaha se haṭṭe nahīn vo. Gānva ke rāja banke ghūmanā cāhate hai."

5. For literature on retributive violence in the context of Dalit assertion, see Mendelsohn and Vicziany 1998; Thorat 2002; Thorat and Newman 2007; and Jaoul 2008.

6. For further references on the link between caste and land struggles, see Mohanty 2001; Waghmore 2013; and Pankaj 2016.

7. Former *khalsa* lands that had been under the direct control of the kingly court (*darbar*), along with nonagricultural lands, fruit orchards, and wells and buildings remained in the possession of former owners.

8. In Hindi: "pahale hamein andara se ṭīka honā hai taba dekhate hai ki kyā kāra sakte hai hama. Shāyada is men kānūna hamārī madada kar sakta hai?"

REFERENCES

Abel, Richard L. 1995. "What We Talk about When We Talk about Law." In *The Law and Society Reader*, edited by Richard L. Abel, 1–10. New York and London: New York University Press.
Abrahams, Ray G. 1998. *Vigilant Citizens: Vigilantism and the State*. Cambridge: Polity Press.
Abrams, Kathryn, and Hila Keren. 2007. "Law in the Cultivation of Hope." *California Law Review* 95 (2): 319–82. https://doi.org/10.15779/Z383D9B.
Acharya, Pranabindu, and Prachi Acharya. 2020. "An Analysis of the Scheduled Castes and Scheduled Tribes (Prevention of Atrocities) Act, 1989." SSRN Scholarly Paper. Rochester, NY. https://doi.org/10.2139/ssrn.3732709.
Affolter, Laura. 2021. *Asylum Matters: On the Front Line of Administrative Decision-Making*. Palgrave Socio-Legal Studies. Cham, Switzerland: Palgrave Macmillan.
Agamben, Giorgio. 1995. *Homo Sacer: Sovereign Power and Bare Life*. Translated by Daniel Heller-Roazen. Stanford, CA: Stanford University Press.
Agnes, Flavia. 1992. "Protecting Women against Violence? Review of a Decade of Legislation, 1980–89." *Economic and Political Weekly* 27 (17): 19–33.
Ahmed, Sara. 2004. *The Cultural Politics of Emotion*. 1st edition. Edinburgh: Edinburgh University Press.
Ajele, Grace, and Jena McGill. 2020. "Intersectionality in Law and Legal Contexts." Toronto: Women's Legal Education and Action Fund (LEAF). https://www.leaf.ca/wp-content/uploads/2020/10/Full-Report-Intersectionality-in-Law-and-Legal-Contexts.pdf.
Alha, Akhil. 2018. "The Other Side of Caste as Social Capital." *Social Change* 48 (4): 575–88. https://doi.org/10.1177/0049085718801490.
Alongi, Briana. 2017. "The Negative Ramifications of Hate Crime Legislation: It's Time to Reevaluate Whether Hate Crime Laws Are Beneficial to Society." *Pace Law Review* 37 (1): 326. https://doi.org/10.58948/2331-3528.1941.
Aloysius, Gnana. 1998. *Nationalism without a Nation in India*. Delhi: Oxford University Press.
Alvarez, Jose. 1999. "Crimes of States/Crimes of Hate: Lessons from Rwanda." *Yale Journal of International Law* 24: 365–483.
Ambasta, Kunal. 2020. "Designed for Abuse: Special Criminal Laws and Rights of the Accused." *NALSAR Student Law Review* 14: 1–19.
Ambedkar, Bhimrao Ramji. 1989a [1917]. "Castes in India: Their Mechanism, Genesis

and Development." In *Dr. Babasaheb Ambedkar, Writings and Speeches*, edited by Vasant Moon, 1:3–22. Bombay: Education Department, Government of Maharashtra.

———. 1989b [1936]. "Annihilation of Caste—with a Reply to Mahatma Gandhi." In *Dr. Babasaheb Ambedkar, Writings and Speeches*, edited by Vasant Moon, 1:23–96. Bombay: Education Department, Government of Maharashtra.

Anandhi, Jeyaranjan, and Rajan Krishnan. 2002. "Work, Caste and Competing Masculinities: Notes from a Tamil Village." *Economic and Political Weekly* 37 (43): 4397–406.

Anjum, Tabeenah. 2022. "Killed for Sporting a Moustache: Dalits in Rajasthan's Feudal Villages Face Rising Tide of Caste Violence." *Article 14* (blog). April 6, 2022. https://article-14.com/post/killed-for-sporting-a-moustache-dalits-in-rajasthan-s-feudal-villages-face-rising-tide-of-caste-violence-624cf9afb65f5.

Antze, Paul, and Michael Lambek. 1996. "Introduction: Forecasting Memory." In *Tense Past: Cultural Essays in Trauma and Memory*, edited by Paul Antze and Michael Lambek, 1st edition, xi–xxxviii. London and New York: Routledge. https://www.routledge.com/Tense-Past-Cultural-Essays-in-Trauma-and-Memory/Antze-Lambek/p/book/9780415915632.

Appadurai, Arjun. 2013. *The Future as Cultural Fact: Essays on the Global Condition*. New York: Verso Books.

Arora, Avneet. 2019. "80 per Cent of All Dowry Cases in India End in Acquittal." *SBS Language*, February 27, 2019. https://www.sbs.com.au/language/punjabi/en/article/80-per-cent-of-all-dowry-cases-in-india-end-in-acquittal/aets82803.

Atak, Kıvanç. 2022. "Racist Victimization, Legal Estrangement and Resentful Reliance on the Police in Sweden." *Social and Legal Studies* 31 (2): 238–60. https://doi.org/10.1177/09646639211023.

Bachmann-Medick, Doris. 2006. *Cultural Turns: Neuorientierungen in den Kulturwissenschaften*. Reinbek bei Hamburg: Rowohlt.

———. 2013. "The 'Translational Turn' in Literary and Cultural Studies: The Example of Human Rights." In *New Theories, Models and Methods in Literary and Cultural Studies*, edited by Greta Olson and Ansgar Nünning, 213–33. Trier: Wissenschaftlicher Verlag Trier.

Bairwa, Sita Ram. 2018. "Atrocities against Dalits in Rajasthan: An Analytical Study of Dausa District." *International Journal of Research in the Social Sciences* 8 (6): 2249–496.

Bajoria, Rishabh. 2018. "Indian Supreme Court Waters Down Legislation Protecting Scheduled Castes and Tribes from Unlawful Discrimination." *Oxford Human Rights Hub* (blog). May 18, 2018.

Balagopal, K. 1991. "Post-Chundur and Other Chundurs." *Economic and Political Weekly* 26 (42): 2399–2401, 2403–5.

Basu, Srimati. 2015. *The Trouble with Marriage: Feminists Confront Law and Violence in India*. Oakland: University of California Press.

Baxi, Pratiksha. 2010. "Justice Is a Secret: Compromise in Rape Trials." *Contributions to Indian Sociology* 44 (3): 207–33. https://doi.org/10.1177/006996671004400301.

———. 2014. *Public Secrets of Law: Rape Trials in India*. Oxford: Oxford University Press.

Baxi, Upendra. 1999. "Constitutionalism as a Site of State Formative Practices." *Cardozo Law Review* 21 (4): 1183–1210.

———. 2012. "Postcolonial Legality: A Postscript from India." *Verfassung und Recht in Übersee/Law and Politics in Africa, Asia and Latin America* 45 (2): 178–94.
Bear, Laura. 2016. "Time as Technique." *Annual Review of Anthropology* 45 (1): 487–502. https://doi.org/10.1146/annurev-anthro-102313-030159.
Bear, Laura, and Nayanika Mathur. 2015. "Remaking the Public Good: A New Anthropology of Bureaucracy." *Cambridge Journal of Anthropology* 33 (1). https://doi.org/10.3167/ca.2015.330103.
Bedard-Gilligan, Michele, Lori A. Zoellner, and Norah C. Feeny. 2017. "Is Trauma Memory Special? Trauma Narrative Fragmentation in PTSD: Effects of Treatment and Response." *Clinical Psychological Science* 5 (2): 2012–225. https://doi.org/10.1177/2167702616676581.
Bej, Srujana, Nikita Sonavane, and Ameya Bokil. 2021."Construction(s) of Female Criminality: Gender, Caste and State Violence." *Economic and Political Weekly*, Engage, 54 (36): 1–13.
Belleau, Jean-Philippe. 2022. "'Neighbor' Is an Empty Concept: How the Neighbourly Turn in Mass Violence Studies Has Overlooked Anthropology and Sociology." *Journal of Genocide Research* 24: 1–21. https://doi.org/10.1080/14623528.2022.2081298.
Beltz, Johannes. 2005. *Mahar, Buddhist and Dalit: Religious Conversion and Socio-Political Emancipation*. Delhi: Manohar.
Berg, Dag Erik. 2014."Karamchedu and the Dalit Subject in Andhra Pradesh." *Contributions to Indian Sociology* 48 (3): 307–449. https://doi.org/10.1177/0069966714540242.
———. 2020. *Dynamics of Caste and Law in India: Dalits, Oppression and Constitutional Democracy in India*. Cambridge: Cambridge University Press.
Berti, Daniela. 2010. "Hostile Witnesses, Judicial Interactions and Out-of-Court Narratives in a North Indian District Court." *Contributions to Indian Sociology* 44 (3): 235–63. https://doi.org/10.1177/006996671004400302.
———. 2015. "Binding Fictions: Contradicting Facts and Judicial Constraints in a Narcotics Case in Himachal Pradesh." In *Regimes of Legality: Ethnography of Criminal Cases in South Asia*, edited by Daniela Berti and Devika Bordia, 91–128. Delhi, India: Oxford University Press.
Berti, Daniela, and Devika Bordia. 2015. "Introduction." In *Regimes of Legality: Ethnography of Criminal Cases in South Asia*, edited by Daniela Berti and Devika Bordia, 1–26. New Delhi: Oxford University Press.
Berti, Daniela, and Giles Tarabout. 2012. "Criminal Proceedings in India and the Question of Culture: An Anthropological Perspective." In *Rechtsanalyse als Kulturforschung*, edited by Werner Gephardt, 193–206. Frankfurt am Main: Vittorio Klostermann.
Béteille, André. 1998. *Society and Politics in India: Essays in a Comparative Perspective*. Oxford: Oxford University Press.
Bharadwaj, Suraj Bhan. 2012. "Myth and Reality of the Khap Panchayats: A Historical Analysis of the Panchayat and Khap Panchayat." *Studies in History* 28 (1): 43–67. https://doi.org/10.1177/0257643013477250.
Bhat, M. Mohsin Alam. 2020a. "Hate Crimes in India." *Jindal Global Law Review* 11 (1): 1–5. https://doi.org/10.1007/s41020-020-00119-0.

———. 2020b. "Mob, Murder, Motivation: The Emergence of Hate Crime Discourse in India." *Socio-Legal Review* 16 (1): 75–108. https://doi.org/10.2139/ssrn.3602509.

Bhat, M. Mohsin Alam, Vidisha Bajaj, and Sanjana Arvind Kumar. 2020. "The Crime Vanishes: Mob Lynching, Hate Crime, and Police Discretion in India." *Jindal Global Law Review* 11 (1): 33–59. https://doi.org/10.1007/s41020-020-00115-4.

Bhatia, Bela. 2006. "Dalit Rebellion against Untouchability in Chakwada, Rajasthan." *Contributions to Indian Sociology* 40 (1): 29–61. https://doi.org/10.1177/006996670504000102.

Bhatia, Gautam. 2019. *The Transformative Constitution: A Radical Biography in Nine Acts*. New Delhi: HarperCollins Publishers India.

Bittner, Egon. 1970. *The Functions of the Police in Modern Society: A Review of Background Factors, Current Practices, and Possible Role Models*. Washington, DC: National Institute of Mental Health, Center for Studies of Crime and Delinquency.

Björgo, Tore. 1994. "Legal Reactions to Racism: Law and Practice in Scandinavia." In *Hate Crime: International Perspectives on Causes and Control*, edited by Mark S. Hamm, 71–90. Cincinnati, OH: Anderson Publishing.

Blichner, Lars Christian, and Anders Molander. 2008. "Mapping Juridification." *European Law Journal* 14 (1): 36–54. https://doi.org/10.1111/j.1468–0386.2007.00405.x.

Bloch, Ernst. 1986. *The Principle of Hope*. Translated by Neville Plaice, Stephen Plaice, and Paul Knight. Vol. 2. 3 vols. Cambridge, MA: MIT Press. https://mitpress.mit.edu/9780262521994/the-principle-of-hope/.

Bob, Clifford. 2007. "'Dalit Rights Are Human Rights': Caste Discrimination, International Activism, and the Construction of a New Human Rights Issue." *Human Rights Quarterly* 29 (1): 167–93.

Botha, Louis, and Anton Kok. 2019. "An Empirical Study of the Early Cases in the Pilot Equality Courts Established in Terms of the Promotion of Equality and Prevention of Unfair Discrimination Act 4 of 2000." *African Human Rights Law Journal* 19 (1): 317–36. https://doi.org/10.17159/1996–2096/2019/v19n1a15.

Bourdieu, Pierre. 1977. *Outline of a Theory of Practice*. Edited by Ernest Gellner, Jack Goody, Stephen Gudeman, Michael Herzfeld, and Jonathan Parry. Translated by Richard Nice. Cambridge Studies in Social and Cultural Anthropology 16. Cambridge: Cambridge University Press.

———. 1986. "The Forms of Capital." In *Handbook of Theory and Research for the Sociology of Education*, edited by John G. Richardson, 241–58. New York and London: Greenwood Press.

Bowling, Benjamin. 1993. "Racial Harassment and the Process of Victimization: Conceptual and Methodological Implications for the Local Crime Survey." *British Journal of Criminology* 33 (2): 231–50.

Boyd, Elizabeth A., Richard A. Berk, and Karl M. Hamner. 1996. "'Motivated by Hatred or Prejudice': Categorization of Hate-Motivated Crimes in Two Police Divisions." *Law & Society Review* 30 (4): 819–50. https://doi.org/10.2307/3054119.

Brass, Paul. 1997. *Theft of an Idol: Text and Context in the Representation of Collective Violence*. Princeton, NJ: Princeton University Press.

Brax, David. 2016. "Motives, Reasons, and Responsibility in Hate/Bias Crime Legislation." *Criminal Justice Ethics* 35 (3): 230–48. http://dx.doi.org/10.1080/0731129X.2016.1243826.

Brax, David, and Christian Munthe. 2015. "The Philosophical Aspects of Hate Crime and Hate Crime Legislation: Introducing the Special Section on the Philosophy of Hate Crime." *Journal of Interpersonal Violence* 30 (10): 1687–95. https://doi.org/10.1177/0886260514555374.

Bryant, Rebecca, and Daniel M. Knight. 2019. *The Anthropology of the Future*. Cambridge: Cambridge University Press.

Cabot, Heath. 2013. "The Social Aesthetics of Eligibility: NGO Aid and Indeterminacy in the Greek Asylum Process." *American Ethnologist* 40 (3): 452–66. https://doi.org/10.1111/amet.12032.

Caldeira, Teresa P. R. 2002. "The Paradox of Police Violence in Democratic Brazil." *Ethnography* 3 (3): 235–63.

Candeub, Adam. 1994. "Motive Crimes and Other Minds." *University of Pennsylvania Law Review* 142 (6): 2071–124.

Card, Claudia. 2004. "The Atrocity Paradigm Revisited." *Hypatia* 19 (4): 212–22.

Carsten, Janet. 1995. "The Politics of Forgetting: Migration, Kinship and Memory on the Periphery of the Southeast Asian State." *Journal of the Royal Anthropological Institute* 1 (2): 317–35. https://doi.org/10.2307/3034691.

Carswell, Grace, and Geert De Neve. 2014. "MGNREGA in Tamil Nadu: A Story of Success and Transformation?" *Journal of Agrarian Change* 14 (4): 564–85. https://doi.org/10.1111/joac.12054.

———. 2015. "Litigation against Political Organization? The Politics of Dalit Mobilization in Tamil Nadu, India." *Development and Change* 46 (5): 1106–32. https://doi.org/10.1111/dech.12190.

Central Press, Government of Rajasthan. 1959. "Report of the State Land Commission for Rajasthan." Jaipur.

Centre for Dalit Rights (CDR) and Programme on Women's Economic, Social and Cultural Rights (PWESCR). 2008. "Dalit Women in Rajasthan: Status of Economic, Social & Cultural Rights." Fact Finding Mission Report 1. New Delhi: Programme on Women's Economic, Social and Cultural Rights (PWESCR). http://www.pwescr.org/Dalit_Report.pdf.

Centre for Dalit Rights (CDR). 2016. "Centre for Dalit Rights (Initiative of Dalit Manavadhikar Kendra Samiti)." Accessed August 11, 2023. http://dmkscdr.org/cms.php?id=226.

Census of India. 2011. *Part XI Rajasthan Census Atlas*. Government of India, Directorate of Census Operations. https://www.census2011.co.in/

Certeau, Michel de. 1984. *The Practice of Everyday Life*. Berkeley, Los Angeles, London: University of California Press.

Chakraborti, Neil, and Jon Garland. 2013. *Hate Crime: Impact, Causes and Responses*. Online edition. London: Sage Publications. https://sk.sagepub.com/books/hate-crime.

Chandhoke, Neera. 2021. *The Violence in Our Bones: Mapping the Deadly Fault Lines within Indian Society*. New Delhi: Aleph Book Company.

Chatterji, Angana P., Thomas Blom Hansen, and Christophe Jaffrelot. 2019. "Introduction." In *Majoritarian State: How Hindu Nationalism Is Changing India*, edited by Angana P. Chatterji, Thomas Blom Hansen, and Christophe Jaffrelot, 1–16. Oxford: Oxford University Press.

Chatterjee, Moyukh. 2017. "The Impunity Effect: Majoritarian Rule, Everyday Legality, and State Formation in India." *American Ethnologist* 44 (1): 118–30. https://doi.org/10.1111/amet.12430.

———. 2023. *Composing Violence: The Limits of Exposure and the Making of Minorities*. Theory in Forms. Durham, NC: Duke University Press.

Chatterjee, Partha. 2001. "On Civil and Political Society in Post-Colonial Democracies." In *Civil Society: History and Possibilities*, edited by Sudipta Kaviraj and Sunil Khilnani, 165–78. Cambridge: Cambridge University Press.

———. 2004. *The Politics of the Governed: Reflections on Popular Politics in Most of the World*. New York: Columbia University Press.

Chattopadhyay, Suhas. 1975. "On the Class Nature of Land Reforms in India since Independence: A Preliminary Examination." In *India—State and Society: A Marxian Approach*, edited by Matthew Kurian, 182–99. New Delhi: Orient Longman.

Cheng, Jesse. 2017. "Humanity's Subtensions: Culture Theory in US Death Penalty Mitigation." *Social Analysis* 61 (3): 73–90. https://doi.org/doi:10.3167/sa.2017.61030.

Chowdhury, Tanzil Z. 2017. "Temporality and Criminal Law Adjudication's Multiple Pasts." *Liverpool Law Review* 38 (2): 187–206. https://doi.org/10.1007/s10991-017-9192-8.

Christie, Pam. 2013. "Space, Place, and Social Justice: Developing a Rhythm Analysis of Education in South Africa." *Qualitative Inquiry* 19 (10): 775–85. https://doi.org/10.1177/1077800413503796.

Cicourel, Aaron. 1968. *The Social Organization of Juvenile Justice*. New Brunswick, NJ: Transaction Publishers.

Ciotti, Manuela. 2012. "Resurrecting Seva (Social Service): Dalit and Low-Caste Women Party Activists as Producers and Consumers of Political Culture and Practice in Urban North India." *Journal of Asian Studies* 71 (1): 149–70. https://doi.org/10.1017/S002191181100297X.

Citizens against Hate. 2018. "Lynching Without End: Report of Factfinding into Religiously Motivated Crime in India." New Delhi. https://citizensagainsthate.org/wp-content/uploads/2018/06/Lynching-Without-End-Reprint.pdf.

Cody, Francis. 2013. *The Light of Knowledge: Literacy Activism and the Politics of Writing in South India*. Ithaca, NY: Cornell University Press. https://www.cornellpress.cornell.edu/book/9780801479182/the-light-of-knowledge/.

———. 2020. "Wave Theory: Cash, Crowds and Caste in Indian Elections." *American Ethnologist* 47 (4): 402–16. https://doi.org/10.1111/amet.12986.

Cohn, Bernard. 1987. "The Census, Social Structure and Objectification in South Asia." In *An Anthropologist among the Historians and Other Essays*, edited by Bernard Cohn, 224–54. New Delhi: Oxford University Press.

Cohen, Lawrence. 2010. "On Transplant Victims, Wounded Communities and the Moral Demands of Dreaming." In *Ethical Life in South Asia*, edited by Anand Pandian and Daud Ali, 253–74. Bloomington: Indiana University Press.

Cole, B. L. 1992. *Census of India 1931: Rajputana Agency—Reports and Tables*. Delhi:

Manohar. https://www.abebooks.co.uk/9788185425948/Census-India-1911-1921-1931-81 85425949/plp.

Comaroff, John L. 2001. "Colonialism, Culture, and the Law: A Foreword." *Law & Social Inquiry* 26 (2): 305–14. https://doi.org/10.1111/j.1747-4469.2001.tb00180.x.

Commonwealth Foundation (CWF). 2019. "Advocacy for Better Implementation of the Prevention of Atrocities Act." https://commonwealthfoundation.com/project/strengthening-advocacy-for-better-implementation-of-the-prevention-of-atrocities-act/ (last accessed December 15. 2022).

Commonwealth Human Rights Initiative (CHRI). 2018. "Scheduled Castes and Scheduled Tribes (Prevention of Atrocities) Act, 1989 & Rules, 1995. As Amended in 2015: A Guide." New Delhi, London, Accra: Commonwealth Human Rights Initiative. https://www.humanrightsinitiative.org/download/1528350081Scheduled%20Castes %20and%20Scheduled%20Tribes%20(Prevention%20of%20atrocities)%20Act,%20 1989.pdf.

Copland, Ian. 2005. *State, Community and Neighbourhood in Princely North India, c. 1900–1950*. New York: Palgrave Macmillan.

Corbridge, Stuart. 2000. "Competing Inequalities: The Scheduled Tribes and the Reservations System in India's Jharkhand." *Journal of Asian Studies* 59 (1): 62–85. https://doi.org/10.2307/2658584.

Corbridge, Stuart, Glyn Williams, Manoj Srivastava, and René Véron. 2012. "Politics of Middlemen and Political Society." In *Re-Framing Democracy and Agency in India: Interrogating Political Society*, edited by Ajay Gudavarthy, 171–200. Anthem Press. https://doi.org/10.7135/UPO9780857289469.009.

Cotterrell, Roger. 1998. "Why Must Legal Ideas Be Interpreted Sociologically?" *Journal of Law and Society* 25 (2): 171–92.

Coutin, Susan Bibler. 1995. "Smugglers or Samaritans in Tucson, Arizona: Producing and Contesting Legal Truth." *American Ethnologist* 22 (3): 549–71. https://doi.org/10 .1525/ae.1995.22.3.02a00050.

Cover, Robert. 1983. "The Supreme Court, 1982 Term—Foreword: Nomos and Narrative." *Harvard Law Review* 97 (1): 4–68.

Crenshaw, Kimberlé. 1989. "Demarginalizing the Intersection of Race and Sex: A Black Feminist Critique of Antidiscrimination Doctrine, Feminist Theory and Antiracist Politics." *University of Chicago Legal Forum* 1989 (8): 139–67.

Crooke, B. A. 1968. *The Popular Religion and Folk-Lore of Northern India*. 2 vols. Chennai, New Delhi, Tirunelveli: Munshiram Manoharlal Publishers.

Csordas, Thomas J. 1994. *Embodiment and Experience: The Existential Ground of Culture and Self*. Cambridge: Cambridge University Press.

Cuno, Kenneth M., and Manisha Desai. 2009. "Introduction." In *Family, Gender, and Law in a Globalizing Middle East and South Asia*, edited by Kenneth M. Cuno and Manisha Desai, xiii-xx. Syracuse, NY: Syracuse University Press. https://www.jstor .org/stable/j.ctt1j5dfd8.

Dale Scott, Peter. 2004. "The Sleep of Reason: Denial, Memory-Work, and the Reconstruction of Social Order." In *Literary Responses to Mass Violence*, edited by Daniel Terris, 35–43. Waltham, MA: Brandeis University.

Das, Veena. 1995. *Critical Events: An Anthropological Perspective on Contemporary India.* New Delhi: Oxford University Press.

———. 2001. "Crisis and Representation: Rumour and the Circulation of Hate."." In *Disturbing Remains: Memory, History, and Crisis in the Twentieth Century*, edited by Michael S. Roth and Charles G. Salas, 37–63. Los Angeles: Getty Research Institute.

———. 2003. "Trauma and Testimony: Implications for Political Community." *Anthropological Theory* 3 (3): 293–307. https://doi.org/10.1177/14634996030033003.

———. 2006. *Life and Words: Violence and the Descent into the Ordinary.* Berkeley, Los Angeles, London: University of California Press.

———. 2007. "Commentary: Trauma and Testimony: Between Law and Discipline." *Ethos* 35 (3): 330–35.

———. 2019. "A Child Disappears: Law in the Courts, Law in the Interstices of Everyday Life." *Contributions to Indian Sociology* 53 (1): 97–132. https://doi.org/10.1177/0069966718812544.

Das, Veena, and Shalini Randeria. 2015. "Politics of the Urban Poor: Aesthetics, Ethics, Volatility, Precarity: An Introduction to Supplement 11." *Current Anthropology* 56 (S11): S3–14. https://doi.org/10.1086/682353.

Datta, Nonica. 1999. *Forming an Identity. A Social History of the Jats.* New Delhi: Oxford University Press.

———. 1997. "Arya Samaj and the Making of Jat Identity." *Studies in History* 13 (1): 97–119. https://doi.org/10.1177/025764309701300104.

Deliege, Robert. 1999. *The Untouchables of India.* Oxford and New York: Berg Publishers.

Derrida, Jacques. 1992. "Force of Law: The 'Mystical Foundations of Authority.'" In *Deconstruction and the Possibility of Justice*, edited by Drucilla Cornell, Michel Rosenfeld, and David Carlson, 3–67. London: Routledge.

Desai, Sonalde, and Veena Kulkarni. 2008. "Changing Educational Inequalities in India in the Context of Affirmative Action." *Demography* 45 (2): 245–70. https://doi.org/10.1353/dem.0.0001.

Devi, Vasanthi. 2017. *Conversations with P. S. Krishnan: A Crusade for Social Justice: P. S. Krishnan Bending Governance to the Deprived.* Chennai: South Vision Books.

Dewey, John. 1958. *Experience and Nature.* Dover Books on Western Philosophy. New York: Dover Publication Inc.

———. 1963. *Reconstruction in Philosophy.* Boston: Beacon Press.

Dhali, Rajshree. 2011. "History, Community and Identity: An Interpretation of Dalibai." *Round Table India: For an Informed Ambedkar Age* (blog). August 9, 2011. http://roundtableindia.co.in.

Dirks, Nicholas B. 1987. *The Hollow Crown: Ethnohistory of an Indian Kingdom.* Cambridge: Cambridge University Press.

———. 2001. *Castes of Mind: Colonialism and the Making of Modern India.* Princeton, NJ: Princeton University Press.

Dixon, Liz, and Larry Ray. 2007. "Current Issues and Developments in Race Hate Crime." *Probation Journal* 54 (2): 109–24. https://doi.org/10.1177/0264550507077251.

Doniger, Wendy. 2014. *On Hinduism.* Oxford: Oxford University Press.

Donner, Henrike. 2011. "Gendered Bodies, Domestic Work and Perfect Families: New Regimes of Gender and Food in Bengali Middle-Class Lifestyles." In *Being Middle-*

Class in India: A Way of Life, edited by Henrike Donner, 47–72. London: Routledge.
Dr. Subhash Kashinath Mahajan v. State of Maharashtra and ANR. 2018, SCC 454 SCC. Supreme Court of India.
Dubois, Vincent. 2018. "The State, Legal Rigor and the Poor: The Daily Practice of Welfare Control." In *Stategraphy: Towards a Relational Anthropology of the State*, edited by Tatjana Thelen, Larissa Vetters, and Kebeet van Benda-Beckmann, 38–55. New York and Oxford: Berghahn Books.
Dutta, Sweta. 2015. "Where One Community Lives in Fear and the Other Is Too Dominant for Parties to Offend." *Indian Express*, June 1, 2015. https://indianexpress.com/article/india/india-others/where-one-community-lives-in-fear-and-the-other-is-too-dominant-for-parties-to-offend/.
Eckert, Julia. 2001. "The Power of Action." *Sociologicus* 51 (1 & 2): 89–122.
———. 2003. *The Charisma of Direct Action: Power, Politics, and the Shiv Sena*. New Delhi and New York: Oxford University Press.
———. 2012. "Rumours of Rights." In *Law Against the State: Ethnographic Forays into Law's Transformations*, edited by Julia M. Eckert, Brian Donahoe, Christian Strümpell, and Özlem Zerrin Biner, 147–70. Cambridge: Cambridge University Press.
Eckert, Julia, and Laura Knöpfel. 2020. "Legal Responsibility in an Entangled World." *Journal of Legal Anthropology* 4 (2): 1–16. https://doi.org/10.3167/jla.2020.040201.
Fairweather, Joan G. 2006. *A Common Hunger: Land Rights in Canada and South Africa*. Calgary: University of Calgary Press.
Faleiro, Sonia. 2021. *The Good Girls: An Ordinary Killing*. London: Bloomsbury Circus.
Fanon, Frantz. 2008. *Black Skin, White Masks*. New York: Grove Press.
Fassin, Didier. 2013. *Enforcing Order: An Ethnography of Urban Policing*. Cambridge: Polity Press.
Fassin, Didier, and Richard Rechtman. 2009. *The Empire of Trauma: Inquiry into the Condition of Victimhood*. Princeton, NJ: Princeton University Press.
Fay, Derrick, and Deborah James. 2008. "The Anthropology of Land Restitution: An Introduction." In *The Rights and Wrongs of Land Restitution: "Restoring What Was Ours,"* edited by Derrick Fay and Deborah James, 1–24. London: Routledge.
Felestiner, William L. F., Richard L. Abel, and Austin Sarat. 1980. "The Emergence and Transformation of Disputes: Naming, Blaming, Claiming . . ." *Law & Society Review* 15 (3/4): 631–54. https://doi.org/10.2307/3053505.
Ferrándiz, Francisco, and Antonius C. G. M. Robben. 2015. *Necropolitics: Mass Graves and Exhumations in the Age of Human Rights*. Philadelphia: University of Pennsylvania Press.
Fiala, Andrew. 2019. "Progress and Meliorism: Making Progress in Thinking about Progress." *Journal of the Philosophy of History* 15 (1): 28–50.
Foucault, Michel. 1980. *Power/Knowledge: Selected Interviews and Other Writings, 1972–1977*. New York: Random House.
Fraser, Nancy. 1998. "Social Justice in the Age of Identity Politics: Redistribution, Recognition, and Participation." Presentation delivered at Stanford University April 30–May 2, 1996. In *The Tanner Lectures on Human Values*, edited by Grethe B. Peterson, 19:1–67. Salt Lake City, Utah: The University of Utah Press. https://tannerlectures.utah.edu/_resources/documents/a-to-z/f/Fraser98.pdf.

Fuchs, Martin. 2019. "Self-Affirmation, Self-Transcendence and the Relationality of Selves: The Social Embedment of Individualisation in Bhakti." In *Religious Individualisations: Historical Dimensions and Comparative Perspectives*, edited by Martin Fuchs, Antje Linkenbach, Martin Mulsow, Bernd-Christian Otto, Rahul Parson, and Jörg Rüpke, 257–88. Berlin: De Gruyter.

———. 2019. "Dhamma and the Common Good: Religion as Problem and Answer—Ambedkar's Critical Theory of Social Relationality." In *Religious Interactions in Modern India*, edited by Martin Fuchs and Vasudha Dalmia, 364–413. New Delhi: Oxford University Press.

Fuchs, Sandhya. 2015. "Between Professionalism and Protest: Reimagining Dalit Activism in the Age of Human Rights." Master of Philosophy (MPhil) Thesis, Oxford, UK: School of Anthropology and Museum Ethnography, Institute of Social and Cultural Anthropology, University of Oxford.

———. 2018. "Indian Supreme Court Curbs One of the World's Most Powerful Anti-Discrimination Laws." *OpenDemocracy*, May 26, 2018. https://www.opendemocracy.net/en/openindia/indian-supreme-court-curbs-one-of-world-s-most-powerful-anti-discrimination-/.

———. 2020a. "'Give Me the Space to Live': Trauma, Casted Land and the Search for Restitution among the Meghwal Survivors of the Dangawas Massacre." *Contemporary South Asia* 28 (3): 392–407. https://doi.org/10.1080/09584935.2020.1801580.

———. 2020b. "'We Don't Have the Right Words!': Idiomatic Violence, Embodied Inequalities, and Uneven Translations in Indian Law Enforcement." *PoLAR: Political and Legal Anthropology Review* 43 (2): 177–94. https://doi.org/10.1111/plar.12373.

———. 2020c. "The Gift of a Bicultural Upbringing." *SAPIENS*, January 10, 2020. https://www.sapiens.org/culture/anthropologist-parents/.

———. 2022. "Rethinking the Atrocities Act: Proving Prejudice and Interpreting Evidence in Rajasthan." *South Asia Multidisciplinary Academic Journal* 28: 146–66. https://doi.org/10.4000/samaj.7884.

Fuller, Christopher J., ed. 1996. *Caste Today*. New Delhi and Oxford: Oxford University Press.

Gadd, David, and Bill Dixon. 2011. *Losing the Race: Thinking Psychosocially about Racially Motivated Crime*. London: Routledge.

Gal, Susan. 2015. "Politics of Translation." *Annual Review of Anthropology* 44 (1): 225–40. https://doi.org/10.1146/annurev-anthro-102214-013806.

Galanter, Marc. 1969. "Untouchability and the Law." *Economic and Political Weekly* 4 (1/2): 131–70.

———. 1984. *Competing Equalities: The Indian Experience with Compensatory Discrimination*. Berkeley, Los Angeles, London: University of California Press.

———. 1989. *Law and Society in Modern India*. Oxford India Paperbacks. Oxford and New York: Oxford University Press.

Garriot, William. 2013. "Introduction: Police in Practice: Policing and the Project of Contemporary Governance." In *Policing and Contemporary Governance*, 1–28. New York: Palgrave Macmillan.

Geertz, Clifford. 1983. "Local Knowledge: Fact and Law in Comparative Perspective."

In *Local Knowledge: Further Essays in Interpretative Anthropology*, edited by Clifford Geertz, 167–234. New York: Basic Books.
Gerlach, Christian. 2006. "Extremely Violent Societies: An Alternative to the Concept of Genocide." *Journal of Genocide Research* 8 (4): 455–71. https://doi.org/10.1080/14623520601056299.
Gill, Kamalpreet Singh. 2018. "A Tale of Two States: Understanding the Complexity of Dalit Politics in India." *Swarajya*, April 7, 2018. https://swarajyamag.com/politics/a-tale-of-two-states-understanding-the-complexity-of-dalit-politics-in-india.
Glenn, Haze. 2016. "Accessing Credibility." *Principles in Practice*, 1–5. https://www.judiciary.uk/wp-content/uploads/2016/01/genn_assessing-credibility.pdf
Gokuldas, Swamiji. 1998. *Meghwansh Itihas*. Ajmer: Shri Saraswati Prakashan.
Goldblatt, Beth. 2015. "Intersectionality in International Anti-Discrimination Law: Addressing Poverty in Its Complexity." *Australian Journal of Human Rights* 21 (1): 47–70. https://doi.org/10.1080/1323238X.2015.11910931.
Goldstein, Daniel M. 2003. "'In Our Own Hands': Lynching, Justice, and the Law in Bolivia." *American Ethnologist* 30 (1): 22–43.
Goody, Jack. 1986. *The Logic of Writing and the Organization of Society*. Cambridge: Cambridge University Press.
Gooptu, Nandini. 1993. "Caste and Labour: Untouchable Social Movements in Urban Uttar Pradesh in the Early Twentieth Century." In *Dalit Movements and the Meanings of Labour in India*, edited by Peter Robb, 277–98. Delhi: Oxford University Press.
Gorringe, Hugo. 2005. *Untouchable Citizens: Dalit Movements and Democratization in Tamil Nadu*. New Delhi, Thousand Oaks, London: Sage Publications India.
Gorringe, Hugo, and Damodaran Karthikeyan. 2014. "Confronting Casteism? Apathy and the Atrocities Act." *Economic and Political Weekly* 49 (4): 74–75.
Gorringe, Hugo, and Irene Rafanell. 2007. "The Embodiment of Caste: Oppression, Protest and Change." *Sociology* 41 (1): 97–114. https://doi.org/10.1177/0038038507074721.
Gottlieb, Nora, Dani Filc, and Nadav Davidovitch. 2012. "Medical Humanitarianism, Human Rights and Political Advocacy: The Case of the Israeli Open Clinic." Special issue: "Migration, 'Illegality,' and Health: Mapping Embodied Vulnerability and Debating Health-Related Deservingness," *Social Science & Medicine* 74 (6): 839–45. https://doi.org/10.1016/j.socscimed.2011.07.018.
Grant, Evadné. 2007. "Dignity and Equality." *Human Rights Law Review* 7 (2): 299–329. https://doi.org/10.1093/hrlr/ngm002.
Greenhouse, Carol J. 2008. "Life Stories, Law's Stories: Subjectivity and Responsibility in the Politicization of the Discourse of "Identity"." *PoLAR: Political and Legal Anthropology Review* 31 (1): 79–95. https://doi.org/10.1111/j.1555-2934.2008.00002.x.
Griffiths, Anne. 2001. "Review of *Remaking Law: Gender, Ethnography, and Legal Discourse*, by Susan F. Hirsch." *Law & Society Review* 35 (2): 495–509. https://doi.org/10.2307/3185411.
Guha, Ayan. 2019. "Recent Debate on Landmark Anti-Caste Legislation in India." *International Journal of Discrimination and the Law* 19 (1): 48–63. https://doi.org/10.1177/1358229118814467.

Gupta, Akhil. 2005. "Narratives of Corruption: Anthropological and Fictional Accounts of the Indian State." *Ethnography* 6 (1): 5–34.

———. 2012. *Red Tape: Bureaucracy, Structural Violence, and Poverty in India*. Durham, NC: Duke University Press.

Gupta, Dipankar. 2004. *Caste in Question: Identity or Hierarchy?* New Delhi, Thousand Oaks, London: SAGE.

Guru, Gopal. 2009. "Introduction: Theorizing Humiliation." In *Humiliation: Claims and Context*, edited by Gopal Guru, 1–19. Oxford: Oxford University Press.

———. 2011. "Liberal Democracy in India and the Dalit Critique." *Social Research* 78 (1): 99–122.

Guru, Gopal, and Anuradha Chakravarty. 2005. "Who Are the Country's Poor? Social Movement Politics and Dalit Poverty." In *Social Movements in India: Poverty, Power, and Politics*, edited by Raka Ray and Mary Fainsod Katzenstein, 135–60. Oxford: Oxford University Press.

Guru, Gopal, and Sundar Sarukkai. 2019. *Experience, Caste, and the Everyday Social*. New Delhi: Oxford University Press.

Guru, Gopal, and Sunder Sarukkai, eds. 2012. *The Cracked Mirror: An Indian Debate on Experience and Theory*. New Delhi: Oxford University Press.

Habermas, Jürgen. 2010. "Das Konzept der Menschenwürde und die realistische Utopie der Menschenrechte." *Deutsche Zeitschrift für Philosophie* 58 (3): 343–58. https://doi.org/10.1524/dzph.2010.58.3.343.

Hall, Nathan. 2013. *Hate Crime*. 2nd edition. London: Routledge.

Hann, Chris M. 1998. "Introduction: The Embeddedness of Property." In *Property Relations: Renewing Anthropological Tradition*, edited by Chris M. Hann, 1–47. Cambridge: Cambridge University Press.

Hansen, Thomas Blom. 2001. *Wages of Violence: Naming and Identity in Postcolonial Bombay*. Princeton, NJ: Princeton University Press.

Hardy, Stevie-Jade, and Neil Chakraborti. 2020. *Blood, Threats, and Fears: The Hidden Worlds of Hate Crime Victims*. Cham, Switzerland: Palgrave Macmillan.

Harriss, John, and Isabelle Clark-Decès. 2011. "Civil Society and Politics: An Anthropological Perspective." In *A Companion to the Anthropology of India*, 389–406. Oxford: Wiley-Blackwell.

Harvey, David. 2006. *Spaces of Global Capitalism: A Theory of Uneven Geographical Development*. London and New York: Verso.

Hasan, Zoya. 2011. *Politics of Inclusion: Castes, Minorities, and Affirmative Action*. Oxford and New York: Oxford University Press.

Heidegger, Martin. 2008 [1962]. *Being and Time*. Reprint edition. Harper Perennial Modern Classics. New York: Harper Perennial Modern Classics.

Helia, Mayur. 2019. "Exploring the Narrative History and Experiences of Meghwal Community: An Ethnographic Study." *Round Table India* (blog). February 24, 2019. https://www.roundtableindia.co.in/exploring-the-narrative-history-and-experiences-of-meghwal-community-an-ethnographic-study/.

Hinchy, Jessica. 2020. "Gender, Family, and the Policing of the 'Criminal Tribes' in Nineteenth-Century North India." *Modern Asian Studies* 54 (5): 1669–1711. https://doi.org/10.1017/S0026749X19000295.

Hinton, Alexander L. 2010. "Introduction: Toward and Anthropology of Transitional Justice." In *Transitional Justice: Global Mechanisms and Local Realities after Genocide and Mass Violence*, edited by Alexander L. Hinton, 1–22. New Brunswick, NJ: Rutgers University Press.

Hirsch, Susan F. 1998. *Pronouncing and Persevering: Gender and the Discourses of Disputing in an African Islamic Court*. Chicago: University of Chicago Press.

Hornberger, Julia. 2013. "From General to Commissioner to General—On the Popular State of Policing in South Africa." *Law & Social Inquiry* 38 (3): 598–614. https://doi.org/10.1111/lsi.12023.

Hota, Pinky. 2019. "Dilution as Political Vitality: Hate Crime Legislation and Right-Wing Populism in India." *Ethnographic Explainers in PoLAR: Political and Legal Anthropology Review* (blog). August 13, 2019. https://polarjournal.org/2019/08/13/dilution-as-political-vitality-hate-crime-legislation-and-right-wing-populism-in-india/.

HT Correspondent Ajmer. 2015. "Dangawas Violence: Meghwals Refuse to Budge on 18 Demands." *Hindustan Times*, May 31, 2015. https://www.hindustantimes.com/jaipur/dangawas-violence-meghwals-refuse-to-budge-on-18-demands/story-iWaVz1xmr3fswQTM6Ib5fO.html.

Human Rights Watch (HRW). 1999. "Broken People: Caste Violence against India's Untouchables." New York, Washington, London, Brussels: Human Rights Watch. https://www.hrw.org/report/1999/03/01/broken-people-caste-violence-against-indias-untouchables.

Husain, Zakir. 2015. "Rajasthan: Dalits Killed, Thrashed in Violence over Land Dispute." *Hindustan Times*, May 17, 2015. https://www.hindustantimes.com/india/rajasthan-dalits-killed-thrashed-in-violence-over-land-dispute/story-w5UXl7euB7BZtXI4zFNGCM.html.

Iganski, Paul, and Spiridoula Lagou. 2014. "The Personal Injuries of 'Hate Crime.'" In *The Routledge International Handbook on Hate Crime*, edited by Nathan Hall, Abbee Corb, Paul Giannasi, and John Grieve, 34-46. London: Routledge.

———. 2001. "Hate Crimes Hurt More." *American Behavioral Scientist* 45 (4): 626–38. https://doi.org/10.1177/0002764201045004006.

Indian Council of Agricultural Research. 2016. "District Profile Udaipur." http://udaipur.kvk2.in/district-profile.html.

Ireland, Emilienne M. 1993. "When a Chief Speaks through His Silence." *PoLAR: Political and Legal Anthropology Review* 16 (2): 19–28.

Iyer, Gopal K. 1995. "Implementation of the Land Ceiling Programme in Rajasthan." In *Land Reforms in India: Rajasthan—Feudalism and Change*, edited by B. N. Yugandhar and P. S. Dutta, 2:133–75. Land Reforms in India Series. New Delhi: SAGE Publications India.

Jackson, Michael. 1996. "Introduction: Phenomenology, Radical Empiricism, and Anthropological Critique." In *Things As They Are: New Directions in Phenomenological Anthropology*, edited by Michael Jackson, 1–50. Bloomington: Indiana University Press.

Jacobs, James B., and Kimberly Potter. 1998. *Hate Crimes: Criminal Law and Identity Politics*. Oxford and New York: Oxford University Press.

Jaffrelot, Christophe. 2003. *India's Silent Revolution: The Rise of the Lower Castes*. New edition. London: C. Hurst.
———. 2006. "The Impact of Affirmative Action in India: More Political than Socio-economic." *India Review* 5 (2): 173–89. https://doi.org/10.1080/14736480600824516.
Jaising, Indira. 2014. "Concern for the Dead, Condemnation for the Living." *Economic and Political Weekly* 49 (30): 34–38.
Jaiswal, Nimisha, Jain Sreenivasan, and Manas P. Singh. 2018. "Under Modi Government, VIP Hate Speech Skyrockets—By 500%." *NDTV India*, April 19, 2018. https://www.ndtv.com/india-news/under-narendra-modi-government-vip-hate-speech-skyrockets-by-500-1838925.
Jakimow, Tanya. 2016. "Clinging to Hope through Education: The Consequences of Hope for Rural Laborers in Telangana, India." *Ethos* 44 (1): 11–31. https://doi.org/10.1111/etho.12110.
James, William. 1981. "Lecture VIII, 12." In *Pragmatism*. Indianapolis, IN: Hackett Publishing Company.
Jaoul, Nicolas. 2008. "The 'Righteous Anger' of the Powerless: Investigating Dalit Outrage over Caste Violence." *South Asia Multidisciplinary Academic Journal* 2: 2–29. https://doi.org/10.4000/samaj.1892.
Jauregui, Beatrice. 2016. *Provisional Authority: Police, Order, and Security in India*. Chicago: University of Chicago Press.
Jenkins, Rob, and James Manor, eds. 2017. *Politics and the Right to Work: India's National Rural Employment Guarantee Act*. London: C. Hurst.
Jodhka, Surinder S. 2015. *Caste in Contemporary India*. New Delhi: Routledge India.
Jodhka, Surinder S., and James Manor, eds. 2017. *Contested Hierarchies, Persisting Influence: Caste and Power in Twenty-First Century India*. New Delhi and Hyderabad: Orient Black Swan.
Joseph, Joychen. 2018. "Dalit Atrocities: NHRC Asks DGP to Submit Report." *Times of India*, January 19, 2018. https://timesofindia.indiatimes.com/city/jaipur/dalit-atrocities-nhrc-asks-dgp-to-submit-report/articleshow/62561157.cms.
Juergensmeyer, Mark. 1982. *Religious as Social Vision: The Movement against Untouchability in 20th-Century Punjab*. Illustrated edition. Berkeley: University of California Press.
Jhunjhunun District Gazetteer. Compiled by Savitri Gupta. 1984. *Directorate of District Gazetteers*. Jaipur: Government of Rajasthan.
Kannabiran, Kalpana. 2012. *Tools of Justice: Non-Discrimination and the Indian Constitution*. New Delhi: Routledge.
Kapadia, Karin. 1995. *Siva and Her Sisters: Gender, Caste, and Class in Rural South India*. Boulder, CO: Westview Press.
Kapila, Kriti. 2008. "The Measure of a Tribe: The Cultural Politics of Constitutional Reclassification in North India." *Journal of the Royal Anthropological Institute* 14 (1): 117–34.
Karandinos, George, Laurie Kain Hart, Fernando Montero Castrillo, and Philippe Bourgois. 2014. "The Moral Economy of Violence in the US Inner City." *Current Anthropology* 55 (1): 1–22. https://doi.org/10.1086/674613.
Karstedt, Susanne. 2012. "Contextualizing Mass Atrocity Crimes: The Dynamics of

"Extremely Violent Societies"." *European Journal of Criminology* 9 (5): 499–513. https://doi.org/10.1177/1477370812454646.

Katri, Ido. 2017. "Transgender Intersectionality: Rethinking Anti-Discrimination Law and Litigation." *University of Pennsylvania Journal of Law and Social Change* 20: 51–79.

Kaur, Satinder. 2020. "Revisiting Intention and Motive in Criminal Law." *International Journal of Law Management & Humanities* 3 (6): 907–16.

Kavedžija, Iza. 2016. "Introduction: Reorienting Hopes." *Contemporary Japan* 28 (1): 1–11. https://doi.org/10.1515/cj-2016-0001.

Kaviraj, Sudipta. 2000. "Democracy and Social Inequality." In *Transforming India Social and Political Dynamics of Democracy*, edited by Francine R. Frankel, Zoya Hasan, Rajeev Bhargava, and Balveer Arora, 89–119. New Delhi: Oxford University Press.

Kelly, Tobias. 2006. "Documented Lives: Fear and the Uncertainties of Law during the Second Palestinian Intifada." *Journal of the Royal Anthropological Institute* 12 (1): 89–107. https://doi.org/10.1111/j.1467-9655.2006.00282.x.

Khan, Dominique-Sila. 1997. *Conversions & Shifting Identities: Ramdev Pir & the Ismailis in Rajasthan*. New Delhi: Manohar Publishers and Distributors.

Khora, Sthabir. 2014. "'Final Reports' under Sec-498A and the SC/ST Atrocities Act." *Economic and Political Weekly* 49 (41): 17–20.

———. 2016. "Removing Discrimination in Universities." *Economic and Political Weekly* 51 (6). https://www.epw.in/journal/2016/6/web-exclusives/removing-discrimination-universities.html.

Kimmel, Michael. 2018. *Healing from Hate: How Young Men Get Into—and Out of—Violent Extremism*. Oakland: University of California Press.

Kirmayer, Laurence J., Robert Lemelson, and Mark Barad. 2007. "Introduction: Inscribing Trauma in Culture, Brain, and Body." In *Understanding Trauma: Integrating Biological, Clinical, and Cultural Perspectives*, edited by Laurence J. Kirmayer, Robert Lemelson, and Mark Barad, 1–20. New York: Cambridge University Press.

Kok, Anton. 2008. "The Promotion of Equality and Prevention of Unfair Discrimination Act 4 of 2000: Proposals for Legislative Reform." *South African Journal on Human Rights* 24 (3): 445–71. https://doi.org/10.1080/19962126.2008.11864965.

Kolsky, Elizabeth. 2010. "'The Body Evidencing the Crime': Rape on Trial in Colonial India, 1860–1947." *Gender & History* 22 (1): 109–30. https://doi.org/10.1111/j.1468-0424.2009.01581.x.

Kooiman, Dick. 2003. *Communalism & Indian Princely States: Travancore, Baroda & Hyderabad in the 1930s*. 1st edition. New Delhi: Manohar.

Kothari, Jayna. 2021. "Intersectionality Matters: The Supreme Court Judgment in *Patan Jamal Vali v State of Andhra Pradesh*." *Centre for Law & Policy Research* (blog). May 14, 2021. https://clpr.org.in/blog/intersectionality-matters-the-supreme-court-judgment-in-patan-jamal-vali-v-state-of-andhra-pradesh/.

Krishnan, Jayanth. 2004. "Book Review. Journal of the National Human Rights Commission, India, Published by: The National Human Rights Commission (India), 2002." *Articles by Maurer Faculty. Paper 378*. https://www.repository.law.indiana.edu/facpub/378.

Krishnan, P. S. 2018a. *Social Exclusion and Justice in India*. New Delhi: Routledge.

———. 2018b. "Need for Avoiding Knee-Jerk Reaction in Face of Agitation against

POA Amendment Act 2018 on Basis of 'False' Cases, Which Are Virtually Non-Existent in Madhya Pradesh—Urgent Action Needed for Implementation of the POA Act for Effective Protection of SCs and STs." Letter to the Chief Minister of Madhya Pradesh.

Krüger, Rósaan. 2011. "Small Steps to Equal Dignity: The Work of the South African Equality Courts." *Equal Rights Review* 7: 25–43. https://www.equalrightstrust.org/ertdocumentbank/ERR7_kruger.pdf

Kumar, A. 2001. *Indian Agriculture: Issues and Prospects*. Delhi: Sarup & Sons.

Lal, Lawrence David. 2023. "Repressed Caste Guilt and Caste Violence in India." In Panel 39, *Citizens at Risk: Caste Violence and State Institutions in India*, Twenty-seventh European Conference on South Asian Studies, July 27, 2023, Turin, Italy.

Lanjewar, Jyoti. 1992. "Caves." In *Poisoned Bread: Translations from Modern Marathi Dalit Literature*, edited by Arjun Dangle, 22. Bombay: Orient Longman.

Larsson, Stefan. 2017. *Conceptions in the Code: How Metaphors Explain Legal Challenges in Digital Times*. New York: Oxford University Press. https://doi.org/10.1093/acprof:oso/9780190650384.003.0003.

Latour, Bruno. 2010. *The Making of Law—An Ethnography of the Conseil d'Etat*. Cambridge: Polity Press.

Lefebvre, Henri. 1991. *The Production of Space*. Translated by Donald Nicholson-Smith. 1st edition. Malden, MA: Wiley-Blackwell.

Legal Correspondent. 2019. "SC/ST Act Can't Be Used to Blackmail or Wreak Vengeance." *The Hindu*, January 31, 2019, sec. Tamil Nadu. https://www.thehindu.com/news/national/tamil-nadu/scst-act-cant-be-used-to-blackmail-or-wreak-vengeance/article26132745.ece.

———. 2020. "All Insults Not Offence under SC/ST Act: Supreme Court." *The Hindu*, November 5, 2020, sec. India. https://www.thehindu.com/news/national/offence-under-scst-act-would-be-made-out-when-a-person-is-abused-in-public-view-supreme-court/article33032722.ece.

Lerche, Jens, and Alpa Shah. 2018. "Conjugated Oppression within Contemporary Capitalism: Class, Caste, Tribe and Agrarian Change in India." *Journal of Peasant Studies* 45 (5–6): 927–49. https://doi.org/10.1080/03066150.2018.1463217.

Lester, Rebecca. 2013. "Back from the Edge of Existence: A Critical Anthropology of Trauma." *Transcultural Psychiatry* 50 (5): 753–62. https://doi.org/10.1177/1363461513504520.

Levitt, Peggy, and Sally Merry. 2009. "Vernacularization on the Ground: Local Uses of Global Women's Rights in Peru, China, India and the United States." *Global Networks* 9 (4): 441–61. https://doi.org/10.1111/j.1471-0374.2009.00263.x

Linkenbach, Antje. 2021. "B. R. Ambedkar's Imaginations of Justice." In *B. R. Ambedkar The Quest for Justice: Legal and Economic Justice*, edited by Aakash Singh Rathore, 75–91. New Delhi: Oxford University Press India.

Lokaneeta, Jinee. 2020. *The Truth Machines: Policing, Violence, and Scientific Interrogations in India*. Hyderabad: Orient Black Swan.

Longkumer, Arkotong. 2020. *The Greater India Experiment: Hindutva and the Northeast*. 1st edition. Stanford, CA: Stanford University Press.

Loomba, Ania. 2016. "The Everyday Violence of Caste." *College Literature* 43 (1): 220–25.

Lopez, German. 2017. "Why It's So Hard to Prosecute a Hate Crime." *Vox*, May 23, 2017. https://www.vox.com/identities/2017/4/10/15183902/hate-crime-trump-law.

Lorenzini, Daniele. 2015. "What Is a 'Regime of Truth'?" *Le Foucaldien* 1 (1). https://doi.org/10.16995/lefou.2.

Lutgendorf, Philip. 1997. "Monkey in the Middle: The Status of Hanuman in Popular Hinduism." *Religion* 27 (4): 311–32. https://doi.org/10.1006/reli.1997.0095.

Lyall, Sir Alfred C. 1884. *Asiatic Studies, Religious and Social*. London: John Murray.

MacDermott, Therese. 2018. "The Collective Dimension of Federal Anti-Discrimination Proceedings in Australia: Shifting the Burden from Individual Litigants." *International Journal of Discrimination and the Law* 18 (1): 22–39. https://doi.org/10.1177/1358229118759712.

MacMullan, Terrance. 2009. *Habits of Whiteness: A Pragmatist Reconstruction*. Bloomington: Indiana University Press.

Malcai, Ofer, and Ronit Levine-Schnur. 2014. "Which Came First, the Procedure or the Substance? Justificational Priority and the Substance-Procedure Distinction." *Oxford Journal of Legal Studies* 34 (1): 1–19.

Mamdani, Mahmood. 2003. "Making Sense of Political Violence in Postcolonial Africa." *Identity, Culture and Politics: An Afro-Asian Dialogue* 3 (2): 1–24. https://doi.org/10.1142/9789812795496_0005.

Mander, Harsh. 2012. "Broken Lives and Compromise: Shadow Play in Gujarat." *Economic and Political Weekly* 47 (8): 90–97.

Mangubhai, Jayshree, and Rahul Singh. 2014. "Justice under Trial: Caste Discrimination in Access to Justice before Special Courts." New Delhi: National Dalit Movement for Justice—(NCDHR) New Delhi. https://www.slideshare.net/jpmangubhai/justice-under-trial-caste-discrimination-in-the-special-courts.

Mani, Rama. 2008. "Editorial: Dilemmas of Expanding Transitional Justice, or Forging the Nexus between Transitional Justice and Development." *International Journal of Transitional Justice* 2 (3): 253–65. https://doi.org/10.1093/ijtj/ijn030.

Manikumar, K. A. 2017. *Murder in Mudukulathur: Caste and Electoral Politics in Tamil Nadu*. New Delhi: LeftWord Books.

Manohar Singh v. State of Rajasthan AIR 2015 SC 1124.

Marks, Susan. 2011. "Human Rights and Root Causes." *Modern Law Review* 74 (1): 57–78. https://doi.org/10.1111/j.1468-2230.2010.00836.x.

Mason, Gail. 2014. "The Hate Threshold: Emotion, Causation and Difference in the Construction of Prejudice-Motivated Crime." *Social & Legal Studies* 23 (3): 293–314. https://doi.org/10.1177/0964663914534459.

Mattei, Ugo, and Laura Nader. 2008. *Plunder: When the Rule of Law Is Illegal*. 1st edition. Malden, MA: Wiley-Blackwell.

Mayans-Hermida, Beatriz E., and Barbora Holá. 2023. "Punishing Atrocity Crimes in Transitional Contexts: Advancing Discussions on Adequacy of Alternative Criminal Sanctions Using the Case of Colombia." *Oxford Journal of Legal Studies* 43 (1): 1–31. https://doi.org/10.1093/ojls/gqac022.

Mbembe, Achille. 2001. *On the Postcolony*. Berkeley and Los Angeles: University of California Press.

McDevitt, Jack, Jack Levin, and Susan Bennett. 2002. "Hate Crime Offenders: An

Expanded Typology." *Journal of Social Issues* 58 (2): 303–17. https://doi.org/10.1111/1540-4560.00262.

McGuirk, Siobhán. 2018. "(In)Credible Subjects: NGOs, Attorneys, and Permissible LGBT Asylum Seeker Identities." *PoLAR: Political and Legal Anthropology Review* 41 (1): 4–18. https://doi.org/10.1111/plar.12250.

McQuade, Joseph. 2021. *A Genealogy of Terrorism: Colonial Law and the Origins of an Idea.* New York: Cambridge University Press.

Meghwanshi, Bhanwar. 2015. "The Dalit Massacre of Dangawas: A Report to the Nation." Translated by Khandelwal, Pankaj. Bhilwara: Rikhya Prashasan.

———. 2015. "Three Dalits Were Mowed down with a Tractor. Why Are Officials Describing This as a 'Group Clash'?" *Scroll India*, May 22, 2015. http://scroll.in/article/728776/three-dalits-were-mowed-down-with-a-tractor-why-are-officials-describing-this-as-a-group-clash.

Mehta, Ashish. 2019. "Woman Jailed for Turning Hostile in Rajasthan Rape Case." *Times of India*, December 25, 2019. https://timesofindia.indiatimes.com/city/jaipur/woman-jailed-for-turning-hostile-in-raj-rape-case/articleshow/72961286.cms.

Mehta, Avantika. 2016. "Family, Police Pressure: Why Most Rape Victims Turn Hostile during Trial." *Hindustan Times*, April 28, 2016. https://www.hindustantimes.com/india/why-most-rape-victims-turn-hostile-during-trial/story-pjYLEJniCxceLIG6w6c8RK.html.

Mendelsohn, Oliver, and Marika Vicziany. 1998. *The Untouchables: Subordination, Poverty and the State in Modern India.* Cambridge: Cambridge University Press.

Merry, Sally E. 1994. "Courts as Performances: Domestic Violence Hearings in a Hawai'i Family Court." In *Contested States: Law, Hegemony, and Resistance*, edited by Mindie Lazarus-Black and Susan F. Hirsch, 35–59. New York: Routledge.

Merry, Sally Engle. 1990. *Getting Justice and Getting Even: Legal Consciousness among Working-Class Americans.* Chicago Series in Law and Society. Chicago: University of Chicago Press. https://press.uchicago.edu/ucp/books/book/chicago/G/bo3774571.html.

———. 2006. "Transnational Human Rights and Local Activism: Mapping the Middle." *American Anthropologist* 108 (1): 38–51. https://doi.org/10.1525/aa.2006.108.1.38.

Michelutti, Lucia, Ashraf Hoque, Nicolas Martin, David Picherit, Paul Rollier, Arild E. Ruud, and Clarinda Still. 2018. *Mafia Raj: The Rule of Bosses in South Asia.* Stanford, CA: Stanford University Press.

Mines, Mattison, and Vijayalakshmi Gourishankar. 1990. "Leadership and Individuality in South Asia: The Case of the South Indian Big-Man." *Journal of Asian Studies* 49 (4): 761–86. https://doi.org/10.2307/2058235.

Mitchell, Jon P. 2007. "A Fourth Critic of the Enlightenment: Michel de Certeau and the Ethnography of Subjectivity." *Social Anthropology* 15 (1): 89.

Miyazaki, Hirokazu. 2006. "Economy of Dreams: Hope in Global Capitalism and Its Critiques." *Cultural Anthropology* 21 (2): 147–72. https://doi.org/10.1525/can.2006.21.2.147.

Mohanty, B. B. 2001. "Land Distribution among Scheduled Castes and Tribes." *Economic and Political Weekly* 36 (40): 3857–68.

Mondal, Amrita. 2021. *Owning Land, Being Women: Inheritance and Subjecthood in India.* Berlin and Boston: De Gruyter.
Montgomery, Heather, Richard A. Wilson, and Jane Cowan. 2001. "Imposing Rights? A Case Study of Child Prostitution in Thailand." In *Culture and Rights: Anthropological Perspectives*, 80–101. Cambridge: Cambridge University Press.
Moore, Erin P. 1993. "Gender, Power, and Legal Pluralism: Rajasthan, India." *American Ethnologist* 20 (3): 522–42.
Moore, Henrietta. 1994. "The Problem of Explaining Violence in the Social Sciences." In *Sex and Violence: Issues in Representation and Experience*, edited by Penelope Harvey and Peter Gow, 138–55. New York and London: Routledge.
Moore, Sally Falk. 1973. "Law and Social Change: The Semi-Autonomous Social Field as an Appropriate Subject of Study." *Law & Society Review* 7 (4): 719–46. https://doi.org/10.2307/3052967.
Mosse, David. 2005. *Cultivating Development: An Ethnography of Aid Policy and Practice.* Anthropology, Culture and Society. London and Ann Arbor, MI: Pluto Press.
———. 2012. *The Saint in the Banyan Tree: Christianity and Caste Society in India.* The Anthropology of Christianity. Berkeley, Los Angeles, London: University of California Press.
———. 2018. "Caste and Development: Contemporary Perspectives on a Structure of Discrimination and Advantage." *World Development* 110: 422–36. https://doi.org/10.1016/j.worlddev.2018.06.003.
Mulla, Sameena. 2014. *The Violence of Care: Rape Victims, Forensic Nurses, and Sexual Assault Intervention.* New York: New York University Press.
Mullard, Jordan C. R. 2010. "Status, Security and Change: An Ethnographic Study of Caste, Class and Religion in Rural Rajasthan." PhD Thesis, London: London School of Economics and Political Science.
Muthukkaruppan, Parthasarathi. 2017. "Critique of Caste Violence: Explorations in Theory." *Social Scientist* 45 (1/2): 49–71.
Mutsaers, Paul. 2019. *Police Unlimited: Policing, Migrants, and the Values of Bureaucracy.* Clarendon Studies in Criminology. Oxford: Oxford University Press.
Myers, Samuel L., Jr., and Vanishree Radhakrishna. 2018. "Hate Crimes, Crimes of Atrocity, and Affirmative Action in India and the United States." In *The Radical in Ambedkar: Critical Reflections*, edited by Anand Teltumbde and Suraj Yengde, 61–86. New Delhi: India Allen Lane.
Nader, Laura. 1990. *Harmony Ideology: Justice and Control in a Zapotec Mountain Village.* 1st edition. Stanford, CA: Stanford University Press.
Nagaur District Gazetteer. Compiled by K. K. Seghal. 1975. *Directorate of District Gazetteers.* Jaipur: Government of Rajasthan.
Nair, Niti. 2018. "Old Laws for New Reasons: The Limits to Free Speech in India." *Berkley Center for Religion, Peace & World Affair* (blog). August 23, 2018. https://berkleycenter.georgetown.edu/responses/old-laws-for-new-reasons-the-limits-to-free-speech-in-india.
National Crime Records Bureau (NCRB). 2016. "Crime in India 2016: Statistics." New Delhi: Ministry of Home Affairs, Government of India. Accessed June 20, 2023.

https://ncrb.gov.in/sites/default/files/Crime%20in%20India%20-%202016%20Complete%20PDF%20291117.pdf.

National Human Rights Commission (NHRC). 2018. "Report on the Open Hearing/Camp Sitting at Jaipur, Rajasthan (18th–19th January, 2018)." Open Hearing Report. https://nhrc.nic.in/sites/default/files/open_hearing_rajathsn_18–19jan2018_25062018_0.pdf.

Natrajan, Balmuri, and Paul Greenough. 2009. *Against Stigma: Studies in Caste, Race and Justice Since Durban*. New Delhi: Orient Black Swan.

Naval, T. R. 2004. *Law of Prevention of Atrocities on the Scheduled Castes and the Scheduled Tribes*. New Delhi: Concept Publishing Company.

Nawsagaray, Nitish. 2018. "Misuse of the Prevention of Atrocities Act: Scrutinising the Mahajan Judgment, 2018." *Economic and Political Weekly* 53 (22): 24–36.

Nayyar, Deepak. 2011. "Discrimination and Justice: Beyond Affirmative Action." *Economic and Political Weekly* 46 (42): 52–59.

Network, Livelaw News. 2022. "Mere Knowledge Of Victim's Caste Does Not Attract SC/ST Act Unless Offence Committed On Basis Of Caste Identity: Chhattisgarh HC Reiterates." *LiveLaw India* (blog). September 26, 2022. https://www.livelaw.in/news-updates/chhattisgarh-high-court-sc-st-act-knowledge-caste-victim-offence-210286.

Ngai, Sianne. 2005. *Ugly Feelings*. New edition. Cambridge, MA, and London: Harvard University Press.

Nordstrom, Carolyn. 2004. *Shadows of War: Violence, Power, and International Profiteering in the Twenty-First Century*. Berkeley, Los Angeles, London: University of California Press.

Olivelle, Patrick. 2011. "Penance and Punishment: Marking the Body in Criminal Law and Social Ideology of Ancient India." *Journal of Hindu Studies* 4 (1): 23–41. https://doi.org/10.1093/jhs/hir011.

Omvedt, Gail. 1980. "Caste, Agrarian Relations and Agrarian Conflicts." *Sociological Bulletin* 29 (2): 142–70. https://doi.org/10.1177/0038022919800202.

———. 1994. *Dalits and the Democratic Revolution: Dr Ambedkar and the Dalit Movement in Colonial India*. New Delhi: SAGE Publications.

———. 1995. *Dalit Visions: The Anti-Caste Movement and the Construction of an Indian Identity*. Hyderabad: Orient Longman.

Ong, Aihwa, and Stephen J. Collier. 2005. "Global Assemblages, Anthropological Problems." In *Global Assemblages: Technology, Politics, and Ethics as Anthropological Problems*, edited by Aihwa Ong and Stephen J. Collier, 3–21. Malden, MA: Wiley-Blackwell.

Oorschot, Irene van, and Willem Schinkel. 2015. "The Legal Case File as Border Object: On Self-Reference and Other-Reference in Criminal Law." *Journal of Law and Society* 42 (4): 499–527. https://doi.org/10.1111/j.1467-6478.2015.00723.x.

Oza, Rupal. 2020. "Sexual Subjectivity in Rape Narratives: Consent, Credibility, and Coercion in Rural Haryana." *Signs: Journal of Women in Culture and Society* 46 (1): 103–25. https://doi.org/10.1086/709214.

———. 2022. *Semiotics of Rape: Sexual Subjectivity and Violation in Rural India*. Durham, NC: Duke University Press Books.

Özkan, Nazlı. 2019. "Representing Religious Discrimination at the Margins: Temporalities and 'Appropriate' Identities of the State in Turkey." *PoLAR: Political and Legal Anthropology Review* 42 (2): 317–31. https://doi.org/10.1111/plar.12313.

Pai, Sudha. 2002. *Dalit Assertion and the Unfinished Democratic Revolution: The Bahujan Samaj Party in Uttar Pradesh.* New Delhi: Sage Publications.

Pande, Ram. 1982. *Peoples Movement in Rajasthan: Selections from Originals.* Vol. 1. Jaipur: Shodhak.

Pande, Rohini. 2003. "Can Mandated Political Representation Increase Policy Influence for Disadvantaged Minorities? Theory and Evidence from India." *American Economic Review* 93 (4): 1132–51.

Pankaj, Ajeet Kumar. 2016. "Land, Labour and Market: Exclusion of Dalits in Uttar Pradesh." *Contemporary Voice of Dalit* 8 (2): 196–205. https://doi.org/10.1177/2455328X16661078.

Parmar, Alpa, Rod Earle, and Coretta Phillips. 2022. "Seeing Is Believing: How the Layering of Race Is Obscured by 'White Epistemologies' in the Criminal Justice Field." *Journal of Criminal Justice Education* 33 (2): 289–306. https://doi.org/10.1080/10511253.2022.2027482.

———. 2023. "'People Are Trapped in History and History Is Trapped Inside Them': Exploring Britain's Racialized Colonial Legacies in Criminological Research." *British Journal of Criminology* 63 (4): 811–27. https://doi.org/10.1093/bjc/azac058.

Parry, Jonathan. 2014. "Sex, Bricks and Mortar: Constructing Class in a Central Indian Steel Town." *Modern Asian Studies* 48 (5): 1242–75. https://doi.org/10.1017/S0026749X1400002X.

———. 2020. *Classes of Labour: Work and Life in a Central Indian Steel Town.* 1st edition. Abingdon, NY: Routledge.

Perry, Barbara. 2001. *In the Name of Hate: Understanding Hate Crimes.* New York and London: Routledge.

Perry, Barbara, and Shahid Alvi. 2012. "'We Are All Vulnerable': The *in Terrorem* Effects of Hate Crimes." *International Review of Victimology* 18 (1): 57–71. https://doi.org/10.1177/0269758011422475.

Perry, Joanna. 2020. "The Migration and Integration of the Hate Crime Approach in India." *Jindal Global Law Review* 11 (1): 7–32. https://doi.org/10.1007/s41020-020-00111-8.

Peteet, Julie. 1994. "Male Gender and Rituals of Resistance in the Palestinian 'Intifada': A Cultural Politics of Violence." *American Ethnologist* 21 (1): 31–49.

Peters, Julie Stone. 2008. "Legal Performance Good and Bad." *Law, Culture and the Humanities* 4 (2): 179–200. https://doi.org/10.1177/1743872108091473.

Pia, Andrea E. 2016. "'We Follow Reason, Not the Law': Disavowing the Law in Rural China." *PoLAR: Political and Legal Anthropology Review* 39 (2): 276–93. https://doi.org/10.1111/plar.12194.

Piliavsky, Anastasia. 2014. *Patronage as Politics in South Asia.* Cambridge: Cambridge University Press.

Pinos, Jaume Castan, and Mark Friis Hau. 2022. *Lawfare: New Trajectories in Law.* London: Routledge.

Pirie, Fernada. 2019. "Legalism: A Turn to History in the Anthropology of Law."

Clio@Themis. Revue électronique d'histoire du droit 15: 221–41. https://doi.org/10.35562/cliothemis.666.

———. 2013. *The Anthropology of Law*. Oxford: Oxford University Press.

Polit, Karin. 2018. "Gifts of Love and Friendship: On Changing Marriage Traditions, the Meaning of Gifts, and the Value of Women in the Garhwal Himalayas." *International Journal of Hindu Studies* 22 (2): 285–307. https://doi.org/10.1007/s11407-018-9234-4.

Povinelli, Elizabeth A. 2002. *The Cunning of Recognition: Indigenous Alterities and the Making of Australian Multiculturalism*. Politics, History, and Culture. Durham, NC: Duke University Press.

Power, Samantha. 2002. *A Problem from Hell: America and the Age of Genocide*. New York and London: Basic Books.

Press Trust of India (PTI). 2016. "Atrocities against Scheduled Castes and Tribes: BJP-Ruled Rajasthan Tops List, UP Follows." *Indian Express*, December 19, 2016. https://indianexpress.com/article/india/atrocities-against-scheduled-castes-and-tribes-bjp-ruled-rajasthan-tops-list-up-follows-4435307/.

Purohit, Dishank. 2018. "Three Years after Dalit Killings, Police Still Stand Guard in Dangawas." *Times of India*, November 2, 2018. https://timesofindia.indiatimes.com/city/jaipur/three-years-after-dalit-killings-police-still-stand-guard-in-dangawas/articleshow/66468111.cms.

Rai, Vibhuti Narain. 2020. "We Have a Brutal and Oppressive Police Because British Masters Designed It as Such." *National Herald*, January 18, 2020. https://www.nationalheraldindia.com/opinion/we-have-a-brutal-and-oppressive-police-because-british-masters-designed-it-as-such.

Rajalakshmi, T. K. 2015. "Murder for Land." *Frontline*, June 10, 2015. https://frontline.thehindu.com/social-issues/murder-for-land/article7297927.ece.

Ralph, Laurence. 2014. *Renegade Dreams: Living through Injury in Gangland Chicago*. Illustrated edition. Chicago and London: University of Chicago Press.

Ram, Kalpana, and Christopher Houston. 2015. "Introduction: Phenomenology's Methodological Invitation." In *Phenomenology in Anthropology: A Sense of Perspective*, edited by Kalpana Ram and Christopher Houston, 1–25. Bloomington: Indiana University Press.

Rameshnathan, N. V. A. 2018. "Dilution of SCs/STs Act." *Economic and Political Weekly* 53 (12): 4.

Rao, Anupama. 2009. *The Caste Question: Dalits and the Politics of Modern India*. Berkeley and London: University of California Press.

Rao, Srinath. 2019. "One in 5 Cops Thinks SC/ST Act Cases False, Motivated: Survey." *Indian Express*, August 31, 2019. https://indianexpress.com/article/india/one-in-5-cops-thinks-sc-st-act-cases-false-motivated-survey-5952730/.

Rao, Ursula. 2002. "Assessing the Past in Search for a Future: The Changing of Caste and the Writing of Caste History in Contemporary Urban India." In *A Place in the World: New Local Historiographies from Africa and South-Asia*, edited by Axel Harneit-Sievers, 347–66. Leiden, Boston, Köln: Brill.

Rawal, Vikas. 2015. "Peasant Struggles in Shekhawati in the Early 20th Century." In

Socio-Economic Surveys of Two Villages in Rajasthan: A Study of Agrarian Relations, edited by Madhura Swaminathan, and Vikas Rawal, 1–8. New Delhi: Tulika Books.

Rawat, Vidya, B. 2017. "Days of Identity in Dalit Politics Are Over, We Need to Focus on Ideology: A Conversation with Bhanwar Meghwanshi, Dalit Activist from Rajasthan." *The Wire*, January 3, 2017. https://thewire.in/politics/the-days-of-identity-in-dalit-politics-is-over-we-need-to-focus-on-ideology.

Rege, Sharmila. 2006. *Writing Caste/Writing Gender: Narrating Dalit Women's Testimonies*. New Delhi: Zubaan Books.

Riles, Annelise. 2005. "A New Agenda for the Cultural Study of Law: Taking on the Technicalities." *Buffalo Law Review* 53 (3): 973–1033.

———. 2011. *Collateral Knowledge: Legal Reasoning in the Global Financial Markets*. Illustrated edition. Chicago and London: University of Chicago Press.

Rodrigues, Valerian. 2002. *The Essential Writings of B.R. Ambedkar*. New edition. New Delhi: Oxford University Press India.

Rubin, Barnett R. 1987. "The Civil Liberties Movement in India: New Approaches to the State and Social Change." *Asian Survey* 27 (3): 371–92. https://doi.org/10.2307/2644810.

Rudolph, Lloyd I., and Susanne H. Rudolph. 2011. "From Landed Class to Middle Class: Rajput Adaptation in Rajasthan." In *Elite and Everyman: The Cultural Politics of the Indian Middle Classes*, edited by Amita Baviskar and Raka Ray, 108–39. New Delhi: Routledge.

———. 1966. "Rajputana under British Paramountcy: The Failure of Indirect Rule." *Journal of Modern History* 38 (2): 138–60.

———.1960. "The Political Role of India's Caste Associations." *Pacific Affairs* 33 (1): 5–22. https://doi.org/10.2307/2753645.

Ruud, Arild E. 2001. "Talking Dirty about Politics: A View from a Bengali Village." In *The Everyday State and Society in Modern India*, edited by Christopher J. Fuller and Veronique Bénéï, 115–36. London: Hurst.

Saberwal, Satish. 2001. "Democracy and Civil Society in India: Integral or Accidental?" *Sociological Bulletin* 50 (2): 183–91. https://doi.org/10.1177/0038022920010202.

Sabea, Hanan. 2013. "A 'Time out of Time': Tahrir, the Political and the Imaginary in the Context of the January 25th Revolution in Egypt." *Editor's Forum: Society for Cultural Anthropology* (blog). May 9, 2013. https://culanth.org/fieldsights/a-time-out-of-time-tahrir-the-political-and-the-imaginary-in-the-context-of-the-january-25th-revolution-in-egypt.

Saikia, Abhinandan, and Noklenyangla. 2015. "In a Fulcrum: Revisiting the Conditions of Manual Scavengers in India." *Journal of Social Research and Policy* 6 (1): 105–10.

Salem, Tomas, and Erika Robb Larkins. 2021. "Violent Masculinities." *American Ethnologist* 48 (1): 65–79. https://doi.org/10.1111/amet.13005.

Samaddar, Ranabir. 2020. "An Insurgent Constitutionalism Is Driving Popular Politics in India Today." *The Wire*, January 26, 2020. https://thewire.in/politics/an-insurgent-constitutionalism-is-driving-popular-politics-in-india-today.

Sanders, Mark. 2002. *Complicities: The Intellectual and Apartheid*. Durham, NC: Duke University Press.

Sankaran, S. R. 2008. "Social Exclusion and Criminal Law." In *Challenging the Rule(s) of Law: Colonialism, Criminology and Human Rights in India*, edited by Kalpana Kannabiran and Ranbir Singh, 121–41. New Delhi: Sage Publications.

Sarukkai, Sundar. 2009. "Phenomenology of Untouchability." *Economic and Political Weekly* 44 (37): 39–48.

Sashittal, Nihar. 2023. "The Enigma of Caste Atrocities: Do Scheduled Castes and Scheduled Tribes Face Excessive Violence in India?" *Oñati Socio-Legal Series* 13 (1): 89–126. https://doi.org/10.35295/osls.iisl/0000-0000-0000-1332.

Satterlee, Michelle. 2006. "Landscape Imagery and Memory in the Narrative of Trauma: A Closer Look at Leslie Marmon Silko's 'Ceremony.'" *Interdisciplinary Studies in Literature and Environment* 13 (2): 73–92.

Scheffer, David. 2007. "The Merits of Unifying Terms: 'Atrocity Crimes' and 'Atrocity Law.'" *Genocide Studies and Prevention: An International Journal* 2 (1): 91–95.

Scheper-Hughes, Nancy. 1992. *Death without Weeping: The Violence of Everyday Life in Brazil*. Berkeley, Los Angeles, London: University of California Press.

Schmidt, Bettina E., and Ingo W. Schröder, eds. 2001. *Anthropology of Violence and Conflict*. London: Routledge.

Scott, James C. 1990. *Domination and the Arts of Resistance—Hidden Transcripts*. New Haven, CT, and London: Yale University Press.

Scroll Staff. 2016. "Dalits and Adivasis Faced Highest Number of Atrocities in Rajasthan between 2013 and 2015." *Scroll India*, December 19, 2016. http://scroll.in/latest/824596/dalits-and-adivasis-faced-highest-number-of-atrocities-in-rajasthan-between-2013-and-2015.

Shade, Patrick. 2001. *Habits of Hope: A Pragmatic Theory*. Nashville, TN: Vanderbilt University Press.

Shah, Alpa. 2007. "'Keeping the State Away': Democracy, Politics, and the State in India's Jharkhand." *Journal of the Royal Anthropological Institute* 13 (1): 129–45. https://doi.org/10.1111/j.1467-9655.2007.00417.x

———. 2009. "Morality, Corruption and the State: Insights from Jharkhand, Eastern India." *Journal of Development Studies* 45 (3): 295–313. https://doi.org/10.1080/00220380802600866.

Shakil, Sana. 2020. "Dalits Are Worst-off in Rajasthan for Last 3 Years." *New Indian Express*, October 13, 2020. https://www.newindianexpress.com/nation/2020/oct/13/dalits-are-worst-off-in-rajasthan-for-last-3-yrs-2209521.html.

Shanmugaratnam, N. 1996. "Nationalisation, Privatisation and the Dilemmas of Common Property Management in Western Rajasthan." *Journal of Development Studies* 33 (2): 163–87. https://doi.org/10.1080/00220389608422461.

Sharma, Brij Kishore. 1990. *Peasant Movements in Rajasthan, 1920–1949*. Jaipur: Pointer Publishers.

Sharma, Jeevan Raj, and Tobias Kelly. 2018. "Monetary Compensation for Survivors of Torture: Some Lessons from Nepal." *Journal of Human Rights Practice* 10 (2): 307–26. https://doi.org/10.1093/jhuman/huy021.

Sharma, Nidhi. 2016. "Crime against Scheduled Castes: Steep Spike in Gujarat, Most Number of Cases in UP." *Economic Times*, July 22, 2016. https://economictimes.india

times.com/news/politics-and-nation/crime-against-scheduled-castes-steep-spike-in-gujarat-most-number-of-cases-in-up/articleshow/53329482.cms?from=mdr.

Sharma, Rajendra. 1999. *Power Elite in Indian Society: Study of the Shekhawati Region in Rajasthan*. Jaipur: Rawat Publications.

Sharma, Smriti. 2015. "Caste-Based Crimes and Economic Status: Evidence from India." *Journal of Comparative Economics* 43 (1): 204–26. https://doi.org/10.1016/j.jce.2014.10.005.

Shoshan, Nitzan. 2016. *The Management of Hate: Nation, Affect, and the Governance of Right-Wing Extremism in Germany*. Princeton, NJ, and Oxford: Princeton University Press.

Shyamlal. 2006. *Untouchable Castes in India: The Raigar Movement (1940–2004)*. Jaipur: Rawat Publications.

———. 2010. *Studies in Social Protest*. Jaipur: Rawat Publications.

Singh, Dilbagh. 1990. *The State, Landlords, and Peasants: Rajasthan in the 18th Century*. New Delhi: Manohar.

Singh, Dool. 1964. *Land Reforms in Rajasthan: A Study of Evasion, Implementation and Socio-Economic Effects of Land Reforms*. New Delhi: Research Programmes Committee, Planning Commission, Government of India.

Singh, Hira. 1998. *Colonial Hegemony and Popular Resistance: Princes, Peasants and Paramount Power*. New Delhi: Sage Publications.

———. 2003. "Princely States, Peasant Protests, and Nation Building in India: The Colonial Mode of Historiography and Subaltern Studies." *Social Movement Studies* 2 (2): 213–28. https://doi.org/10.1080/1474283032000139788.

———. 2014. *Recasting Caste: From the Sacred to the Profane*. New Delhi: Sage Publications.

Singh, Lakshmi Narayan, and Reena Gupta. 2014. "Dalit Access to Land in Rajasthan: Land Reform as Redistributive Justice since Independence." *International Research Journal of Management Sociology and Humanity* 5 (10): 309–20.

Singh, Rahul. 2020. "A Quest for Justice: Implementation of SC/ST (Prevention of) Atrocities Act 1989 and Rules 1995 Status Report 2009–2018." Status Report. New Delhi: Swadikhar: National Dalit Movement for Justice—(NCDHR) New Delhi. https://www.indiaspend.com/wp-content/uploads/2020/09/NCDHR_REPORT-NEW2.pdf.

Sinha, Mrinalini. 1995. *Colonial Masculinity: The "Manly Englishman" and the "Effeminate Bengali" in the Late Nineteenth Century*. 1st edition. Manchester and New York: Manchester University Press.

Sisson, Richard. 1969. "Peasant Movements and Political Mobilization: The Jats of Rajasthan." *Asian Survey* 9 (12): 946–63. https://doi.org/10.2307/2642561.

———. 1972. *The Congress Party in Rajasthan: Political Integration and Institution-Building in an Indian State*. Berkeley, Los Angeles, London: University of California Press.

Smith, Amber. 2016. *The Way I Used to Be*. Export edition. New York: Margaret K. McElderry.

Snodgrass, Jeffrey G. 2006. *Casting Kings: Bards and Indian Modernity*. Illustrated edition. Oxford and New York: Oxford University Press.

Somek, Alexander. 2011. *Engineering Equality: An Essay on European Anti-Discrimination Law*. Oxford and New York: Oxford University Press.

Special Statistics for EPW. 2014. "2013 Legislative Assembly Elections, Rajasthan." *Economic and Political Weekly* 43 (6): 90–93.

Srinivas, M. N. 1962. *Caste in Modern India and Other Essays*. London: Asia Publishing House.

Srinivas, Mysore N. 1952. *Religion and Society among the Coorgs of South India*. Oxford: Clarendon Press.

Statistical Handbook of Jhunjhunu: 2020. https://jhunjhunu.rajasthan.gov.in/content/raj/jhunjhunu/en/about.

Still, Clarinda. 2011. "Spoiled Brides and the Fear of Education: Honour and Social Mobility among Dalits in South India." *Modern Asian Studies* 45 (5): 1119–46. https://doi.org/10.1017/S0026749X10000144.

———. 2017a. *Dalit Women: Honour and Patriarchy in South India*. London and New York: Routledge.

———. 2017b. "Dalit Women, Rape and the Revitalisation of Patriarchy?" In *Dalit Women: Vanguard of an Alternative Politics in India*, edited by S. Anandhi and Karin Kapadia,189–217. New Delhi: Routledge India.

Stroud, Scott R. 2023. *The Evolution of Pragmatism in India: Ambedkar, Dewey, and the Rhetoric of Reconstruction*. Chicago: University of Chicago Press.

Sukirtharani, S. 2012. "Portrait of My Village." In *The Oxford Anthology of Tamil Dalit Writing*, edited by Ravikumar and R. Azhagarasan, 27. Oxford: Oxford University Press.

Suresh, Mayur. 2019a. "The 'Paper Case': Evidence and Narrative of a Terrorism Trial in Delhi on JSTOR." *Law and Society Review* 53 (1): 173–201. https://doi.org/10.1111/lasr.12378.

———. 2019b. "The Social Life of Technicalities: 'Terrorist' Lives in Delhi's Courts." *Contributions to Indian Sociology* 53 (1): 72–96. https://doi.org/10.1177/0069966718812523.

Suresh, Mayur R. 2023. *Terror Trials: Life and Law in Delhi's Courts*. 1st edition. New York: Fordham University Press.

Swiffen, Amy. 2018. "New Resistance to Hate Crime Legislation and the Concept of Law." *Law, Culture and the Humanities* 14 (1): 121–39. https://doi.org/10.1177/1743872114534017.

Tate, Winifred. 2007. *Counting the Dead: The Culture and Politics of Human Rights Activism in Colombia*. Berkeley, Los Angeles, London: University of California Press.

Taylor, Charles. 2004. *Modern Social Imaginaries*. Public Planet Books. Durham, NC: Duke University Press.

Teitel, Ruti. 2008. "Editorial Note-Transitional Justice Globalized." *International Journal of Transitional Justice* 2 (1): 1–4. https://doi.org/10.1093/ijtj/ijm041.

———. 2000. *Transitional Justice*. New York: Oxford University Press.

Teltumbde, Anand. 2008. *Khairlanji. A Strange and Bitter Crop*. New Delhi: Navayana Publishers.

———. 2011. *The Persistence of Caste: The Khairlanji Murders & India's Hidden Apartheid*. New Delhi: Navayana Publishers.

———. 2018a. "Judicial Atrocity?" *Economic and Political Weekly* 53 (15): 14–16.

———. 2018b. *Republic of Caste: Thinking Equality in the Time of Neoliberal Hindutva*. New Delhi: Navayana Publishers.

Tenhunen, Sipra. 2003. "Culture and Political Agency: Gender, Kinship and Village Politics in West Bengal." *Contributions to Indian Sociology* 37 (3): 495–518. https://doi.org/10.1177/006996670303700304.

Thorat, Sukhadeo. 2002. "Oppression and Denial: Dalit Discrimination in the 1990s." *Economic and Political Weekly* 37 (6): 572–78.

———. 2017. "Discrimination and Atrocities against Dalits in Maharashtra: Analysis of Magnitude, Causes and Solution." New Delhi (unpublished).

Thorat, Sukhadeo, and Katherine S. Newman. 2007. "Caste and Economic Discrimination: Causes, Consequences and Remedies." *Economic and Political Weekly* 42 (42): 4121–24.

Thorat, Sukhadeo, and Nidhi S. Sabharwal. 2014. *Bridging the Social Gap: Perspectives on Dalit Empowerment*. Classism & Social Exclusion, South Asia Studies. New Delhi: Sage Publications India. https://doi.org/10.4135/9789351508083.

Thorat, Sukhadeo, and Umakant, eds. 2004. *Caste Race and Discrimination: Discourse in the International Context*. New Delhi and Jaipur: Rawat Publications.

Times News Network. 2016. "CBI Gets Nod to Arrest 34 for Killing 6 Dalits in Dangawas." *Times of India*, October 18, 2016. https://timesofindia.indiatimes.com/city/ajmer/CBI-gets-nod-to-arrest-34-for-killing-6-Dalits-in-Dangawas/articleshow/54908306.cms.

———. 2019. "Find Dangawas Accused, Get Rs 50,000 Reward: CBI." *Times of India*, December 1, 2019. https://timesofindia.indiatimes.com/city/ajmer/rewards-of-rs-50k-each-on-10-wanted-for-dangawas-killings/articleshow/72313497.cms.

Times Press News. 2019. "SC/ST Act: Supreme Court Recalls Directions of Mar 2018 Verdict." *Economic Times*, October 1, 2019. https://economictimes.indiatimes.com/news/politics-and-nation/sc/st-act-supreme-court-recalls-directions-of-mar-2018-verdict/articleshow/71391987.cms.

———. 2019. "Will Not Dilute Provisions of SC/ST Act: Supreme Court." *Economic Times*, October 3, 2019. https://economictimes.indiatimes.com/news/politics-and-nation/will-not-dilute-provisions-of-sc/st-act-supreme-court/articleshow/71425412.cms?from=mdr.

Tod, James. 1920. *Annals and Antiquities of Rajasthan: Or the Central and Western Rajput State of India*. Vols. 1–3. Edited by William Crooke. London, Edinburgh, Glasgow, New York, Toronto, Melbourne, Bombay: Humphrey Milford and Oxford University Press.

Trivedi, Prashant K. 2016. "Introduction: Ensuring Land to the Tiller." In *Land to the Tiller: Revisiting the Unfinished Land Reforms Agenda*, edited by Prashant K. Trivedi, 1–12. New Delhi: ActionAid India. https://www.actionaidindia.org/publications/land-to-the-tiller/.

Trouillot, Michel-Rolph. 2000. "Abortive Rituals: Historical Apologies in the Global Era." *Interventions* 2 (2): 171–86. https://doi.org/10.1080/136980100427298.

Tsing, Anna L. 2005. *Friction: An Ethnography of Global Connection*. Princeton, NJ: Princeton University Press. https://press.princeton.edu/books/paperback/9780691120652/friction.

Turner, Victor. 1969. "Liminality and Communitas." In his *The Ritual Process: Structure and Anti-Structure*, 94–113. Chicago: Aldine Publishing.

Udaipur District Gazetteer. Compiled by B. S. Agarwal. 1979. *Directorate of District Gazetteers*. Jaipur: Government of Rajasthan.

Vissmann, Cornelia. 2008. *Files: Law and Media Technology*. Translated by Geoffrey Winthrop-Young. Stanford, CA: Stanford University Press.

Vyas, Vijay S., Sarthi Acharya, and Surjit Singh. 2007. "The Quest for Sustainable Development." New Delhi: Academic Foundation.

Wade, Peter. 2004. "Human Nature and Race." *Anthropological Theory* 4 (2): 157–72. https://doi.org/10.1177/1463499604042812.

Waghmore, Suryakant. 2013. *Civility against Caste: Dalit Politics and Citizenship in Western India*. New Delhi: Sage Publications India.

———. 2018. "From Hierarchy to Hindu Politeness: Caste Atrocities and Dalit Protest in Rural Marathwada." In *Contested Hierarchies, Persisting Influence: Caste and Power in the Twenty-First Century*, edited by Surinder S. Jodkha and James Manor, 111–39. Hyderabad: Orient Black Swan.

Wagner, Sarah. 2010. "Identifying Srebrenica's Missing: The 'Shaky Balance' of Universalism and Particularism." In *Transitional Justice: Global Mechanisms and Local Realities after Genocide and Mass Violence*, edited by Alexander L. Hinton, 25–48. Brunswick, NJ: Rutgers University Press.

Walters, Mark Austin. 2022. *Criminalising Hate: Law as Social Justice Liberalism*. Palgrave Hate Studies. London: Palgrave Macmillan.

Walters, Mark Austin, Rupert Brown, and Susann Wiedlitzka. 2016. "Causes and Motivations of Hate Crime." 102. Manchester, UK: Equality and Human Rights Commission. https://www.equalityhumanrights.com/sites/default/files/research-report-102-causes-and-motivations-of-hate-crime.pdf.

Walters, Mark Austin, Abenaa Owusu-Bempah, and Susann Wiedlitzka. 2018. "Hate Crime and the 'Justice Gap': The Case for Law Reform." *Criminal Law Review* 12: 961–86.

Watt, Carey Anthony. 2005. *Serving the Nation: Cultures of Service, Association and Citizenship*. New Delhi and New York: Oxford University Press.

Waughray, Annapurna. 2022. *Capturing Caste in Law: The Legal Regulation of Caste Discrimination*. London and New York: Routledge.

Weber, Max. 1978. *Gesammelte Aufsätze zur Religionssoziologie II: Hinduismus und Buddhismus*. Tübingen: Mohr.

Welton-Mitchell, Courtney, Daniel N. McIntosh, and Anne P. DePrince. 2013. "Associations between Thematic Content and Memory Detail in Trauma Narratives." *Applied Cognitive Psychology* 27 (4): 462–73. https://doi.org/10.1002/acp.2923.

Whitehead, Ann. 1984. "Women and Men, Kinship and Property: Some General Issues." In *Women and Property—Women as Property*, edited by Renee Hirschon, 176–92. New York: Palgrave Macmillan.

Whitehead, Neil. 2004. "Introduction: Cultures, Conflicts and the Poetics of Violent Practice." In *Violence*, edited by Neil Whitehead, 3–24. Santa Fe, NM: School for Advanced Research Press.

Wilkerson, Isabel. 2020. *Caste: The Origins of Our Discontents*. London: Penguin Books UK.

Wire Staff. 2018. "High Acquittal in SC/ST Atrocities Cases Due to Failure of Police,

Prosecution: Centre to SC." *The Wire*, November 21, 2018. https://thewire.in/caste/high-acquittal-in-sc-st-atrocities-cases-due-to-failure-of-police-prosecution-centre-to-sc.

———. 2019. "My Birth Is My Fatal Accident: Rohith Vemula's Searing Letter Is an Indictment of Social Prejudices." *The Wire*, January 17, 2019. https://thewire.in/caste/rohith-vemula-letter-a-powerful-indictment-of-social-prejudices.

Wright, Fiona. 2018. *The Israeli Radical Left: An Ethics of Complicity*. Philadelphia: University of Pennsylvania Press.

Zedner, Lucia. 2004. *Criminal Justice*. Clarendon Law Series. Oxford and New York: Oxford University Press.

Zutshi, Chitralekha. 2009. "Re-Visioning Princely States in South Asian Historiography: A Review." *Indian Economic & Social History Review* 46 (3): 301–13. https://doi.org/10.1177/001946460904600302.

INDEX

Adivasi: affirmative action for, 7, 287; as discussed in this book, xii–xiv; protection under Prevention of Atrocities Act, 3, 8–9, 15, 50, 53–54; 57–62, 64, 66, 68, 114, 119, 133, 135, 156–57, 185, 226, 252, 254; in Rajasthan, 30–31, 34
affirmative action: controversies around, 124, 185; and Dalit assertion, 288; Indian program of, 7, 14; Meghwal economic accumulation through, 37, 40, 82; and Prevention of Atrocities Act, 255
Agamben, Giorgio, 117–18
All India Dalit Mahila Manch (AIDMAM), xviii, xxi, 4, 25, 31–32, 83, 221, 285
Ambedkar, Bhimrao Ramji: drafting of constitution, 6, 50, 116 (*see also* constitution); movement led by, 35, 82, 228; theory of caste oppression, 6, 288
anticaste legislation: conversion of, 15, 18, 143 (*see also* Berg, Dag-Erik); controversy around, 64, 249, 252; and definition of Prevention of Atrocities Act, 49, 50; in relation to hate crime law, 50–51, 58
antidiscrimination law: vs. hate crime law, 49, 255; in other postcolonial nations, 159, 250, 255; problems with, 100, 254–56
aspiration: economic and social conditions of, 219, 221; and hope in anthropological debates, 219; through legal texts, 61, 221

assertion: and caste atrocities, 54, 192–93, 206; of Dalits in Rajasthan, 21, 25, 75, 81, 246, 288, 289, 291; fragility of, 192, 208; as performance of masculinity, 126; and resignation, 211–13; tactical forms of, 176, 178. *See also* tactics
atrocity: conceptualization in international law, 50, 55; crime statistics involving Dalits in Rajasthan, 25; definition in Indian context of caste violence, 53–54; 56; relation to hate crime, 56–57

bail: anticipatory forms of, 132; rules in atrocity cases, 66, 275–76; Supreme Court of India judgments on Prevention of Atrocities Act, 132–33, 291. *See also* Supreme Court of India
Balai jāti (subcaste), xxiii, 34–35, 219, 224–25, 233
Baxi, Pratiksha, 9, 14, 20, 52, 54, 75, 95, 144, 163, 166, 249. *See also* gender; hostility; sexual violence
Berg, Dag Erik, 9, 14, 15, 42, 50–51, 131, 136,143, 148, 180, 206, 247
Bhat, Mohsin Alam, 9, 14, 50, 57, 65, 99, 119, 134
Brahmin caste: involvement in atrocity cases, 1, 63, 133, 156, 168, 174, 214, 222; in Jhunjhunu and Shekhawati, 31, 204; status in Indian caste system, 2, 143
caste: as basis of competition; 37–41, 111, 192–95, 202–6; hierarchy of, 1–2, 6, 14,

323

caste (*cont.*)
    23; and law, 16–17; in Rajasthan, 10; and violence, x, 4, 7–8, 9, 13, 19–20. *See also* jāti
caste associations: colonial role of, 81; in Jhunjhunu, 37, 70, 77–82; as local modes of political organization, 80–81; role in atrocity cases, 77–82, 180, 182
caste violence: escalation into mass aggression, 8, 50, 53, 54–57; everyday forms of, 8, 12, 56, 108, 211; intersections with gender-based violence, xii, 21, 42, 74, 101, 242, 290 (*see also* intersectional violence); land-related forms of, 189–213
Center for Dalit Rights (CDR), xvii, 26, 30, 85, 98, 127, 139–40, 159, 161, 168, 178, 180–81, 221, 223–24, 231–33, 239, 255, 285
Central Bureau of Investigation (CBI), 190, 199, 285
Certeau, Michel, de, 175–76
Chamar: as derogatory term, 2, 146, 215, 287; jāti (subcaste) in Jhunjhunu, 31, 289; relation to Meghwal community, 35, 289
charge sheet, 85, 114, 116, 147, 199, 200, 270, 275, 278, 285
class: and affirmative action, 7 (*see also* affirmative action); and caste, 2, 39, 136, 143, 144–48; and intracaste inequality, 182–84; in police recruitment, 120–21; role in atrocity cases, 20, 45, 109, 125, 129–30, 136, 143, 144, 148; and urban upward mobility of Dalits, 216, 222
Code of Criminal Procedure of 1973 (CrPC), 51–52, 83, 85, 95, 114, 132, 149, 155, 231, 285, 290
cognizable offence, 57, 113, 150, 285
colonialism: evolution of Indian criminal law, 13–14, 51–53, 65; history of Rajasthan's Shekhawati region, 28, 37–41, 81; history of Rajasthan's Udaipur district, 105, 111–12; implications for Prevention of Atrocities Act, 8, 12, 14, 49, 253–56; and Indian constitution, 6, 50; masculinity in, 126, 131; policing structure in, 120–21 (*see also* police); postcolonial comparisons in law, 253–56; and race, 121–22
compensation: for atrocity victims, 85–86, 172; of land in post-independence India, 40, 205; Rajasthan state scheme, 85; for rape victims, 85
compromise: and activists, 98–100, 160–63; in atrocity cases, 85, 93, 181, 184–86, 235–37; good vs. bad, 163–68, 180–82, 183, 252; in literature on rape, 95, 165; and netas, 95–98; and non-compoundable offences, 95; as out-of-court negotiation, 85, 167; as tactical agencies, 175–77, 181, 252
constitution: as counter-hegemonic and insurgent, 6, 17, 18, 137, 159, 255; drafting of Indian, 6, 50, 116 (*see also* Ambedkar, Bhimrao Ramji); as juris-generative, 44, 178
courts: colonial, 14 112, 290, 291; exclusive special courts for atrocity cases, 30, 52, 87, 116; judgments on the Prevention of Atrocities Act, 62–65, 67, 132–35, 155–56; magistrate's courts, 83; perjury in, 95; procedure in atrocity complaints, 113–14; special courts, 52, 65; system in India, 29–30. *See also* Supreme Court of India
credibility, 44, 89, 109, 126, 134–36, 142–45, 147, 153–56, 158–59, 161, 249, 291
criminal law: vs. civil, 49, 250, 255; Code of Criminal Procedure of 1973 (CrPC), 51–52, 83, 85, 95, 114, 132, 149, 155, 231, 285, 290; continuation with colonial law in India, 13–14, 51–53, 65; Indian Evidence Act of 1872 (IEA), 52, 253, 264; Indian Penal Code of 1860 (IPC), 8, 51, 72, 95, 114, 139, 146, 157, 170, 199, 231, 260, 263, 264, 269, 271, 274, 282–83, 285, 290; main pillars of, 51–52; special criminal laws, 8, 17–19, 49, 51–52, 62, 65–67, 161, 179, 248, 255. *See also* Code

of Criminal Procedure of 1973; Indian Evidence Act of 1872 (IEA); Indian Penal Code (IPC) of 1860; special criminal laws

Dalit: communities in Rajasthan, 28, 31, 34 (see also under jāti); history of term, 6–7; organizations in Rajasthan, xvii, 26, 30, 85, 98, 127, 139–40, 159, 161, 168, 178, 180–81, 221, 223–24, 231–33, 239, 255, 285 (see also Centre for Dalit Rights); pattern of violence against, 6, 7–8; in Shekhawati, 35–41; usage of term in Rajasthan, xv
Dangawas massacre: background behind, xxiii, 44, 189, 195–200; media coverage of, 190, 192, 199, 213
Deputy Superintendent of Police (DSP), 114–15, 160, 171, 279, 285. See also police
Dewey, John, 10, 22, 220, 232, 288. See also pragmatism
discretion: of judiciary in atrocity cases, 62–64; of police in atrocity cases and hate crimes, 118–19
Director General of Police (DSP), 243, 285. See also police
Dowry Prohibition Act of 1961, 67, 238

embodiment. See language
equality: as right and as policy in India, 7; as spatial restitution, 191–93
evidence: accessibility for Dalits, 140–44; in Indian criminal law, 52, 135, 142–43; and language, 116–17, 119, 129; and memory, 88–89; special consideration in hate crime cases, 156–59; special criminal laws, 64–66, 179–80. See also motive

false cases: Indian Supreme Court judgment on, 65, 67, 132–33, 157; relationship to police recording practices, 133, 140, 142; rumors of, 67, 134, 148, 154–58; truth of, 149–54. See also Supreme Court of India

Final Report (FR): and false cases, 139–40, 150, 155; filing procedure for, 114–16; meaning of, 285; role in production of police statistics, 121, 135, 155. See also National Crime Records Bureau
First Information Report (FIR): filing procedure of, 113–15, 270, 277; importance of, 118, 142; meaning of, 60, 72
Fraser, Nancy, 41, 56, 193, 201

gender: intersectionality with caste violence, 25, 64, 74–77, 100 (see also intersectional violence; sexual violence); patriarchal structures in Rajasthan, 19–20, 72, 75–76; and power in atrocity cases, 19–22; special laws regarding, 64, 67, 238
Gujar caste: involvement in atrocity cases, 146–148, position in Jhunjhunu and Shekhawati, 38, 145
Guru, Gopal, x, 7, 54, 57, 68, 75, 87, 124, 128, 211, 288

hate crime: as affect, 12; as communicative violence or messenger crime, 41, 185–86, 193–94, 203, 222; conceptual history of, 12–13, 62; as gendered, 72–74, 219; issues of evidence around, 13, 16–17, 72, 99–101, 119–20, 131, 156–57, 250 (see also motive); legal response to, 13, 59, 62–64; as method of oppression, 12, 56–57, 185–86, 193–94; as mode of boundary making, 12; in postcolonial contexts, 13–14, 111, 121–26, 253–56; relationship to atrocity crimes under international law, 54–57; relationship to Prevention of Atrocities Act, 8, 49–53, 99, 131, 156–57
hierarchy: between activists and survivors, 4, 20–21, 98–100, 160–63; of caste, 1–2, 6, 10, 14, 23; between netas and survivors, 21, 40, 89–95, 98–100, 110

Hinduism: and caste, 1–2, 36, 51, 55–56, 62, 207, 291; dharma and law, 227, 229–30; and Meghwals in Rajasthan, 35, 81, 228–30, 233; and nationalist politics, xiv, 9, 245
honor: and gender, 20, 75–76 38–87, 97, 215, 226; production through law, 4, 42, 85, 89, 100, 129, 175–76, 226–27, 234, 246
hope: in anthropological literature, 218–19, 232; fragility of, x, 21–22, 192, 209, 257; and meliorism, 10, 16, 22, 45, 217–18, 220, 247, 233–35, 239, 258, 288
hostility: in cases involving intersectional caste and sexual violence, 75, 87; category of, 163; and compromise, 91, 95, 164; as hate, 55
human rights: as Dalit Rights xviii, 24–25, 286; hearings, 45, 241–46, 286 (see also National Human Rights Commission); and legal aid NGOs, xvii, xxi, 4, 25–26, 30, 31–32, 83, 85, 98, 105, 127, 139–40, 159, 161, 168, 178, 180–81, 206, 221, 223–24, 231–33, 239, 241, 255, 285. See also All India Dalit Mahila Manch; Center for Dalit Rights; See National Campaign on Dalit Human Rights
humiliation, 7–8, 51, 57, 61, 86–87, 98, 106, 127–28, 146, 150, 166, 170, 178, 180, 197. See also Guru, Gopal

impunity, 5, 137, 163, 167, 177, 180, 203, 235, 246
Indian Evidence Act of 1872 (IEA), 52, 253, 264
Indian National Congress (INC), 39–40, 90, 92, 291
Indian Penal Code (IPC) of 1860, 8, 51, 72, 95, 114, 139, 146, 157, 170, 199, 231, 260, 263, 264, 269, 271, 274, 282–83, 285, 290
intent (*mens rea*): in criminal law, 13, 156; vs. motive, xiii, 13, 63–64, 65, 67, 119, 156–57, 248. See also motive

intersectional violence: in context of patriarchal structures and dynamics of class, 25, 64, 74–77, 100 (see also gender; sexual violence); intersectional vs. intrasectional, 74–77

Jaipur princely state, 29
Jat caste: agricultural influence In Jhunjhunu, 34, 37–41, 84–85, 138; and caste atrocities, 34, 37–41, 70, 77, 138–44, 149–52, 168–70, 189, 195–200; power in Nagaur district, 202–6; relationship to Meghwals and other Dalit communities in Shekhawati, 34, 37–41, 81–82, 92; role in peasant revolts, 38–41
Jāti (subcaste): Dalit jātis in Shekhawati, 31, 33–34, 35–41; statistical representation in atrocity cases in Jhunjhunu, 34, 35–41, 70, 77, 138–44, 149–52, 168–70, 189, 195–200
Jauregui, Beatrice, 14, 74, 108–9, 120–21, 127, 129, 199. See also police
Jhunjhunu district: boundaries and subdistricts of, 33; caste relations in, 31, 33–34, 36–41; Dalit land ownership in, 40–41, 92; demographics of, 31, 36–27; fieldwork in, 26, 29–31; history of, 29, 33–34, 36–41; Jhunjhunu Ambedkar Society, 34, 70, 78, 79, 138; Jhunjhunu Meghwal Samaj, 34, 70, 79; Jhunjhunu Meghwal Sangharsh Samiti (JMSS), xxiv, 34, 70, 73, 77–80, 85, 89–91, 93, 255, 285; role of peasant revolts, 38–41
Jodhpur princely state, 204–5
justice: accountability of hate crime law, 76, 101; competing visions of, 11, 19, 21–22, 66–68, 85, 90, 99, 166; through legal texts, 227–31; legal understanding of, 134–35, 156; as micro agencies, 165, 167, 173, 174, 177, 181, 184; and police, 117–19; and Prevention of Atrocities Act, 11,15, 17, 19, 25, 42, 44, 66, 68, 96–99, 128, 136, 161, 164; as restitution, 11, 16, 21, 22, 43, 165, 190, 192, 194–95, 210, 212, 218, 236, 257

Kannabiran, Kalpana, 17, 137, 159. *See also* constitution; strategic disobedience
Karauli district, 27, 168–69, 180–82
Khairlanji murders, 192
Khetri tahasīla (subdistrict) of Jhunjhunu, 33, 145
kinship: family disagreements around atrocity cases, 76–77, 83–87; political versions of, 73–74, 76–77, 89–95
Krishnan, P. S., xviii, 5, 53, 62, 162, 211, 287

land: as casted space, 191, 204–7, 291; jagirdari system, 37–39, 111, 138, 289; khalsa lands, 111–12; land tenure system in Rajputana agency, 28, 37–39, 111, 289; Rajasthan Tenancy Act of 1955, 196–97, 205; redistribution of, 39–40, 196, 205, 237; reforms in post–independence India: 38–40, 112, 138, 145, 204–6, 237; resistance to; 204–6
language: body language, 16, 43, 74, 90, 108–9, 124–126, 129, 158, 247–48; legal registers, 109, 117–18, 128
legal aesthetics, 109, 131, 143
legal registers. *See* language

masculinity: in context of Dalit activism and politics, 19–20, 250; and police performance, 109, 126, 131; relationship to colonial history, 125; symbols of, 62
media: and police, 96, 116, 154, 170; role in atrocity cases, 30, 34, 54, 77, 91, 96, 116, 154–55, 170, 173–74, 180–81, 190, 192, 199, 225, 235
medical report, 140–41
Meghwal: caste history of, 35–36; in census data, 35; economic and social status in Shekhawati, 31, 34, 36–41, 81, 82; in jagirdari system, 37–38; Jat relations, 34, 37–41, 81–82, 92; origin of name, 35; relationship with other Dalit jātis in Shekhawati, 34–35; relationship to Ramdev Pir, 36, 113, 126, 289;

religious affiliation, 35, 81, 228–30, 233 (*see also* Hinduism); visibility in legal proceedings, 34
meliorism: as concept in pragmatist philosophy, 10, 22, 218, 220, 247, 288; as perspective on justice in atrocity cases, 10, 16, 45, 217–18, 233–35, 239, 258; in relation to legal habits, 22, 45, 218, 220, 231–35, 239, 251–52
Member of Legislative Assembly (MLA), 90, 96, 196
motive, xiii, 13, 63–64, 65, 67, 119, 156–57, 248

Nagaur district, 27, 29, 44, 189–90, 196, 202, 203–4, 291
National Campaign on Dalit Human Rights (NCDHR), xviii, 24, 286
National Crime Records Bureau (NCRB), 25, 133, 135, 155
National Human Rights Commission (NHRC), 45, 241–46, 286
netas (big men): in anthropological literature, 76–77; and Dalit activists, 21, 98–100; involvement in atrocity cases, 21, 89–95, 110; in Jhunjhunu's Meghwal community, 40, 89–91
noncompoundable offence, 58, 95, 163, 286

Oza, Rupal, 65, 67, 165, 178, 290

Pancayata (village council), 151, 173–174, 198, 225, 235, 290
Perry, Barbara, 12, 13, 41, 50, 56–57, 59, 193. *See also* hate crime
police: Commissionerate of, 29, 154; Deputy Superintendent of, 114–15, 160, 171, 279, 285; Director General of, 243, 285; global theories of policing, 107–8, 120; Indian structure of; 120–21; role in categorizing atrocity complaints, 113–16, 121, 133, 135, 139–40, 142, 150, 155, 270, 277; Superintendent of, 30, 286, 290, 291

328   *Index*

postcolonial law: and constitutionalism, 254, 255; continuity with colonial categories, 253–54; and hate crime legislation, 253–54, 255–56; in India, 13–14, 51–53, 65, 253–54; postcolonial comparisons in law, 253–56. *See also* colonialism
Pradhan. *See* sarpanca
pragmatism, 10, 22, 220, 232, 288. *See also* Dewey, John
princely states: colonial systems of governance in; 28–29; definition of, 28; Jaipur princely state, 29; Jodhpur princely state, 204–5; source material on, 28; Udaipur princely state 112. *See also* Rajasthan; Rajputana Agency
procedural law, 51–52, 74
Promotion of Equality and Prevention of Unfair Discrimination Act of 2000 (South Africa), 159, 255
Protection of Children from Sexual Offences Act (POCSO), 73
Protection of Civil Rights Act (PCR) of 1976, 58, 279

Rajputana Agency: caste relations in, 28–29, 35; land tenure systems in, 28, 37–39, 111, 289; organization of, 28; and princely states, 28–29. *See also* princely states
restitution, 11, 16, 21, 22, 43, 165, 190, 192, 194–95, 210, 212, 218, 236, 257. *See also* justice
Rajasthan: bordering states, 27; caste relations in, 25–26; colonial history of, 28–29; demographic and geographical markers, 26, 27–33, 37, 289; modern state foundation, 28; party politics among Meghwals, 21, 39–40, 80, 90; relationship with Indian National Congress (INC), 39–40, 90, 92, 291. *See also* Rajputana Agency.
Rajput caste: in colonial Rajputana Agency, 28–29, 38, 40, 62, 81, 128, 289 (*see also* Rajputana Agency);

involvement in atrocity cases, 106–7, 110, 139–40, 143, 173, 177, 219, 225, 226, 234–36, 242, 288; in Nagaur district, 204, 206; Shekhawat Rajputs, 29; in Shekhawati and Jhunjhunu 31, 82; status in Indian caste system, xxii, xxiii, 62, 226; in Udaipur district, 106–7, 110, 112–13, 126–27, 129, 289, 290. *See also* Jhunjhunu district; Nagaur district; Rajasthan; Shekhawati region; Udaipur district
Rao, Anupama, 8, 14, 15, 35, 51, 58, 124, 131, 135, 252
rumors: of false cases in India, 43, 132, 135, 143–44, 148, 154–56; role in Supreme Court judgments, 132–35, 156. *See also* false cases; Supreme Court of India
rupture. *See* trauma; temporality

sarapanca (village head), xxii, 145–46, 168, 169, 173, 174–75
Scheduled Castes/Scheduled Tribes (Prevention of) Atrocities of 1989: amendments to, xiv, 8, 29, 59, 63, 107, 133, 157, 259; central features of, 59, 60–62; genealogy of, 49–68; legislative predecessors to, 56–60; main Supreme Court judgments on, 62–65; and myth of false cases (*se also* false cases); political polarization around, 18–19, 65, 132–37; as special criminal law, 65–68
sexual violence: against Dalit women, 19–20–22, 69–73, 75–76; intersection with caste violence, xii, 21, 25, 42, 64, 74–77, 100, 101, 242, 290; rape as non-compoundable offence, 58, 95, 163, 286. *See also* gender; intersectional violence
Sikar district, 27, 29, 37, 219, 224–27, 229, 233–35, 236, 237, 289
Shekhawati region: and Arya Samaj reform movement, 81; boundaries and location, 27, 29; climate and demographics, 27–29, 37; fieldwork in, 26–41; Jaipur princely state, 29; Jat Meghwal relations in, 37–41; Marwari

trader caste economic and educational investment in; 33–34, 36–37; Meghwals in, 31, 34, 36–41, 81, 82; peasant revolts in, 38–41, 81, 92, 138; reigning Rajput clan in colonial era, 29
social imaginary, 19 26, 74, 239. *See also* Taylor, Charles
sociality: casted forms, 207, 210, 237; and hopeful habits, 224, 231–35; and new activist networks, 75, 165, 167, 177–78; new modes in atrocity cases, ix, 10, 26, 42, 75, 165, 167, 177, 224, 231–35, 252; rupture of, 177, 195, 207, 210, 237
space: and caste atrocities, 203–6, 210; for Dalit experiences in law, xiii, 16–19, 137, 248, 257; of institutional discretion, 62–65, 119, 130, 158; as justice, 44, 165, 191, 193, 195, 200–2, 203, 206–8, 210, 212, 218, 236, 257; for tactics, 175–76, 184, 186
special criminal laws: controversies around, 8, 18–19, 49, 51–52, 62, 65–67, 161, 179, 248, 255; definition of, 8, 17, 52. Dowry Prohibition Act of 1961; other examples of, 65–68; Unlawful Activities (Prevention) Act of 1967 (UAPA), 65–66, 179. *See also* criminal law; Dowry Prohibition Act of 1961; Unlawful Activities (Prevention) Act of 1967
Special Public Prosecutor, 60–61
strategic disobedience, 43, 132, 137, 152–59, 252. *See also* Kannabiran, Kalpana
substantive law, 51
success: amplitudes of, 22, 251; and compromise, 184–86; contestations in atrocity cases, 4, 5, 9–11, 21, 44, 101, 178; gendered notions of, 19, 74; normative visions of, 165, 167–68
suicide: abetment of, 3, 216, 225, 243; Rohit Vemula suicide note, 223
Superintendent of Police (SP), 30, 286, 290, 291. *See also* police
Supreme Court of India: amendments to Prevention of Atrocities Act, xiv, 8, 29, 59, 63, 107, 133, 157, 259; judgment in *Subhash Kashinath Mahajan v. Union of India* of 2018, 65, 67, 132–34, 155–57; key judgments in atrocity cases, 132–33, 62–65, 132–34, 157. *See also* false cases; Scheduled Castes/ Scheduled Tribes (Prevention of) Atrocities Act of 1989
Suresh, Mayur, xii–xiii, 51, 52, 65–66, 134, 136, 142, 152, 158, 167, 179, 223, 248. *See also* Unlawful Activities (Prevention) Act of 1967 (UAPA)

tactics, 175–76. *See also* Certeau, Michel, de
Tahasīla (subdistrict), 33, 106
Taylor, Charles, 26, 74, 239
Teltumbde, Anand, 14, 50, 115, 119–20, 134, 142, 163, 192, 288. *See also* Khairlanji murders
temporality: in criminal law, 16,18, 42–43, 45, 137, 148, 153, 158–59; of discrimination, 11, 137, 148; of hope 235–39
Thorat, Sukhadeo, xviii, 13, 24, 163, 223, 288, 291
constitutionalism, 6, 250. *See also* constitution
transitional justice, 44, 194, 209, 213
translation: of caste violence into law, 76; and embodiment, 43, 121–26; by police officers, xiii, 108–9, 114, 117–20
trauma: in anthropological literature, 72, 88–89; of casteism, 3–4, 72, 75–76, 128, 190; and fieldwork, 24–25, 32; and forgetting, 87–88; post-traumatic suffering, 87, 190–95
truth: accountability in this book, xv; deep truths of discrimination, 16–17, 18, 43, 68, 133–35, 137, 148, 149–52, 159, 218, 246, 248–49; and evidence, 16–17, 42, 135, 142–43, 145, 154–57; legal regimes of, xiii, 5, 10, 11, 42–43, 135, 152–54, 158, 218, 221. *See also* evidence

Udaipur princely state, 112
Unlawful Activities (Prevention) Act of 1967 (UAPA), 65–66, 179
untouchability: abolishment of, 6, 7, 57; modes of violence around, 7–8 (*see also* atrocity); phenomenology of, x, 122; practice of, 2, 6, 7
Untouchability Offences Act (UOA) of 1955, 57–58

Vidhan Sabha (State Legislative Assembly), 78, 92, 95
village: caste dependencies in Rajasthan, 31, 37–38, 84, 94, 97, 109, 138, 151, 172–73, 183, 191, 221; fieldwork village, 31–32, 40, 93; involvement in atrocity cases, 72, 172–74; as privileged collective, 20, 176–78; as treacherous homes for Dalits, 207, 223

Waghmore, Suryakant, 41, 174, 192, 207–8, 288, 291
witness: credibility of 156, 162; rights and protections under Prevention of Atrocities Act, 59, 261, 264, 270, 274, 276–78; turning hostile, 75, 87, 91, 95, 163–64

ALSO PUBLISHED IN THE SOUTH ASIA IN MOTION SERIES

Resistance as Negotiation: Making States and Tribes in the Margins of Modern India
Uday Chandra (2024)

Breathless: Tuberculosis, Inequality, and Care in Rural India
Andrew McDowell (2024)

Labors of Division: Global Capitalism and the Emergence of the Peasant in Colonial Panjab
Navyug Gill (2024)

The Political Outsider: Indian Democracy and the Lineages of Populism
Srirupa Roy (2024)

Qaum, Mulk, Sultanat: Citizenship and National Belonging in Pakistan
Ali Usman Qasmi (2023)

Boats in a Storm: Law, Migration, and Decolonization in South and Southeast Asia, 1942–1962
Kalyani Ramnath (2023)

Life Beyond Waste: Work and Infrastructure in Urban Pakistan
Waqas Butt (2023)

Colonizing Kashmir: State-building under Indian Occupation
Hafsa Kanjwal (2023)

Dust on the Throne: The Search for Buddhism in Modern India
Douglas Ober (2023)

Mother Cow, Mother India: A Multispecies Politics of Dairy in India
Yamini Narayanan (2023)

The Vulgarity of Caste: Dalits, Sexuality, and Humanity in Modern India
Shailaja Paik (2022)

Delhi Reborn: Partition and Nation Building in India's Capital
Rotem Geva (2022)

*The Right to Be Counted: The Urban Poor and
the Politics of Resettlement in Delhi*
Sanjeev Routray (2022)

*Protestant Textuality and the Tamil Modern: Political Oratory
and the Social Imaginary in South Asia*
Bernard Bate, Edited by E. Annamalai, Francis Cody, Malarvizhi
Jayanth, and Constantine V. Nakassis (2021)

*Special Treatment: Student Doctors at the All
India Institute of Medical Sciences*
Anna Ruddock (2021)

From Raj to Republic: Sovereignty, Violence, and Democracy in India
Sunil Purushotham (2021)

The Greater India Experiment: Hindutva Becoming and the Northeast
Arkotong Longkumer (2020)

Nobody's People: Hierarchy as Hope in a Society of Thieves
Anastasia Piliavsky (2020)

*Brand New Nation: Capitalist Dreams and Nationalist
Designs in Twenty-First-Century India*
Ravinder Kaur (2020)

Partisan Aesthetics: Modern Art and India's Long Decolonization
Sanjukta Sunderason (2020)

For a complete listing of titles in this series, visit the
Stanford University Press website, www.sup.org.

The authorized representative in the EU for product safety and compliance is:
Mare Nostrum Group
B.V Doelen 72
4831 GR Breda
The Netherlands

www.ingramcontent.com/pod-product-compliance
Lightning Source LLC
Chambersburg PA
CBHW031753220426
43662CB00007B/392